A GUIDE TO CORPORATE GOVERNANCE

A GUIDE TO CORPORATE GOVERNANCE

N GOPALSAMY
(FCS)

NEW AGE MANAGEMENT

An Imprint of

NEW AGE INTERNATIONAL (P) LIMITED, PUBLISHERS

LONDON • NEW DELHI • NAIROBI

Bangalore • Chennai • Cochin • Guwahati • Hyderabad • Kolkata • Lucknow • Mumbai

Visit us at **www.newagepublishers.com**

Published by New Age International (P) Ltd., Publishers
First Edition: 2009
Reprint: 2017

GLOBAL OFFICES

- **New Delhi** **NEW AGE INTERNATIONAL (P) LIMITED, PUBLISHERS**
  7/30 A, Daryaganj, New Delhi-110002, (INDIA)
  Tel.: (011) 23253771, 23253472, **Telefax:** 23267437, 43551305
  E-mail: contactus@newagepublishers.com • Visit us at www.newagepublishers.com
- **London** **NEW AGE INTERNATIONAL (UK) LTD.**
  27 Old Gloucester Street, London, WC1N 3AX, UK
  E-mail: info@newacademicscience.co.uk • Visit us at www.newacademicscience.co.uk
- **Nairobi** **NEW AGE GOLDEN (EAST AFRICA) LTD.**
  Ground Floor, Westlands Arcade, Chiromo Road (Next to Naivas Supermarket)
  Westlands, Nairobi, KENYA, **Tel.:** 00-254-713848772, 00-254-725700286
  E-mail: kenya@newagepublishers.com

BRANCHES

- **Bangalore** 37/10, 8th Cross (Near Hanuman Temple), Azad Nagar, Chamarajpet, Bangalore- 560 018
  Tel.: (080) 26756823, **Telefax:** 26756820, **E-mail: bangalore@newagepublishers.com**
- **Chennai** 26, Damodaran Street, T. Nagar, Chennai-600 017, **Tel.:** (044) 24353401, **Telefax:** 24351463
  E-mail: chennai@newagepublishers.com
- **Cochin** CC-39/1016, Carrier Station Road, Ernakulam South, Cochin-682 016, **Tel.:** (0484) 2377303, **Telefax:** 4051304
  E-mail: cochin@newagepublishers.com
- **Guwahati** Hemsen Complex, Mohd. Shah Road, Paltan Bazar, Near Starline Hotel, Guwahati-781 008,
  Tel.: (0361) 2513881, **Telefax:** 2543669, **E-mail: guwahati@newagepublishers.com**
- **Hyderabad** 105, 1st Floor, Madhiray Kaveri Tower, 3-2-19, Azam Jahi Road, Near Kumar Theater, Nimboliadda Kachiguda, Hyderabad-500 027, **Tel.:** (040) 24652456, **Telefax:** 24652457
  E-mail: hyderabad@newagepublishers.com
- **Kolkata** RDB Chambers (Formerly Lotus Cinema) 106A, 1st Floor, S N Banerjee Road, Kolkata-700 014
  Tel.: (033) 22273773, **Telefax:** 22275247, **E-mail: kolkata@newagepublishers.com**
- **Lucknow** 16-A, Jopling Road, Lucknow-226 001, **Tel.:** (0522) 2209578, 4045297, **Telefax:** 2204098
  E-mail: lucknow@newagepublishers.com
- **Mumbai** 142C, Victor House, Ground Floor, N.M. Joshi Marg, Lower Parel, Mumbai-400 013
  Tel.: (022) 24927869, **Telefax:** 24915415, **E-mail: mumbai@newagepublishers.com**
- **New Delhi** 22, Golden House, Daryaganj, New Delhi-110 002, **Tel.:** (011) 23262368, 23262370, **Telefax:** 43551305
  E-mail: sales@newagepublishers.com

ISBN: 978-81-224-2572-7
C-16-08-9594

Printed in India at Saras Graphics, Rai, Haryana.
Typeset at Printex India, Delhi.

NEW AGE INTERNATIONAL (P) LIMITED, PUBLISHERS
7/30 A, Daryaganj, New Delhi-110002
Visit us at **www.newagepublishers.com**
(CIN: U74899DL1966PTC004618)

TO MY TEACHER AND MENTOR:

The Hindu and its Group of Publications.

Preface

Good corporate governance is an amalgam of the adoption of best practices, creation and maximization of wealth, better accountability and investor protection. Corporate governance largely depends on the following: The quality of the promoters, the intentions of the promoters, the systems and procedures adopted, the transparency in the activities and the quality of the persons at the helm of day-to-day affairs. In the matter of board functioning, Corporate governance is based on the following fundamentals issues:

(a) Transparency in respect of the company's affairs with full and complete disclosure of all factors affecting a company adversely or positively.

(b) Accountability of the directors for all matters concerning the company whether it be the business performance or compliance with the laws of the land or servicing of the shareholders or the creditors.

(c) Fairness in respect of all dealings of the company whether it be with the business clients or whether it be with the consumers or the investors at large.

(d) Responsibility on part of the directors to ensure that the company is answerable for all matters of its business dealings.

The Institute of Company Secretaries of India, which has also taken many pioneering steps to promote sound corporate governance principles and practices, had recommended institutionalising corporate governance as a way of corporate life. Some of the governance practices recommended by it are: The Baord meeting once a year without the Chief Executive Officer to discuss all issues without any bias, the Board undertaking an annual revaluation of itself, linking directors compensation to performance, instituting orientation programmes and training for directors, defining the roles and responsibilities for board, chairman and the CEO, formal evaluation process of members of board and its committees, succession planning, ESOPs to be fair and progressive and developing appropriate work culture.

A corporate governance country assessment for India was carried out in the year 2004, as part of the joint World Bank IMF programme of Report on the observance of standards and codes. Its objective was to benchmark the observance of corporate governance by India against the OECD principles of corporate governance. The OECD principles are considered as benchmark on corporate governance by the World Bank. The report brought out assessees India's compliance with each of the OECD principles of corporate governance. The assessment team had found Indian corporates to be only 'partially observant' of the OECD principles. The report has made several policy recommendations. The report recommends sanctions and enforcements should be credible deterrents for the corporates to carry out their business practices within the applicable laws and regulations, the directors upgrading their knowledge and skill, strong focus on professionalism of directors, institutional investors who are in the fiduciary capacity adhering to the comprehensive corporate governance policy etc. The comments given in the report with regard to the statement that Indian companies are 'partially observant' of the OECD principles, state that doubts persist about the effectiveness of legal remedies for the shareholders when they approach SEBI/Company Law Board, enforcement of insider trading regulations as problematic, misuse of the corporate assets and abuse in related party transactions remaining a problem, long delays and backlogs for redressal through civil and High Courts, multiple board membership interfering with performance of directors etc. Since these observations do not augur well for good corporate governance, the Government has been compelled to initiate necessary new regulatory measures or strengthening of existing ones.

In August 2003, after deliberating on and incorporating the views of at least three expert committees, SEBI decided to make companies comply with specified governance standards. These standards, among other things were for purposes like benchmarking companies against international norms on matters such as the composition of the board of directors, a fixed percentage of them comprising independent directors with clearly defined profiles and roles in governance, the company's principal officers to be held personally responsible for certain acts of omission and commission, working of subsidiary companies being reviewed by the audit committees of the parent etc. All companies whose shares were quoted on domestic stock exchanges would be required to comply with the new provisions and it was for the designated stock exchange to ensure that it was done. To a large extent these proposals have been objected to and industry associations made a strong case for modifications, particularly the stringent rule regarding independent directors. Family owned businesses are reluctant to induct outsiders to their boards and they have pointed out that it would be difficult to find competent people to serve as independent directors. In the light of these developments SEBI has deferred by nine montshs the insitutionalization of new governance standards, that is to say the SEBI Board has given time till December 31, to be fully compliant. SEBI, during the process of implementaiton of the new regulatin, is willing to look at the need for making minor modificaitons, if any problems arise. The major new provisions included in the new Clause 49 are: The board will lay down a code of conduct for all board members and senior management of the company to compulsorily follow, the CEO and CFO will certify the financial statements and cash flow statements of the company, at least one independent director of the holding company will be a member of a material non-listed subsidiary, the audit committee of the listed company to review the financial statements of the unlisted subsidiary, in particular its investments and in case the prescribed accounting standards are not followed, an explananation for the some in the corporate governance report.

Some industry people believe that corporate governance is largely an issue of ethic and hence difficult to enforce. They prefer self governance and instead of regulatory bodies bringing out various guidelines and rules, they should be allowed to govern themselves from within the organization. In support of this view it has been contended that "Corporate governance is clearly not merely the number of board meetings held, the number of hours the meetings lasted or the number of persons attending such meetings. Good governance is an amalgam of the adoption of best practices." However there are major question marks about the quality and state of current corporate governance practices, both within the country and outside, as could be noticed from the following:

- There are many examples where senior executives of prominent firms have been identified helping themselves to generous chunks of salaries and bonuses.

- Many investors are wondering how credit rating agencies grant investment status to borrowing companies on the basis of poor and questionable financial information.
- Enron, Worldcom, Sunbeam, Tyco have all become by words for financial skullduggery and outright cheating of stakeholds, who suffered heavily in the wake crash that followed inevitably.
- There are cases where there was negligence or connivance of many of the well-known audit firms, financial institutions and investment banks, which led to the further ballooning of misdeeds. Morgan Stanely provides the case in point.
- Fraudulent financial reporting, have taken place, despite audit and accounting standards. In such cases deception such as manipulation, falsification or alteration of accounting records have taken place. This is in addition to misrepresentation or intentional omission from financial statements of events and transactions. Such actions get reflected in the bottom-line of an entity.
- SEBI, till April 2005, has passed orders against 100 vanishing companies and 378 directors debarring them from accessing the capital market. There are proposals to treat as violations inviting monetary penalty, where the end-use of funds raised have been in a manner other than the disclosed in the prospectus. SEBI and MCA are looking at the prospects of referring large value cases of vanishing companies to the Serious Frauds office so that investors can get back their money quickly.
- Experts have often suggested that a code of best practice for government owned enterprises may be desirable; also review of law and organizational set up in regard to the publicly owned financial institutions, to make them consistent with good corporate governance practices. This is on the basis that 'If government has to be a model employer, it should also be a model corporate governance practitioner'.

Therefore the choice is to opt for all or any of the following four methods: legislation, regulation, self-discipline and societal pressure. The effectiveness of corporate governance would then largely depend upon the optimum blend of these methods. Further there can be no two opinions that Indian companies must strive to match global standards of governance. While doing so, the new regulatory measures and rules for better governance have to be consistent with Indian ground realities. Merely transplanting ideas and regulation from the West may prove counterproductive. In the West, investor awareness and shareholder activism have generally kept company managements on their toes; this has discouraged unethical behaviour. These factors are still extremely weak in India. The authorities, have therefore been advised, at the present juncture, to prioritise core standards that must be followed while leaving the rest to be adopted voluntarily. Similar approach has also been advocated in a leading editorial in the following words, "But perhaps SEBI needs to make a short list of mandatory provisions, with the more contentious proposals being left as non-mandatory recommendations. This could set the stage for competition in corporate governance, with investors and the markets rewarding companies that voluntarily adopt a higher standard."

SEBI may still have to keep a watchful eye whether corporates in general adhere and follow time-honoured values like honesty, accountability, transparency, trust etc and whether corporate actions are invariably consistent with stakeholdes interest. The face of corporate financial report is also changing and the trend established by Infosys should percolate down to family-managed companies. The regulators therefore carry the obligation to enforce compliance of suitable rules, including corporate governance code strictly. Investors, while conceding that the audited financial statements constitute an important component of corporate governance, also prefer that this could be supplemented by the currently accepted model of financial reporting by electronic information systems providing financial and other forms of information which would be widely available via the Internet.

The book, a part from providing a general introduction on the subject in a summary form, also covers key areas and concepts like the concept of corporate governance, various compliance requirements, Board composition, its role and accountability, how the concept is sought to be applied in so far as the functioning of banks and public enterprises are unconcerned/and also the relevance of social responsibility and ethics. In addition, very useful reference material have been provided in other sections, under the following headings: General reference, Current developments, Company law and company precedents, Board management, Committee reports and awards. Thus the book which is a comprehensive one, apart from providing necessary insight into the subject, also offers appropriate guide for all concerned as to the best corporate practices that could be followed and adopted in the day to day management of corporates and which would simultaneously be in the best interest of all the stakeholders.

N. GOPALSAMY

CONTENTS

PART - I

GENERAL INTRODUCTION

General Introduction

CHAPTER 1: CORPORATE GOVERNANCE: INTRODUCTION

The concept of corporate governance is gaining momentum because of various factors as well as the changing business environment, The question of corporate governance in India has come up mainly in the wake of economic liberalisation and deregulation of industry and business, as well as the demand for a new corporate ethos and stricter compliance with the law of the land. In the context of a unique situation obtaining in India, where financial institutions hold substantial stakes in companies, the accountability of directors including non-executive directors and nominees, has come into sharp focus, "The need for good governance is not something that is typical to our country or economy. Even in the countries where regulatory mechanisms are more demanding in their content and more vigilant in their implementation, flagrant violations under the veil of corporate impenatrability have generated a strident demand for better governance. The advent of information age has created an awakened shareholder, vigilant public and an almost predatory journalistic fervour. Depending upon the model of corporate disclosure followed by different legal frameworks, the right to information has forced corporates to divulge more than they ever did."[1]

The Indian scenario of Corporate governance, dealt with in the book 'Directors and Corporate Governance' also summarised the weaknesses in the system in the following words, "In India although weakness' in the system such as-undesirable stock market prices, boards of directors without adequate fiduciary responsibilities, poor disclosure practices, lack of transparency and crony capitalism, – were crying for reforms and improved governance, there was no real push. The momentum gathered albeit slowly, once the economy was opening up and the liberalisation processes got initiated. The credit should go Ito Confederation of Indian Industries. It was rightly believed that the ongoing measures, already implemented or under implementation are far too inadequate to icombat the deep-rooted weaknesses in the system."

What is Corporate Governance?

The following definition should help us to understand the concept:

"Corporate governance is not just corporate management, it is something much broader to include a fair, efficient and transparent administration to meet certain well defined objectives. It is a system of structuring, operating and controlling a company with a view to achieve long-term strategic goals to satisfy shareholders, creditors, employees, customers and suppliers, and complying with the legal and regulatory requirements, apart from meeting environmental and local community needs. When it is practised under a well-laid out system, it leads to the building of a legal, commercial and institutional framework and demarcates the boundaries within which these functions are performed."[2]

---

1 Proceedings of the Silver Jubilee National Convention of ICSI, Chartered Secretary, October 1997.

2 'Corporate Governance: Time for a Metamorphosis', *The Hindu*, July 9, 1997.

The above definition may further be elaborated, thus:

"Corporate governance can be defined as a set of systems and process which ensure that a company is managed to the best interests of all stakeholders — employees, shareholders, customers, creditors and community. It stipulates parameters of accountability, control and reporting functions of the board of directors and encompasses the relationship among the various participants of a corporation — the board, the management team, shareholders and other stakeholders. In the latest survey of the United States, the Paris based OECD comprising 28 rich industrial countries, defined corporate governance as the resolution of a conflict between the goals of the corporate and the differing objectives of the various agents who play a role in their operation. It is the need to ensure enlightened corporate behaviour rather than the compliance of specific laws that is behind corporate governance. Simply stated, it involves the framing of a code of management practices that would be used as a reference by individual companies. In their treatment of stakeholders. Although there are various attributes of corporate governance, yet some important rules and practices include the concentration of ownership and control and the constitution of boards and their roles, information to shareholders and disclosure obligations to potential shareholders and investors, corporate takeovers, corporate restructuring etc. It calls for setting up behaviour standards ably supported' and protected by structural system under full glare of public accountability."[3]

Investor concerns

Board of directors are supposed to represent shareholders' interest as fiduciaries; they also have oversight responsibility for executive management. Independent auditors are to provide assurance that reported financial performance is consistent with accepted accounting principles. Directors have been made responsible for ensuring that investors are not misled and are given all the Information they might need to assess the performance of companies they own; Directors should regularly monitor management's actions for investors, However the integrity of the system has in practice been found to be violated by particular cases of egregious misfeasance and even fraud. Therefore more stringent regulation, stricter enforcement, and harsher penalties can solve the current crisis in investor confidence or not remains open for debate. Therefore, the public opinion is, without dramatic changes in behaviour of executives and directors, laws and regulations will exist only to be circumvented and broken again. The investors and public expect that the business leaders would police themselves to avoid stricter regulations. Directors have avoided transparency through sheer complexity of modern-day corporations, selective disclosure of information and careful crafting of earnings definitions to control stock prices. They have used and abused – stock options to inflate their personal earnings at a great cost to others, Individual investors have suffered more relative pain than institutional investors in the process, Individual investors lack the experience, access to information and ability to convert information to knowledge leading to the better decision-making capacity, when compared to institutional counterparts.

---

[3] Background paper for the Regional Conference of SIRC of ICSI held on 9-10 May 1997 at Thiruvananthapuram.

Duties of directors: It has been suggested that directors on corporate boards must meet two standards to fulfill their fiduciary obligations to shareholders, namely "duty of loyalty" and "duty of care". Duty of loyalty requires directors to demonstrate unyielding loyalty to the company's shareholders. The duty of care requires directors "to exercise due diligence" in making decisions. They must discover as much information as reasonably possible on the issues they face and be able to show that in reaching a decision they have considered all reasonable alternatives. The courts also rely on the "business judgment rule, which holds that if directors make decisions based on their loyalty to shareholders and to the company (instead of to management) and act with care, it is assumed that they have used their best judgment and are not liable for their decisions. The courts have also consistently held that duty of loyalty imposes far broader requirements than simply avoiding self-dealing. It is preferred that a majority of a board's directors come from outside the company and not from the company's executive management team. A simple majority of independent directors, it is believed, would be more likely in a position to assure duty of loyalty for the whole board. The general belief is that to fulfill the duty of care standard, directors must continually ask probing questions and be skeptical. No doubt regulations and legislations are needed to support better governance and higher standards. But that is not enough. Directors should accept that they now have a larger obligation to diligently exercise duty of loyalty and duty of care because other mechanisms that ought to protect investors' interests have been compromised.

Why governance reform?

The integrity of our corporate system has been violated by many cases of egregious misfeasance and even fraud, In order to minimise the likelihood of such failures, improvements have been advised. This is in the wake of the system getting developed as 'managers capitalism' in which the corporations came to be run to profit its managers, in complicity if not conspiracy with accountants and the managers of other companies or corporations. The conversion of a system of 'owners capitalism' into a system of 'managers capitalism' was made possible because of (1) the diffusion of corporate ownership among a large number of investors, non holding a controlling share of the voting power and (2) the unwillingness of the agents of the owners -the boards of directors - to honour their responsibility to serve above all else the interests of their principals, the shareholders themselves. The resulting power vacuum quickly got filled by corporate managers. The governance reform therefore demanded independent directors who could be "business-savvy, interested and shareholder-oriented," as one of the measures. We need not only good managers of corporate India, but good owners, who should work together to restore the integrity of the system. SEBI has made many regulatory changes which also covers stock exchange listing obligations and regulations. Company law reforms have also been contemplated. New standards for audit committees, compensation committees have also been set. In addition various other suggestions also have also been made from time to time and these include investors, particularly institutional investors becoming better owners, behaving as responsible corporate citizens, voting their proxies thoughtfully and communicating their views to corporate managements. Companies should have an independent board chairman and higher standards of director independence. Owners and managers should unite in returning the focus of corporate information to long term financial goals, cash flows, intrinsic values and strategic direction. There should be demand for full disclosure of the impact of significant accounting policy decisions. It has been suggested to "bring back dividends" since higher dividend payouts are actually associated with higher future returns on stocks. While improving the practices of governance, we must also establish a higher set of principles.

Principles of good governance

Now we turn to some sound principles of good governance, Good governance comes from developing the right relationships among the directors, management and shareholders. The rule-making exercise and frequent amendments is only because of the failure to achieve the desired relationships among all concerned. A principles-based system of corporate governance relies on trust, depends on fiduciaries and requires validation. It has been asserted that 'Corporate governance is not a science subject to immutable rules, but it is a culture of relationships'. In the following lines, some of the principles of good governance and how management, boards and investors could live upto those principles have been briefly covered.

- Directors should make a public commitment by executing an oath of independence and care annually. A trade-off between full disclosure with transparency and the need to preserve a competitive advance has to be ensured.
- Investors and professional fund managers who serve as fiduciaries for many investors all have to share a certain degree of responsibility for ensuring good governance.
- Nominating committees or the selection of independent directors should extend beyond the sole jurisdiction of the CEO and instead, it should be on the basis of soliciting input and suggestions from shareholders and others who have a stake in how the company is run. The category of 'Independent director' should be willing and able to devote the time and effort required to collect, analyse and understand all reasonably available information with regard to the company or to oversee such processes, to make informed business judgments. Several respected governance experts have also suggested that shareholders be given the right to directly nominate one or more directors by popular vote.
- It has also been suggested that directors should disclose dissenting opinions on important issues and explain decisions that may not appear to reflect the collective will of the shareholders. Each board should establish policies and procedures to disclose board votes as soon as practical.
- It may also be necessary to ensure independent board leadership with adequate procedures and guidelines and maintaining a true and healthy system of checks and balances.

The board, as the shareholder's watchdog, must demonstrate great diligence in seeking out problems, ask many detailed questions and collect and analyse information not supplied by management. If they fail in these duties, they are not fulfilling their obligation to be a deterrent to unethical behaviour and fraud, nor will they have a way to know if either has occurred. In practice, boards have made many decisions that have raised significant shareholder concerns. These include approving poison pill provisions to guard against hostile takeovers; paying greenmail (repurchasing stock at a premium to prevent takeover); establishing classified boards, which encourages continuity through long terms of service, eliminating cumulative voting, approving excessive compensation etc., While some of the actions may be justified in specific instances, these practices have been found to be resorted to entrench existing managements and boards. Obviously shareholders have no effective recourse against them other than expensive litigation or proxy contests, which are not economical for single shareholders.

CHAPTER 1: Corporate Governance: Introduction deals with the following topics: The concept of corporate governance, corporate governance abuses, the objectives of corporate governance, code convergence in Asia, the various developments in India and also at the end, 'good governance and value addition'. Very useful material have also been included and covered in the sections, carrying the headings: General developments and Current developments.

CHAPTER 2: CORPORATE GOVERNANCE AND COMPLIANCE REQUIREMENT

Listing Agreement

The Securities and Exchange Board of India has made an overhaul of Clause 49 of the listing agreement by way of a Circular dated 29th October 2004. This new clause which supersedes all earlier circulars issued by SEBI on Clause 49 of the listing agreement is a key instrument as it lays down many important compliance requirements and new prescriptions. Some of the salient features cover the definition of the term independent director being widened in its scope and application, prior approval of shareholders to pay fees/compensation to non executive directors/independent directors, the board being required to review compliance reports of all laws applicable to the company, the board adopting a code of conduct for the directors/senior management, two thirds of audit committee shall be independent directors, related party transactions being placed before the audit committee periodically, management providing explanations when prescribed accounting standards are not followed, the company laying down procedures to inform the board member about the risk assessment and minimization procedures, disclosing to the audit committee the uses and application of funds when applied for purposes like capital expenditure out of money raised through an issue, Board certification regarding review of financial statements and cash flow statements, submission of a quarterly compliance report to the stock exchanges etc. Some of the key requirements may be elaborated in the following paragraphs.

Code of Conduct: The requirement is the board shall adopt a code of conduct for the directors as well as member of senior management of the company. This requirement is based on the belief that ethical conduct of business should be interest of all concerned and therefore all directors and senior management personnel should be governed by the prescribed code of conduct. The code, it is believed, would promote honest and ethical conduct of business, avoid conflicts of interest between personal and professional relationships, fair disclosure in reports and documents, compliance with applicable laws and regulations, enabling appropriate actions for violations and adherence through accountability. The various clauses of such a code may cover major clauses like honesty and integrity, confidentially of information, personal transactions and no misuse of information, position and property, disclosure of interest, compliance with law and lawful and ethical behaviour. Compliance procedures are laid so that the code is followed as a general company policy and these are adhered by all concerned and also making it clear that failure to adhere, would result in appropriate disciplinary action.

In the company law section, the code adopted by the New York Stock Exchange Board of directors has been included for necessary reference.

OECD Principles of Corporate Governance

In early 2004, a corporate governance country assessment for India was carried out as part of the Joint World Bank IMF Programme of Report on the observance of standard and codes. The objective was to benchmark the observance of corporate governance by India against OECD principles of corporate governance. The assessment team had found Indian corporates to be only 'partially observant' of the OECD principles. The following comments may be mentioned: While shareholders can approach SEBI, the Company Law Board etc., doubts persist about the effectiveness of legal remedies; while insider trading is a criminal offence, the enforcement is problematic; the misuse of corporate assets and abuse in related party transactions remain a problem; Redress through civil and high courts, there are long delays and backlogs; special training and certification programme for audit committee members should be considered. Some of the important policy recommendations have also been made. These include: The existing provisions on sanctions in the Companies Act are considered inadequate, the existing three-tiered supervision system should be reviewed, the directors should upgrade their skill and knowledge and there should be focus on professionalism, institutional investors should form a comprehensive corporate governance policy, board rooms are invariably filled with 'yes' men and the report also has drawn attention to the Auditing and assurance standard 4 (Revised) on auditor's responsibility to consider fraud and error in an audit of financial statements. Disclosures in financial statements should be such that these statements do not deceive financial statement users.

Naresh Chardra Committee Recommendations

The Ministry of Finance and Company Affairs constituted in year 2002 a high powered committee to examine the Auditor-company relationship and regulating auditors etc., and this committee deliberated under the chairmanship of Shri Naresh Chandra (former Cabinet Secretary). The recommendations of the committee, if approved and implemented, was expected to carry tremendous impact on the role, functioning and effectiveness of professionals like chartered accountants, company secretaries and cost accountants, legal practitioners, CFOs etc. The committee has recommended drastic changes in corporate disclosures, corporate responsibility and corporate governance which will have significant ramifications for the future of the Indian economy; the general opinion was that if the recommendations were faithfully implemented, it could lead to the strengthening the functioning and standards of corporate governance in the country, apart from restoring investors confidence in the corporate sector.

Concept Paper on the Companies Act

The concept paper on the new Companies Act has retained some of the controversial provisions in the companies (Amendment) Bill, 2003 includign appointing about 50 per cent independent directors in a company's board and prohibiting multi-layered subsidiaries. The suggestions covered pruning number of sections to 289 from the present 658, board having at least 50% independent directors, investment may be routed through more than one subsidiary, no retirement age for directors, no approval for raising managerial remuneration and also proposing consolidation of accounts and rationalizing penalties. According to experts, there were a number of welcome measures which aimed to bring about better corporate governance and enhanced shareholder participation in order to keep the legal framework in line with international practices but at the same time greater autonomy was needed by companies to ensure speedy decision making; The move to de-link procedural aspects of a law from substantive law was favoured, as it would help in addressing the problems of a routine nature by administrative action. The concept paper empowered the government to make rules and regulations for many of the proposed provisions.

Vanishing Companies

The Government and the regulatory agencies have initiated several measures to tackle the menace of vanishing companies. However still sustained and stepped up efforts, according to experts, are required to ensure that companies do not vanish in the way they have in the past. SEBI and Department of Company Affairs provided the following criteria to term a company as vanishing company: Non compliance with the listing requirement with the respective stock exchange and ROC for two years. Non submission of required reports with the regional exchanges for two years; and Non availability at the registered office for inspection by the stock exchanges. As per the study conducted by Prime database during the period 1st April 1992 to 31st March 1996, as many as 205 issues were not traded at all and 2987 issues were traded below the offer price. The total market capitalization of all these illiquid scrips amounted to Rs. 37,799 crores. Besides 118 companies proved to be vanishing companies that collected the public money and vanished. It was reported that investors including financial institutions have lost around Rs. 15000 crores in the stock market in the post 1994 period. The various actions taken by SEBI included debarring 96 companies from all activities of capital market for a period of five years from 29.9.03, introduction of Electronic Data Information filing and Retrieval system, introduction of Central Database of market participants regulations, 2003 etc. A high powered central coordination and monitoring committee has been set up to monitor the action taken against the vanishing companies and unscrupulous promoters who misused the funds raised from the public. In order to tackle this menace, suggestions like providing individual corporate identity account numbers for promoters/ directors of listed companies, post–issue monitoring of funds by SEBI with wide powers etc have been made. The vanishing companies, being a scar on the face of the Indian capital market, it has been emphasized that the regulators and the public at large should coordinate and work together to remove the scar permanently.

Better Governance and Terrible Governance

The warning signals provided by some expert runs as follows, "Guidelines and checklist, and checking the boxes has little or nothing to do with good governance. By checking the right boxes, companies can give the appearance of improved governance; some may believe they actually have improved. But-by-the numbers conformance to guidelines, in and of itself, does not prevent terrible governance." Boards wanting compliance assistance would find it readily available either through rating services or other professionals. Perhaps, the solution may lie in making the board and directors effective in their onerous functions; What makes a Director effective?

"A director should have requisite expertise so that he can make a contribution to the functioning of the board. Directors should measure themselves in terms of their value add to the organization. Directors should be articulate and persuasive. Of course, they should be team players who could carry conviction. They may be required at times to play the role of a rebel, a devil's advocate, or even (Parkinson's) abominable no-man to ensure thorough and comprehensive analysis of issues that need-attention at the board level. Their effectiveness will also depend on the information systems, procedures and culture of transparency in the organization. It may be worthwhile to focus especially on this issue and train directors on their role so that maximum benefits all round are obtained. Ultimately, the effectiveness of a person in an organization depends on three factors: motivation, ability or expertise, and role clarity."[4]

CHAPTER 2 which deals with compliance requirements, covers various areas which may be considered to be relevant in the above context, particularly the following: quality and composition of the board, board governance and more particularly, finding the answer to the question, 'Has CG remained more in paper?'. The amended clause 49 is to be found in one of the Appendices.

CHAPTER 3: BEST BOARDS

Codes of Corporate Governance

The Corporate Governance principles are said to revolve around three key basic principles, namely integrity and fairness, transparency and disclosures and accountability and responsibility. In evolving good corporate governance practices, these principles become the core issues. Although, voluntary codes may be ideal, in practice written down legislation and regulation have been found to be essential. The compliance of codes of corporate governance stipulated by the regulators like SEBI has therefore become an essential condition for fulfilling the introduction of sound governance practices. In so far as the principle of integrity and fairness goes, the top management has to inculcate a culture of ethical practices so that the same can percolate to other levels in the organization. In respect of the second principle, 'transparency and disclosures' the board is expected to reveal all key activities and results in a periodic manner. The effectiveness of the disclosures, in turn, would depend upon strong MIS, active role of audit committees, proper internal control, supported by systems and procedures. Accountability and responsibility, categorised as the third pillar in the essence of good corporate governance demands that the executive management is accountable to the board and the board being accountable to the shareholder and other stakeholders. Where the company follows high ethical standars, it is emboldened to be accountable to all stakeholders, even for their omissions and commissions. In practice, it is noticed that companies having high standards of integrity and good performance record, do have concerns for the society and they actively undertake socially responsible activities. Good governance practices provide sufficient strength to the management to

---

4 What make a Director effective: p. 51 Corporate Boards and Governance.

withstand pressures under recessionatry trends. No doubt performance parameters of corporates may exhibit swings with the cycles of business in a market based economy but rating agencies have evolved methodologies to evaluate stakeholder value creation and corporate governance practices in different conditions and thus are in a position to provide a fair assessment.

Managerial Excellence: The Intangible. There are success stories of best companies in each industry. The reasons for their success may be different, not least because they operate in very different industries. The qualities needed for being successful in the utilities business, for instance, are different from those required to beat the competition in the fast moving consumer good industry. Nevertheless it is possible to identify some common characteristics of businesses that are at the very top of their respective industries. The most common factor is that all of them have strong balance sheets and cash flows. But that is more the result of their success than a reason for it–years of strong profit growth should result in robust balance sheets, providing a cushion for any company to ride out the storms that come sometime or the other. Success, in short, builds success. It is not good balance sheet that builds a strong business, but a good business that builds a strong balance sheet. Therefore corporate boards and the management should be in a continuous move to seek and post high profits and growth, year after year. How do we seek managerial excellence? The road map runs as follows:

"Another lesson is that managements that learn from their mistakes can win again. Exhibit one is the story of Bajaj Auto catching up with Hero Honda in terms of market capitalization after losing market leadership in two wheelers. It is trite to say that global reach is what distinguishes the winners in the IT sector from the second-rung players, but it is, nevertheless, true. Transparency and good corporate governance are other qualities that come readily to mind when talking of leaders in the IT business. Global reach is a factor in the pharmaceutical industry, too, but the competition between Ranbaxy and Dr. Reddy's shows that markets prefer a less risky, more steady and diversified model of growth than a high-risk, high reward one. Size is important as seen when we compare Tata Motors with Ashok Leyland, but not all important, as illustrated by a comparison between HDFC Bank and the State Bank of India, or when we put Tata Steel next to SAIL. In short, while there is no one reason for excellence, perhaps the critical distinguishing feature lies in that intangible: managerial excellence".[5]

Checks and balances

It has been noticed that enormous consolidated power in the hands of CEO underscores the need for an effective system of checks and balances. It has been observed "The relationship between directors and CEOs, as it has evolved, seems convoluated. Directors serve to provide management oversight, but when the CEO holds the power to hire, pay and fire directors, the director's ability to act independently is certainly compromised. Because independence is a hallmark of fiduciary responsibility, anything that diminishes independence is a major governance problem". Boards of directors should therefore beware when a CEO achieves star status because their ability to discipline or replace that CEO, when circumstances demand, is greatly compromised. Even if the board has legitimate reasons for wanting to make a change in CEO, they

---

5 Pointers to excellence, the Business Standard dated 19th August 2004.

may feel hamstrung by the probability of a stock price decline in the near term. In view of their vast numbers and geographic dispersion, shareholders cannot supervise every move that management makes. Instead, they rely on the board of directors, which they elect-at least ostensibly-to do that for them. To hold them accountable, shareholders need a mechanism to assess the board's performance as a group and as individuals. That, in turn, requires that shareholders have accurate and timely information about what the board does and why.

The legal and capital market system provides investors an alternative to voting with their feet to force good governance. Through a proxy contest, shareholders can propose a new slate of directors, when they feel that a company is not being managed for the investor's benefit. Such exercise/options, unfortunately are very expensive and often fail because institutional investors are reluctant to vote against the incumbent management. Also few shareholders stand to gain more from proxy contest than they would from selling their shares. Institutional investors, portfolio managers for pension funds, mutual funds, life insurance companies and the like who control or hold considerable percentage of equity securities, should analyse not only the information reported by the companies but also and more important, information available from other independent sources. One might expect that such managers would be the investor's advocates for better governance. Encouraging good governance is not only in the interest of professional investors, it is also their obligation as participants in the economic system. Corporate governance experts, when they are hired whether for financial expertise, audit committee support, compensation advice, succession planning or other corporate governance issues, they help resolve tensions and improve governance, through information, analysis and discussion. Such expert advice and actions on their advise, should also be covered in the Director's Report/Corporate governance discussion.

Training and Research Institutions

Training and research institutions, everyone would agree provide the mechanism to propagate the best models of corporate governance. The cabinet decision to set up a National Foundation for corporate governance is a welcome step as this foundation can actively promote the required training and research activities in corporate governance. The above step augurs well for revolutionizing the concept of best practices and for ushering in an era of good corporate governance. In the reference section, readers would find more details about the Corporate governance centers that are being established.

CHAPTER 3: Best Boards, among other things, cover the need for a balanced board, governance code, role of nominee directors, how do we evaluate individual director's performance, the role of the board and also the features of good corporate governance. In the Appendices, some topics which can help in the formation of 'Best Boards' have been included.

CHAPTER 4: CORPORATE GOVERNANCE AND BANKING SECTOR

Corporate governance and Public sector banks

The public sector banks in India are insulated by the 'safe wall' provided by government ownership. Therefore discipline enforced by market forces carries a limited role. The objective of the Government as the major stakeholder of a public sector banks has been to balance the constraints imposed by its accountability to parliament on behalf of these institutions, with the statutory mandate of nominate the board of these institutions in such a manner, as to ensure effective management. In so far as it concerns standards of 'transparency and disclosures', such disclosures in financial statements are guided by Schedule II of Section 29 of Banking Regulation Act, 1949, RBI guidelines, Listing agreement in case of listed banks, accounting standards and guidelines issued by the Institute of Chartered Accountants of India (ICAI) etc. In addition to the statutory disclosures, banks give additional information by way of Director's Report, about the bank's overall performance, its business strategies, its services, products and risk management etc., It may be mentioned that Narasimham committee in its first report had recommended sweeping changes in the norms to be followed by banks for making them viable and internationally competitive. Further, as per the RBI's guidelines, various disclosures and the business ratios (Tier I and Tier II), percentage of net NPAs to net advances, interest income as % to working funds, operating profit as % to working funds, return on assets, business per employee, profit per employee, amount of subordinate debt eligible for tier II capital and details of provisions and contingencies appearing in profit and loss account. Bank, since March 2000, have started to disclose among other things, the maturity profile of assets/liabilities, movement in NPAs and associated provisions and lending exposure to sensitive sectors. Banks are now required to submit half yearly review/report to the RBI/A listed bank is also required to prepare cash flow statement in accordance with the requirements of the Listing Agreement (clause 32). If we turn to the 'Accounting Standards' it means the standards of accounting recommended by the Institute of Chartered accountants of India and prescribed by the Central government in consultation with the National Advisory committee on accounting standards. Indian GAAP is largely drawn from the International Accounting Standards) ICAI is also making efforts to have industry specific accounting standards. It has been suggested that Indian public sector banks could adopt USGAAP to address fundamental corporate governance issues. Stronger public sector banks may choose to voluntarily adopt 'Transparency Disclosures' as per USGAAP and address many of the fundamental corporate governance issues. The Hampel committee (UK) has recommended that boards should introduce procedures for assessing their own collective performance and that of individual directors. Reference may also be made to the recent failure of USA's leading company–Enron, mainly due to creating accounting, impropriety and lack of transparency; it also highlighted the failure of the 'Internal Audit committee' of the board to police their auditors.

Code for Corporate Governance for PSBs

It has also been suggested that a code for corporate governance for PSBs would enable them to achieve high standards of corporate behaviour and bring about openness, integrity and accountability in their working. The stock exchanges can make compliance statement from the public sector banks a condition for listing. The code would provide boards of PSBs with a check list against which to measure their standing in matters of governance and give shareholders, particularly the institutional shareholders, an agenda to pursue in their dialogues with the boards. A suggested model code of best practices for PSBs, would probably cover the following areas: Bifurcation of the posts of chairman and managing director, a minimum tenure of

3 years for them, a formal schedule of matters reserved for them for decisions making, active non-executive directors carrying defined responsibilities, non-executive directors offering independent judgement on issues of strategy, performance, resource planning, key appointments and standards of conduct, re-appointment of non-executive directors based on an appraisal of their contribution, effective audit committee. Institutional investors like mutual funds, UTI, LIC, GIC and FIIs playing an effective and useful role, improving quality of shareholders' communication, reasonable fees and compensation to directors etc.

As regards the impact of the code for corporate governance on boards of PSBs, the following may be stated: "The issue of corporate governance for PSBs has come into prominence mainly in the wake of competitive environment ushered in by the financial sector reforms. In an increasingly Competitive world, survival of PSBs will not be guaranteed merely by virtue of the fact that government is the majority shareholders for them. In such a scenario, the PSBs would have to transform themselves into outperforming organizations. The functioning of the boards of PSBs needs to undergo a change if they are to meet the growing expectations of their stakeholders. There has to be increasing synergy between executive and non-executive director's institutional shareholders and external auditors. A formal code of corporate governance would be a first step in this direction. Being a document of self-discipline, it would be free from bureaucratic rigidities and be flexible enough to undergo a change as and when the situation warrants."[6]

Reforms of banking sector

Reforms initiated in the 1990 covered deregulation of interest rates, introduction of new products, relaxation in investment norms for financial intermediaries, especially banks, emergence of new institutions such as primary dealers and mutual funds. Bank's foreign currency investments were eased, in addition to withdrawal of reserve requirements on inter-bank borrowings. Various reform measures also helped sharp growth of the foreign exchange market. Steps were taken to make capital market safer. RBI permitted entry of new private banks and foreign banks; the size of non-bank intermediation expanded considerably. Several DFIs have been permitted to access the domestic and international capital markets. DFIs can now offer a host of new products and services to meet the needs of industrial enterprises. The scheduled commercial banks and DFIs are now following the prudential norms as means to maintain their financial health, credit concentration, asset classification, income recognition etc., In future there would be qualitative changes and there would be sharper, information technology-based and knowledge centric, risk reward paradigm rather than process-based administration. Banks would adopt new skills similar to competitors, in technology, sales and marketing enterprises.

In order to bring the banking industry to global levels, the Government is contemplating new initiatives to bring substantive changes in the banking sector. According to the Finance Minister, public sector banks were seriously evaluating consolidation as one of the strategies to increase competitiveness and ad value. It was

---

6 Corporate governance in public sector banks, p 333, Emerging trends in International Business and Financial services.

pointed out that revision in the foreign direct investment limit from 49 to 74 per cent in private sector banks would create an enabling environment for higher FDI inflows. It would result in infusion of new technology and management practices resulting in enhanced competitiveness. According to the Finance Minister, consolidation would allow economies of scale in terms of footprint, manpower and other resources. Large size enables facing international competition more easily, apart from better management of risk. Small and weak banks posed systemic risks with their low capital adequacy ratio and high non performing assets.

Basel II and containing risk

Banks in India have recently been asked by the RBI to adopt, by March 31, 2007, a new, proactive approach towards risk management as laid down by the Basel committee on bank supervision. The Basle Committee on Banking supervision in its report has recommended that banks in their financial reports and disclosures to the public must provide timely information which would facilitate market participants (depositors and investors) to assess the risks associated with a bank. Risk management, by whatever name called, has been basic to banking business, which is more leveraged than any other comparable business. Banks create a multiplier effect by lending (and investing) more than what their level of deposits would normally permit. It is in that context that banking regulators hit upon the idea of asking banks to adjust their capital (the other critical component alongside deposits on the liabilities side of their balance sheets) in line with their risks profile. The more risks a bank took on, the more it had to provide for by way of capital and reserves. The new Basel II norms address these two deficiencies and to quote, "A multi-pronged strategy will recognize all types of risks and comprise measures to contain them. The new approach also recognizes the need to supplement regulatory stipulation of capital adequacy requirements—still the first pillar of a more comprehensive framework—with other tools. Better regulation and inculcating market discipline among banks have come to be recognized as equally important; they constitute the second and the third pillars. The three mutually reinforcing elements, it is hoped, will pave the for a superior risk containment strategy."[7]

The Economic Survey presented on February 25, 2005 calls for greater competition and efficiency in banking to bring spreads down, reduce non performing assets and improve the credit culture an better credit appraisal skills to identify future winners among start ups and small scale units. Almost all PSBs have listed their shares and a few including Punjab National Bank are now in the market to raise fresh resources. The interests of the non-government shareholders will have to be reckoned with.

CHAPTER 4 explains why corporate governance is more of an imperative in banking sector and the topics relating to financial sector reforms, Reserve Bank of India, proposals to improve corporate governance, banking turnaround, diversified services, DFIs and corporate governance. In the Appendices, the methodology for ranking banks in India and also bank scams and frauds, have been covered in addition to other topics.

---

7 Basel II and containing risk, The Hindu dated March 4, 2005.

CHAPTER 5: CORPORATE GOVERNANCE AND PUBLIC ENTERPRISES

Public Sector Reforms

The fiscal and financial problem of may countries after the second oil shock of 1979 forced governments to refocus on their public sector enterprises (PSEs). They were forced to address the following issues: Could PSEs be reformed and made more accountable to market discipline without dilution of state ownership whether ownership per se was critical factor in relatively poor performance? Was there something intrinsic in government ownership that created poor incentives for managers and workers, reduced the efficacy of monitoring and altered the rules of governance resulting in lower corporate value? The first question paved the way for maintaining the public sector with greater autonomy, less ministerial interference. Profitability and management by objectives through the process of memorandum of understanding provided some tools. In due course it become clear that experiments with government ownership and greater autonomy was at best a half way house. PSEs did not have the incentive structure to differentiate between rents that are necessary to promote efficiency and those which merely reward unproductive rent seeking activities. The second issue, whether state ownership is critical to efficiency has resulted in disinvestments, privatization, restructuring etc., Such experiments were found to be applied specially in countries like UK, Mexico, Chile, Argentina, Poland and the Czech republic and others. It was felt that competitive pressures could improve performance if PSEs faced hard budgets. Therefore measures like hardened budgets by reducing or eliminating direct subsidies, putting access to credit on a more commercial basis, strengthening regulation of PSE monopoly prices were applied. The reforms also focused on strengthening supervision and regulation, relaxing controls over interest rates and reducing direct credit. The measures also included increased managerial autonomy and signed explicitly performance agreements.

The ruling United Progressive Alliance released its common minimum programme on 27th May 2004 and the highlights covered: Privatisation to be on a case by case basis, Generally profitable PSUs not be privatized, LIC and GIC to remain public sector entities, PSU banks to be given full managerial autonomy, automatic hire and fire regime ruled out but labour laws and Industrial Disputes Act to be reviewed etc. It declared that the Navratnas (IOC, ONGC, HPCL, BPCL, NTPC, BHEL, SAIL etc.), would, in particular be retained in the public sector fold and no PSU would be privatized if it leads to the emergence of a monopoly or restricts competition. The President in his address to the parliament also mentioned that PSU privatization would be on case-by-case basis and there would be full autonomy to profit making PSUs. The Government believes that there must be a direct link between privatization and social needs – like, for example, the use of privatization revenues for designated social sector schemes. Public sector companies and nationalized banks will be encouraged to enter the capital market to raise resources and offer new investment avenues to retain investors. In the budget for 2005-06, it was emphasized that investment is the paramount requirement to consolidate the growth process and in agriculture, public and private investment in the infrastructure would be enhanced to support expansion, diversification and value addition. In the industrial sector, both the public sector and the private sector were to play the leading role in providing and facilitating investment in public goods such as roads, railways, power, seaports and airports. The government proposed to provide equity support of Rs. 14,040 crore and loans of Rs. 3,554 crore to Central Public enterprises including Railways. It was brought out that capital market, banks, insurance companies, pension funds and superannuation funds would have a crucial role in mobilizing and disbursing the financial resources required to sustain high investment.

Sound Corporate Governance

Some issues/proposals which related to disinvestment, privatization and restructuring of public sector units may be mentioned, in the following lines:

- Reforming PSUs without privatization may be difficult via Memorandum of Understanding, because of the near impossibility of Indian political leaders ever voluntarily going into a 'self-denial mode' and refraining from interfering in the functioning of enterprises. For the disinvestments to be successful, there should be appropriate corporate governance systems and functional autonomy. According to some studies, privatization can enhance enterprise performance if corporate governance is sound.
- For restructuring to succeed, it depends on factors like degree of product competition, availability of external finance for restructuring and the degree of firm independence from the government. Other factors also mattered and these covered state of technology, stock of human capital, internal resources/retained earning etc.,
- Public enterprises suffering from chronic losses and those with cumulated losses equal to or more than their net worth need a more urgent attention for their rehabilitation/restructuring without delay. Enterprises which cannot be rehabilitated need liquidation rather than resturucturing. PSUs with internal financial resources and operating in growth sectors eg. Software, need strategic restructuring including diversification;
- PSUs in which minority disinvestments are accompanied by handing over the management control to private sector strategic partners, may have to be subjected to laws regarding monitoring and control of monopolistic, restrictive, anti-competitive, unfair trade practices and competition policy, subjected to laws regarding monitoring and control of monopolistic, restrictive, anti-competitive, unfair trade practices and competition policy.

Policy Review

Some important policy pronouncements on the working of public sector enterprises may be noted and these include:

- **Granting PSUs special status:** The department of public enterprises has decided to review the criteria companies have to fulfil to qualify for 'ratna' status. Navratna or mini-ratna status or public sector units secures them greater autonomy. This would help the proposals to provide greater autonomy to Power Grid corporation of India Ltd., Power Finance Corporation and National Hydro electric Power corporation.

- **PSUs must face market test:** It was proposed to throw open government enterprises to greater participation in the market economy. The public sector units should have their shares traded on the stock exchange.
- **Dividends from PSUs:** The Finance ministry is eager to ensure that public sector undertakings including cash rich oil companies and state owned banks, cough up the government's share of dividend during a year when their profits are soaring.

The Prime Minister also advocated the need for greater functional autonomy to public sector CEOs. He said, "Many of our public sector enterprises have very talented and committed leaders. We must strengthen their hands so that they can provide effective leadership and manage public resources more efficiently. They must be cost effective if they are to serve the interests of the people. However the real strength of any organization lies in the commitment and capability of its many functionaries."

CHAPTER 5 which covers the topic of Corporate governance in public enterprises discusses various issues like autonomy and accountability, restructuring public sector, privatisation and disinvestment and also about developing a culture of better corporate governance. Useful reference material have been provided both in the Appendices and in the reference section of the book.

CHAPTER 6: BUSINESS ETHICS AND SOCIAL RESPONSIBILITY

What is Ethics?

Ethics according to the Concise Oxford Dictionary means "a set of principles of morals, science of morals, moral principles, rules of conduct, the whole field of moral science." The development of moral principles and codes of conduct is a progress which is directly linked with the development of a society. Depending upon the conditions prevailing in a society what was considered moral and ethical at a given point of time may no longer be considered as moral and ethical. In fact there is the school of thought which holds that the entire issue of morals is situational. All persons, whether in business, government or any other enterprise are concerned with ethics. BUSINESS ETHICS is concerned with truth and justice and has a variety of aspects, such as the expectations of society, fair competition, advertising, public relations, social responsibility, consumer autonomy, and corporate behaviour.

Corporate scandals such as those of Enron and Worldcom have shaken the confidence of investors. While the investors in Worldcom, Global Crossing and other telecommunication companies where referring, however, top managers of these companies got rich. Because of such improprieties, the United States initiated a new legislation — Sarbanes-Oxley law; According to this law, CEOs and CFOs are required to certify the correctness of the reports to regain the confidence of investors. Business week ("After-Enron: The Ideal Corporation," Business week, August 26, 2002, pp 68-74) therefore suggests several idea for the creation of the ideal corporation, which must be built on integrity, ethics, fairness and trust. The new corporate model must be more transparent for investors, suppliers, customers and employees. Performance data need to be accurate so that investors can trust the members. Executive pay must be perceived as being fair. The more open corporate culture needs to emphasise accountability, and employees must feel free to report unethical and unfair practices. For the purpose of institutionalizing ethics, the following three ways have been suggested" (1) Establishing an appropriate company policy or a code of ethics, (2) Using a formally appointed ethics committee, and (3) teaching ethicisin management development programmes. A code is set to comprise a statement of policies, principles, or rules that guide behaviour. Mention should also be made about 'whistle blowing' which means making known to outside agencies about unethical company practices. Its objective is to protect and defend persons who disclose actions harmful to the environment and public health.

What is Social Responsibility of Business?

"Corporate social responsibility is not philanthropy. It is not charity. It is an investment in our collective future." — Dr. Manmohan Singh

Conceptually, social responsibility implies an objective concern for the community that restrains corporate behaviour from causing destructive and harmful activities, however profitable they may be immediately and leads to the direction of positive contributions to human betterment defined in various ways. This broad definition of Kenneth Andrew underlines the fact that corporate business activities cause damage to environment by polluting noise, air and water, destroying forests, hazards to health because of the nature of the products and the conditions of work in factories.

Corporate responsibility is still equated with 'social welfare' instead of being seen as related to core business issues of competitiveness and risk management. However, major groups such as Birla Group, the Tata Group, the Jindal group and ITC and banks such as Samsung and ICICI have earned recognition by their support of sustainable development. In their ethical business practices and also through trickle-down effect on the community around them. Some people would like to see such major groups and industry association talk about how to help India meet the Millennium Development goals. Corporate social responsibility, helps companies develop new competencies, builds reputations and enhance relations with the government, the investors and the general public. It is an exercise in goodwill that reaps rich rewards in the long run. Corporates are required to have specific policies with regard to environment, education, social welfare, anti-discrimination and community development, apart from occupational/health/safety and human right concerns. Numerous companies have established independent trusts and partnering with non governmental organizations to make positive contributions to society. Companies like Infosys., the Tata and Birla group of companies, Reliance, Wipro and Hindustan Lever are doing exemplary service to society.

CHAPTER 6 which is on Business ethics and social responsibility covers the following topics: Ethical principles, ethical propositions, ethics and corporate governance, ethics code and corporate social responsibility. Case studies/illustrations have been provided in the Appendices. In other sections of the book also, reference material have been provided and this includes "Arguments for social involvement of business and arguments against social involvement of business".

1

Corporate Governance: Introduction

1.1 CORPORATE GOVERNANCE: THE CONCEPT

The concept of corporate governance is gaining momentum because of various factors as well as the changing business environment. The EEC, GATT and WTO regulations have also contributed to the rising awareness and are compelling us to think in terms of adhering to the good governance practices. Corporate governance, by the very nature of the concept, cannot be exactly defined. However, there can be no two opinions that "effective accountability to all shareholders is the essence of corporate governance."

The following definition should help us to understand the concept better. "Corporate governance is not just corporate management, it is something much broader to include a fair, efficient and transparent administration to meet certain well-defined objectives. It is a system of structuring, operating and controlling a company with a view to achieve long-term strategic goals to satisfy shareholders, creditors, employees, customers and suppliers, and complying with the legal and regulatory requirements, apart from meeting environmental and local community needs. When it is practised under a well-laid out system, it leads to the building of a legal, commercial and institutional framework and demarcates the boundaries within which these functions are performed."[1]

Corporate governance cannot disregard the diverse interests—shareholders, lenders, employees, government, etc. It is believed that shareholders would increasingly assert their rights, hitherto virtually unknown; similarly the lending institutions, having to justify their performance in a market-driven environment, have no choice but to demand effective and efficient corporate governance; besides FIIs with substantial foreign investment in India would demand greater transparency and internationally recognised, sound corporate practices. The new paradigm of governance to bring about quality corporate governance is not only a necessity to serve the diverse corporate interests, but it is also a key requirement in the best interests of the corporates themselves.

Corporate practices in the matter of disclosure, transparency, group accounting, role of directors, degree of accountability to the shareholders, lenders and overall public good are some of the critical issues which require a fresh and closer look. A framework for addressing concerns public good, such as regard for environment, overall conservation of resources, cost effective managerial input—all these would, among other things form part of the core of corporate governance. Government can play a catalytic role in creating the enviroment for quality governance through an appropriate regulatory framework. Corporate leadership and its mindset would also determine the sort of governance that would ultimately evolve.

---

1 Corporate governance: Time for a Metamorphosis' The Hindu July 9, 1997.

The Cadbury committee has also defined the term "Corporate Governance" and according to the committee, it means,

"(It is) the system by which companies are directed and controlled." It may also be defined as a system of structuring, operating and controlling a company with the following specific aims:-

(i) Fulfilling long-term strategic goals of owners;

(ii) Taking care of the interests of employees;

(iii) A consideration for the environment and local community;

(iv) Maintaining excellent relations with customers and suppliers;

(v) Proper compliance with all the applicable legal and regulatory requirements.

We may also note what the CII constituted committee has to say on the definition, "Corporate governance deals with laws, procedures, practices and implicit rules that determine a company's ability to take informed managerial decisions vis-à-vis its claimants–in particular, its shareholders, creditors, customers, the State and employees. There is global consensus about the objective of 'good corporate governance: maximising long-term shareholder value." Further the Kumar Mangalam Birla committee constituted by SEBI has observed that, "Strong corporate governance is indispensable financial reporting structure." According to ICSI, "We may define 'corporate governance as a blend of rules, regulations, laws and voluntary practices that enable companies to attract financial and human capital, perform efficiently and thereby maximise long term value for the shareholders besides respecting the aspirations of multiple stakeholders including that of the society."[2]

In India, the question of corporate governance has come up mainly in the wake of economic liberalisation and deregulation of industry and business, as well as the demand for a new corporate ethos and stricter compliance with the law of the land. In the context of the unique situation in India where the financial institutions hold substantial stakes in companies, the accountability of the directors, including non-executive directors and nominees, has come into sharp focus."[3]

In the UK and USA the corporate system and structure is characterised by diffused ownership and shareholding, as a large percentage of shares is subscribed by the public. They have a well developed capital market with active shareholder participation. Firms are subject to strict disclosure norms and investor protection. The focus of good governance in these countries 'is the code of best practices.' However, the Japanese and German models are somewhat different. There is a close association between the financial institutions and the firms, as with the predominant shareholders. Both have close relationship towards their commitment to a philosophy of lifetime association. In India, a strident demand for evolving a code of good practices by the corporates themselves is emerging. In the global perspective, it may constitute a necessity to cut through the maze of prevalent questionable practices, indefensible management attitudes to stakeholders and penetrable non-disclosures.

---

2 Corporate Governance Reporting (Model Formats) by ICSI 2003.

3 Corporate Governance: The new paradigm Charted Secretary October 1997.

1.1.1 Corporate Governance Abuses and the General Scene

In the Indian business groups, the concept of dominant shareholders is more amorphous. The promoters' shareholding is spread across several friends and relatives and also corporate entities. It may be difficult to establish the total effective holding of this group. However, the aggregate holding of all these entities taken together is typically swell below a majority stake. Since financial institutions have historically played a passive role, it paves the way for the promoters acting as the dominant shareholders, despite they may not even be the largest single shareholder. The promoters are thus enabled to play all the games that a dominant shareholder can play, namely structuring of businesses and transfer of assets between group companies, preferential allotments of shares to themselves, payment for "services" to closely held group companies and the like. This has led to the situation of what could be termed, "There may be many financially sick companies but no financially sick promoters". Thus corporate governance abuses perpetrated by a dominant shareholder poses a difficult regulatory dilemma; The regulatory intervention is therefore required to be concerned with micro—management which are related to routine business decisions. The general scene with regard to the Indian corporate sector, as perceived by Dilip Kumar Sen may be noted, which are as follows: [4]

- Companies are often run as if they were the managing director's or CEO's personal freedom;
- Those at the helm are only about the principal shareholders' interests, any benefit to other shareholders is only consequential;
- Majority of directors are unaware that they are agents of shareholders and their position is one of trust and faith
- Participation of non-executive directors in meetings whether of the board or any committee thereof is inversely proportional to the health of the bottom line—better the bottom line lesser the participation.
- Most directors do not consider it necessary to update themselves on changes in laws, regulations;
- Non executive directors do not see themselves as watch-dog of the owners.
- Boardrooms are invariably filled up by 'yes' men who do not raise relevant questions.
- Except in a crisis even nominee directors tend to play a passive role at board meetings and do not oppose the proposals of the management.

Therefore, the author of the above article, concludes, "Hence, no amount of regulation can enforce the true spirit of good corporate governance practices in a company unless it comes from within the organisation".

1.1.2 What are the objectives of corporate governance?

The development of corporate governance concept is naturally and essentially related to the 'objectives of corporate governance' and it may be important to note what the 'Introductory framework' has to say on this:[5]

---

4 A Few leaves of Corporate governance, The Hindu Business Line dated 2nd October 2003.

5 Corporate Governance Reporting (Model formats) by ICSI 2003.

"Good governance is integral to the very existence of a company. It inspires and strengthens investor's confidence by ensuring company's commitment to higher growth and profits. It seeks to achieve following objectives:

(i) That a properly structured Board capable of taking independent and objective decisions is in place at the helm of affairs;

(ii) That the Board is balanced as regards the representation of adequate number of non-executive and independent directors who will take care of the interests and well being of all the stakeholders;

(iii) That the Board adopts transparent procedures and practices and arrives at decisions on the strength of adequate information.

(iv) That the Board has an effective machinery to subserve the concerns of stakeholders;

(v) That the Board keeps the shareholders informed of relevant developments impacting the company;

(vi) That the Board effectively and regularly monitors the functioning of the management team; and

(vii) That the Board remains in effective control of the affairs of the company at all times.

The overall endeavour of the Board should be to take the organisation forward, to maximise long-term value and shareholders' wealth."

1.1.3 Code convergence in Asia

The points of convergence, according to 'Code Convergence in Asia: Smoke or Fire?'[6], the following observation has been made:

"Although Asian countries are not moving towards identical systems of governance, there is a striking agreement among the proponents of reform in each country on the centrality of certain principles and these include:

- Enhancing shareholder value as the primary focus of companies, and upholding or extending shareholder rights (this is accepted, even in places like China, as a fundamental prerequisite for the development of capital Markets).
- The need for non-executive and independent non-executive directors to provide an "outside" view on strategic direction and to counterbalance the executives on the board (or to help strengthen the supervisory board vis-à-vis the management board in two-tier systems).
- The usefulness of board committees responsible for audit, nomination and compensation and comprising a majority of independent directors.
- The importance of higher levels of information disclosure from listed companies.
- Allowing or encouraging institutional investors to act as a check against management and a lever for enhancing board independence.

---

[6] Corporate Governance International, Vol. 3 Issue 1, March 2000, pp. 23-37.

Some of these principles have been incorporated into laws and regulations governing companies and securities trading, or have been expressed in the listing rules of stock exchanges. Most are now included in codes of best practice developed over the past two years, and may or may not be mandatory."

The Cadbury Committee. A spate of scandals and financial collapses in the UK in the late 1980s and early 1990s made the shareholders and banks worry about their investments. The UK Government therefore recognised the insufficiency of existing legislation role of self-regulation as a measure of controlling scandals and financial collapses. In order to prevent recurrence of business failures, the Cadbury committee was set up by the London stock Exchange in May 1991 inter alia to help raise standards of corporate governance. The "Code of best practices" (1992) of the Cadbury committee report spelt out the methods of governance needed to achieve a balance between the essential powers of the Board and their proper accountability.

1.1.4 Developments in India

On account of the interest generated by Cadbury committee report and also in the wake of Government initiatives to respond to corporate developments world over, the following major developments have taken place:

- The Confederation of Indian Industries (CII), the Associated Chambers of Commerce and Industry and the Securities and Exchange Board of India constituted committees to recommend initiatives in corporate governance. The CII, in 1996, took a special initiative on corporate governance. It was the first institutional initiative in Indian industry. The objective being to develop a code for corporate governance to be adopted by the Indian companies (private sector, the public sector,banks and fiancial institutions which are corporate entities), a code by CII carrying the title "Desirable Corporate Governance" was released.
- The SEBI appointed committee, known as the Kumar Mangalam Birla committee's recommendations led to the addition of Clause 49 in the Listing Agreement. Compliance of provisions of Clause 49 was largely made mandatory by listed companies. The committee recommended that there should be a separate section on Corporate governance in the Annual Report of companies. This section was required to detail the steps taken to comply with the recommendations of the committee and thus inform the shareholders of specific initiatives taken to ensure corporate governance. The committee accorded recognition to the three vital aspects of corporate governance, namely accountability, transparency and equality of treatment for all stakeholders.
- The Department of Company Affairs (DCA) appointed a study group on 15.5.2000 under the Chairmanship of the then Secretary DCA to suggest ways and means of achieving corporate governance. The study group appointed a task force. The study group recommended the setting up of an independent, autonomous centre for corporate excellence with a view to accord accredition and promote policy research and studies, training and education and awards etc., in the field of corporate excellence through improved corporate governance. It favoured greater shareholders' participation, formal recognition of corporate social responsibility, non-executive directors being charged with strategic and oversight responsibilities,

minimisation of interest–conflict potential, and also suggested application of corporate governance principles to public sector.

- The Department of Company Affairs also constituted on August 21, 2002 a high level committee, popularly known as Naresh Chandra committee, to examine various corporate governance issues and to recommend changes in the diverse areas such as the statutory auditor-company relationship, rotation of statutory auditors, procedure for appointment and determination of audit fees, restrictions if necessary on non-audit fees, independence of auditing functions, ensuri presentation of 'true and fair' statement of the financial affairs of compani certification of financial statements and accounts, regulation of oversig functionaries, setting up an independent regulator and the role of independent directors. The committee has made very significant recommendations for changes, inter alia, in the Companies Act.
- Yet another major development includes the constitution of a committee by SEBI under the Chairmanship of Shri N.R. Narayana Murthy, for reviewing the implementation of corporate governance code by listed companies. The mandatory recommendations of the committee on various matters are detailed in the Annexure.
- The Department of Company Affairs also has set up a proactive standing company law advisory committee to advise on issues like inspection of corporates for wrong doings, role of independent directors and auditors and their liability, suggesting steps to enhance imposition of penalties. A High powered Central Coordination and Monitoring committee (CCMC) co-chaired by Secretary DCA and Chairman SEBI was also set up to monitor action against vanishing companies and unscrupulous promoters, who misused funds raised from public.
- SEBI has also undertaken a project for development of a comprehensive instrument by a reputed rating agency for rating the good corporate governance practices of listed companies.

1.1.5 Good Governance and Value Addition

What benefits or value addition, the corporates are likely to achieve through sound and effective corporate governance practices? The answer, as provided by ICSI runs as follows and the road map is Factors which add greater value through good governance, may be summarised as follow:[7]

- Adoption of good governance practices stability and growth to the enterprise.
- Good governance system, demonstrated by adoption of good corporate governance practices, builds confidence amongst stakeholddders as well as prospective stakeholders. Investors are willing to pay higher price to the corporate demonstrating strict adherence to internationally accepted norms of corporate governance.

---

[7] Corporate Governance Reporting (Model Formats) by ICSI 2003.

- Effective governance reduces perceived risks, consequently reduces cost of capital; it also enables board of directors to take quick and better decisions which ultimatley improves bottom line of the corporates.
- In to-day's knowledge driven economy, demonstrating excellence in skills has become the ultimate tool in the hands of board of directors to leverage competitive advantage.
- Adoption of good corporate governance practices provides long-term sustenance and strengthens stakeholders' relationship.
- A good corporate citizen becomes an icon and enjoys a position of respect.
- Potential stakeholders aspire to enter into relationships with enterprises whose governance credentials are exemplary.

Appendices

1.1 HISTORY OF CORPORATE GOVERNANCE[8]

The seeds of modern Corporate Governance were probably sown by the Watergate scandal in the United States. As a result of subsequent investigations, US regulatory and legislative bodies were able to highlight the control failures that had allowed several major Corporations to make illegal political contributions and to bribe government officials. This led to the development of the Foreign and Corrupt Practices Act of 1977 in USA that contained specific provisions regarding the establishment, maintenance and review of systems o f internal control.

This was followed in 1979 by the Securities and Exchange Commission of USA's proposals for mandatory reporting on internal financial controls. In 1985, following a series' of high profile business failures in the USA. the most notable one of which being the Savings and Loan collapse, the Treadway Commission was formed. Its primary role was to identify the main causes of mis-representation in Financial Reports and to recommend ways of reducing incidence thereof. The Treadway Report published in 1987 highlighted the need for a proper control environment, independent Audit Committees and an objective Internal Audit function. It called for published reports on the effectiveness of internal control. It also requested the sponsoring organizations to develop an integrated set of internal control criteria to enable companies to improve their controls. Accordingly COSO (Committee of Sponsoring Organizations) was born. The report produced by it in 1992 stipulated a control framework, which has been endorsed and refined in the four subsequent UK reports: Cadbury, Rutteman, Hampel and Turnbull. While developments in the United States stimulated a debate in the UK, a spate of scandals and collapses in that country in the late 1980s and early 1990's led the Shareholders and Banks to worry about their investments. These also led the Government in UK to recognize that the then existing legislation and self-regulation were not working.

The issue of corporate governance became particularly significant in the context of globalisation because one special feature of the late 20th century/21st century globalisation is that in addition to the traditional three elements of the economy, namely physical capital in terms of plant and machinery, technology and labour, the volatile element of financial capital invested in the emerging markets and in the third world countries is an important element of modern globalisation and has become particularly powerful. Thanks to the ubiquitous application of information technology, at the touch of a computer mouse, it is possible now to transfer billions of dollars across borders. The significance and the impact of the volatility of the financial capital was realised when in June 1997 the currency of South East Asian countries started melting down in countries like Thailand, Indonesia, South Korea and Malaysia. It was realised by the World Bank and all investors that it is not enough to have good corporate management but one should have also good corporate governance because the investors want to be sure that

---

8 Extract from Dharma in Corporate Governance Charted Accountant, December 2003.

the decisions taken are ultimately in the interest of all stake holders. Honesty is the best policy is a fact that is now being re-discovered.

In practical terms, corporate governance has meant that there should be at the board level non-official directors who arc professionals and who have no conflicting interests and who can particularly operate the two key committees, the Ethics Committee and the Finance Committee to see that there is greater transparency in the management of the enterprise. Corporate governance ultimately has to come to mean better transparency in the operations without sacrificing business strategy or business secrets which are necessary for success in the market place, and absolutely ethical behaviour where the conduct of the company will not only be legal but also ethical.

1.2 CORPORATE GOVERNANCE RATING/BENCHMARKING CORPORATE GOVERNANCE

According to SEBI sources,SEBI has no intention to making rating of governance of listed companies mandatory. According to SEBI, it may be wrong to conclude that governnce norms compelled companies to sacrifice long-term interests or outlook in the pursuit of short-term interests and responses to market signals. SEBI has commissioned a study to determine the cost of compliance incurred by companies in respect of the regulatory framework, including Clause 49 of the listing agreement. The Narayana Murthy committee on corporate governance code had gone about its work in a highly professional and democratic manner and SEBI wanted that the professionals should study the issues raised and its recommendations, including the proposal for facilitation of 'whistle blowing'; ICRA which rated companies, adopted certain parameters and procedures for the purpose and the agency clarified that it normally required four to six weeks and the rating was not an audit or certification of regulatory compliance by the listed company and the exercise was not a guarantee against fraud. Its primary focus in the rating was on the business processes. Key variables analysed in rating included the shareholding structure, governance structure, management processes, board structure and processes, stakeholder relationship, transparency and disclosures and financial discipline. The starting point was an assessment of the corporate's compliance with statutory regulations as laid down in clause 49 of the listing agreement. Feedback from independent directors was a 'key part' of the rating process. International Finance Corporation, Washington which also carried out rating of companies followed OECD guidelines. The corporation faced the task of adopting the model and developing best practices suited to companies in emerging economies. Global experience showed that good governance helped corporates in accessing capital, especially long-term finance and equity. The IFC , as a major lender, looked at corporate governance as a tool to reduce investor risk and took account of the risk to reputation arising from bad governance. It was observed that companies which focused much on short term profits tended to lose in the long-term. Further according to international research, corporates with sound governance practices received higher premium for the shares in the stock market.

Measuring Corporate governance practice: It may be noted that Standard & Poor has recently launched a new service, known as Corporate Governance Scores, to evaluate corporate governance practices, both at a country and at a company level. In the case of country governance assessment, the analysis starts with an evaluation of governance issues at the country level. Depending upon the level of support, a country would be assessed as providing "strong support", "moderate support" or "weak support". The primary focus of this analysis is at the country or national level. However when the external environment is affected by the policies of regional/state governments, the focus of analysis would be modified to consider such influences. In the country governance analysis the following four main areas are considered: legal infrastructure, regulation, information infrastructure and market infrastructure.

The second part of the analysis is concerned with company analysis which is concerned with evaluating the practices at individual companies. Standard and Poor assigns scores to a company's overall practices using a synthesis of the OECD's and other international codes and guidelines of corporate governance practices. The analysis has four main components. These four components and sub categories are as follows:

Component 1 concerned with ownership structure, relates to transparency of ownership structure, concentration and influence of ownership.

Component 2 concerned with financial stakeholder relations , has subcategories such as regularity of, access to, and information on shareholder meeting, voting and shareholder meeting procedures and ownership rights.

Component 3 concerned with financial transparency and information disclosure comprises sub-categories like quality and content of public disclosure, timing of, and access to, public disclosure and independent and standing of the company's auditor.

Component 4, concerned with board structure and process, is related to Board structure and composition, role and effectiveness of board, role and independence of outside directors and directors and executives compensation, evaluation and succession policies.

The Anglo-Saxon system focuses primarily on the shareholder, while others, such as the German system, attempt to achieve a greater balance of interest between shareholders and other external stakeholders (creditors, employees, the community, the environment etc.). By addressing the interest of both creditors and shareholders, the scoring model recognises the importance of stakeholder's right beyond the rights of the shareholder. Finally how can corporate governance scores can benefit different sections? Investors can use the scores to identify and compare corporate governance standards of different companies in their portfolios or the risk characteristics associated with the corporate governance practices of potential investments. Corporate governance scores and the accompanying analysis also helps investors understand how a company's management treats the interest or shareholders, including minorities.

2

Corporate Governance and Compliance Requirements

2.1 IMPORTANCE OF LEGAL AND REGULATORY SYSTEMS

According to the Confederation of Indian Industry's code on corporate governance 'corporate governance' goes far beyond law. The code prepared by CII has focused on many key issues and this is at a time when corporate ethics has touched a new low in the wake of damning revelation of the misdeeds of some company managements. The recent collapse of CRB Capital Markets is a good example of what individual dishonesty plus system failure can do to shareholders. Given India's dismal law and order scenario, it has often been found that directors, managers, auditors and regulators are together engaged in asset stripping, profit diversification, sometimes leading to bankruptcy, thus causing heavy damage to the interests of small shareholders. It is believed that internal monitoring will achieve nothing when external legal and regulatory systems are lax. Corporate governance, according to experts, can be brought to shape, the moment penalty for corporate misbehaviour is hiked, liquidation and bankruptcy proceedings and takeovers become hassle-free and enforcement, rigorous. This works worldwide. Nordic nations like Finland and Sweden which have the best developed audit and enforcement systems, have the lowest rates of company misdemeanour. Sprucing up law enforcement and administration, in the Indian context, would therefore be an urgent need.

2.2 QUALITY AND COMPOSITION OF THE BOARD

It has been stressed that corporate governance is an inter-play among companies, their shareholders, creditors, capital markets and the company law. Corporates financed by public funds have their obligations to their shareholders, employees, creditors and the community at large. Differences are bound to be there between the Anglo-American, European, Japanese or South Korean models of corporate governance; however for good corporate governance, the quality and composition of the company's board of directors constitutes uniformly the most important key element. Radical structural changes in the composition of the corporate boards, improvements in the quality of information the managements are willing to share with their boards, a commitment to managerial disclosure with transparency are some of the new demands that have been stressed. Traditional Indian business houses are bound to be sceptical about the new demands or ideas. But taking cognizance of some of the sensitive issues facing the corporate sector may be timely and unavoidable.

2.3 BOARD GOVERNANCE AND PRACTICES

"At the lower end of the scale, a normal board would perform its basic duties and stay clear of prosecutions, but a growing company at the top of the industry would have a board with very high professional standards and have a very low levels of violations of law, but most important, it would not stop with maximising shareholder value, but will adopt in reaching its corporate goals and means as are consistent with current requirements of social responsibilities."[1]

Directors are generally exposed to many common claims: Civil rights violations, anti-trust violations, interference with contractual rights, misleading representations, imprudent investment, inadequate supervision of illegal payments, and such claims could be from outsiders, shareholders or employees. A diligent director, when he is in no way negligent, or privy to the breach, should invariably demand enforcement of a system of control and review of designated duties of senior employees. He cannot remain content with a certificate of compliance of statutory requirements.

The role of the Board of Directors, as explained by Wheelan and Hunger, can be in terms of a continuum, and accordingly, the board's involvement in the continuum ranges from non-involvement to a high degree of involvement at the two extremes. A phantom board is one having no involvement. It is a passive body which has no idea of what its role is. Next is the continuum is a Board that permits officers to make all decisions and then votes for the action issues recommended by them. This board has a 'rubber stamp' type role. Minimal review of issues that officers may bring to the Board's attention is another possible role of the Board. Involvement to a limited extent in the performance or review of selected key decisions constitutes what may be called 'nominal participation ' of the Board in strategic management.

Active participation of a still higher degree implies decisions on mission, objectives, policy and strategy. A highly involved board acts as a 'catalyst', initiating, evaluating, influencing and monitoring strategic decisions and actions and also advising management, when necessary. In the case of most private sector companies, we have relatively passive boards in the country with low degree of involvement. "Our experience in joint stock companies was mixed and going by the performance of the companies in the country, it could be said that joint stock companies had not been used for effective growth in the past. There was enough past evidence of company mismanagement putting the government in difficult situations."[2]

2.4 EVOLVING A CODE OF GOOD CORPORATE PRACTICES

The desirability of bringing out a voluntary code of good corporate practices was identified and recognised by the Institute of Company Secretaries of India, as its theme in the year 1997. In advocating such a code in the best interests of corporates themselves, the ICSI President has conceded that it was a complicated task as many corporates in India were family managed and only some were professionally managed. There may be no scope for imposition of such a code but the need to evolve such a code by the corporates themselves, nonetheless, appears to be both relevant and important. Thus, a code of good corporate practices becomes relevant along with efforts for meaningful disclosure of information to shareholders.

---

1 Ramappa, T., Corporate Governance, Task before the Directors.

2 'Companies Bill for better corporate governance', The Hindu Business Line October 26, 1997.

Referring to the specifics of the proposed code, he had suggested that this might include, inter alia, induction of more professionals as independent directors on the boards of companies, pro-active role for nominee and non-executive directors through audit and legal compliance committees, regular flow of information to the board about the overall operational activities of the company, filing of legal compliance certificates at every board meeting by the chief executive and the company secretary and meaningful disclosure of information to shareholders in the annual report on a voluntary basis, etc., he had also suggested that in order to strengthen the interactive role of board of directors and shareholders, Sec. 292 of the Companies Act, which prescribes certain powers to be executed by the board only at a meeting of the board and the restrictions placed on powers of the board by requiring shareholders' approval in respect of matters mentioned in Sec. 293 of the Act, be enlarged. The financial institutions, as major stockholders and lenders of finance whose nominee directors are on the boards of assisted companies, should also share the responsibility in evolving a good corporate practices code so as to suit the needs of industry and the economy.

Several countries, particularly those with developed capital markets, have documented minimum corporate code requirements appropriate to their needs. Reports such as the Treadway Report, the Cadbury Report and others may be mentioned and these reflected the needs and moods of respective countries around the time these committees were appointed. The reports were often in the nature of reactive response to extraordinary events or discoveries that shook up the particular country. It may neither be possible nor desirable to adopt another country's norms.

2.5 WORKING GROUP RECOMMENDATIONS

The Union Finance Minister, in his budget speech made in July 1996, annouced constitution of a working group to re-write the Companies Act, 1956. The working group report, which was unanimous, looked at a company, as if it was an organic entity and looked at it, through the life cycle from birth to eventual demise. It focussed matters relating to classification and incorporation, issues that relate to raising capital, internal management of companies, non-financial disclosures to companies shareholders, the constitution and working of board of directors, conduct of meetings, some basic disclosures that must be made, recommendations regarding accounts, audit and financial disclosures.

It also analysed issues relating to corporate restructuring of viable companies, winding up of non-viable ones, monitoring and enforcement, and also the role of central government. In explaining the objectives of the report, it has been stated that the main emphasis was on re-writing the Companies act to facilitate a healthy growth of the Indian corporate sector under a liberalised, fast changing and highly competitive environment, to bring out the latent dynamism of Indian companies to make them grow, and also to enhance shareholder value.

The group has sought to achieve a balance that recognises an international trend:

More flexibility and greater self-regulation, subject to better disclosures, more efficient enforcement and tougher penalties. According to the report, "Growth and flexibility are to be catalysed through many novel provisions and procedures—introducing a more appropriate re-classification of companies, expediting mergers and de-mergers, enabling fast-tract restructuring, removing barriers to create economies of scale and scope, allow for greater flow of inter-corporate loans and investments, recognize hybrids, derivatives and options as means of corporate funds, to name a few."

The group also recognised the need for moving towards greater corporate transparency and has, therefore, proposed norms that will accelerate the trend of greater disclosure of relevant financial information. Before moving to the main body of the report, the Group also made three basic recommendations, which were as follows:

- First, the corporate scene is changing very rapidly, and will do so at an even faster pace in the future. Hence it is essential that the Companies Act be reviewed once in every five years.
- Second, in spite of the best of intentions and adept drafting, laws tend to have the characteristic of being carved in stone. Laws do not change seamless with the times, while businesses do. Thus, desirable corporate governance and practices need legal support as well as evolution of internal standards.
- Third, the report be widely disseminated and discussed. The group commits itself to consider the various suggestions before finalising the Bill that is to be eventually tabled in Parliament.

It could thus be concluded that the Working Group report has suggested sweeping changes in the Act.

2.6 CORPORATE GOVERNANCE THROUGH LISTING AGREEMENT

The SEBI had appointed a committee on corporate governance on May 7, 1999 under the Chairmanship of Shri Kumar Mangalam Birla. The terms of reference of the committee particularly included reference to the amendments needed in the listing agreement executed by the stock exchanges with the companies, continuous disclosure of material information, both financial and non-financial, responsibilities of independent and outside directors, a draft code of corporate best practices and safeguards to be provided against insider trading. Its primary aim was to view corporate governance from the perspective of the investors and shareholders and to prepare a code suited to Indian corporate environment. The committee identified three key constituents of corporate governance namely the shareholders, the board of directors and the management and identified their roles and responsibilities as well as their rights in the context of good corporate governance. Rightly recognition was accorded to the three vital aspects of corporate governance, namely accountability, transparency and equality of treatment for all stakeholders.

The committee recommended that there should be separate section on Corporate Governance in the Annual Report of companies, which should detail the steps taken to comply with the recommendations of the committee with the objective to inform the shareholders of specific initiatives taken to ensure corporate governance. The recommendations were divided into two parts as mandatory recommendations and non-mandatory recommendations; the mandatory recommendations were to be implemented immediately while the non-mandatory ones were to be implemented in due course to be in tune with subsequent company law changes. It was obligatory to highlight non-compliance of any mandatory recommendations with reasons thereof and also the extent to which the non-mandatory recommendations have been adopted. The aim was to enable the shareholders and the securities market participants to assess for themselves the standards of corporate governance followed by a company.

The SEBI which considered the recommendations of the Birla committee adopted the recommendations at its Board meeting held on January 25, 2000. SEBI also decided to implement the recommendations through the medium of listing agreement entered into by the stock exchanges with the listed companies. The stock exchanges have included the directions on Corporate Governance as Clause 49 in the listing agreement

SEBI had estimated that when the first phase of implementation was completed by March 31, 2001, it would cover companies representing more than 80% of market capitalisation. The SEBI directions are to be implemented by March 31, 2003 in the case of all listed companies with a paid up capital of Rs 3 crores. The steps to be taken by listed companies pursuant to clause 49 of the listing agreement have been detailed in the Annexure under the following heads:

I. Board of Directors;
II. Audit committee,
III. Remuneration of directors,
IV. Board procedure;
V. Management,
VI. Shareholders,
VII. Report on Corporate Governance and
VIII. Compliance.

The Annexure cover various compliance requirements and the following are the highlights of the Code:[3]

- Boards to have an optimum combination of Executive and non-Executive directors with not less than fifty per cent of the Board of directors comprising non-executive directors.
- All pecuniary relationship or transactions of the non-executive directors with the company should be disclosed in the annual report.
- Companies to set up a qualified and independent Audit committee and the Company Secretary to act as the secretary to the said committee. All members of the audit committee shall be non-executive directors with the majority of them being independent, and with at least one director having financial and accounting knowledge. Chairman of the committee shall be an independent director.
- Audit committee shall have power to investigate any activity within its terms of reference, to seek information from any employee, to obtain outside legal or other professional advice. The committee will review with the management, the external

---

[3] Reproduced from Corporate Governance Reporting (Model formats) by ICSI.

and internal auditors, the adequacy of internal control systems, internal audit function including the structure of internal audit department, staffing and seniority of official heading the department, reviewing the findings of any internal investigations by the internal auditors, discussions with external auditors, to review company's financial and risk management policies and to look into the reasons for substantial defaults in the payment to the depositors, debenture holders, shareholders and creditors.

- As part of the director's report or as an addition thereto, a management discussion and analysis report should form part of the Annual Report to the shareholders.
- Remuneration of Non-executive directors to be decided by the Board.
- Board meetings to be held at least four times a year.
- Shareholders to be provided prescribed information about the appointment of new directors and re-appointment of directors.
- Companies to provide in Annual Report a separate section on Corporate Governance.
- Companies to obtain a compliance certificate from an auditor and to attach it with Directors' Report.
- Management must disclose to the board all important financial and commercial transactions
- Information like quarterly results and presentations made by the company to analysts, shall be put on the company's website or shall be sent in such a form as to enable the stock exchange on which the company is listed to put it on its own website.
- To expedite the process of share transfers, the Board shall delegate the power of share transfer to an officer or a committee or to the registrar and share transfer agents.

2.7 COMPLIANCE CERTIFICATE

The Companies (Amendment) Act, 2000 has inserted a proviso to sub-section (l) of Section 383A of the Companies Act, 1956. Accordingly, every company having a paid up capital of Rupees ten lakh or more and not required to employ a whole-time Secretary is required to file with the Registrar of Companies a compliance certificate from a Secretary in whole-time practice and also attach a copy of that certificate with Board's report. In this connection, the provisions of Section 217 of the Companies Act 1956 and the Companies (Compliance Certificate) Rules, 2001 providing the form of certificate, time within which it is to be filed with the Registrar of Companies and the conditions to be complied with by the companies may be referred. The compliance certificate is required to be laid by the company in the Annual general meeting. The format in which the compliance certificate is to be issued (under Rule 3 of the rules referred to above) is given in the Annexure and it would be obvious from the same that onerous responsibilities have been cast on the Company Secretary in whole-time-practice, since the object of such appointment is to guide smaller companies who easily become prey to violations of the provisions of the Companies Act in the absence of professional support as compared to companies which employ a qualified Company Secretary.

The Secretary in whole time practice appointed for the purpose of issue of certificate under Section 383A shall have right to access at all times whether kept in pursuance of the Companies Act or otherwise, to the registers, books, papers, documents and records of the company. He is also entitled to require from the company such information or explanations as he may think necessary for the purpose of such certificate. Where it is considered necessary, he may make qualifying or adverse remarks or make reservations on the matters contained in the form of the certificate. The successive Annual Reports on the working and administration of the Companies Act, 1956 reveal that a large number of documents are returned for rectification of defects and in such cases, there are a large number of errors and omissions on account of mis-interpretation or ignorance of the provisions of law. It may therefore be possible to appreciate the significance of compliance certificate issued by the Company Secretary in whole-time practice and more so with reference to the following, "Compliance certificate is therefore, salutary as it creates an awareness among companies to comply with the provisions of the Companies Act and thus helps in effective corporate governance amongst smaller companies. Compliance certificate also provides a mechanism for self-regulation by companies. Compliance certificate not only acts as an effective mechanism to ensure that the legal and procedural requirements under the Companies Act are duly complied with but also instills professional discipline in the working of the company besides building up the necessary public confidence in the state of affairs of companies. It relieves the company and its directors including nominee directors from the consequences of unintended non-compliance of the provisions of the Companies Act."[4]

However the existing anomaly in the case of companies having paid up capital of Rs two crores and above has been pointed out as no such certification similar to the ones having a paid up capital of ten lakhs of Rupees or more has been prescribed and this should be removed; in this connection the following observations may be noted: It is of interest to observe that the substantive provision regarding employing a whole time company secretary "by companies having prescribed amount of paid up capital (at present rupees two crores and above) does not provide for any certification by such secretary or by any other person on compliance by the company of all the provisions of the Act. This is anomalous as such companies are likely to be larger in size and more in complexity." (Taxmann's Company law and Practice, 2003)

Compliance of conditions of Corporate governance: Under the listing agreement, the auditors render a compliance certificate regarding the compliance of conditions of corporate governance; In such certificates, the auditors usually state that the compliance of conditions of corporate governance is the responsibility of management and in their opinion, such compliance is neither an assurance as to the future viability of the company nor the efficiency or effectiveness with which the management has conducted the affairs of the company. This appears to be in accordance with what the ICAI President has stated that henceforth the auditors have to include a disclaimer in their reports to the effect that the auditor's opinion does not amount to an assurance regarding future viability of the enterprise or efficiency or effectiveness with which the management has run the business. This does not appear to be a happy situation; one of the solution could be appropriate empowerment of auditors for the purpose; the desired

---

4 Corporate Governance Reporting (Model formats) by ICSI.

role of auditors should be given a fresh look, since such stand by auditors are apparently as a result of the fallout of Enron Corporation disaster in the U.S.A. and similar other cases.

2.8 STRENGTHENING THE CORPORATE GOVERNANCE SYSTEM

The following measures have been suggested to strengthen the Corporate Governance system:[5]

- Apart from integrity and timeliness in financial reporting, auditors can play a key role in ensuring transparency and insist upon adherence to accepted norms and practices. Within the existing framework, they can suggest improvements in presentation and clarity, so that the intended message is conveyed without any ambiguity.
- It may be possible to bring about greater coordination under the aegis of the audit committee, so that the statutory and internal auditors can work in unison towards desired corporate and reporting objectives.
- CFOs should make valuable contribution, performing the twin functions—those of supporting the organisational strategies and processes, and those of ensuring transparency transactions and adherence to accepted norms.
- Apex chambers and associations should be in a position to take the initiative to devise the norms, learning from others who have already traversed this path, and at the same time, taking due cognizance of the country's unique requirements.
- The Company law provisions laying down the ground rules for the independence, whether of non-executive directors or auditors or accountants, if corporate governance initiatives are to succeed.
- In addition, numerous changes in the present corporate and capital market legislations and regulations would be called for, to provide an appropriate environment in which new expectations are to be achieved
- Corporate governance is based on corporate democracy; shareholders' concurrence should be prescribed for major decisions.
- Corporate governance is only a subset of overall political and societal standards of integrity and transparency. An orderly and transparent corporate environment, lies not so much in the number of Acts, rules, regulations and codes, as in the manner in which these could be administered, and compliance enforced.

The above measure appear to be all the more necessary in the light of corporate frauds lapping at our shores with the formerly inviolate Tatas embroiled in a financial controversy and Xerox's Indian subsidiary involved in bribing Government officials. The country has also faced a spate of such scams in recent years. In the case of multinationals mired in financial fraud, action has been taken by the market regulators, the courts and the US Government. Enron, Worldcom and Anderson have not been able to wriggle out of their quagmire and entire global conglomerates are being wound up. In our country, there have been too many scams in the Indian financial markets and too little effort to ensure that anyone is actually punished for wrong doing. This is despite

---

[5] Corporate governance: The new paradigm, Wheeler Publishing.

the institutional mechanism, through the Securities and Exchange Board of India emerging and seeking to protect the investors' interests. The most widely publicised scandal concerns securities scam involving the Reserve Bank of India, high-profile stock market brokers such as the Big Bull, Harshad Mehta, and several banks. It is a well-known fact that despite the unending parade of testimony before a joint parliamentary committee, it took years for a single conviction to actually take place. The banking system also went through turmoil during the period as several reputed banks were involved in routing the funds through their systems. Some small banks collapsed in the process and middle class depositors saw their life's savings wiped out. It has therefore been suggested that the Government should seriously look at eradicating corporate fraud; the present efforts to set up a Serious Frauds office is a good signal that the government is determined to bring corporate criminals to book. Simultaneously, good governance within the Government itself has been suggested particularly in the context of "improper payments" to government officials remaining the norm rather than the exception in dealings with Government agencies which continue to have regulatory powers; therefore ensuring good governance within the Government is another focal point, and we may note what Sushma Ramachandran, has to say on this, "It is thus essential for the government to look at corporate fraud from both sides of the lens. Not just from the perspective of good corporate governance, which is undoubtedly essential, but also from the viewpoint of good governance within the government. In this context, it must be pointed out that leading software companies such as Infosys are noted for good corporate governance but these are also the ones with the least interface with the government. Even Pramod Mahajan has conceded that the success of the Indian information technology sector may have been due to the lack of governmental interference."[6]

2.9 CORPORATE GOVERNANCE PRACTICES

The following have been suggested as some more effective corporate practices by ICSI to strengthen the corporate governance systems.[7]

- To institutionalise corporate governance as a way of corporate life.
- The Board of Directors to meet once a year without the Chief executive officer and discuss all issues without any bias.
- Undertaking by the board of an annual revaluation of itself
- Linking director compensation to performance.
- Instituting Board orientation programmes and training
- Clear definitions of the roles and responsibilities for board, chairman and the CEO
- Introduction of formal evaluation process of members of Board and its committees.
- Succession planning at all senior levels
- ESOPs to be fair, progressive, based on merit and market value

---

6 Corporate Fraud, The Hindu dated 26th August 2002.

7 Corporate Governance Reporting (Model formats) by the ICSI, 2003.

- Developing work culture to discourage hierarchy, promote openness and encourage free management access.

Further it has also been suggested that in order to reflect a company's commitment to upgrade its governance practices in line with international standards, there should be no hesitation on the part of companies to voluntarily make additional disclosures and also adopt suitably other corporate governance codes such as Cadbury committee, CII code, Blue ribbon committee recommendations, Euro shareholders corporate governance guidelines, 2000 etc.

2.10 HAS CG REMAINED MORE IN PAPER?

According to some writers, 'CG has remained more in paper and almost negligible in real practice' and in support of the same, reference has been made to the following:

(i) As per the observations made by the Advisory committee of RBI "a Distinguishing feature of the Indian Diaspora is implicit Acceptance that corporate entities belong to founding families"; In the Indian scenario the promoters dominate governance in every possible way".

(ii) The securities scam of 2002 which followed the same modus operandi as the scam of 1992 exposed the hollowness of the surveillance and enforcement of the Companies Act 1956 and the Listing agreement. It is interesting to point out here that CG in form of clause 49 was already introduced in the year 2000.

(iii) The total amount of money duped by the vanishing companies (companies which vanished after collecting monies through the public offerings) is calculated to be Rs 66861 crores.

(iv) Non performing assets of scheduled commercial bank amounted Rs. 58,554 crores as on the 31st March 1999.

(v) As per the Transparency International Corruption perception index 2000 India ranks 69th of the 70 countries.

CG in India: much celebrated but hardly implemented, Chartered Secretary August 2003

However, some of the important observations of the Narayana Murthy committee observations support the view that CG is a sine qua non for corporate success. The observations may be noted here:

1. CG is beyond the realm of law. It stems from the culture and mindset of the management and cannot be regulted by legislation alone. CG deals with conducting the affairs of a company such that there is fairness of all stakeholders and its actions benefit the greatest number of stakeholders. It is all about openness, integrity and accountability.
2. CG is the key element in improving the economic efficiency of a firm. Good CG makes the Board accountable to the shareholders.
3. The failure to implement CG can have a heavy cost beyond regulatory problems. Evidence suggests that companies that do not employ meaningful CG procedures can pay a significant risk premium when competing for scarce capital in the public markets.

4. The credibility offered by CG also helps tomaintain the confidence of the investors – both foreign and domestic to attract more patient long term capital and this will reduce the cost of the capital.

In strengthening the process of corporate compliance more effectively, it may be necessary to aim at the following steps:

Effective external check against friendly compensation committees: "If one were to believe the gossip, unaccounted cash generation and legal and illegal ways and means of milking companies are widespread evils, Even, if one were to discount the gossip, official managerial compensations are getting rapidly westernised, Managers, particularly owners, of some publicly listed companies draw financial compensation that is much higher then that received, even in dollar terms by managers of companies of much larger sizes in the west. Most are unjustified by measures of performance that assign high weight to shareholder value creation and building lastining businesses. Friendly compensation committees cooperate. Neither shareholder activism, unfortunately because of passive role played by state controlled financial institutions which are dominant shareholders, nor board independence is such as to provide effective external check.[8]

- Aiming at well functioning and competent board of directors: "Regulator driven corporate governance, with all its associated shortcomings and susceptible to political interference would impact honest managers and spirit of enterprise and innovation the most. In my judgment, the principal pillar of good voluntary corporate governance is a well functioning and competent board of directors."
- Convergence between interests of managers and other shareholders: "The art part of corporate governance lies in establishing convergence between interests of managers and other stakeholders and selecting boards that can provide this crucial link, ensuring that managers do not abuse their authority nor feel suffocated to such an extent that they are reduced to mediocrity."
- As recommended by the Naresh Chandra committee, the constitution of Serious Frauds office and incorporating necessary provisions in the Companies Act, supporting the principle of ill-gotten gains being disgorged from the wrongful gainers.
- Code of conduct for the Board: The Narayana Murthy committee has recommended that it should be obligatory for the board of a company to lay down a code of conduct for the board members and the senior management of the company.
- According to the Report of the Narayana Murthy committee, "Effectiveness of a system of corporate governance cannot be legislated by law nor can any system of corporate governance be static. In a dynamic environment, systems of corporate governance need to be continually evolved. The committee believes that its recommendations raise the standards of corporate governance in Indian firms and make them attractive for domestic and global capital."

---

8 P.1146, Chartered Secretary, August 2003.

Appendices

2.1 CLAUSE 49 OF LISTING AGREEMENT

1. All Stock Exchanges ore hereby directed to amend the Listing Agreement by replacing the existing Clause 49 of the listing agreement (issued vide circulars dated 21st February, 2000, 9th March 2000, 12th September 2000, 22nd January, 2001, 16th March 2001 and 31st December 2001) with the revised Clouse 49 given in Annexure I through I D to this circular- SEBI Circular no. SEBI MRD/SE/31/ 2003/26/08 dated August 26, 2003 (which has been since deferred) is hereby withdrawn. The revised Clause 49 also specifies the reporting requirements for a company.
2. Please note that this is a master circular which supersedes all other earlier circulars issued by SEBI on Clause 49 of the Listing Agreement.
3. The provisions of the revised Clouse 49 shall be implemented as per the schedule of implementation given below :
   (a) For entities seeking listing for the first time, at the time of seeking in-principle approval for such listing.
   (b) For existing listed entities which were required to comply with Clause 49 which is being revised, i.e., those having a paid up share capital of Rs. 3 crore and above or net worth of Rs. 25 crores or more at any time in the history of the company, by April 1, 2005.

   Companies complying with the provisions of the existing Clause 49 at present (issued vide circulars dated 21st February, 2000, 9th March 2000, 12th September 2000, 22nd January, 2001, 16th March 2001 and 31st December 2001) shall continue to do so till the revised Clause 49 of the Listing Agreement is complies with or till March 31, 2005 whichever is earlier.
4. The companies which are required to comply with the requirements of the revised Clause 49 shall submit a quarterly compliorce report to the stock exchanges as per sub Clause VI (ii), of the revised Clause 49 within 15 days from the and of every quarter, The first such report would be submitted tor the quarter ending June 30, 2005. The report shall be signed either by the Compliance Officer or the Chief Executive of the company.
5. The revised Clause 49 shall apply to all the listed companies, in accordance with the schedule of implementation given above. However; for other listed entities which are not companies, but body corporate (e.g. private and public sector banks, financial institutions, insurance companies etc.) incorporated under other statutes, the revised Clause 49 will apply to the extent that it does not violate their respective statutes and guidelines or cirectives issued by the relevant regulatory authorities. The revised Clause 49 is not applicable to Mutual Funds.

6. The Stock Exchanges shall ensure- that all provisions of the revised Clause 49 have been complied with by a company seeking listing for the first time, before granting the in-principle approval for such listing. For this purpose, it will be considered satisfactory compliance if such a company has set up its Board and constituted committees such as Audit Committee, Shareholders/lnvestors Grievances Committee etc. in accordance with :ne revised clause before seeking in-principle approval for listing.
7. The Stock Exchanges shall set up a separate monitoring cell with identified personnel to monitor the compliance with the provisions of the revised Clause 49 on corporate govemcnce. The cell, after receiving the quarterly compliance reports from the companies which are required to comply with the requirements of the revised Clause 49, shall submit a consolidated compliance report to SEBI within 60 days from the end of each quarter.

Parag Basu

Deputy General: Manager, SEBI

ANNEXURE I CLAUSE 49-ORPORATE GOVERNANCE

The company agrees to comply with the following provisions

I Board of Directors

(A) Composition of Board

(i) The Board of directors of the company shall have an optimum combination of executive and non-executive directors with not less than fifty percent of the board of directors comprising of non-executive directors.

(ii) Where the Chairman of the Board is a non-executive director, at least one-third of the Board should comprise of independent directors and in case he is an executive director at least half of the Board should comprise cf independent directors.

(iii) For the purpose of the sub-clause the expression inddependent director' shall mean a non-executived airector of the company who:

(a) apart from receiving director's rermuneration does not have material pecuniary relationships or transaction with the company, its promoters, its directors, its senior management or its holding company, its subsidiaries and assocctes which may affect independence of the director;

(b) is not related to promoters or persons occupying management positions at the board level or at one level below the board;

(c) has not been an executive of the company in the immediately preceding three financial years;

(d) is not a partner or an executive or was not partner or an executive during the preceding three years of any of the following :

- the statutory audit firm or the internal audit firm that is associated with the company, and

- the legal firm(s) and consulting firm(s) that have a material association with the company.

(e) is not a material supplier, service provider or customer or a lessor or lessee of the company, which may affect independance of the director; and

(f) is not a substantial shareholder of the company i.e. owning two percent or more of the block of voting shares.

Explanation

For the purposes of the sub-clause (iii)

(a) Associate shall mean a company which is an "associate" as defined in Accounting Standard (AS) 23, "Accounting for Investments in Associates in Consolidated Financial Statements', issued by the Institute of Chartered Accountants of India.

(b) "Senior management" shall mean personnel of the company who are members of its core management team excluding Board of Directors. Normally, this would comprise all members of management one level below the executive directors, including all functional heads.

(c) "Relative" shall mean "relative" as defined in section 2(41) and section 6 read with Schedule IA of the Companies Act, 1956.

(d) Nominee directors appointed by an institution which has invested in or lent to the company shall be deemed to be independent directors.

Explanation

"Institution" for this purpose means a public financial institution as defined in Section 4A of the Companies Act, 1956 or a "corresponding new bank" as defined in section 2(d) of the Banking Companies (Acquisition and Transfer of Undertakings) Act, 1970 or the Banking Companies (Acquisition and Transfer of Undertakings) Act, 1980 both Acts."

(B) Non-executive Directors' Compensation and Disclosures

All fees/compensation, if any paid to non-executive directors, including independent directors, shall be fixed by the Board of Directors and shall require previous approval of shareholders in general meeting. The shareholders' resolution shall specify the limits for the maximum number of stock options that can be granted to non-executive directors, including independent directors, in any financial year and in aggregate.

(C) Other Provisions as to Board and Committees

(i) The board shall meet of least four times a year, with a maximum time gap of three months between any two meetings. The minimum information to be made available to the board is given in Annexure-IA.

(ii) A director shall not be a member in more than 10 commitees or act as Chairman of more than five committees across all companies in which he is a director. Furthermore it should be a mandatory annual requirement for every director to inform the. company about the committee positions he occupies in other companies and notify changes as and when they take place.

Explanation

1. For the purpose of considering the limit of the committees on which a director can serve, all public limited companies, whether listed or not, shall be included and all other companies including private limited companies, foreign companies and companies under Section 25 of the Companies Act shall be excluded.
2. For the purpose of reckoning the limit under this sub-clause, Chairmanship/ membership of the Audit Committee and the Shareholders' Grievance Committee alone shall be considered.
3. The Board shall periodically review compliance reports of all laws applicable to the company, prepared by the company as well as steps taken by the company to rectify instances of non-compliances.

(D) Code of Conduct

(i) The Board shall lay down a code of conduct for all Board members and senior management of the company. The code of conduct shall be posted on the website of the company.

(ii) All Board members and senior management personnel shall affirm compliance with the code on an annual basis. The Annual Report of the company shall contain a declaration to this effect signed by the CEO.

Explanation

For this purpose, the term "senior management" shall mean personnel of the company who are members of its core management team excluding Board of Directors. Normally, this would comprise all members of management one level below executive directors, including all functional heads.

II Audit Committee

(A) Qualified and Independent Audit Committee

A qualified and independent audit committee shall be set up, giving the terms of reference subject to the following:

(i) The audit committee shall have minimum three directors as members. Two-thirds of the members of audit committee shall be independent directors.

(ii) All members of audit committee shall be financially literate and at least one member shall have accounting or related financial management expertise.

Explanation 1

The term "financially literate" means the ability to read and understand basic financial statements i.e. balance sheet, profit and loss account, and statement of cash flows.

Explanation 2

A member will be considered to have accounting or related financial management expertise if he or she possesses experience in finance or accounting, or requisite professional certification in accounting, or any other comparable experience or background which results in the individual's financial sophistication, including being or having been a chief executive officer, chief financial officer or other senior officer with financial oversight responsibilities.

(i) The Chairman of the Audit Committee shall be an independent director;

(ii) The Chairman of the Audit Committee shall be present at Annual General Meeting to answer shareholder queries;

(iii) The audit committee may invite such of the executives, as it considers appropriate (and particularly the head of the finance function) to be present at the meetings of the committee, but on occasions it may also meet without the presence of any executives of the company. The finance director, head of internal audit and a representative of the statutory auditor may be present as invitees for the meetings of the audit committee;

(iv) The Company Secretary shall act as the secretary to the committee.

(B) Meeting of Audit Committee

The audit committee should meet at least four times in a year and not more than four months shall elapse between two meetings. The quorum shall be either two members or one third of the members of the audit committee whichever is greater, but there should be a minimum of two independent members present.

(C) Powers of Audit Committee

The audit committee shall have powers, which should include the following:

(i) To investigate any activity within its terms of reference.

(ii) To seek information from any employee.

(iii) To obtain outside legal or other professional advice.

(iv) To secure attendance of outsiders with relevant expertise, if it considers necessary.

(D) Rote of Audit; Committee

The role of the audit committee shall include the following:

1. Oversight of the company's financial reporting process and the disclosure of its financial information to ensure that the financial statement is correct, sufficient and credible.
2. Recommending to the Board, the appointment, re-appointment and, if required, the replacement or removal of the statuatory auditor and the fixation of audit fees.
3. Approval of payment to statutory auditors for any other services rendered by the statutory auditors.
4. Reviewing, with the management, the annual financial statements before submission to the board for approval, with particular reference to:

   (a) Matters required to be included in the Director's Responsibility Statement to be included in the Board's report in terms of clause (2AA) of section 217 of the Companies Act, 1956.

   (b) Changes, if any, in accounting policies and practices and reasons for the some.

(c) Major accounting entries involving estimates based on the exercise of judgment by management.

(d) Significant adjustments made in the financial statements arising out of audit findings.

(e) Compliance with listing and other legal requirements relating to financial statements.

(f) Disclosure of any related party transactions.

(g) Qualifications in the draft audit report.

5. Reviewing, with the management, the quarterly financial statements before submission to the board for approval.
6. Reviewing, with the management, performance of statutory and internal auditors, adequacy of the internal control systems.
7. Reviewing the adequacy of internsl audit function, if any, including the structure of the internal audit department, staffing and seniority of the official heading the department reporting structure coverage and frequency of internal audit.
8. Discussion with internal auditors any significant findings and follow up there on.
9. Reviewing the findings of any internal investigations by the internal auditors into matters where there is suspected fraud or irregularity or a failure of internal control systems of a material nature and reporting the matter to the board.
10. Discussion with statutory auditors before the audit commences, about the nature and scope of audit as well as post-audit discussion to ascertain any area of concern.
11. To look into the reasons for substantial defaults in the payment to the depositors, debenture holders, shareholders (in case of non payment of declared dividends) and creditors.
12. To review the functioning of the Whistle Blower mechanism, in case the same is existing.
13. Carrying out any other function as is mentioned in the terms of reference of the Audit Committee.

Explanation 1

The term "related party transactions" shall have the some meaning as contained in the Accounting Standard 18, Related Party Transactions, issued by The Institute of Chartered Accountants of India.

Explanation 2

If the company has set up an audit committee pursuant to provision of the Companies Act, the said audit committee shall have such additional functions/features as is contained in this clause.

(E) Review of information by Audit Committee

The Audit Committee shall mandatorily review the following information:

1. Management discussion and analysis of financial condition and results of operations;

2. Statement of significant related party transactions (as defined by the audit committee), submitted by management;
3. Management letters/letters of internal control weaknesses issued by the statutory auditors;
4. Internal audit reports relating to internal control weaknesses; and
5. The appointment, removal and terms of remuneration of the Chief internal auditor shall be subject to review by the Audit Committee.

III Subsidiary Companies

(i) At least one independent director on the Board of Directors of the holding company shall be a director on the Board of Directors of a material non listed Indian subsidiary company.

(ii) The Audit Committee of the listed holding company shall also review the financial statements, in particular, the investments made by the unlisted subsidiary company.

(iii) The minutes of the Board meetings of the unlisted subsidiary company shall be placed at the Board meeting of the listed holding company. The management should periodically bring to the attention of the Board of Directors of the listed holding company, a statement of all significant transactions and arrangements entered into by the unlisted subsidiary company.

Explanation 1

The term "material non-listed Indian subsidiary" shall mean an unlisted subsidiary, incorporated in India, whose turnover or net worth (i.e. paid up capital and free reserves) exceeds 20% of the consolidated turnover or net worth respectively, of the listed holding company and its subsidiaries in the immediately preceding accounting year.

Explanation 2

The term 'significant transaction or arrangement" shall mean any individual transaction or arrangement that exceeds or is likely to exceed 10% of the total revenues or total expenses or total assets or total liabilities, as the case may be, of the material unlisted subsidiary for the immediately preceding accounting year.

Explanation 3

Where a listed holding company has a listed subsidiary which is itself a holding company, the above provisions shall apply to the listed subsidiary insofar as its subsidiaries are concerned.

IV Disclosures

(A) Basis of Related Party Transactions

(i) A statement in the summary form of transactions with related parties in the ordinary course of business shall be placed periodically before the audit committee.

(ii) Details of material individual transactions with related parties which are not in the normal course of business shall be placed before the audit committee.

(iii) Details of material individual transactions with related parties or others, which are not on an arm's length basis should be placed before' the audit committee, together with Management's justification for the same.

(B) Disclosure of Accounting Treatment

Where in the preparation of financial statements, a treatment different from that prescribed in an Accounting Standard has been followed, the fact shall be disclosed in the financial statements, together with the management's explanation as to why it believes such alternative treatment is more representative of the true and fair view of the underlying business transaction in the Corporate Governance Report.

(C) Board Disclosures - Risk management

The company shall lay down procedures to inform Board members about the risk assessment and minimization procedures. These procedures shall be periodically reviewed to ensure that executive management controls risk through means of a properly defined framework.

(D) Proceeds from Public Issues, Rights Issues, Preferential Issues etc.

When money is raised through an issue (public issues, rights issues, preferential issues etc.), it shall disclose to the Audit Committee, the uses/applications of funds by major category (capital expenditure, sales and marketing, working capital, etc.), on a quarterly basis as a part of their quarterly declaration of financial results. Further, on annual basis, the company shall prepare a statement of funds utilized for purposes other than those stated in the offer document/prospectus/notice and place it before the audit committee. Such disclosure shall be made only till such time that the full money raised through the issue has been fully spent. This statement shall be certified by the statutory auditors of the company. The audit committee shall make appropriate recommendations to the Board to take up steps in this matter.

(E) Remuneration of Directors

(i) All pecuniary relationship or transactions of the non-executive directors vis-a-vis the company shall be disclosed in the Annual Report.

(ii) Further the following disclosures on the remuneration of directors shall be made in the section on the corporate governance of the Annual Report

(a) All elements of remuneration package of individual directors summarized under major groups, such as salary, benefits, bonuses, stock options, pension etc.

(b) Details of fixed component and performance linked incentives, along with the performance criteria.

(c) Service contracts, notice period, severance fees.

(d) Stock option details, if any - and whether issued at a discount as well as the period over which accrued and over which exercisable.

(iii) The company shall publish its criteria of making payments to non-executive directors in its annual report. Alternatively, this may be put up on the company's website and reference drawn thereto in the annual report.

(iv) The company shall disclose the number of shares and convertible instruments held by non-executive directors in the annual report.

(v) Non-executive directors shall be required to disclose their shareholding (both own or held by/for other persons on a beneficial basis) in the listed company in which they are proposed to be appointed as directors, prior to their appointment. These details should be disclosed in the notice to the general meeting called for appointment of such director.

(F) Management

(i) As part of the directors' report or as an addition thereto, a Management Discussion and Analysis report should form part of the Annual Report to the shareholders. This Management Discussion & Analysis should include discussion on the following matters within the limits set by the company's competitive position

(a) Industry structure and developments.

(b) Opportunities and Threats.

(c) Segment-wise or product-wise performance.

(d) Outlook

(e) Risks and concerns.

(f) Internal control systems and their adequacy.

(g) Discussion on financial performance with respect to operational performance.

(h) Material developments in Human Resources/Industrial Relations front, including number of people employed.

(ii) Senior management shall make disclosures to the board relating to all material financial and commercial transactions, where they have personal interest, that may have a potential conflict with the interest of the company at large (for e.g. dealing in company shares, commercial dealings with bodies, which have shareholding of management and their relatives etc.).

Explanation

For this purpose, the term "senior management" shall mean personnel of the company who are members of its core management team excluding the Board of Directors).

This would also include all members of management one level below the executive directors including all functional heads.

(G) Shareholders

(i) In case of the appointment of a new director or re-appointment of a director the shareholders must be provided with the following information

(a) A brief resume of the director;

(b) Nature of his expertise in specific functional areas;

(c) Names of companies in which the person also holds the directorship and the membership of Committees of the Board; and

(d) Shareholding of non-executive directors as stated in Clause 49 (IV) (E) (v) above.

(ii) Quarterly results and presentations made by the company to analysts shall be put on company's web-site, or shall be sent in such a form so as to enable the stock exchange on which the company is listed to put it on its own web-site.

(iii) A board committee under the chairmanship of a non-executive director shall be formed to specifically look into the redressal of shareholder and investors complaints like transfer of shares, non-receipt of balance sheet, non-receipt of declared dividends etc. This Committee shall be designated as 'Shoreholders/ Investors Grievance Committee'.

(iv) To expedite the process of share transfers, the Board of the company shall delegate the power of share transfer to an officer or a committee or to the registrar and share transfer agents. The delegated authority shall attend to share transfer formalire in a fortnight.

V CEO/CFO Certification

The CEO, i.e. the Managing Director or Manager appointed in terms of the Companies Act, 1956 and the CFO i.e. the whole time Finance Director or any other person heading the finance function discharging that function shall certify to the Board that:

(i) They have reviewed financial statements and the cash flow statement for the year and that to the best of their knowledge and belief

(a) these statements do not contain any materially untrue statement or omit any material fact or contain statements that might be misleading;

(b) these statements together present a true and fair view of the company's affairs and are in compliance with existing accounting standards, applicable laws and regulations.

(ii) There are, to the best of their knowledge and belief, no transactions entered into by the company during the year which are fraudulent, illegal or violative of the company's code of conduct.

(iii) They accept responsibility for establishing and maintaining internal controls and that they have evaluated the effectiveness of internal control systems of the company and they have disclosed to the auditors and the Audit Committee, deficiencies in the design or operation of internal controls, if any, of which they are aware and the steps they have taken or propose to take to rectify these deficiencies.

(iv) They have indicated to the auditors and the Audit committee

(a) significant changes in internal control during the year;

(b) significant changes in accounting policies during the year and that the same have been disclosed in the notes to the financial statements; and *(c)* instances of significant fraud of which they have become aware or the involvement therein, if any, of the management or an employee having a significant role in the company's internal control system

VI Report on Corporate Governance

(i) There shall be a separate section on Corporate Governance in the Annual Reports of company, with a detailed compliance report on Corporate Governance. Non-compliance of any mandatory requirement of this clause with reasons thereof and the extent to which the non-mandatory requirements have been adopted should be specifically highlighted. The suggested list of items to be included in this report is given in Annexure-I C and list of non-mandatory requirements is given in Annexure-I.

(ii) The companies shall submit a quarterly compliance report to the stock exchanges within 15 days from the close of quarter as per the format given in Annexure I B. The report shall be signed either by the Compliance Officer or the Chief Executive officer of the Company.

VII Compliance

1. The company shall obtain a certificate from either the auditors or practicing company secretaries regarding compliance of conditions of corporate governance as stipulated in this clause and annex the certificate with the directors' report, which is sent annually to all the shareholders of the company. The same certificate shall also be sent to the Stock Exchanges along with the annual report filed by the company.

2. The non-mandatory requirements given in Annewre-I D may be implemented as per the discretion of the company. However, the disclosures of the compliance with mandatory requirements and adoption (and compliance)/non-adoption of the non-mandatory requirements shall be made in the section on corporate governance of the Annual Report.

ANNEXURE I A INFORMATION TO BE PLACED BEFORE BOARD OF DIRECTORS

1. Annual operating plans and budgets and any updates.
2. Capital budgets and any updates.
3. Quarterly results for the company and its operating divisions or business segments.
4. Minutes of meetings of audit committee and other committees of the board.
5. The information on recruitment and remuneration of senior officers just below the board level, including appointment or removal of Chief Financial Officer and the Company Secretary.
6. Show cause, demand, prosecution notices and penalty notices which are materially important.
7. Fatal or serious accidents, dangerous occurrences any material effluent or pollution problems.

8. Any material default in financial obligations to and by the company, or substantial nonpayment for goods sold by the company.
9. Any issue, which involves possible public or product liability claims of substantial nature, including any judgement or order which, may have passed strictures on the conduct at the company or taken an adverse view regarding another enterprise that can have negative implications on the company.
10. Details of any joint venture or collaboration agreement.
11. Transactions that involve substantial payment towards goodwill, brand equity, or intellectual property.
12. Significant labour problems and their proposed solutions. Any significant development in Human Resources industrial Relations front like signing of wage agreement, implementation of Voluntary Retirement Scheme etc.
13. Sale of material nature, of investments, subsidaries, assets, which is not in normal course of business.
14. Quarterly details of foreign exchange exposures and the steps taken by management to limit the risks of adverse exchange rate movement, if material.
15. Non-compliance of any regulatory, statutory or isting requirements and shareholders service such as non-payment of dividend, delay in share transfer etc.

ANNEXURE I B FORMAT OF QUARTERLY COMPLIANCE REPORT ON CORPORATE GOVERNANCE

Name of the Company

Quarter ending on:

Particulars	Clause of Listing agreement	Compliance Status Yes/No	Remarks
I. Board of Directors	49 I		
(A) Composition of Board	49(IA)		
(B) Non-executive Directors' compensation & disclosures	49 (IB)		
(C) Other provisions as to Board and Committees	49 (IC)		
(D) Code of Conduct	49 (ID)		
II. Audit Committee	49 (II)		
(A) Qualified & Independent Audit Committee	49 (IIA)		
(B) Meeting of Audit Committee	49 (IIB)		
(C) Powers of Audit Committee	49 (IIC)		
(D) Role of Audit Committee	49 II(D)		
(E) Review of Information by Audit Committee	49 (IIE)		
III. Subsidiary Companies	49(111)		
IV. Disclosures	49 (IV)		
(A) Basis of related party transactions	49 (IV A)		
(B) Board Disclosures	49 (IV B)		

(C) Proceeds from public issues, rights issues, preferential issues etc. (D) Remuneration of Directors (E) Management (F) Shareholders	49 (IV C) 49 (IV D) 49 (IV E) 49 (IV F)		
V. CEO CFO Certification	49 (V)		
Vi. Report on Corporate Governance	49 (VI)		
Vii. Compliance	49 (VII)		

Note

1. The details under each head shall be provided to incorporate all the informotion required as per the provisions of the Clause A9 of the Listing Agreement.
2. In the column No. 3, compliance or non-compliance may be indicated by Yes/No/N.A. For example, if the Board has been composed in accordance with the Clause 49 1 of the Listing Agreement, "Yes" may be indicated. Similarly, in case the company has no related party transactions, the words "N.A." may be indicated against 49 (IV A).
3. In the remarks column, reasons for non-compliance may be indicated. for example, in case of requirement related to circulation of informotion to the shareholders, which would be done only in the AGM, EGM, it might be indicated in the "Remarks" column as – "will be complied with at the AGM". Similarly, in respect of matters which can be complied with only where the situation arises, for example, "Report on Corporate Governance" is to be a part of Annual Report only, the words "will be complied in the next Annual Report" may be indicated.

ANNEXURE I C SUGGESTED LIST TO BE INCLUDED IN THE REPORT ON CORPORATE GOVERNANCE IN THE ANNUAL REPORT OF COMPANIES

1. A brief statement on company's philosophy on code of governance
2. Board of Directors
   (i) Composition and category of directors, for example, promoter, executive, non-executive, independent non-executive, nominee director, which institution represented as lender or as equity investor.
   (ii) Attendance of each director at the Board meetings and the last AGM.
   (iii) Number of other Boards or Board Committees in which he/she is a member or Chairperson
   (iv) Number of Board meetings held, dates on which held.
3. Audit Committee
   (i) Brief description of terms of reference
   (ii) Composition, name of members and Chairperson
   (iii) Meetings and attendance during the year

4. Remuneration Committee
   (i) Brief description of terms of reference
   (ii) Composition, name of members and Chairperson
   (iii) Attendance during the year
   (iv) Remuneration policy
   (v) Details of remuneration to all the directors, as per format in main report.
5. Shareholders Committee
   (i) Name of non-executive director heading the committee
   (ii) Name and designation of compliance officer
   (iii) Number of shareholders' complaints received so far
   (iv) Number not solved to the satisfaction of. shareholders
   (v) Number of pending complaints
6. General Body meetings
   (i) Location and time, where last three AGMs held.
   (ii) Whether any special resolutions passed in the previous 3 AGMs
   (iii) Whether any special resolution passed last year through postal ballot details of voting pattern
   (iv) Person who conducted the postal ballot exercise
   (v) Whether any special resolution is proposed to be conducted through postal ballot
   (vi) Procedure for postal ballot
7. Disclosures
   (i) Disclosures on materially significant related party transactions that may have potential conflict with the interests of company at large.
   (ii) Details of non-compliance by the company, penalties. strictures imposed on the company by Stock Exchange or SEBI or any statutory authority, on any matter related to capital; markets, during the last three years.
   (iii) Whistle blower policy and affirmation that no personnel has been denied access to the audit committee.
   (iv) Details of compliance with mandatory requirements and adoption of the non-mandatory requirements of this clause.
8. Means of communication
   (i) Quarterly results;
   (ii) Newspapers wherein results normally published;
   (iii) Any website, where displayed;
   (iv) Whether it also displays official news releases; and
   (v) The presentations made to institutional investors or to the analysts.

9. General Shareholder information
   (i) AGM: Date, time and venue
   (ii) Financial year
   (iii) Date of Book closure
   (iv) Dividend Payment Date
   (v) Listing on Stock Exchanges
   (vi) Stocks Code
   (vii) Market Price Data High., Low during each month in last financial year
   (viii) Performance in comparison to broad-based indices such as BSE Sensox, CRISIL index etc.
   (ix) Registrar and Transfer Agents
   (x) Share Transfer System
   (xi) Distribution of sharoholding
   (xii) Dematerialization of shares and liquidity
   (xiii) Outstanding GDRs/ADRs/Warrants or any Convertible instruments, conversion date and likely impact on equity
   (xiv) Plant Locations
   (xv) Address for correspondence.

ANNEXURE I D NON-MANDATORY REQUIREMENTS

1. The Board
   (i) A non-executive Chairman may be entitled to maintain a Chairman's office at the company's expense and also all reimbursement of expenses incurred in performance of his duties.
   (ii) Independent Directors may have a tenure not exceeding, in the aggregate, a period of nine years, on the Board of a company.
2. Remuneration Committee
   (i) The board may set up a remuneration committee to determine on their behalf and on behalf of the shareholders agreed terms of reference, the company's policy on specific remuneration packages for executive directors including pension rights and any compensation payment.
   (ii) To avoid conflicts of interest, the remuneration committee which would determine the remuneration packages of these executive directors may comprise of at least three directors, all of whom should be non-executive directors, the Chairman of a committee being an independent director.
   (iii) All the members of the remuneration committee could be present at the meeting,
   (iv) The Chairman of the remuneration committee could be present at the Annual General Meeting, to answer the shareholder queries However, it would be up to the Chairman decide who should answer the queries.

3. Shareholder Rights

A half-yearly declaration of financial performance include summary of the significant events in last six-months, may be sent to each household of shareholders.

4. Audit qualifications

Company may move towards a regime of unqualified fine statements.

5. Training of Board Members

A company may train its Board members in the business model of the company as well as the risk profile of the business parameters of the company, their responsibilities as directors, and the best ways to discharge them.

6. Mechanism for evaluating non-executive Board Members

The performance evaluation of non-executive directors could be done by a peer group comprising the entire Board of Directors, excluding the director being evaluated; and Peer Group evaluation could be the mechanism to determine whether to extend/continue the terms of appointment of non-executive directors.

7. Whistle Blower Policy

The company may establish a mechanism for employees report to the management concerns about unethical behaviour actual or suspected fraud or violation of the company's code of conduct or ethics policy. This mechanism could also provide adequate safeguards against victimization of employees who avail of the mechanism and also provide for direct access to the Chairman of the Audit committee in exceptional cases. Once established, the existence of the mechanism may appropriately communicated within the organization.

2.2 FORM: COMPLIANCE CERTIFICATE

FORM

Compliance Certificate

(See Rule 3)

To,

The Members

..............(Name of the Company)

I/We have examined the registers, records, books and papers of .... Limited (the Company) as required to be maintained under the Companies Act, 1956 (the Act) and the rules made there under and also the provisions contained in the Memorandum and Articles of Association of the Company for the financial year ended on 31st March, 20.... In my/our opinion and to the best of my/our information and according to the examinations carried out by me/us and explanations furnished to me/us by the company, its officers and agents, I/We certify that is respect of the aforesaid financial year:

1. the company has kept and maintained all registers as stated in Annexure 'A' to this certificate as per the provisions and the rules made thereunder and all entries therein have been duly recorded.

2. the company has duly filed the forms and returns as stated in Annexure 'B' to this certificate with the Registrar of Companies, Regional Director, Central Government, Company Law Board or other authorities within the time prescribed under the Act and the rules made thereunder.
3. the company being private limited company has the minimum prescribed paid-up Capital and its maximum number of members during the said financial year was ...... excluding its present and past employees and the company during the year under scrutiny.
   (i) has not invited public to subscribe for its shares or debentures; and
   (ii) has not invited or accepted any deposits from persons other than its members, directors or their relatives.
4. the Board of Directors duly met ....times on ....(dates) in respect of which meetings proper notices were given and the proceedings were properly recorded and signed including the circular resolutions passed in the Minutes Book maintained for the purpose.
5. the company closed its Register of Members, and/or Debenture-holders from ... . to ....and necessary compliance of section 154 of the Act has been made.
6. the annual general meeting for the financial year ended on was held on ....after giving due notice to the members of the company and the resolutions passed thereat were duly recorded in Minutes Book maintained for the purpose.
7. ....extraordinary meeting(s) was/were held during the financial year after giving due noticc to the members of the company and the resolutions passed thereat were duly recorded in the Minutes Book maintained for the purpose.
8. the company has advanced loan amounting to Rs. ....to its directors and/or persons or firms or companies referred in the section 295 of the Act after complying with the provisions of the Act.
9. the company has duly complied with the provisions of section 297 of the Act in respect of contracts specified in that section.
10. the company has made necessary entries in the register maintained under section 301 of the Act.
11. the company has obtained necessary approvals from the Board of Directors, members and previous approval of the Central Government pursuant to section 314 of the Act wherever applicable.
12. Board of Directors or duly constituted Committee of Directors has approved the issue of duplicate share certificates.
13. the Company has :
    (i) delivered all the certificates on allotment of securities and on lodgement thereof for transfer/transmission or any other purpose in accordance with the provisions of the Act.
    (ii) deposited the amount of dividend declared including interim dividend in a separate bank account on ....which is within five days from the date of declaration of such dividend.
    (iii) paid/posted warrants for dividends to all the members within a period of 30 (Thirty) days from the date of declaration and that all unclaimed/unpaid

dividend has been transferred to Unpaid Dividend Account of the Company with ....Bank on ....

(iv) transferred the amounts in unpaid dividend account, application money due for refund, matured deposits, matured debentures and the interest accrued thereon which have remained unclaimed or unpaid for a period of seven years to Investor Education and Protection Fund.

(v) duly complied with the requirements of section 217 of the Act.

14. the Board of Directors of the company is duly constituted and the appointment of directors additional directors, alternate directors and directors to fill casual vacancies have been duly made.

15. the appointment of Managing Director/Whole-time Director/Manager has been made in compliance with the provisions of section 269 read with Schedule XIII to the Act and approval of the Central Government has been obtained in respect of appointment of .... not being in terms of Schedule XIII.

16. the appointment of sole-selling agents was made in compliance of the provisions of the Act.

17. the company has obtained all necessary approvals of the Central Government, Company Law Board, Regional Director, Registrar or such other authorities as may be prescribed under the various provisions of the Act as detailed below:-

18. the directors have disclosed their interest in other firms/companies to the Board of Directors pursuant to the provisions of the Act and the rules made thereunder.

19. the company has issued ....shares/debentures/other securities during the financial year and complied with the provisions of the Act.

20. the company has bought back ....shares during the financial year ending .... after complying with the provisions of the Act.

21. the company has redeemed ....preference shares/debentures during the year after complying with the provisions of the Act.

22. the company wherever necessary has kept in abeyance rights to dividend, rights shares and bonus shares pending registration of transfer of shares in compliance with the provisions of the Act.

23. the company has complied with the provisions of sections 58A and 58AA read with Companies (Acceptance of Deposit) Rules, 1975/the applicable directions issued by the Reserve Bank of India/any other authority in respect of deposits accepted including unsecured loans taken, amounting to Rs. .... raised by the company during the year and the company has filed the copy of Advertisement/ Statement in lieu of Advertisement/necessary particulars as required with the Registrar of Companies .... on ....The comp has also filed return of deposit with the Registrar of Companies/Reserve Bank of India/other authorities.

24. the amount borrowed by the Company from directors, members, public, financial institutions, banks and others during the financial year ending - is/are within the borrowing limits of the company and that necessary resolutions as per section 293(1)(*d*) of the Act have been passed in duly convened annual/extraordinary general meeting.

25. the company has made loans and investments, or given guarantees or provided securities to other bodies corporate in compliance with the provisions of the Act and has made necessary entries in the register kept for the purpose.
26. the company has altered the provisions of the memorandum with respect to situation of the company's registered office from one state to another during the year under scrutiny after complying with the provisions of the Act.
27. the company has altered the provisions of the memorandum with respect to the objects of the company during the year under scrutiny and complied with provisions of the Act.
28. the company has altered the provisions of the memorandum with respect to name of the company during the year under scrutiny and complied with the provisions of the Act.
29. the company has altered the provisions of the memorandum with respect to share capital of the company during the year under scrutiny and complied with the provisions of the Act.
30. the company has altered its articles of association after obtaining approval of members in the general meeting held on.... and the amendments to the articles of association have been duly registered with the Registrar of Companies.
31. a list of prosecution initiated against or show-cause notices received by the company for alleged offences under the Act and also the fines and penalties or any other punishment imposed on the company in such cases is attached.
32. the company has received Rs. ....as security from its employees during the year under certification and the same has been deposited as per provisions of section 417(1) of the Act.
33. the company has deposited both employee's and employer's contribution to Provident Fund with prescribed authorities pursuant to section 418 of the Act.

Note: The qualification, reservation or adverse remarks, if any, may be stated at the relevant places.

Place: Signature

Date: Name of the Company Secretary

C.P. No.

Annexure A

Registers as maintained by the Company

1. .... u/s ....
2. .... u/s ....
3. .... u/s ....

Annexure B

Forms and Returns as filed by the Company with the Registrar of Companies, Regional Director, Central Government or other authorities during the financial year ending on 31st March, 20....

1. Form No ....Filed u/s ....for ....
2. Form No ....Filed u/s ....for ....
3. Form No ....Filed u/s ....for ....

THE FIRST SCHEDULE

[See sections 21(4) and 22]

PART I

Professional misconduct in relation to members of the Institute in practice

A company secretary in practice shall be deemed to be guilty of professional misconduct, if he

1. allows any other person to practise in his name as a company secretary unless such other person is a company secretary or is a member of such other recognised profession as may be prescribed in this behalf, and is in partnership with or employed by him;
2. pays or allows or agrees to pay or allow, directly or indirectly, any share, commission or brokerage in the fees or profits of his professional work to any person, other than a member of the Institute or a partner or a retired partner or the legal representative of a deceased partner.

   Explanation In this item, "partner" includes a person residing outside India with whom a company secretary in practice has entered into partnership which is not in contravention of item (4) of this Part;
3. accepts or agrees to accept, except from a member of the institute or from any one belonging to any of the recognised professions prescribed for the purpose, any part of the profits, fees or other remuneration arising out of the work which is not of a professional nature;
4. enters into partnership with any person other than a company secretary in practice or a member of any other recognised profession as may be prescribed or a person resident outside India who but for his residence abroad would have been entitled to be registered as a member of the institute under clause (e) of sub-section (1) of section 4 or whose qualifications are recognised by the Central Government or the Council for the purpose of membership of the Institute provided that the company secretary shares in the fees or profits of the professional work of the partnership both within and outside India;
5. secures, either through the services of a person not qualified to be his partner or by means which are not open to a company secretary, any professional work;
6. solicits, clients or professional work, either directly or indirectly, by circular, advertisement, personal communication or interview or by any other means;
7. advertises his professional attainments or services or uses any designation or expression other than company secretary on professional documents, visiting cards, letter heads or sign boards, unless it be a degree of a university established by law in India or recognised by the Central Government or a title indicating membership of the Institute or of any other Institution that has been recognised by the Central Government or may be recognised by the Council;
8. accepts the position of a company secretary in practice previously held by another company secretary in practice without first communicating with him in writing;
9. charges or offers to charge, accepts or. offers to accept, in respect of any professional employment fees which are based on a percentage of profits or which

are contingent upon the findings or results of such employment, except in cases which are permitted under any regulations made under this Act;

10. engages in any business or occupation other than the profession of company secretary unless permitted by the Council so to engage;

    Provided that nothing contained herein shall disentitle a company secretary from being a director of a company except as provided in the Companies Act;

11. accepts a position as company secretary in practice previously held by some other company secretary in practice in such conditions as to constitute under-cutting;

12. allows a person not being a member of the Institute in practice or a member not being his partner to sign on his behalf or on behalf of his firm anything which he is required to certify as a company secretary, or any other statements related thereto.

PART II

Professional misconduct in relation to members of the Institute in service

A member of the Institute (other than a member in practice) shall be deemed to be guilty of professional misconduct, if he, being an employee of any company, firm or person–

1. pays or allows or agrees to pay, directly or indirectly, to any person any share in the emoluments of the employment undertaken by the member;
2. accepts or agrees to accept any part of fees, profits or gains from a lawyer, a company secretary or broker engaged by such company, firm or person or agent or customer of such company, firm or person by way of commission or gratification;
3. discloses confidential information acquired in the course of his employment otherwise than as required by any law for the time being in force or as permitted by his employee.

PART III

Professional misconduct in relation to members of the Institute generally

A member of the Institute whether in practice or not shall be deemed to be guilty of professional misconduct, if he –

1. includes in any statement, return or form to be submitted to the Council any particulars knowing them to be false;
2. not being a Fellow styles himself as a Fellow;
3. does not supply the information called for or does not comply with the requirements asked for by the Council or any of its Committee;
4. defalcates or embezzles moneys received in his professional capacity.

2.3 WHAT CONSTITUTES GOOD GOVERNANCE?

Overall corporate governance should be considered as a delicate balance between statutory compliance and the concept of fiduciary duties. Finally, there must also be a mindset for obeying the law. Because if legislation alone were enough, then India would be among the most reformed societies. Whether legally ordained structures can succeed? The answer is, "Welcome as these regulatory approaches are, it ought to be realised that the creation of rules and structures by itself does not enhance governance standards.

Without a formal structure, some Indian companies have been following sound practices. But even the most deftly drfted codes can be violated in spirit if not in letter. The crying need therefore is to create simultaneously a climate in which companies will view corporate governance codes as a way of life rather than as mere legally-ordained structures."[9]

The adequacy and the quality of corporate governance have a bearing on the Financial markets and therefore on the economy. In large measure followed by successful companies in the advanced countries, it has now come to be viewed as an integral part of the Indian corporate scene. Companies have started realising that the meticulous observance of standards will be rewarding in a financial sense too and even over a comparatively short time-frame. The Infosys experience stands out, as a model. Its Chairman has underlined most of the beliefs and practices, which, along with abundant technical skills, have taken Infosy's share prices to dizzy heights, both in India and abroad. They include non-violation of the trust in public institutions, eschewing the use of corporate resources for personal purposes and adoption of straight forward and sound value system. Many other companies in diverse sectors, especially those in today's glamorous industries such as software and media, profess to follow the same ideals. Infosys has earned all the kudos not because of the hype built around information technology but because of the steadfast belief in sound practices.

In promoting good corporate governance, various practical steps are to be , such as ensuring right composition of the board, adherence to standards and best practices and accurate disclosures and review of audit plans. Global governance standards are driven by a system of accountability, checks and balances and the role of the management in achieving greater shareholder value. Adherence to governance standards is important to regulators and exchanges because of competition for foreign portfolio investment . There is also evidence to suggest that investor behaviour is influenced by superior governance, resulting in better prices. The UK model stresses the role of directors, the directors' remuneration, relations with shareholders, accountability and audit and institutional investors. Accordingly there must be an effective board to lead and control the company, a separation of the Chairman and CEO posts and a system of formal and transparent appointments/re-election, as well as timely supply of appropriate information since there is shareholder concern or anxiety over the CEO's pay, the directors remuneration should be sufficient and attractive but not excessive; these may have to be linked to corporate and individual performance. There must be documentation of existing practices against governance principles, standards and best practices; compliance checklists and an accurate disclosure of existing governance, besides an annual review of market best practices.

---

9 Corporate Governance, The Hindu dated 14th February 2000.

3

Best Boards

3.1 INTRODUCTION

As a board of directors is concerned with policy framing and directing the operations at the highest level, it is necessary to plan for its success and affectiveness, being a committee form of organisation. The Board should be large enough to promote deliberations and include the breadth of expertness required for its onerous jobs but no so large as to waste time or foster indecision. The members selected should be representative of the interests they are intended to serve and possess the requisite authority and they must also be able to perform well in a group, The Board is not a medium for exercising managerial functions and this should be left to the chief executive. A good Chairman can avoid many of the wastes and drawbacks, as he can set the tone and integrate the deliberations. An effective chief executive does not allow the board to run amuck but contains conflicts, cultivates group interests (for results) and above all makes use of the high authority and status of the board to fashion it to his own managerial purpose, as well as for enterprise objectives.

3.2 MOVING TOWARDS A BALANCED BOARD

Clause 49-I(A) of the Listing Agreement stipulates that the board of directors of a company shall have an optimum combination of Executive and non-Executive directors, It also prescribes not less than 50 per cent of total number of directors on the board should comprise non-executive directors. Further in the listing agreement, there is considerable emphasis on the induction of independent directors on the boards. According to Explanation to Clause 49-1(A), the expression "independent director" means directors which apart from receiving director's remuneration, do not have any other material pecuniary relationship or transactions with the company, its promoters, its management or its subsidiaries, which in the judgment of the board may affect independence of judgment of the director. The induction of independent directors, it is believed, not only adds value to the board but results in more objective and fair decision making process; in the process, outsiders also gain confidence in the functioning of the board, The following suggestions have been made in order to make the Boards 'well balanced':[1]

- The Company should clearly spell out the maximum size of the Board and then leave it to the Board to decide the actual size within the limit
- Age limit for retirement of directors from the Board should be clearly prescribed,
- The Board members should have a balance as regards the representation of business leadership skills vis-à-vis specialist, technical or other expertise;

---

1 Corporate Governance Reporting (Model formats) by ICSI p.25.

- The non-executive directors should be persons drawn from amongst professionals having expertise in business, finance, law etc.

3.3 GOVERNANCE CODE AND INDEPENDENT DIRECTORS

The Kumar Mangalam Birla committee extensively debated on the issue of independent directors. It felt that the touchstone of the independence is the material pecuniary relationships or transactions of the non-executive directors with the company. Independent directors, according to the committee, are "who apart from receiving director's remuneration do not have any other material pecuniary relationship or transactions with the company, its promoters, its management or its subsidiaries, which in the judgment of the board may affect their independence of judgment. Further, Clause 49 of the listing agreement has bracketed 'institutional directors' or nominee directors with that of independent directors, whether the institution is an Investing Institution or lending Institution. It may be important to mention that the Naresh Chandra Committee, which examined various definitions of independence, has come to the conclusion that the definition can be made more precise than what is contained in Clause 49 of the Listing Agreement and the committee has provided its own definition of what is meant by an independent director. Further the Kumar Mangalam committee treats nominee directors as Independent, the Naresh Chandra committee excuses them in calculating the percentage of independent directors on the board of a company. Therefore without further diluting on the arithmetic component of 'independent directors', in the board, it may suffice to note that they constitute a necessary component of a balanced board and various governance codes have also underlined the significance of associating independent directors on the board.

3.4 CRIMINAL LIABILITY OF INDEPENDENT DIRECTORS

Various statutes make directors criminally liable for acts of commission and omission. In the case of Independent directors, the Naresh Chandra committee has recommended a different approach as in its view independent directors are not managers; they are fiduciaries who perform wider supervisory functions over management and executive directors. It has observed that amore practical view has to be taken, as otherwise it would be very difficult to attract high quality independent directors on the boards of Indian companies, it they have to constantly worry about serious criminal liabilities under different Acts.

The committee favours inserting suitable provisions in the definition chapter of certain Acts, such as the Companies Act, Negotiable Instruments Act, Provident Funds Act, Employees State Insurance Act, Factories Act, Industrial Disputes Act and the Electricity Supply Act, to specifically exempt non-executive directors and independent directors from certain criminal and civil liabilities. It has wanted that independent directors should also be indemnified for litigation and other related costs. The Naresh Chandra committee, with some exceptions, has also recommended that Audit committees of all listed companies, as well as unlisted public limited companies with a paid up share capital and free reserves of Rs. 10 crones and above, or turnover of Rs. 50 crore and above, should consist exclusively of independent directors. As per listing agreement, it is obligatory that all pecuniary relationships or transactions of non-executive directors with the company should be disclosed in the Annual Report. This is in addition: to the disclosure obligations contemplated under Sec. 299 of the Companies Act 1956, whereby every director of a company is required to make a disclosure on the nature of his concern or interest, at a meeting of the board of directors, of his direct and indirect concern or interest in a contract or arrangement or proposed contract or arrangement entered into or to be entered into, by or on behalf of the company.

3.5 ROLE OF NOMINEE DIRECTORS

Recognising the importance of the role to be played by the nominee directors in promoting good corporate governance in companies, the Ministry of. Law, Justice and Company Affairs, Department of Company Affairs (vide letter No 2/5/2001-CL V; General Circular No 8/2002 dated 22.3.02 exempting Nominee directors appointed on the boards of assisted concerns or other public companies by (a) public financial Institutions within the meaning of S.4A of the Companies act, 1956 (b) Central or State Government; and (c) Banks), while exempting them from the applicability of-disqualification of sub-clause (g) of Clause (1) of Section 274 of the Companies Act 1956, has expected that the Nominee directors shall comply with the following:

(i) to work assiduously towards observance of good corporate governance practices in the company with due regard to legitimate interests of the various stakeholders. The nominee directors should study the provisions relating to good corporate governance introduced in the Companies Act /Rules/ Regulations and Clause 49 of the Listing agreement introduced by the SEBI and have them implemented.

(ii) to ensure that the operations of the company are conducted in consonance with public policy.

(iii) to ensure strict compliance in letter and spirit of all statutory provisions of the Companies Act, and the regulations and clarifications etc., issued thereunder, The nominee directors should acquaint themselves fully with the relevant provisions of the Companies Act and ensure that measures are instituted to monitor and certify that these statutory provisions are being observed.

(iv) To see that important committees of the board of directors are constituted and are functioning effectively such as Audit committee, nomination committee, remunertion committee etc., The nominee directors are expected to seek membership of these important committees and through their active participation in such committees ensure that objectives of setting up these committees are being achieved.

(v) To regularly attend and actively participate: in the proceedings of the board and in the committee on which they are included. Their frequent absence for insufficient reasons from the meetings of the Board of directors/committees would negate the purpose of their nomination by the nominating institution and they would not be able to perform the various duties.

(vi) To duly safeguard the interest of the Government/Banks/Financial Institutions, which they represent. To ensure proper utillsation of financial assistance by the assisted company and prevent any misuse/diversion of funds by the promoters/management of the companies.

(vii) To provide adequate feedback to the nominating Institutions/Banks/ Companies on the affairs and operations of the assisted concerns.

(viii) The Financial Institutions are expected to closely monitor the participation by the Nominee Directors in the Boards/Committees as above and to ensure that they are discharging their responsibilities as listed out above. In case any Nominee director fails to discharge his/her responsibilities, the nominating institutions are also expected to take steps to replace him/her. The institutions are expected to six monthly reports to the Department of Company Affairs (DCA) bringing out the steps taken by them to ensure that their nominee directors are discharging their responsibilities. The financial Institutions should also in a separate section of Annual Report clearly bring out the measures instituted by them for ensuring that the system of Nominee directors is functioning effectively.

3.6 HOW TO EVALUATE DIRECTORS' INDIVIDUAL PERFORMANCES?

"One reasonable sound alternative appears to be a peer evaluation, where each director on the board evaluates, preferably anonymously, every other colleague, on a number of parameters: attendance, contribution, participation, preparedness, commitment, connections, financial skills, business acumen, and so on. In order that the feedback is free and uninhibited, it may be worthwhile to seek an external consultant to design and process the appraisal forms and responses, and leave it to the non-executive chairman to share the collective perceptions of the board with each director individually. If remuneration is dependent upon such performance appraisals, this would also serve as an objective and impartial format for deciding the quantum of reward. As an incidental bonus, directorial independence would also largely be protected in this system, since the rewards would not be seen as some largesse only from the CEO."[2]

3.7 INTEGRATED CORPORATE GOVERNANCE MODEL

Sir Adrian Cadbury has put it in a 1993 Ernest Sykes Memorial Lecture, "the board is juxtaposed between the shareholders or owners on the one hand and the executives, managers and employees on the other and thus corporate governance, basically has to do with power and accountability who exercises power on whose behalf, and how such exercise is controlled." In India the Securities and Exchange Board of India's code of corporate governance, reiterates the fundamental objective of corporate governance as being the enhancement of shareholder value, keeping in view the interests of other stakeholders. There is increasing recognition that the shareholder primacy dictum and its wealth maximisation goals should not be pursued to the exclusion of the claims and interests of other stakeholders. The OECD guidelines on corporate governance, while accepting and emphasising creation of long-term economic gain to enhance shareholder value, as their central mission, also postulate "corporations must function in the larger society." The following six groups have commonly been distinguished as stakeholders: providers of funds (shareholders), employees, general pubic, government, customers and suppliers. However, in the context of corporate governance debate, particular attention has been bestowed on two of these six groups, namely the shareholders and employees. In developing countries the public as stakeholder group has often been given a short

---

2 Corporate boards and Governance, Sterling Publishers, p. 231.

shrift though societal activism is on the rise. The Government is often left to fend for itself through its own regulatory and punitive measures, Suppliers as a group, in terms of corporate accountability, seem to have been ignored, particularly in the context of outsourcing and sub-contracting.

The identification of stakeholders comprising six groups as mentioned above has thus made all concerned to think and move towards an integrated corporate governance model, The beginning of an integrated corporate governance model emerging could be noticed from the successful stories of various corporations, as narrated in "Corporate Governance: An International Perspective".[3]

"Could this be the beginning of an integrated corporate governance model that seeks to straddle the competing claims of shareholder primacy and stakeholder stridency? Certainly, it would appear to be the most balanced approach to corporate governance in recent decades. There is indeed striking evidence that successful corporation has almost always practised these percepts without perhaps labelling them with such clarity. Illustratively, General Electric Company, currently the world leader in terms of market capitalisation, is an impressive case, Its long-time CEO Ralph Cordiner called its top management a trustee responsible for managing the enterprise "in the best balanced interest of shareholders, customers, employees, suppliers and plant community cities." Decades later, its current CEO, Jack Welsh, presides over the company, which is rated the Most Admired Company in the world in a 2000 Fortune survey, the judgment criteria of which includes some of the key stakeholder measurements as well.

In India, the five-year vision of Wipro Corporation, again among the top in terms of market capitalisation, puts "its people first" and has a whopping 78% of its employees affirming the company to be the best organisation for them to be in. Its compatriot Infosys Technologies thrives on its objective of making thousands of its employees millionaires through the company's stock sharing programmes, while retaining a top slot in the capital market and attracting international investors."

3.8 FUNDAMENTAL FEATURES OF GOOD CORPORATE GOVERNANCE

The governance principles should take into account the cultural, developmental, social and other country specific dimensions; It cannot be standardised whole sale on a one-size-fits all basis; The following fundamental features of good corporate governance may be noted, as we could take them to be fairly acceptable:

- In a competitive capitalistic form of society, shareholders as residual claimants are the principal owners of the corporation to whom the board of directors and the management team are accountable, though in upholding this obligation, boards and companies ought to keep in view the interests of other stakeholders as well.
- The Board collectively is responsible for the stewardship of the corporation and towards this end it should take responsibility for adoption of the company's strategic planning process, its risk management, appointment, training and monitoring of the company's senior management, the company's communication policies, and the integrity of corporate internal and management information systems.

---

[3] Seminar on Corporate Governance: Backgrounder, SIRC August 26, 2000.

- To enable better and more focused attention to the affairs of the corporation, the Board should be assisted by committees, largely comprising independent external directors (as opposed to executive directors); in several countries where the ownership-control-separation may not be as robust as in other better developed economies, it is recognised that some of the non-executive directors may not be independent by rigorous criteria.
- To ensure non-executive directors have adequate time to devote to the affairs of their companies, such directorship numbers must be limited; In the interests of attracting the right people and to demand their contribution to the company, such non-executive directors should be adequately compensated, with the whole or at least a major part of such compensation being tied to future stock ownership.
- The positions of Board Chair and the CEO should be separated and where it is not; appropriate justifications must be made to the shareholders.
- Adequate and timely information should be provided to the directors to enable them to discharge their duties diligently; they should be allowed to seek external independent professional advice where they deem it necessary.
- There should be transparency of information reporting to the shareholders through meaningful, and timely dissemination of such information
- Greater participation by shareholders should be encouraged in major decisions of the corporations that require shareholder approval.
- A corporation's objective is to maximise shareholder value, which implicitly requires superior competitive performance, and responsiveness to 'the demands and expectations of other stakeholders.
- Corporations need to recognise, and discharge their social obligations as good corporate citizens.

3.9 ROLE OF THE BOARD

While the fundamental features of good corporate governance, as noted above are important to be followed, the next question would be, What should be the purpose of the Board and its functions? The board is accountable in various ways to a number of different stakeholders in a company; they are required to achieve a balance between competing interests. Directors' legal duties and responsibilities are not only onerous but are growing significantly over the years. According to the views of some eminent Chairmen of Boards in UK, the board function is essentially viewed in terms of 'strategic direction', establishing objectives and strategy and subsequently, monitoring and reviewing their achievement. The following have been highlighted to be the role of the unitary board of a medium to large sized UK Company: [4]

- Determine a distinctive purpose for the company, a rationale for its continued existence, and articulate and share a compelling vision.
- Establish achievable and measurable objectives derived from the vision, and formulate a strategy for their achievement.

---

[4] Creating an offensive Board, Corporate Boards and Governance, Sterling Publishers Private Ltd. 1999.

- Ensure the company has adequate finance, people, organisation, supporting technology, and management and business processes to implement the agreed strategy.
- Appoint a management team and establish the framework of policies and values within which the management operates.
- Agree and review plans, and monitor performance against agreed targets, taking corrective action where appropriate.
- Safeguard the physical, financial and intellectual assets of the company, and ensure ethical conduct (While most boards safeguard the former, they are relatively naive when it comes to safeguard the former, they are relatively naive when it comes to protecting their most promising ideas).
- Ensure renewal, learning and the development of key competencies occur, and if significant change is required, the company has the support of appropriate learning and transformation partners.
- Report performance to various stakeholders in the company, particularly to those with 'ownership rights' and a legal entitlement to certain information.

Thereafter a strategy review process could be used to ensure that both planning and implementation issues are addressed.

3.10 A FORMAL CODE

A formal and written code of conduct has been suggested in order to bind members and those serving at various positions in the company to achieve certain values; According to 1CSI, the following principles have been found to occur in most of the companies, while preferring the exact code details to be evolved by each organisation independently:

- Avoidance of compromising on commercial relationship;
- Avoidance of unlawful agreements;
- Avoidance of offering or receiving monetary or other inducements
- Demonstration of unquestionable personal ethics.
- Maintenance of confidentiality;
- Collection of Information from legitimate sources only.

It has also advocated value-based corporate practices, such as striving for excellence, Responsiveness and decisiveness. A political organisation that is thinking of company, customers and shareholders before one's own interests, mutual respect and teamwork, transparency in all actions and high ethical standards and behaviour and personal integrity. In addition, the existence and enforcement of rules relating to insider trading by companies may enhance the quality of company's governance. Some companies have already formulated a code of insider trading to deal with transactions in shares of the company.

3.11 THE EMERGING MESSAGE

What is the emerging message for a socially unconscionable corporation? "The emerging message seems to be quite clear. Take care of your customers; do not ignore your suppliers. Your employees are your most important partners in the wealth creation process; share your potential prosperity with your people. Meet your debt service obligations promptly and on schedule. All these are imperative in ensuring shareholder wealth maximisation, which is indeed the primary goal of the corporation, At the end of the day, as former ABB Chairman Percy Barnevik puts it, "there has to be one clear responsibility and that is to the shareholders, the owners of the company," But in order to sustain such achievements, working within and as part of society is all important. Otherwise, just as the human body rejects an incompatible implant, society will reject the socially unconscionable corporation, often sooner than later. Such are the challenges and opportunities for corporations in the twenty first century."[5]

Thus creating necessary societal value-addition would mean a company or corporation striving its ways through efficient pursuit of their core business activities, social investment and philanthropy pursuits and also contributing to the public policy debate through helping government and other bodies develop appropriate fiscal, regulatory and institutional structures that facilitate achieving desired objectives.

---

5 P.51 Seminar on corporate governance, Backgrounder, SIRC Aug 26, 2000.

Appendices

3.1 THE ESSENTIAL PROPOSITIONS OF ACCOUNTABLE BOARDS: WHAT YOU WILL LEARN[6]

What You Will Learn

As we set out the Policy Governance framework, you will be introduced to some perspectives on governance that will be of interest whether or not your board ultimately decides to use them. To give you a flavor of what is to come, we offer the following propositions:

- Significant advances in governance will occur only when people recognize that governance is not a subcategory or extension of management but a subcategory or extension of ownership. *The nature of board work, then, is not management one step up but ownership one step down.*
- A board must be an active, deciding, independent link in chain of authority from owners to operators. *Accountable boards, then, are commanders, not advisers.*
- Assertive fulfillment of the board's authority need not yield weak management. *Proper delegation, then, must result in board control and management empowerment simultaneously.*
- As long as governance is CEO-centric or chair-centric, excellence in representing owners will remain beyond reach. *Responsible governance, then, must be board-centric and board controlled.*
- The proper chair is not boss but first among equals as the board's crucial servant-leader, responsible to the board for ensuring that it successfully governs. Tomorrow's *chair, then, is not top management but is best conceived as-and, even better, titled as chief governance officer (CGO).*
- Leading a group of equals to define and demand successful execution is an entirely different process front leading subordinates in achieving successful execution. *Clear separation of the roles of chair and CEO, then, is critical even when the positions arc combined in one person.*
- Transparency with owners and with society is impeded when the *board* does not make its values explicit and available or allows the management of information or performance to be hidden. *Transparency outside then,* is markedly dependent on transparency inside.
- Traditional practices, even best practices, though clearly a collection of wisdom, are limited in how much improvement they can offer because they are not derived from a conceptually sound whole. *More mature governance, then, will be designed from a coherent paradigm* instead of *assembled from parts.*
- Although structure, process, and practice *matter,* significant advances in governance will come an out only from rethinking the very nature of the board job. *Powerful governance, then,* will *derive from* consideration of *the value the board should add plus a design of the job rigorous enough to produce that value.*

---

6 Extract from Corporate Boards that create value, p. introduction 19.

3.2 SEBI GUIDELINES FOR FAIR PRACTICES/CODE OF CONDUCT FOR PUBLIC REPRESENTATIVE AND SEBI NOMINEE DIRECTORS

GENERAL MANAGER
SECONDARY MARKET DEPARTMENT
E-MAIL: RAVI@SEBI.GOV.IN

SEBI/SMD/SEAD/Cir-29/2003/03/07
July.03.2003

The Managing Directors and Executive Directors of all the Stock Exchanges
Dear Sir,

Sub: Guidelines for Fair Practices/Code of Conduct for Public Representative and SEBI Nominee Directors

Please refer to SEBI order dated April 20, 1993 passed under section 8 of the Securities Contracts (Regulation) Act, 1956 directing the stock exchanges to amend their Rules or Articles of Association inter alia to provide for the constitution of the Governing Board including not more than three members to be nominated by the Central Government or the Board in accordance with the Act and three public representatives to be nominated by the Board.

It has been decided that the Rules or Articles of Association, as the case may be, of the stock exchanges shall provide for Guidelines for Fair Practices/ Code of Conduct for Public Representatives and SEBI Nominee Directors in order to ensure that the affairs of the stock exchanges are conducted on healthy lines, with the highest standards of professional conduct, business ethics and morality to inspire and sustain the confidence of the investing public. A copy of Guidelines for Fair Practices/ Code of Conduct for Public Representative and SEBI Nominee Directors is enclosed as Annexure.

Accordingly, the Exchanges are directed to make necessary amendments to the Rules or Articles of Association for the implementation of the above decision.

This circular is being issued in exercise of powers conferred by section 11(1) of the Securities and Exchange Board of India Act, 1992 to protect the interests of investors in securities and to promote the development of, and to regulate the securities market.

Yours faithfully

D. RAVIKUMAR

Encl: a/a

GUIDELINES FOR FAIR PRACTICES/CODE OF CONDUCT FOR PUBLIC REPRESENTATIVE AND SEBI NOMINEE DIRECTORS

Public Representative/SEBI Nominee Directors shall

(A) Meetings and minutes

(a) endeavour to attend all the board meetings and shall be liable to vacate his office if he remains absent for three consecutive meetings of the Board of Directors or does not attend 75% of the total meetings of the Board in a calendar year.

(b) not participate in the discussion of any subject matter in which any conflict of interest exists or arises, whether pecuniary or otherwise, and in such cases the same shall be disclosed and recorded in the minutes of the meeting.

(c) not encourage the circulation of agenda papers during the meeting, unless circumstances requires.

(d) meet themselves at least once in 6 months separately, if necessary, to exchange views on critical issues.

(e) offer their comments on the draft minutes and ensure that the same are incorporated in the final minutes.

(f) insist on the minutes of the previous meeting being placed for approval in subsequent meeting.

(g) endeavour to have the date of next meeting fixed at each Board Meeting in consultation with other members of the Governing Board.

(h) endeavour that in case where all the items of the agenda of a meeting were not covered for want of those, the next meeting is held within 15 days for considering the remaining items.

(B) *Strategic Planning*

(a) participate in the formulation and execution of strategies in the best interest of the exchange and contribute towards pro-active decision making at the Board level.

(b) give benefit of his experience and expertise to the exchange and provide assistance in strategic planning and execution of decisions when the Board is in the throes of a raging controversy.

(C) *Regulatory Compliances*

(a) endeavour to ensure that the Exchange abides by all the provisions of the SEBI Act, Securities Contracts (Regulation) Act, Rules, Regulations framed there under and the Circulars, directions issued by the Government/SEBI from time to time.

(b) endeavour compliance at all levels so that the regulatory system does not suffer any breaches.

(c) endeavour to ensure that the Exchange takes commensurate steps to honour the time limit prescribed by SEBI for corrective action.

(d) not support any decision in the meeting of the Governing Board which may adversely affect the interest of investors and shall report forthwith any such decision to SEBI.

(e) endeavour that the arbitral award is given within the period stipulated in the bye Laws, rules or regulations of the Exchange and in any case, the award is delivered within 15 days after the final meeting.

(D) *General Responsibility*

(a) be punctual and participate actively in the proceedings of the Meetings.

(b) place priority for redressing Investor Grievance, encourage fair trade practice, to become engine for the right growth of the securities industry.

(c) make use of every reasonable opportunity to enhance and improve his level of knowledge and endeavour to analyse and administer the exchange issues with professional competence, fairness, impartiality, efficiency and effectiveness,

(d) submit the necessary disclosures/statement of holdings/dealings in securities as required by the Exchange from time to time as per their Rules or Articles of Association.

(e) unless otherwise required by law, maintain confidentiality and shall not divulge/ disclose any information obtained in the discharge of their duty. Further, no such information shall be used for personal gain.

(f) maintain the highest standards of personal integrity, truthfulness, honesty and fortitude in discharge of his duties in order to inspire public confidence and shall not engage in acts discreditable to his responsibilities.

(g) avoid any interest or activity which is in conflict with the conduct of his official duties.

(h) perform his duties in an independent and objective manner and avoid activities that may impair, or may appear to impair, his independence or objectivity.

(i) perform his duties with a positive attitude and constructively support open communication , creativity, dedication, and compassion.

(j) not engage in any act involving moral turpitude, dishonesty, fraud, deceit, or misrepresentation or any other act prejudicial to the administration of the exchange.

Chief General Manager

Market Intermediaries Regulation

& Supervision Department

3.3 DIFFERING ROLES OF COMPANY BOARDS AND CADBURY CODE

The Board meets at least four times a year, the minimum statutorily required. Its principal objective is enhancing shareholder value; it concerns itself with issues like maintaining an expected rate of return on assets and company profitability, keeps track of cash flow and head count, besides overseeing legal compliance.

Reviewing strategy which includes sharpening the market definition and commenting on product development are areas where, particularly in the absence of a joint venture partner, directors contribute based on their expertise with reference to local market operations. They serve as a sounding board and provide a second opinion on issues where executive directors feel the need. The presence and participation of non-executive directors enhances the credibility of the board in the eyes of financial institutions and the parent company. The parent complies with the best practices of corporate governance in its home country, the United Kingdom (see Box), but the Indian subsidiary, by itself, still has a long way to go before fully emulating the parent. On the other hand, to the extent the subsidiary fits into the reporting and governance structure of the holding company, it can claim to be broadly in line with such compliance requirements.

Courtaulds and the Cadbury Code

The parent company complies with some of the principal provisions of the Cadbury Committee code on matters relating to the constitution of the Board, Board committees, adoption of going concern concept and internal control.

Board of Directors

The Board holds regular meetings in alternate months. The roles of chairman and chief executive have been separate since 1991. In addition to the chairman and other executive directors, the Board includes several non-executive directors who are independent of the company, who do not participate in stock option schemes or qualify for pension benefits; normally, non-executive directors serve for no more than six years.

The CEO has a service contract with a fixed term. Each of the other executive directors has a service contract which can be terminated at two years' notice.

There is an agreed procedure for directors to take independent legal or other professional advice at the company's expense, and this principle is incorporated in -the articles of association. All directors have access to the advice and services of the company secretary, who is also responsible for ensuring that board procedures are followed, and that applicable rules and regulations are complied with.

Board Committees

Audit Committee, comprising the chairman and all the non-executive directors. The committee functions to ensure as far as possible that the annual accounts, the interim statement, and any other major financial statements put out in the name of the Board follow generally accepted accounting principles, and give a fair and meaningful account of the group's affairs. It aims to satisfy itself as to the adequacy and effectiveness of the group's audit and control procedures, and towards this end, it meets regularly with the external and internal auditors, with the finance director, and with other directors as appropriate.

Nomination Committee comprises the chairman, the chief executive and all *the* non-executive directors. The committee's functions are to make recommendations to the board about future appointments of non-executive directors and of **the** chairman and the chief executive, and to consider recommendations from the chief executive to the Board about future appointments of executive directors.

Remuneration Committee comprises the chairman and all the non-executive directors. The committee's principal functions are to authorise the remuneration, bonuses, and other benefits of executive directors, and to grant awards under the Courtaulds Long Term Incentive Scheme.

Going Concern concept is for the preparation of the company's financial statements; towards this, the directors review the company's budget for the year and also its forecasts for two subsequent years. This process includes an analysis of the business operating plans for the relevant periods, including proposed capital' expenditure, and of the associated cash flow projections. It also includes a comparison of these projections, and the resultant gearing ratios, with the company's committed borrowing facilities.

Internal Control is inherent in Courtauld's established financial systems which complements the group's decentralised management and legal structures. The components of this system include:

Financial Reporting

A formal and detailed budgeting process for all group businesses culminating in an annual group budget approved by the Board. Results for the company and for its main constituent businesses are reported monthly against this budget to the Board and revised forecasts for the year arc prepared each quarter.

Financial and Accounting Standards

A comprehensive financial and accounting standards manual setting out the principles of, and minimum standards for, effective financial control, and defining financial and accounting policies to be applied throughout Courtauld's. Compliance with the policies and procedures set out in the manual is reviewed or, a regular bass by external and internal audit.

Financial Controls Assurance

A formal mechanism, based on self-assessment, for the measurement and assessment of the principal financial controls across the group to complement the existing internal and external audit procedures with the evaluation of risk forming an integral part of this assessment.

Capital Investment

Defined procedures for the appraisal, review and control of capital expenditure, particularly with projects of over £ 1m requiring approval of three Courtaulds directors, and projects of over £ 10 m requiring the approval of the board.

The Code of Best Practice

1. The Board of Directors

(i) The board should meet regularly, retain full and effective control over the company and monitor the executive management.

(ii) There should be a clearly accepted division of responsibilities at the head of a company, which will ensure a balance of power and authority, such that no one individual has unfettered powers of decision. Where the chairman is also the chief executive, it is essential that there should be a strong and independent element on the board, with a recognized senior member.

(iii) The board should include non executive directors of sufficient calibre and number for their views to carry significant weight in the board's decisions.

(iv) The board should have a formal schedule of matters specifically reserved to it for decision to ensure that the direction and control of the company is firmly in its hands.

(*v*) There should be an agreed procedure for directors in the furtherance of their duties to take independent professional advice if necessary; at the company's expense.

(*vi*) All directors should have access to the advice and services of the company secretary, who is responsible to the board for ensuring that board procedures are followed and that applicable rules and regulations are complied with. Any question of the removal of the company secretary should be a matter for the board as a whole.

2. Non-Executive Directors

(*i*) Non-executive directors should bring an independent judgement to bear on issues of strategy, performance, resources, including key appointments, and standards of conduct.

(*ii*) The majority should be independent of management and free from any business or other relationship which could materially interfere with the exercise of their independent judgement, apart from their fees and shareholding. Their fees should reflect the time which they commit to the company.

(*iii*) Non-executive directors should be appointed for specified terms and re-appointment should not be automatic.

(*iv*) Non-executive directors should be selected through a formal-process and both this process and their appointment should be a matter for the board as a whole.

3. Executive Directors

(*i*) Directors service contracts should not exceed three years without shareholders approval.

(*ii*) There should be full and clear disclosure of directors total emoluments and those of the chairman and highest-paid UK director, including pension contributions and stock options. Separate figures should be given for salary and performance related elements and the basis on which performance is measured should be explained.

(*iii*) Executive directors' pay should be subject to the recommendations of a remuneration committee made up wholly or mainly of non-executive directors.

4. Reporting and Controls

(*i*) It is the board's duty to present a balanced and understandable assessment of the company's position.

(*ii*) The board should ensure that an objective and professional relationship is maintained with the auditors.

(*iii*) The board should establish an audit committee of at least three non-executive directors with written terms of reference which deal clearly with its authority and duties.

(*iv*) The directors should explain their responsibility for preparing an account next to a statement by the auditors about their reporting responsibilities.

(*v*) The directors should report on the effectiveness of the company's system of internal control.

(*vi*) The directors should report that the business is a going concern, with supporting assumptions or qualifications as necessary.

3.4 SHOULD CORPORATE GOVERNANCE RATINGS BE MADE MANDATORY?

While efforts are on by regulators and chambers and rating agencies, it may take a while before the corporate sector buys the concept of corporate governance ratings (CGR). According to ICRA Ltd., what is restraining the corporate sector from embracing the CGR is the fear that the regulator may decide to make it mandatory; The officials of the Federation of Indian Chambers of Commerce and Industry, companies should be allowed to weigh the pros and cons of the CGR model before adopting it. They felt that corporate governance ratings should not be made mandatory. The cost of compliance also worried them. It was pointed that "as it is companies are required to deal with so many disclosure norms under various provisions of the company law. If CGR is made mandatory, it would eat into the profit margins of the corporates. However setting aside the apprehensions of the corporate sector, ICRA felt that it does not add to the compliance cost but will only improve the cost of capital. Besides, market studies reveal that investors are willing to pay a premium for those companies which have a good corporate governance record.

In fact companies such as ITC, Wipro, Godrej consumer products, PNB Gilts, ESSAP Ltd., and Infosys Technologies Ltd., have gone ahead with such ratings. Though not all have gone for CGR, some have opted for a rating that evaluates the stakeholders' value creation. To understand the market mood, ICRA had carried out a survey of 35 leading institutional investors and large brokerage houses during the period October – December 2003. According to survey, an overwhelming majority felt that contrary to the apprehensions aired by the corporate sector, the current emphasis on corporate governance is desirable and will play a major role in making the capital markets a safer place for investors. From the investor's viewpoint, 'integrity of accounting statements' and 'stress on ethical behaviour were identified as the key objectives of good corporate governance. Over 85 per cent of the respondents felt that corporate governance is as important as quantifiable factors, such as likely growth in earnings, from the point of view of investment decision. "The facts that well-governed corporate entities are less likely to indulge in malpractice and are more likely to protect the interests of minority shareholders were some of the other contributory reasons cited by the respondents". The key variable in ICRA's rating methodology for corporate governance includes shareholding structure, governance structure and management process, board structure and process, stakeholders relationship, transparency and disclosure and financial discipline.

4

Corporate Governance and Banking Sector

4.1 INTRODUCTION

The banking sector, which is the largest segment of the financial system consists of state owned banks, state sponsored co-operative and regional rural banks and private and foreign banks. In addition the informal sector consists of non-bank finance companies, nidhis and chit funds. These intermediaries are the repositories of the nation's savings; they help to ensure furthering growth of investment, production and creation of wealth. They are also responsible for managing the country's payment system. The banking system has the responsibility to ensure an adequate level of credit for the economy. In so far as the matter relates to banking sector reforms, these are largely required to conform to the global initiatives of the Bank for International Settlements in terms of micro and macro prudential norms. Banking sector functioning is also crucially related to matters like credit repression, central banking autonomy etc. Financial repression relates to credit controls, regulation of interest rates, nationalisation of major banks and insurance, restricting entry into the financial sector, directed credit and pre-empting bank's deposits for financing government deficits; Credit repression is concerned with the restriction of credit to commercial sector/private sector, resulting in credit repression.

4.2 WHY CORPORATE GOVERNANCE IS MORE OF AN IMPERATIVE IN THE BANKING SECTOR?

There are so many identified factors which specifically apply to the functioning of Banks and financial institutions and these have been considered to be imperative to understand the special nature of their functional environment:

To quote:

(i) Banks exhibit strong linkages with the real sector of the economy and they are a major source of funding for all types of economic activity. They are the backbones of the national payment system.

(ii) Given their importance to the economy, these banks and other financial intermediaries are under the regulatory purview of the Central Bank of the country not only in India, but in most other countries. As it is a relatively more regulated sector, some laxity is witnessed on the corporate governance front at the board level as also the senior management level.

(iii) Interest of the depositors is of paramount importance as far as the banks are concerned, unlike in the case of corporates. Banks have a fiduciary relationship with their customers. This creates additional principal agent relationship with banks that generally do not exist with the non-financial firms.

(iv) In times of distress, banks are generally given access to the safety net arrangements by the Reserve Bank of India or the Government of India. The

safety net has become inescapable to protect the integrity of the payments system and secondly to protect the interest of depositors.

(v) Banking sector exhibits large public ownership, since they were nationalised in two phases and several social obligations were placed on them.

Given the fact that banks are highly leveraged entities and also that their failure would have a contagions effect on the entire financial system, with attendant adverse impact on the real sectors of the economy, it is felt that the corporate governance systems and procedures are required to be much higher in the banks and financial institutions."[1]

4.3 FINANCIAL SECTOR REFORMS

What constituted the agenda of financial sector reforms? The agenda runs as follows:

"The major policy thrust was to improve the operational and allocative efficiency of the financial system as a whole by correcting many of the exogenous and structural factors affecting the performance of the financial institutions. Easing the external constraints such as administered interest rate structures and reserve requirements for banks, strengthening the financial base of the financial institutions, facilitating the entry of new institutions, exploring indirect monetary policy instruments and strengthening prudential regulations were some of the items on the agenda of the financial sector reforms."[2]

The reforms in the banking sector which started during the last decade is gathering momentum. Such reforms were introduced to enable banks to operate more efficiently in a market oriented competitive environment. These reforms began in 1991 on the basis of the recommendations of the Narasimhm Committee-I as part of the general economic reform. RBI introduced a large package of reform, covering the entire financial system.

Both structural and functional changes were brought about in the capital market, banking sector as also in the external sector and foreign exchange market. In the capital market, new national stock exchange was introduced and the SEBI instituted as the principal monitor of capital market in 1988. SEBI became the dominant institution to control the equity market. National Securities clearing corporation and National securities Depository Ltd., are the two important agencies set up for offering guarantees to broker firms and maintaining the ownership records. Entry of foreign institutional investors, emergence of mutual funds, primary dealers along with corporate houses and banks and financial intermediaries together have made the stock market quite sensitive and extensive after the economic reform.

On functional front important instruments like certificate of deposits and commercial papers provided the opportunity to corporate houses for mobilising resources. The call market, debt market and the foreign exchange markets were brought closer with continuous flow and reverse flow of funds in the market. Use of rolling settlements and introduction of derivatives helped to maintain the liquidity requirements. In so far as

---

1 Governance in banks and financial institutions, Corporate Governance Reporting, ICSI.

2 p.141 Governance in banks and financial institutions, Corporate Governance Reporting (Model formats) ICSI.

foreign exchange market is concerned, banks were permitted to borrow from and invest abroad upto 15 per cent of the Tier-1 capital and to arrange to hedge risks for corporate clients through derivative instruments. Extending forward cover for participants through rupee-forex swaps is an important instrument to reduce uncertainties and hedging risk in the forex market. Some public sector banks have been selected for autonomous status so that they can function openly in the competitive market. The government is also in favour of banks raising capital from capital market and ceasing to provide fund for recapitalisation of the sick banks. RBI has implemented the capital adequacy norms of Basel International standard and the banks are trying to catch up with those norms. RBI has directed the banks to provide more information with the balance sheet regarding maturity pattern of loans and advances, investment securities, deposits and borrowings, foreign currency, assets and liabilities and NPA. The financial institutions have also been brought under the reform package and the measures included grooming Multi-faceted institutional structure. Term lending institutions and NBFIs have been given power to mobilise resources, to open subsidiaries such as mutual funds. Liberalisation of the insurance sector and the current account convertibility further opens the possibility of foreign investors in the financial sector.

The second phase of financial reform: It concentrated on three aspects:

(a) Strengthening the foundation of the banking system by clearing the assets, accounts and capital structure;

(b) technological upgradation and human resource development and

(c) structural change from lower level of co-operative finance to the top level, the RBI.

The actions indicated covered the transfer of NPAs to Asset Reconstruction Company, the accounts and Balance sheets of the banks and financial institutions to be brought under strict scrutiny so as to plug the loopholes for corruption etc., The big scam of the financial market was considered as the outcome of the existence of accounting window dressing. The measure laid emphasis on new Basle Norms of capital adequacy and these should be fully implemented in Banks, DFIs and NBFCs. The Basle norms carried three main objectives viz. enhancing competitive quality, promotion of safety and soundness and comprehensive approach to addressing risk. The important imperatives for that are minimum capital requirement, supervisory review process and the effective use of market discipline. RBI started encouraging Universal Banking both for profitability as well as for the purpose of meeting customer demand for multi-dimensional financial services. The Narasimham committee Reports I and II have recommended the restructuring of the banks and DFIs at several stages. Suggestion has been made for elevating banks to the international standard, as at present only the SBI is considered of international standard. It has also been suggested that mergers and acquisitions should be guided so that international and national banks are strengthened. All DFIs, NBFIs and RFIs should be brought under one overall common framework such as the Board for Financial Supervision.

4.4 RESERVE BANK OF INDIA

RBI has taken upon itself a wide variety of developmental and promotional functions. It has performed a magnificent task of developing the Indian money market; in the present reform regime, it has moved forward for international integration. The important task of

RBI now is regulation and supervision of the vastly heterogeneous market players. Monetary regulation is carried through the monetary instruments and it is a prime task of the RBI as the central bank. The reform regime has changed the functions of the RBI, with new foreign banks, insurance companies and foreign financial institutions emerging in the Indian financial scene. Foreign capital is changing the lending and borrowing of the financial institutions and banks. Indian firms are participating in international stock market. The extension of money and commodity market pave the way for the multinational financial institutions and firms seriously attempting to control the resource mobilisation and allocation in the Indian financial system. The interest rate, exchange rate, and security prices will continually be affected by global forces. Central bank, under such circumstances, has to work with undivided attention for maintaining stability through necessary flexibility and restrain.

The inflation rate, exchange and interest rate, growth rate, debt management – carry a set of conflicting objectives and RBI has to tackle them effectively. RBI is often at a fix as to which objectives has to be pursued in a conflicting and chaotic condition. RBI has also been made to undertake the debt obligation of the Government. The borrowing programme of the government is routed through the RBI. It has therefore the obligation to check the mobilisation problem and monetary growth.

It may also be important to refer the suggestions made by the advisory group chaired by M Narasimham which has set out a momentous agenda for reform, which comprise: RBI ceasing to be an extended arm of the government, RBI Act being given a fresh look to be consistent with liberalisation moves, government taking over the debt management policy decisions, RBI while managing inflation, multiple objectives being not thrust on it, enhancing the efficiency of the forex market by revealing direct and indirect intervention programme, RBI publishing supervisory information relating to financial institutions to ensure market discipline. Financial fraud and wide corruption are taken to be the outcome of inefficient supervision and regulation.

4.5 PROPOSALS TO IMPROVE CORPORATE GOVERNANCE

RBI vide its Monetary and Credit Policy Statement of October 2001 constituted a consultative group of directors of banks and financial institutions under the chairmanship of Dr. AS Ganguly, to review the supervisory role of boards of banks and financial institutions. The review proposed a feed back on the functioning of boards vis-à-vis compliance, transparency, disclosures, audit committees etc. Some of the major recommendations may be mentioned:

- On appointment of directors, due diligence of the directors of all banks, be they in public or private sector, should be done in regard to their suitability for the post;
- There is urgent need for making boards of banks more contemporarily professional by inducting technical and specially qualified individuals.
- The independent/non-executive directors should raise in the board meetings critical questions relating to business strategy, important aspects of the functioning of the bank and investor relations.
- An undertaking from directors to the effect that they have gone through the guidelines defining the role and responsibilities of directors, as a step towards effective corporate governance.

- The level of remuneration payable to the directors should be commensurate with the time required to be devoted to the bank's work.
- It may be desirable to separate the office of Chairman and Managing Director in respect of large sized public sector banks.
- The information furnished to the Board should be wholesome, complete and adequate to take meaningful decisions.
- It would be desirable if the exposures of a bank to stockbrokers and market makers as a group, are reported to the board regularly.
- There could be a supervisory committee of the board in all banks to monitor credit and investment, review of adequacy of risk management process etc.

It may also be mentioned that the Government proposes to enforce Parliamentary scrutiny on most acts of the financial regulator. In this connection, mention may be made to the Banking Regulation (Amendment) and Miscellaneous Provisions Bill, 2003. Autonomy and market orientation have been emphasised in the functioning of RBI and the following may be quoted to underline their importance:

"Central banks which are mandated to pursue monetary and financial stability should enjoy autonomy in the execution of policy and be accountable for the achievement of the objective. Central banks while defining benchmarks or anchors to guide policy to achieve monetary and financial stability have to take into account the increasing constraints that result from the growing power of markets to arbitrage across currencies, instruments and institutions as well as across legal, regulatory and tax jurisdictions. The increasing power of markets put a premium on transparency to guide market expectations, market incentives and credibility of policies. The market orientation of the framework has to be strengthened by: Enlisting and upgrading the markets disciplinary mechanism; Enlarging the domain and improving the quality of public disclosure; Designing regulatory constraints such as capital standards so as to make them less vulnerable to financial arbitrage; and Limiting the impact of those forms of intervention that provide protection without commensurate oversight which reduce incentive to prudent behaviour."[3]

4.6 BANKING TURNAROUND

Public sector banks continue to be dominant force in Indian banking; their share in a competitive environment continues to remain above 80 per cent of the total deposits and advances. Government owned banks are now making their presence felt in areas they previously shunned. The stock market was one area where these banks had but a marginal presence. The reform era and the compulsions to tap resources from non-government sources made the majority of public sector banks access the capital market. Till recently, only the better performing banks could invite public subscription. Now it is the turn of even the laggards. Recently two banks, Indian overseas Bank and United commercial bank, successfully completed their share offers after charging a premium. Now IOB and most other public sector bank stocks are quoting at record levels, contributing in a significant measure to the current bullishness in the stock markets. In addition, two rating agencies Standard and Poor's and its local affiliate CRISIL, have

---

3 Modern Commercial Banking, HT Machiraju, Vikas 2001.

been upbeat on public sector banks. There has already been plenty of investment interest, domestic and foreign, in these banks. The government-owned banks, it may be seen, are also adapting skillfully to the requirements of the reform agenda. Slow in adopting technology, they are now in race with one another and with the private banks in rolling out technology oriented products and customer initiatives. As they have been forced to comply with regulatory norms, they have much more transparent balance sheets than earlier. All have increased their capital in line with evolving international norms. The biggest change has come about in their reorientation towards profitable goals. They have been helped by proactive changes in government policies and regulatory initiatives.

4.7 DIVERSIFIED SERVICES

The banking reforms ended the euphoria of posting profits on accrual basis, as they were never realised in full. The new measures brought to the focus the intrinsic health of advances. It created a wave of competition to improve commercial efficiency, demanded maintenance of a minimum capital of eight per cent on the risk weighted assets akin to international standards. Technology absorption was accelerated; Development of specialised skills in forex management, treasury management and merchant banking were given more importance. The cascading effect of these measures compelled the union/associations to work in cohesion for organisational development. The new opportunities encouraged banks to diversify their services to earn more Non-interest income and resulted in opening specialised bank branch for international business, industrial finance, corporate banking, personal banking and hi-tech agro branches. Subsidiaries were floated to manage mutual funds, credit card services, housing finance factoring and similar specialised services. Banks started to be customer specific and started building the required infrastructure to integrate into global banking. Banks started to think in terms of attaining commercial efficiency and to operate under an autonomous and deregulated environment rather than for socio-economic development.

4.8 DFIs AND CORPORATE GOVERNANCE

DFIs have created an ideal platform for other corporate groups to emulate. The following may be mentioned as to the way in which they have created good corporate governance practices: the boards comprising eminent persons drawn from different spheres like banking, finance, economics, management, public administration, industries etc. Bifurcation of the post of CEO and Chairman, the full board meeting at intervals of two/three months, use of formally articulated mission statement to specify objectives and providing a clear mission statement and set of values that guide the total organisation. ALM committees study and monitor liquidity risk, foreign exchange risk in a coordinated manner. The committee regularly Monitors the interest rate/liquidity profiles of maturing assets and liabilities and decisions regarding interest rate and maturity of incremental lending and borrowings are calibrated with a view to achieve the desired interest rate and liquidity profile of assets and liabilities. In ICICI, for example, the Chief General Manager and his teamwork closely with the audit committee, implements comprehensive firm wide risk methodologies and coordinates all divisions that conduct activities involving credit risks. The group is also responsible for internal audit and corporate governance.

Appendices

4.1 CA DIRECTOR IN A PUBLIC SECTOR BANK[4]

The operational areas in which the contributions of the CA director would be of particular importance are:

- *Internal Audit and Inspections*: As member of the audit committee of the board, the CA director is expected to guide the total audit function of the bank.
- *Treasury Management*: Being a finance specialist, the CA director is expected to help in the formulation of investment and funds management strategies of the bank.
- *Corporate and Credit Plans*: The CA director would be expected to guide the bank in preparing the 'corporate and credit plans' and the 'performance obligations and commitments report'.
- *Internal Control and Housekeeping:* The CA director would have the responsibility of developing or demanding a feedback and advisory mechanism.
- *Review of Half-Yearly and Annual Accounts*: The CA director would have to ensure that these accounts have been prepared in the light of the directives and circulars of the RBI. Additionally, the director would have to check compliance with the standards of the ICAI.
- *Statutory Audit*: The CA director would have to interact with statutory auditors at the time of finalization of accounts.
- *Turnaround Strategy (for loss-making branches)*: The CA director would be expected to chart out turnaround strategies for loss-making branches, keeping the government policy of directed credit in view.
- *Restructuring of Capital Funds and Risk Assets*: The CA director would be expected to restructure capital funds and risk assets, keeping the capital adequacy norms in view.
- *Prevention of Fraud*: The CA director would be expected in focus on strategies to prevent fraud in the light of the recommendations made by the Ghose Committee.
- *Change Management*: The CA director would be expected to guide the older-generation bank in meeting the challenges of the emerging marketplace.

It is not difficult to identify such operational areas of contribution by other specialized professionals/nominee directors in sectors of operations other than banking so that the organization concerned are benefited with the professional knowledge and experience of such nominee directors. This can no doubt bring about perceptible improvement in the standards of corporate governance in the concerned organization.

4.2 RANKING BANKS IN INDIA[5]

Ranking banks in India could easily amount to comparing the incomparable. For one, there is no level playing field. The foreign banks have autonomy and can be aggressive

---

[4] Banking on the CA Director, The Chartered Accountant, July 1997.

[5] Source: Business India November 24-December 7, 2003.

and innovative, the new private banks lack muscle, and the public sector banks have a sovereign backing, making them big and safe but restricting their freedom of operation. Further, ranking is complicated by the absence of uniform accounting and disclosure norms and the lack of transparency in balance sheets. Strictly speaking, apples cannot be compared with oranges. The task was tough-avoid bias, find uniform criteria for comparison, and (of course) simplify the data for the reader. Hence, *Business India* adopted the internationally renowned cramel model (with minor modifications) for evaluating banks. CRAMEL stands for Capital adequacy, Resources deployed, Asset quality, Management, Earnings quality, and Liquidity.

Capital Adequacy

Simply stated, this is each bank's leverage calculated after assigning different risks, generally announced by Reserve Bank of India (RBI), to assets. Banks in India must currently have a minimum capital adequacy ratio (CAR) of 8 per cent. Capital is classified as tier-1 and tier-2 for computation of the CAR. Tier-1 capital comprises the equity capital and free reserves, while tier-2 capital comprises subordinated debt of 5-7 year tenure. The higher the capital adequacy ratio, the stronger the bank. However, a very high CAR indicates that the bank is conservative and hasn't utilised the full potential of its capital. In the initial years of business for a new bank, the CAR may be relatively high on account of the minimum capital requirement stipulated.

Banks have been ranked based on their reported CARS as on 31 March 2002. Other ratios which have a bearing on the CAR have been calculated as below:

- **Debt-equity ratio:** calculated as the proportion of total outside liability to net worth.
- **Advances-to-assets:** shows a bank's aggressiveness in improving its credit-deposit ratio by higher advances, which determine profitability.
- **G-secs-to-investments:** relevant in view of the nil risk for government securities earlier and the risk weightage that is now being introduced in a phased manner.

Resources Deployed

In banking, the size of the balance sheet is very significant. The ranking on this parameter is based on total assets.

The other factors that have a bearing on resources and, in turn, on efficient deployment have been computed as below:

- **Liquid assets:** Total proportion of resources deployed in liquid assets, which generate relatively low yields. For this survey liquid assets have been defined as cash ABD balances with RBI plus balances with banks and money at call and short notice.
- **Investments:** Proportion of resources deployed in investments, indicating the aggressiveness of banks.
- **Advances:** Proportion of resources deployed as advances.
- **Fixed assets:** Proportion of resources deployed in fixed assets, thus contributing indirectly to profitability.
- **Other assets:** Proportion of resources deployed in other assets which generate relatively low yields.

Asset Quality

Asset quality is also another very important aspect of the evaluation of banks. Net non-performing advances (NPAs) to Net Advances is the best indicator of the quality of a banks assets and its real worth. Banks in India provide for NPAs as per income recognition norms stipulated by the RBI. Many of the foreign banks who do business with few clients have nil NPA levels. Other parameters:

- **Advances-to-assets:** Used to gauge the credit disintermediation of a bank - a higher ratio indicates that the bank is aggressive in its lending operations.
- **Advances-to-growth:** A bank's ambition to grow faster has an impact on asset quality.
- **Advances yield:** Indicates quality of assets - a higher yield on advances suggests that the bank may be taking a higher risk than a bank with a lower yield. Lending rates increase in direct proportion to the risk perception of the assets,
- **Investments-to-assets:** Indicates how a bank is leveraging its resources to credit and investment. In the past few years' banks have been inclined to increase their investment activities as this cushions banks from NPA problems.

Efficiency/Management

Although any evacuation of management is subjective, we have tried to segregate parameters which best reflect the quality of management based on the information available in the balance sheets.

- **Credit-deposit ratio:** Total advances as proportion of total deposits. Indicates the management's aggressiveness to improve income.
- **Return on average net worth:** Prime indicator of a management's capability to provide adequate returns. Net profit as percentage of average net worth (simple average of opening and closing net worth).
- **Employee efficiency:** There are two parameters here. First is net profit per employee. A high ratio suggests that the manpower is efficiently utilised by the bank. Business per employee. The higher the better. Business here means advances plus deposits.

Earnings Quality

Improvement in profitability. Banks are ranked on profit after tax and provisions. The other parameters are:

- **EPS growth:** To factor in equity dilution, if any
- **Spread:** Spreads are, in fact, the operating margin of banks. Spread is net interest income/total assets expressed as a percentage.
- **Other-income-to-net-interest-income:** Indicates a bank's ability to generate non-fund-based income.
- **Net profit-to-total-average-assets:** This ratio reflects asset productivity.

Liquidity

As banks are in the business of borrowing and lending, an asset-liability mismatch can wreak havoc on a bank's operation. The more liquid the assets the better, while, on the liability (deposits) side, the longer the maturity period the better. Here the banks are ranked on proportion of liquid assets to total assets. For this survey liquid assets have been defined as cash and balances with RBI plus balances with banks and money at call and short notice. Other ratios which have a bearing are governments securities and approved securities.

4.3 BANK SCAMS AND FRAUDS

The Sensex-the index of 30 of the key and most traded scripts in the country was nearly 2000 In January 1992, crossed 3,350 on March 9 and had crossed 4,300 in April 20, 1992. The government considered the stock exchange boom to be a reflection of the welcome accorded to the 1992-93 budget. However, in fact it was a manipulated stock exchange boom. Unscrupulous brokers in the stock exchange, colluding with some bank officials, violated established rules and guidelines and siphoned off bank funds for speculative transactions in the stock market. These irregularities and frauds are popularly called 'securities scam'. RBI set up the Janakiraman committee and the committee identified several types of irregularities in securities transactions which were used to siphon off funds out of the banking system. The following irregularities may be mentioned:

- Purchases were made by banks and their subsidiaries of securities and other instruments where the counter-party was ostensibly another bank but when in reality the proceeds were directly or indirectly credited to the accounts of brokers.
- Ready forward (sale and purchase) transactions were entered into either on their own or on clients' accounts by banks with brokers who used these funds for speculative activity.
- Brokers in the stock exchanges were directly financed by banks by discounting bills, not supported by genuine transactions.
- Banks and other Institutions showed large payments as call money to other banks. However, in the books of the receiving banks, there was no record of call money acceptances. The amounts were credited to the accounts of individuals.
- Banks and other institutions rediscounted bills of exchange held by other banks and Institutions but the proceeds and repayments were routed through brokers' accounts.
- Sums received as inter-corporate deposits and under portfolio, management scheme by merchant banking subsidiaries of public sector and other banks were passed on to brokers through ready-forward deals.

The extent of unreconciled amounts were estimated to be around Rs. 4000 crores and the irregularities were committed by public sector banks, private sector banks and foreign banks.

The scam showed that even the State Bank of India was found wanting in this respect. Analytical tools for the evaluation of securities are now available. It should be noted that screen-based trading will bring in changes in practices and a whole set of new products will come on the market. The banks may be required to strengthen their investment departments by infusion of well-trained staff. The bank managements may be required to ensure that there is well-integrated management information system, clear cut policy guidelines, limits on counter party exposures and critical analysis *of all products.* The Government took immediate steps to identify and punish those responsible for the irregularities and fraudulent transactions. A Special court was appointed to try all matters relating to the securities scam. It appointed a custodian for prompt disposal of the attached assets. The CBI was asked to take over investigation of all the frauds and underhand dealings. In addition, a joint parliamentary committee (JPC) was set up to enquire into all aspects of the scam, to fix responsibility and to make suggestions about future reforms of the banking system, Thus the Government took steps to minimise the adverse effects of the scam on the economy and on the working of the financial sector. On receipt of Janaki Raman committee report, RBI took steps to improve internal control mechanisms in the banks and to strengthen the supervisory system so as to prevent the recurrence of such problems in the future. A series of structural reforms were also worked out to prevent the systemic pressures on the system.

Non-performing Assets (NPAs)

Banks are also facing the problem of non-performing assets. An asset is categorised as NPA if the loan is not recovered from the borrower or payment of either principal or the interest amount or both are overdue to the bank. The growing size of these assets are causing concern and the problem has become a threat to the banking sector. Another tip of the big NPA iceberg is the loans to public sector enterprises owned by central and state governments, Whenever a PSE is in financial trouble, the concerned government freely gives its guarantee for the advances given by banks to the PSE but when the time comes for paying up the guarantee, on default, the guaranteeing government rarely pays up the amount on demand. Lack of proper laws enabling, banks to sell the security charged to them has been one cause for the NPA figure persisting at a fairly high level. The recent enactment of the securities legislation enabling banks to sell the security at short notice, without even getting the court's permission, has considerably strengthened the hands of banks. It has been reported that between June 21 2002 when the Act (The Securitisetion and Reconstruction of Financial Assets and enforcement of Securities Interest Act, 2002) was passed and as on 31st March 2003, a mere0.5 percent or Rs. 450 crore of the total non-performing assets with the banking system amounting to over Rs. 1,00,000 crore was recovered. Some of the reasons for the NPA problem are said to be on account of diversion of funds, time or cost overruns in project completion, supply bottlenecks in raw materials, infrastructure, market failure, poor recovery of receivables, Industrial recession and the liquidity crunch. The problem of NPA has many facets. Banks have been well advised to considerably tone up their systems and procedures for ensuring that their systems and procedures for ensuring that their officers take reasonable precautions before granting a loan and once a loan is granted, to monitor effectively to identify weakness in time. There is now a growing consensus among the bankers and borrowers alike that more stringent debt recovery measures will follow in the future. This augus well for the backlog of NPAs with the banking,

4.4 BANKING INDUSTRY; PROFITABILITY AND PRODUCTIVITY

In view of the changing competitive environment, the importance of improved efficiency has assumed a critical significance for the survival and sustained viability of commercial banks in India. Various measures such as imposition of prudential norms, strengthening of supervisory system, liberalisation of interest rate and new competitive environment has brought about a significant change in bank's attitude towards profitability, productivity and risk. Indian banks are therefore striving hard to improve their efficiency at all levels of their banking operations. One way of examining the commercial bank's efficiency could be by relating operating costs to output. Output by bank is measured in terms of aggregate deposits, total number of deposit accounts, total credit, number of credit accounts and the number of branches opened during a particular period. The responsiveness of change in operating cost to output may be taken as a measure of operational efficiency. If we should take using a bank's resources wisely and in a cost-effective manner as connoting its efficiency, efficiency can be measured on the basis of the following three criterion: Profitability, productivity and financial management.

Profitability. A higher profitability is required for higher dividend payments and return on equity. Banks also require higher profits to compensate the higher operating costs and overhead expenses, etc. The following indicators are usually selected to represent the efficiency in profitability:

1. Net profit as percentage to total income (NPI)
2. Return on assets: net profit/total assets (ROA)
3. Return on equity: Net profits/(Capital plus Reserves) ROE
4. Net profit as percentage to deposits (NPD)
5. Net profit as percentage to spread (NPS)

Profitability criterion has been represented by 'net profit' instead of 'gross profit ' since net profits account for provisions for non-performing assets (NPAs).

Productivity: Banking is a multi-service industry. The output therefore should be summation of every service it provides or generates. Diversity of services provided by a bank renders the measurement of output in a bank rather difficult. However, financial intermediation that is getting funds from various sources and deploying them into various uses can be assumed to be the main function of a bank. It may therefore be reasonable to take the 'volume of business' (deposits plus advances) as a surrogate measure of output of a bank. The major input for any bank being its employees, number of employees working in a particular bank constitute the denominator of the productivity equation. The following may be taken as indicators representing the productivity efficiency.

1. Volume of business per employee (BPE)
2. Income per employee (IPE)
3. Spread per employee (SPE)
4. Number of accounts per employee (ACPE)

Profit making banks (foreign and private banks) try to reduce the per account servicing cost by concentrating upon only large borrowers. Public sector banks on the other hand have to service a large number of credit accounts on account of their obligations under the priority sector lending programmes.

Financial Management: Financial management in banking industry is concerned with the planning and controlling of bank's financial resources. The object is maximization of shareholder's wealth. The following are the indicator selected to represent the efficiency in financial management:

1. Yield on assets: Interest income/total assets (YOA)
2. Yield on advances: Interest earned on advances/total investment (YOI).
3. Yield on investments: Income from investment/total investment. (YOI).
4. Spread percentage to establishment expenses (SPEST).
5. Spread as percentage to total assets (SPTA).

4.5 WHY DFIs SHOULD BE STRENGTHENED?

Revealing the findings of a survey on meeting the needs of the Indian industry, the FICCI has pressed the Government to make a portion of long-term funds available to the development financial institutions (DFI) to enable them to meet the financial requirement of a large number of mid-sized Indian companies looking for fresh investments. The President of FICCI said there were thousands of mid-sized Indian companies to-day looking for fresh investments for which they needed long term competitive finance. If a portion of long term funds such as Provident Fund /Pension/Gratuity fund and postal savings fund is made available to the DFIs, it will facilitate corporate financing better. The survey on 'Long-term financing needs of the Indian industry and the role of DFIs, says that the long term debt market should be developed so that in future the market itself is in a position to support these institutions. The DFIs should also be given tax concessions with respect to their bond issues and be exempted from tax on their profits. On the various sources of debt finance, term loans from banks found favour with 59 per cent of the respondents. Another 46 per cent said they would also avail of the term loans from financial institutions. Voicing concern of the low levels of activity of the DFIs, revival and strengthening of DFIs was pressed by the respondents.

5

Corporate Governance and Public Enterprises

5.1 INTRODUCTION

The key features of corporate governance in the public sector as identified in Corporate boards and governance are as follows:

1. The equity shares are owned wholly or substantially (meaning 51 per cent or more) by the government.
2. The boards of public sector undertakings, appointed for all practical purposes by the controlling administrative ministry, comprise of three categories of directors:
   (i) functional directors, who are full time employees of the concerned public sector undertaking,
   (ii) government directors who are bureaucrats from the controlling administrative ministry, and
   (iii) outside directors.
3. There is, in general, a good deal of political and bureaucratic influence over the management of public sector undertakings. As a result, the autonomy of the management is often substantially eroded.
4. Public sector undertakings are constrained by various regulations and administrative guidelines. Further, they are subject to the GAG audit and are accountable to parliament. This leads to an excessive emphasis on observing rules, regulations, and guidelines. Efficiency and performance are often sacrificed at the altar of propriety.
5. Chief executives of public sector undertakings have short tenures often one to five years; it is uncommon to find a chief executive (typically designed as Chairman and Managing Director) who has been at the helm of affairs for more than five years. Such a short tenure, coupled with limited freedom, leads to a myopic outlook. It is therefore, rare to find a visionary leader guiding the destiny of a public sector undertaking with a long planning horizon, Most of the chief executives seem to be concerned with fulfilling short-term targets emanating from the Memorandum of understanding (MOUs), which themselves appear to be the outcome of an elaborate budgetary game between the management and the government.
6. In general, performance standards are soft, compensation levels low, incentives for performance poor, and 'real' accountability weak.

In summary, the corporate governance system in the public sector may be characterised as the 'transient system' with the key players, viz. politicians' bureaucrats, and managers taking a myopic view of things.

Public enterprises are 'generally autonomous bodies' are owned and managed by the government and which provide goods or services for a price. The ownership of the government extends to 51 per cent, or more, in order to make it a public enterprise/entity. Public enterprises are considered as important instruments for self-reliant economic growth. They also help speed up economic growth, provide the required infrastructure, act as tools achieve various social objectives like better distribution of income, expansion employees employment opportunities, removal of regional imbalances, reducing concentration etc., The Indian Companies Act, which was basically meant to regulate the affairs of the private sector, by a legal fiction, it was extended to state owned enterprises as well in 1956. A number of new provisions were introduced and these covered the following sections:

S.617 Definition of Government companies

S.619 Application of sections 224 to 233 to Government companies

S.619A Annual reports on Government companies

S.620 Power to modify Act in relation to Government companies

The various exemptions provided to Government companies are carried in the following Sections of the Act: Sections 198, 255-259, 263, 264, 294, 370, 166(l) and 619B (Provisions of Section 619 to apply to certain companies).

The various public enterprises originated in a number of ways -new ventures in fields like steel, aluminum, export trading, cement, fertilizers and electronics; nationalisation of private sector units such as coal mines; acquisition by government as in the case of Indo-Burma Petroleum, Hindustan Petroleum, etc. Thus, state-ownership or takeover of various production activities were on account of different factors such as preference of public ownership in essential services, preventing competition in essential services, control of resources for effective economic planning, control of economic power arising from control over large enterprises, state ownership to meet defence needs, the requirement for massive injection of capital in important industries like coal, steel, railways and the like. The genesis of setting public enterprises in most countries has been a combination of political, social, economic and historical factors and these have been categorised as follows:[1]

(i) To pursue a specific socio-political model

(ii) To accelerate economic development and compensate private sector inadequacies

(iii) Natural monopoly and infrastructural need

(iv) Government revenue and economies of scale

(v) Commanding heights, self -reliance and reducing foreign domination

(vi) Employment and regional employment

The multiple objectives prescribed embraced infrastructure needs for rapid development, creation of employment opportunities, development of backward areas, Import-substitution, strengthening indigenous capability, acting as a countervailing force to concentration of economic power, etc., Therefore, the broader considerations of national policy under which the development of public sector was undertaken, both for

---

1 Public Enterprises Management, BP Mathur, Macmillan 1999.

economic growth and social justice, cannot be ignored and it is beyond doubt that they played an extremely valuable role in the growth of the national economy in the last four decades.

This contribution, however, cannot undermine the present demand for making the public sector units economically efficient and viable and, at the same time, socially accountable and responsible. Basically, there can be no disagreement between the objectives of generating a surplus while being socially responsible. The need for profitability as distinct from profiteering is thus increasingly being stressed upon in relation to these enterprises.

5.2 REFORMS AND COMPETITION

The Industrial policy Resolution 1956 had given primacy to the public sector; Apart from direct responsibility for setting up new industrial undertakings, all industries of basic and strategic importance were in the public sector, The Industrial policy statement 1991, however, moved towards liberalisation and the policy paved the way for removing unnecessary bureaucratic controls. It was proposed to abolish monopoly of any sector in the field of manufacture except for strategic or military considerations; otherwise all manufacturing activities were open to competition. The public sector was to be run on business lines; the liberalisation measures covered, among other things, amendment of MRTP Act, foreign technology agreements in high priority industries, enhancing the limit of foreign direct investment. In order to ensure private sector participation, the government announced liberalisation of government policy towards highways, bridges, tourism, power generation and distribution, telecom services, telecom equipment manufacturing.

In due course, the involvement of the public sector in all sectors had come to be criticised due to low productivity, high costs, dismal return on capital employed The enterprises showed a profitability (gross profit on capital employed of 14-53 percent and net profitability of 4-11 percent. The private sector-taken-over sick units accounted for approximately one-third of the total losses of the central public enterprises. Sector-wise analysis of profitability indicated that gross profitability declined for various sectors except those for power as well as petroleum companies; agrobase and textile enterprise reported loss. Over the years, the net profitability reduced and turned out to be negative over the years for engineering, fertilizers, chemicals and pharmaceutical, textiles and agro-based industries and while power and petroleum sectors maintained their positive profitability. The poor performance were reported to be, due to poor project management overmaning, inadequate attention to R&D, lack of human resources development and also the policies of the government. In addition, comparison of manufacturing public enterprises with private manufacturing companies by Onkar Goswami had shown that wage costs were comparatively higher in the public sector and in the case of fixed costs, even higher by bigger margin. Bad management is the reason for these developments. The World Bank in its 1991 report concluded that public enterprise performance could be improved without changing ownership by laying down clear commercial goals, imposing a hard budget, necessary power to managers to attain goals, exposing the enterprises to competition and rewarding managers for results, The commercialisation process exposes public enterprises to maximise profits in a competitive environment.

5.3 AUTONOMY AND ACCOUNTABILITY

The PE Boards are also weak in regard of various entrepreneurial and innovative decisions. The government directors are often risk-averse and want to play safe, The board lays special emphasis on rules, procedures, precedents and consideration of each and every possible dimension of a decision involving uncertainty, it is also taken to be doubtful whether members of the board come prepared for the board meeting and ask discerning questions to reach at the bottom of the issues which confront each enterprise. However, with many heterogeneous entities, it may be difficult to generalise about their working, as there are varied situations and the boards comprising different and diverse personalities. Broadly, the conclusion would be that the PE boards do not often exhibit the freedom, dynamism and speed required to them, which usually form the hallmarks of boards of large-scale private enterprises.

Do public enterprises have autonomy to take decisions? Whether their accountability is well defined? Public enterprises, no doubt are considered autonomous; their board is also supposed to be a policy making body.

But the enterprises are mostly subjected to various types of controls including different forms of audits and parliamentary control. On paper they enjoy larger autonomy but in practice informal and formal involvement of ministers and departments take place in areas wholly within the decision making powers of such enterprises. In a private enterprise, the owners define the business charter, set business objectives, appoint and remove directors, approve annual accounts and declare dividends on the recommendations of the board; the board has a strategic role to achieve objectives, monitor performance and to appoint chief executive; the chief executive along with his team has an operating role to manage business in accordance with agreed objectives; public enterprises, despite having similar organisational structures, government as owners 'invariably encroach on the strategic and operational functions'. Their involvement in operational matters is time consuming for an overstretched bureaucracy; the ministers also lack information and the business perspective to make the correct decisions.

The Arjun-Sengupta committee therefore recommended that "it is necessary to evolve a set of rules and conventions by which the government can help in the better functioning of public enterprises by reducing the points of intervention without minimising the government's right to have needed information for evaluating performance. The government should primarily be concerned with overall strategic planning and policy, rather than with day-to-day functioning of the enterprises." In the year 1986, the MOU (Memorandum of Understanding) system was designed to give operational autonomy and to enforce accountability, commensurate with authority for results. MOU served as an instrument to enumerate a list of agreed indicators and targets and to arrive at a composite performance evaluation measure. It was claimed as a major instrument of the rollback of state involvement in running public enterprises. Despite MOUs, the performance of public enterprises, have not improved and the problems relating to autonomy and accountability continue to remain; it has been stated that much more is needed than MOUs to distance the government from the actual running of the public enterprises.

In the above context, the Swedish example is cited and it is reported that they have one of the most decentralised system of public enterprise evaluation system and providing a good example of managerial autonomy. Under this system, a professional supervisory agency, called a "Unit for State Participation", as part of Ministry of Industry is delegated the responsibility to execute the ownership role of the state industries. The unit of state participation acts in the best interests of the enterprise and do not overpower the board with their ownership role; it increases involvement in decision making only in times of crisis and when public enterprises require state financial support. The Swedish model carries the following features:

1. A supervisory board of professionals and experts should be vested with the responsibility to perform the role of public enterprises, viz to set overall business objectives, to appoint chief executive, full time directors and to monitor performance. The supervisory board reporting to a committee of elected representatives, which in turn reports to the Parliament.
2. The supervisory board should appoint Chief executive and the team, without the involvement of the government and the process of appointment committee of Cabinet and the Public Enterprises Selection Board.
3. The tenure of the Chief Executive and other directors should be for a period of five years, long enough to show results.
4. Wage fixation should be such that there is autonomy, but within the overall policy of the government; the remuneration package for directors should be comparable with private sector enterprises.
5. The organisation should be designed in such a way so that there is no undue political or bureaucratic interference.
6. In respect of financial autonomy, this requires laying down financial objectives, capital structure, social objectives and subsidies and performance measurement. Financial ratios can be developed and integrated with the performance measurement indicator. From time to time the regulating authority examining whether the social objectives and subsidies are serving the purpose.

5.4 PERFORMANCE EVALUATION

In the evaluation of public enterprises, the evaluating agencies could be broadly divided into two, namely as external agencies and internal agencies. The external agencies comprise Parliament, Minister and the Administrative ministry and user ministries, finance and planning. Internal agencies comprise the governing board, the divisions or units and the division level or unit level managers. In the case of internal agencies, the performance evaluation is co-related to corporate objectives and how for these have been achieved over a period and in the case of others, they are related to unit objectives and budgets and micro-level objectives. In the case of external agencies, while the minister is concerned with political short-term goals, the Parliament is concerned with national and socio-economic objectives; the others are concerned with budgetary objectives and plan objectives. Because of such variances in the objectives, the evaluation also have to have different yardsticks when the evaluation is done by different evaluating agencies. To solve the problem, what is called an 'organisational index approach' has been suggested and the Appendix provides the characteristics and how the index is to be constructed.

Mention should be made regarding 'Navratnas' by which greater freedom has been provided to selected enterprises; the freedom includes power to enter into strategic alliances or technology, financial joint ventures, to incur capital expenditure or purchasing technology or winding up posts up to the directors level or to raise debt from domestic market, as these would enable them to be more competitive with the private sector. At present, there is demand for according such status to more and more public enterprises. In the case of enterprises reserved for the public sector, it has been suggested that there could be partial privatisation, as this would help to raise resources to meet budgetary deficits and also to bring in competitiveness in such enterprises.

5.5 RESTRUCTURING PUBLIC SECTOR

The public sector undertakings have demanded a level playing field and ending the state of suspended animation vis-à-vis their existence due to globalisation measures. The PSUs have demanded implementation of the Rangarajan committee report on PSU disinvestment and suggested a number of measures to make them competitive. Suggestions for important reforms have been made and these include portfolio restructuring, reforms in financial engineering and organisational set up, empowerment of boards and their constitution, vigilance and audit, MOU pattern wage policy and disposal of sick units.

The memorandum submitted by them offered a number of suggestions to make the company boards more effective, empowering them to decide on strategic alliances, floating of joint ventures, floating of joint acquisition and disposal of assets, changing product profile and raising of capital in the cases of sick units. The MOU has pointed out that the delay in making decisions is only resulting in money being doled out to sustain some employment. The memorandum particularly highlighted the following aspects for quick remedial actions: Quick dispensation of cases at BIFR, professionalisation of management, redesigning of the MOU system, empowerment of boards, disinvestment to improve PSU efficiency, financial restructuring measures such as adoption of strict cost reduction. Freedom to raise internal resources, reduction of equity base, where needed, freedom for disposal or acquisition of properties, acquisition of equity in other organizations, hiving–off some of the business, if needed, raising of capital from the market, including from the foreign market and achieving a wide dispersal of shares.

5.6 DISINVESTMENT AND PRIVATISATION

According to the working group, the policy options for reforming PSUs included restructuring and privatisation. The group also recommended that Comptroller and Auditor-General audit be made optional for PSUs and done only for submission of report to Parliament, saying statutory audit should be considered sufficient for compliance of Companies Act. In the far reaching recommendation for autonomy to PSU boards in decision making for investment, joint venture, selling and acquisition assets and raising resources from the market, the group said in the new role for PSUs in liberalised economy, the selection of Chief Executives should be purely on the basis of merit. Not only the Chief Executive should be given an opportunity to select his own team and reallocate work among the functional directors, there should also be free movement between the public sector and the private sector, it said adding that there should be performance contract between the Chief Executive and the Government

5.6.1 Steps for Effective Privatization

Privatisation, to be successful, needs strong will on the part of the governments and also a consensus across political parties. It requires co-operation from the labour as it may involve a reduction of workforce, restraining change of technology, or a combination of all these. Privatisation also requires capital market support to absorb new securities, financial expertise to evaluate PSUs assets, organisational restructuring, and the like, to make the process attractive to private investors.

In some countries as in Mexico, privatisation became a part of the process of fundamentally altering the organisation of production with benefits for consumer and the economy, as a whole. The strategies would have to aim at building competitive markets for the long-term rather than maximising short-term revenue. There have to be transparent procedures which should ensure disposal of assets through competitive bidding or other acceptable methods which should be kept open to outside scrutiny. Selling assets to meet current liabilities cannot be a good criteria, as it may affect the future of the company. There should be a widespread distribution of shares to nationals and foreigners with proper timing and distribution to maximise the revenue from disinvestments. The committee appointed under the Chairmanship of Mr. C Rangarajan (1993) to study and recommend measures to make privatisation more effective has made the following observations:

- Units to be disinvested need to be identified.
- There is need for government to retain majority holding in equity of undertakings in areas such as defence and atomic energy. In others, disinvestment can be upto any level.
- Disinvestment shall be in stages and the sales are to be staggered so as to fetch the best possible prices from the bidders.
- Worker's interests need to be protected. Employees of the privatised units are to be allowed to buy shares.
- Disinvestment must be transparent.
- An autonomous body needs to be set up to monitor the process of disinvestment.

Disinvestment implies sale of shares of the public sector enterprises to outsiders conferring the right of ownership to these units; the disinvestment may be either partial sale or shares or all shares to the private entrepreneurs. A number of reasons for such disinvestment have occurred but these principally cover: sickness in the public sector, enterprises which are incurring losses from year to year as in the case of FCI, HMT etc. Inefficiency in running the enterprises due to poor use of physical and human resources, under utilised capacity where the units are not able to ensure more than fifty per cent of plant capacities, excess manpower, lack of professional management, lack of autonomy or lack of proper autonomy and also lack of accountability.

When the expectation that the public sector would contribute to economic growth and social stability had not been borne out in actual practice, the alternatives were given consideration; the privatisation route helped the State to minimise its role and paved the way for private sector participation and orderly withdrawal of the state from activities that could be better managed by private entrepreneurs. There were external pressures from international donors and banking agencies, in the context of growing debts and poorly-run state owned enterprises. Privatisation of public enterprises were pressed as a condition for providing support and financial assistance. Privatisation is referred to liberalisation of different regulations to unleash forces of competition and introduction of market forces into an economy. It may also be referred as a structural adjustment programme for the economy. In a narrow sense of the term, it refers. to 'divestiture' or denationalisation, meaning transfer of ownership from state to private hands. The ways and means for the purpose involve any one of the following methods or their combination:

- Transfer of shares of public enterprises to public;
- Private placement of shares;
- Additional investment in public enterprises by private hands;
- Sale of PE assets;
- Reorganisation of PE into separate entities (holding or subsidiary companies);
- Management/employee buyout;
- Privatisation of management either by lease or by management contract.

The decision and method would depend upon the objectives and circumstances of each case of 'privatisation'. Some of the instances of privatisation proposals maybe mentioned The Government accepted in principle the privatisation of air travel and issued licences to four private sector companies to fly air taxis, though partial privatisation of Indian Airlines and Air India by offering 49% equity to public was rejected. Indian Oil Corporation had proposed to the government to disinvest 25% of its capital, either by public issue route or private placement. Indian Petrochemicals Corporation had proposed to the government to offer equity to the public to raise Rs 1000 crores for funding the Eighth Plan projects. In the banking sector, the proposal covered privatising five public sector banks, giving more freedom to private sector banks etc., In addition mention may also be made regarding commercialisation of infrastructure projects; Financing of construction is done by organisations like Infrastructure Leasing and Financial Services (IL&FS) and such commercialisation is an extension of Build, own, operate and transfer (BOOT). BOOT schemes are common for the oil exploration sector.

Privatisation may not be taken as a panacea for all the weakness of public sector enterprises. Apart from political and social resistance, legal confusion, concentration of buyer in a given sector of the economy, non-preservation of the interest of the State are encountered in the process. Privatisation thus depends more on government policy and the political will would be the determining factor. Introduction of market forces, as a form of privatisation, is considered a safer course and to turn inefficient units as effiicient units. Privatisation should not merely result in shifting a terminally sick enterprise to another place without prior diagnosis and therefore long term policies may be required by giving consideration to all the ramifications of privatisation.

5.7 DISINVESTMENT BLUES

It may be mentioned that as against a budgetary target of Rs. 13,200 crores for the year 2003, the disinvestment programme has raked in just over Rs. 1000 crores, including Rs 900 crores from Maruti's "big ticket" divestment. The disinvestment process of HPCL and BPCL would have helped to bridge the gap but the Supreme Court judgment in September 2003 ruling that the government cannot privatise HPCL and BPCL without the approval of Parliament, has come as a blow to the disinvestment process. The two oil companies have been the centerpieces of the disinvestment agenda over the past two years. These companies belonged to the strategic sector, made profits and were listed on the stock exchange. Their sale had become controversial; the criticism was on account of the preference that only loss making and unviable companies should be sold; in the case of these oil companies, it was more over the method chosen by the Government for divesting its stake. The strategic sale route involving the handing over of the management along with a chunk of equity to the successful bidder had come to be preferred method recently. Initially both the oil companies were to be sold through that route but the opposition forced the government to seek a compromise, by adopting a strategic sale for HPCL and a public offer route for BPCL. The public offer route, which was widely followed in the initial stages of the disinvestment programme, enabled the government to divest its stake through the stock exchanges in phases. Had the Government succeeded in its move forward with the divestment of its stake in the two oil companies, it would have built upon the momentum it had generated by the successful strategic sale of some important public sector enterprises such as VSNL and IPCL and the uniquely fashioned disinvestment method adopted in the case of Maruti Udyog. In that case strategic bidders including those from abroad, would have received the right signals.

5.8 SYNTHESIS OF "PUBLIC" AND "ENTERPRISE" CONCEPT

A public enterprise has two dimensions: the public dimension which implies not only public ownership but also implies public control and purpose and (ii) the enterprise dimension, which implies concept of a business firm. The public dimension concept involves three aspects: non-private accretion of net benefits, public decision-making and social accountability. The net benefits of the activity undertaken by the enterprise do not go to the enrichment of a private group of individuals. In the case of public decision making, the entrepreneurial and other major decision making activity shifts from the level of private group of persons brought together as owners and managers to some public level at which no such personal interest exists. The attempt is to move from financial profitability to total national profitability; Under the third element, which is social accountability, the enterprise is accountable to the public for its performance. Any private or partisan gains are to be avoided. On the other hand, the enterprise concept suggests two elements: financial viability and the cost price equation. The financial viability implies efforts of an enterprise to raise net revenues, without damaging the long-term financial interest of the enterprise. The cost price equation attaches significance to the relationship that prices bear to costs. Public enterprises in the above context should therefore be a synthesis of 'public' and 'enterprise' concept so that it becomes an institution 'clothed with the power of the government but possessed of the initiative and flexibility of private enterprise.

5.9 DEVELOPING A CULTURE OF BETTER CORPORATE GOVERNANCE

Systems and procedures ensure transparency and this should be made to fit with the values of the organisation. In addition, laying down appropriate performance reporting mechanisms ensures that such requirements are met by operating management. In the governance of PSUs, however, it may be observed that there is total irrelevance of the board in the governance; the Board has very little say in the selection of CEO or in the composition of the Board. The Government, as the majority shareholder, takes these decisions through the concerned Ministry with the help of PSE. As far as audit is concerned, the dominant role is that of the Comptroller and Auditor General, leaving very little for an Audit committee to do. The delegation of financial and operating powers to the CEO are very limited. The system is not for an effective Board, but the board being pushed into managing, which is clearly different from its legitimate function of directing. The current governance structure rather allows the Board to play a highly obstructive role if it chooses to oppose on operational matters. A meaningful strategic role is absent since all strategic decisions are taken by the dominant shareholder through concerned ministry.

Some of the essential components for making Corporate Governance a success in public enterprises may be mentioned and these are:

- Directors should measure themselves in terms of value addition to the organisation; they should be team players. The effectiveness however, would depend on the information systems, procedures and the culture of transparency in the organisation. Motivation is another essential, which can be ensured by selecting people who are committed to the welfare of the organisation. Ability has to be ensured by screening the track record of selected persons, may be through PSEB.
- Laying down and following appropriate code of ethics prescribing standards of integrity and conduct that applies to all the PSE managers; Apart from other matters, the Code would require employees refraining from decisions in respect of which they have reason to believe that it is calculated to benefit any particular person or party at the expense of the public interest; the code would require them to ensure effective and efficient use of public money; continuous improvement through professionalism and teamwork; the organisation would reward good work and punish any dereliction of duty and obligations based on objectives and transparent criteria.
- *Separate law for Government companies*: It has been observed that company law provides a very inadequate basis for regulating the affairs of a Government company. Therefore the need for promulgating a separate law for regulating the affairs of Government companies is being pressed. Some of the provisions, it is pointed out are having a merely ritualistic application. In this connection, the United States enacting a Government Corporation Control Act in 1945 to put the government's commercial activities on a sound footing is cited.
- *Two tier system*: In Japan, West Germany and Britain, there is a great deal of insistence that the top decision making body should consist of professionals who are drawn from within the industry and have an intimate knowledge of its

problems. Some of the progressive public enterprises like BHEL have a two-tier system of management comprising the policy making body and the executive committee; where possible this course may be adopted. With the two-tiered board system, the present control system having a multiplicity of control agencies could be done away with.

Leadership and strategic vision: An effective board is possible only with an effective leader. "The key to corporate success is a leader with strong will to manage, who inspires able people to work purposefully and effectively through traditional managing process that are integrated into a management system tailored to the nature and environment of the business". Only 'strategic vision' has made it possible for the General Motors and IBM to become one of the most successful companies in the world.

Appendices

5.1 PRIVATISATION AND CORPORATE GOVERNANCE OF STATE OWNED ENTERPRISE ASSETS

The Deputy Chairman of the Planning commissio described the progress on privatisation as not quite satisfactory and noted that it had encountered "significant roadblocks, making the process slow and painful." (November 2003). He felt there had not been any significant improvement in operational efficiencies of these units. Inaugurating a conference on privatisation and corporate governance of state owned assets, he said the process was still facing issues such as method of disinvestments, or how to optimise the basic objective of privatisation. He said there were no templates that could be readily adopted. The Indian experience suggested that the targets of disinvestment had often not been met and the process had not resulted in significant improvement of efficiency in these units. The concept of strategic sale had also been criticised particularly in regard to the sale price of real assets of public sector enterprises.

The Deputy Chairman maintained that changing the organisational culture and incentive structure was more important than the ownership of PSEs. Referring to the Chinese system of converting PSEs into corporations, he said it had led to slowing down of total productivity due to the frequent changes and conversion of ownership patterns. Such results were feared to have led to a setback to reforms in China and fuelled the argument for full scale privatization.

Global experience, he felt, indicated that reforms of state-owned enterprises of privatization depended upon the interlinked reform package encompassing the entire economy and also upon expectation that exist regarding the outcome. In this context, he said corporate governance was one of the most crucial factors required for rapid and sustained growth and development and the Planning Commission had placed it at the centre of development strategy of the Tenth Plan. He said the Commission had identified lack of good governance as the cause of unfulfilled expectations and missed development opportunities in economic spheres as well as in improving the quality of social life.

5.2 MEMORANDUM OF UNDERSTANDING

The Memorandum of Understanding is a formal agreement between the administrative ministry and the public enterprises with regard to the code of conduct regulating the autonomy and accountability of the public sector *vis-à-vis.* the government. It is a charter of mutual accountability or mutual obligation. It specifies the objectives, mission, goals, targets, resources, parameters of evaluation, monitoring system and indicators and review modalities.

The MoU is reviewed yearly. The credit for evolving MoU is given to France, which invented the mechanism known as 'The Contract Plan'. The contract plan is a negotiated performance agreement between the government as owner of public enterprise and the directors of the enterprise. The World Bank took the initiative to spread the MoU concept to developing countries. The contract plan system also drew the attention of the Indian government.

In the year 1984, the government appointed a Committee under the Chairmanship of Dr. Arjun Sen Gupta to review the policy for public enterprises. The committee considered that the issues of accountability and autonomy were interrelated. It felt that the form of organizational structure. Government interference and intervention and performance were all interrelated matters, and therefore, the accountability should be designed in terms of performance criteria and the code of conduct, regulating relations between the government and the public sector.

The committee wanted the role of the government to be confined to overall strategic planning and policy matters rather than day-to-day functioning of the public enterprises. It favoured their functioning consistent with plan objectives. Once the goals were mutually agreed upon, it wanted the enterprise to be allowed to operate without government interference.

The Economic Administration Reforms Commission (Jha Commission) also went into the question of evaluation of public enterprises some time in 1984 and also suggested that for each public enterprise there should be a document setting forth the basic expectations of the government in arriving at the relevant investment decision, and the PEs attempting a corporate statement, of goals and objectives. The Commission recommended that with reference to such a governmental charter and corporate statement, each enterprise should attempt an annual self-evaluation, to be published as part of its annual report. This should be followed-once in three years-by an appraisal of the performance by a multi-disciplinary group of experts.

The MoU system sought to achieve: Clarity of objectives, provide a methodology and machinery for the evaluation of performance, and also altering the quality of the relationship between the government and the PEs, thus paving the way for a quasi-contractual relationship. The components and MoU carry the following sections–the first section giving a brief statement of the corporate mission and objectives of the PE, the second setting out the performance representing the aspects of activities which are regarded as important by both parties; the relative importance of the different indicators is shown by the weights attached to each; these weights make it possible to combine the performance into an overall evaluation. The third section mentions the obligations of the other party of the MoU, namely, the Government. The fourth one indicates the information flow expected and the monitoring arrangements which will be in force.

It may be added that there is no standardized set of indicators which are applicable across the board to all the PEs. The MoU is enterprise-specific, and is essentially a system of management audit. It helps evaluate the performance of the management in a given year with reference to the commitments against specific indicators made in the MoU in that year. The system is operated through the Department of Public Enterprises which is the nodal agency in government for all general issues relating to PEs. The examination of the draft MoU is done in two stages. In the first stage, the appropriateness of the chosen indicators, their relative weights, and stipulations made by the PEs concerned are examined. In the second round, which takes place in the month of March, the MoU targets, their conformity to the plan/budget documents and their acceptability, etc. are examined. The signed MoU are placed before Parliament.

When performance data with reference to the MoU targets, become available, each PE is expected to indicate its actual performance against the MoU targets: attempt a self-evaluation; work out a composite score, and submit these along with supporting material to the DPE. When the evaluation reports are finalized, gradings are given to PEs as excellent, very good, etc. These reports are included in' the Public Enterprises Survey; which is then placed before Parliament along with the budget documents.

It may be useful to note the following essential features of MoUs, as outlined by the Government, vide Document No. 1 (31)/88 Fin (PPU) New Delhi, dated September 16, 1996.

The preconditions for successful MoUs

- Coherent/consistent corporate strategy.
- Fully elaborated development strategy and policy for the sector in which the public sector unit works.
- Administrative ministries to improve their capacity to assess and discuss corporate strategies with PSU management and ensure their contribution to sectoral/national priorities.
- Contract between equal partners.
- Duration-annual (should be preferably for two years with targets covering 3-5 years).
- Enterprise-specific, based on the corporate strategy of the PSU.

Hence, for detailed guidelines or standard formats, MoUs are not suitable. MoUs should contain all essential objectives assigned to PSUs. The target can be of the following types:

- *Quantitative* (Financial targets, physical efficiency indicators, investment programmes).
- *Qualitative* (Purpose of Pre-appraisal of projects, strategy, diversification, corporate restructuring, reallocation of resources, labour aspects, training, R & D, other national priorities).
- *Non-commercial objectives* Specificity and its impact on profitability. The contract will contain commitments regarding.
- Magnitude of autonomy.
- Financing of non-commercial obligations.
- Budget support in the first year of implementation of preapproved projects.

The contracts will also specify:

- Requirements/frequency of reporting/monitoring.
- Detailed economic policy assumptions underpinning targets assigned to PSUs.
- Performance parameters for determining managerial bonuses.

The other critical aspects of performance contracts are:

- They are executing instruments and not a substitute for strategic decisions which are the preconditions for success.

They must supersede, not supplement, the existing mechanisms and systems of authorization.

They must contain all entries to be used for performance evaluation.

5.3 ORGANISATION INDEX APPROACH[2]

The organisational index approach presented below has the following characteristics:

(a) aims at evaluating the performance at an individual enterprise level;

(b) takes into account the different expectations of various interest groups (hence multiple objectives, both financial and non-financial in nature) for giving due weightages to different performance criteria;

(c) shows trends in total performance;

(d) tries to serve all purposes of a performance evaluation exercise (to learn, to judge, to control, to motivate, and to. identify areas for further improvement);

(e) facilitates an outsider's as well as insider's evaluation;

(f) is simple and can be implemented within the given structure, systems, staff, and skill, available in public enterprises;

(g) facilitates the setting up of a proper regard and punishment system.

In constructing an anisational index, the following steps are to be taken sequentially:

(a) Spell out the mission of the enterprise.

(b) Derive its broad objectives, and obligations.

(c) Delete objectives which will have to be evaluated with subjectivity.

(d) Specify objectives which are amenable for performance evaluation.

(e) Identify possible performance parameters for each of the specific objectives.

(f) Check data availability on actual performance with regard to each of the possible performance parameter.

(g) Specify performance parameters and their quantification.

(h) Ascertain the weights to be assigned to each of the selected performance parameter by interest groups (Nijkamp, 1980).

(i) Calculate the weighted average weights of each. performance parameter.

(j) Tabulate the actual performance data on all the performance parameters as required.

(k) Calculate the performance scores by multiplying the actual performance with the weighted average weights of all the performance parameters.

(l) Total up the performance, scores of all performance, parameters, and this total is what is called an organisational Index.

---

2 *Source*: Public sector restructuring and Privatisation, Kanishka Publishers and distributors

6

Corporate Governance: Business Ethics and Social Responsibility

6.1 INTRODUCTION

'Ethics' commonly means rules and/or principles that define right and wrong conduct. Business ethics refers to the system of moral principles and rules of conduct applied to the business. Business being a social organ, shall not conduct itself in a way detrimental to the interests of the society and the business sectors itself. The following definition of ethics may also be noted:[1] "Ethics is a fundamental trait which one adopts and follows as a guiding principle or basic Dharma in one's life. It implies moral conduct and honourable behaviour on the part of an individual. Ethics in most cases runs parallel to law and shows due consideration to other's rights and interests in a civilised society. Compassion on the other hand may induce a person to give more than what ethics might demand."

According to the speakers at the 4th International conference on Governance organised by the Indian Merchant's Chamber and the Asian Centre for Corporate Governance in Mumbai, the fundamental issue of corporate governance is of ethics and therefore, good governance cannot be imposed by legislations and it should come from within. A mere quantitative compliance is not enough; there must also be intellectual honesty and qualitative compliance. The SEBI Chairman, participating in the conference, has emphasised the need for a dynamic approach towards framing governance and compliance standards. According to him, these are shaped by the environment and hence must evolve with time. "Corporate governance is about delivering, satisfying and satiating the expectations of all stake-holders–including customers, employees suppliers and the society at large," he said. "But a regulator cannot legislate ethics; we can lay down the rules and define the structure, but good governance has to emerge from the people who manage the interests of the stakeholders." A company's activities must at all times, be ethical, honest and trustworthy—because corporate governance is the "fundamental pillar' on which the growth of the company is built, he added. According to Mr. Mervyn E King, author of King Committee report on corporate governance and former Judge of the Supreme court of South Africa, guidelines for governance are needed, as the corporate has to be seen as discharging its responsibilities. He said, mere compliance is not enough, as it was to found to be otherwise in the case of Enron. Enron had all the trappings of governance and had quantitatively complied with the guidelines, and it was functional, because it was dishonest and failed to discharge good faith, care skill and diligence. Mr. King said, " There must be intellectual honesty, and qualitative compliance." "Good governance is a journey, not the destination." According to him, the questions that directors need to ask

---

1. Ethics, Business and professions, Charted Secretary November 2003 p. 1673.

themselves are: is there any conflict; do I have all the facts to enable me to make a decision; is the decision in the best interests of the company; is the communication to stakeholders transparent; is the company acting as a good steward of the company's assets.

6.2 ETHICAL PRINCIPLES

The following are some of the most important and well accepted ethical principles that a business should follow:[2]

- Ensure that the customers are not cheated or deceived by substandard or defective products, by under measurement or by any other means
- Businessmen and traders must not get together and hold stocks of items that are in short supply
- Conform to fair and undistorted competition
- Discourage unfair practices to tarnish the image of competitors
- Competing businessmen should not form cartels—which fix prices at which their products are to be sold.
- Make accurate business records available to all authorised persons
- Pay taxes and discharge other obligations promptly
- Ensure sincerity in advertising and, labelling and packaging and
- Competing businessmen should not agree to carve out market shares between themselves.

There are three parameters for analysis of ethical reasoning. These are:

(i) ethics of social utility,

(ii) ethics of human rights, and

(iii) ethics of justice and fairness.

The ethics of social utility, although difficult to measure, has to be analysed in terms of "whether the benefit accrued to the society exceeds the cost of the society." Human rights are another basis for judging ethics. The most basic human rights are those claims or entitlements that enable a person to survive, to make free choice, and to realise one's potential as human being. Where a company carelessly disposes of hazardous waste, it may be guilty of ignoring the human rights. Justice or fairness refers to the fair distribution of benefits among the people in a society; if minority and women are treated unequally it is social injustice and unethical.

Embedding ethics into a company's standard operating procedures and policies is closely related to corporate social responsiveness. In some organisations a permanent board level committee is created to consider ethical dimensions of the company's policy and procedures. They are called "public policy" or "social responsibility" committees. Such committees serve as a symbolic function that communicates to employees and external stakeholders, about the company's formal commitment to given ethics. Ethics scholars recommend that companies should not only identify the generic questions of

---

[2] Managerial tools for corporate leadership, Himalaya Publishing House.

ethical nature but these should be integrated with usual questions on matters relating to legal, financial and marketing areas, in which company operates.

6.3 ETHICAL PROPOSITIONS

Integrating ethics into corporate governance is considered important, as the exercise makes the propositions more robust than a stultified view of corporate governance as a box-ticking process. The following ethical propositions may be taken into consideration for the purpose:

- Ethical conflicts and choices are inherent in business decision making.
- Proper ethical behaviour exists on a plane above the law. The law merely specifies the lowest common denominator of acceptable behaviour.
- There is no single satisfactory standard of ethical action agreeable to everyone that a manager can use to make specific operational decisions.
- Managers should be familiar with a wide variety of ethical standards.
- The discussion of business cases or of situations having ethical implications can make managers more ethically sensitive.
- There are diverse and sometimes conflicting determinants of ethical action. These stem primarily from the individual, from the organisation, from professional norms, and from the values of the society.
- Individual values are the final standard, although not necessarily the determining reason for ethical behaviour.
- Consensus regarding what constitutes proper ethical behaviour in a decision-making situation diminishes as the level of analysis proceeds from abstract to specific.
- The moral tone of an organisation is set by top management.
- The lower the organisational level of a manager, the greater the perceived pressure to act unethically.
- Individual managers perceive themselves as more ethical than their colleagues.
- Effective codes of ethics should contain meaningful and clearly stated provisions, along with enforced sanctions for non-compliance.
- Employees must have a non-punitive, fail-safe mechanism for reporting ethical abuses in the organisation.
- Every organisation should appoint a top-level manager or director to be responsible for acting as an ethical director in the organisation.

6.4 ETHICS AND CORPORATE GOVERNANCE

Are ethics and corporate governance inter-related? What provides an ethical base for business? How the emerging trends in corporate governance and related developments are relevant? Let us note the following answers.

"Corporate governance will empower an effective role for the independent directors to review and reorient the policies of the company. The institutional directors will start working for the company as a whole instead of merely protecting their investment interests. As a corollary, periodical performance appraisals, environmental and energy audits and effective legal compliances would become part of corporate governance, providing an ethical base for business. Good corporate governance, in so far as it caters to all interests, is an integral part of Business Ethics. Business owes it to the community."[3]

As far as the emerging trends in corporate governance are concerned, "The Companies Act 1956, the listing agreement and SEBI rules and regulations have undergone radical changes in the recent years, in order to promote better corporate governance. The emerging concepts of independent directors, Audit committee, Remuneration committee, Directors' responsibility statement in the Directors' Report, Corporate governance, compliance certificate as part of Directors' Report—all these and more have brought about radical changes in the art of corporate management. The corporate boards are now required to manage the affairs of corporate bodies with better accountability to shareholders and transparency of operations with better disclosure of both financial and non-financial data through annual and other periodical reports. The Naresh Chandra and Narayanamurthy committee reports propose to carry further the ongoing reforms aimed at corporate re-structuring. All these developments will usher in a more effective and purposeful role for the professionals in general and the Company Secretaries in particular."[4]

6.5 ETHICS CODE

An ethics code describes the general value system and ethical rules that the organisation tries to apply. These codes are developed to define organisational purpose, establish a uniform ethical climate within the organisation and provide for consistent decision making. Written codes are important for large organisations, branch units and franchisers, as these companies tend to have complex structures. A code is preferably drawn after consulting the employees; when poorly handled, the ethics code may retard and encourage unethical practices. The Code of Ethics promulgated by the PHD Chamber of Commerce reads as follows:

- Business must maintain highest standards of behaviour so that their actions and decisions result in the benefits for industry, employees, customers, shareholders and society.
- Goods and services must conform to the commitment promised to customers. Business must be realistic and truthful in stating claims.
- Customers must be given best possible service and treated with respect and fairness.
- Best way of promoting high standards of business practices is through self-regulation. The code has been designed as an instrument of self—regulation to serve as voluntary guideline towards better quality of life and higher standards of business practices.

---

3 Ethics, Business and professions, Chartered Secretary, November 2003 (p.1673)

4 Chartered Secretary, p.1679 November 2003.

The document prepared by Department of Administrative Reforms and Public Grievances has laid emphasis on the following principles in its "Code of ethics for the Public Services in India":

- **Selflessness:** Holders of public office should take decisions solely in terms of the public interest. They should not do so in order to gain financial or other material benefits for themselves, their family or their friends.
- **Integrity:** Holders of public office should not place themselves under any financial or other obligation to outside individuals or organisations that might influence them in the performance of their official duties.
- **Objective:** In carrying out public business, including making public appointments, awarding contracts or recommending individuals for rewards and benefits, holders of public office should make choice on merit.
- **Accountability:** Holders of public office are accountable for their decisions and actions to the public and must submit themselves to whatever scrutiny is appropriate to their office.
- **Openness:** Holders of public office should be as open as possible about all the decisions and actions that they take. They should give reasons for their decisions and restrict information only when the wider public interest clearly demands.
- **Honesty:** Holders of public office have a duty to declare any private interest relating to their public duties and to take steps to resolve any conflicts arising in a way that protects the public interest.
- **Leadership:** Holders of public office should promote and support these principles by leadership and example.

These principles apply to all aspects of public life.

6.6 CORPORATE SOCIAL RESPONSIBILITY

The following definition may be noted: "Corporate social responsibility is operating a business in a manner which meets or excels the ethical, legal, commercial and public expectations that a society has from the business."[5]

Corporate social responsibility is nothing but what an organisation does to positively influence the society in which it exist. It could take the form of community relationship, volunteer assistance programmes, special scholarships, preservation of cultural heritage and beautification of cities. The philosophy is basically to return to the society what it has taken from it, in the course of its quest for creation of wealth. Essentially, it is an inter—disciplinary subject in nature and encompasses in its fold:

- Social, economic, ethical and moral responsibility of companies and managers,
- Compliance with legal and voluntary requirements for business and professional practice,
- Challenges posed by needs of the economy and socially disadvantaged groups, and

---

5 Corporate social responsibility (Corporate Governance Reporting (model formats) The ICSI Ist ed. May 2003.

- Management of corporate responsibility activities.

Commerce requires the external defence and internal order and an agreed set of rules and regulations, all of which are provided by the society. While society is expected to provide the environment in which the business can safely operate and develop, Business is expected to create wealth; supply markets; generate employment; innovate its competitiveness, while contributing to the maintenance of the community in which it operates. The various factors and developments, such as the State rolling back its functions in favour of the private sector and the growth of modern corporations, some times even considered bigger than some States/countries, their size and wealth should enable them to easily discharge their social responsibilities.

6.7 IS GOOD GOVERNANCE CONFINED TO CORPORATE EXCELLENCE ONLY?

Good governance is not simply about corporate excellence. It is the key to economic and social transformation. The corporations of today are no longer sheer economic entities. These are the engines of economic and social transformation. Kenichi Ohmae argued in "The borderless world: Power and Strategy in the Interlined Economy" that:

"A Corporation is a social Institution whose responsibilities extend far beyond the well being of its equity owners to giving security and a good life to its employees, dealers, customers, vendors and subcontractors. Their whole life hinges on the well being of the corporation."

Corporations are the powerhouses that generate employment, provide education and health care, and given sustenance to the society. Globalisation has given multinational overwhelming power at the expenses of democratically elected governments. Good governance needs to ensure that the corporations take into account the interests of all constituencies in which they operate. A business enterprise's corporate actions must be compatible with long term societal needs such as the quality of environment and welfare of local community.[6]

---

6 Corporate governance, concept and dimensions, Snow White, 2003.

Appendices

6.1 SOCIAL RESPONSIBILITY OF CORPORATES

It is believed that a business firm must view itself as a socially responsive entity and assume wider responsibilities. This is based on the following three premises:

- A company operates with the franchise given to it by the society, and hence, the society legitimately expects it to shoulder social responsibility.
- It is in the enlightened self-interest of a company to promote public welfare.
- If a business assumes social responsibility, it mitigates the pressure for as well as the incidence of governmental regulations.

Kenneth Andrews, an eloquent advocate of social responsibility says: "Corporate executives of the calibre, intelligence and humanity required to run substantial companies cannot be expected to confine themselves to the narrow economic activity and to ignore its social consequences."[7]

This view of explicitly and implicitly is subscribed to by a large number of companies that make commitments to various social programmes and projects.

According to the emerging consensus on the matter, corporates should have the social responsibility of giving due weightage, to protect the environment and safeguard the interests of customers, employees, suppliers and the community, rather than concentrating on maximization of profits. There is an increasing resistance from different groups against business outfits' incessant drive to maximize profits. The industry should shed its traditional attitude of exploiting the customer and adopt the customer's perspective in every action of business. Similarly, there is a need to provide work to the employees in a manner that is dignified, fulfilling and meaningful. In this context, social responsibility and corporate governance should become the philosophy of the corporate entities in carrying out the following:

- It is a prime social responsibility of business to set standards of quality and integrity which give the customer a fair deal. A manufacturer who short - changes his customer would over time, find himself out of business through the forces of competition.
- The social responsibility in respect of the physical environment in which we live. The callous and irresponsible manner in which we pollute air and water, denude forests and other natural resources, reflects social responsibility of a high order.
- The business should not wait, for radical legislation or aggressive unionism to share the surplus. The sharing of surplus should not become a political game, a trial of strength between organized forces rather than a mature adult dialogue, where the organization's capacity and constraints become prime factors influencing such decisions.
- The dignity and worth of every' human being working in the organization should be recognized. The cast-iron barriers between the blue-collar and white-collar workers should be removed.

---

7 Andrews, B. Kenneth, The Concept of Corporate Strategy, Homewood, Illinois, Dow Jones Irwin.

- The business should evolve organization structures where individuals can find professional and emotional satisfaction out of doing a job.
- The business also should use its talents and resources to innovate products and services designed to meet the unfulfilled needs of the community. Attention can be directed towards cheap, appropriate building materials for housing, low cost, mass-produced protein foods, clean drinking water, programmed literacy, low-cost indigenous medicines, and so on.

Corporate bodies thus should treat their suppliers as business partners and protect the interests of investors by adding value to their investments. Corporate governance is nothing but ushering in better relations among the shareholders, members of the board, suppliers, employees and customers, besides being environment-friendly. In this connection, the social responsibilities of management stated by Drucker may be noted:

- The first responsibility of management of society is to operate at a profit and ensure growth of the enterprise on the ground that business is the wealth-creating and wealth-producing organ of society.
- For the same reason, management has a public responsibility to make sure of tomorrow's management without which resources would be mismanaged, and the corporate would lose wealth-producing capacity and finally be destroyed.
- Management is responsible for conducting the enterprise so as not to undermine the social beliefs and cohesion, e.g., to keep open the opportunity for individuals to rise from the bottom according to ability and performance, and not demand absolute and total allegiance from employees.
- It should be the responsibility of the management of 'large companies to develop a capital expenditure policy which tends to counteract the extremes of business cycles.
- Management also has a responsibility to develop policies that will overcome the deep-seated hostility to profits, which is a threat to the economic and social system of free enterprise.

The corporate sector should accord utmost importance to moral and ethical values and function with a social responsibility. According to the President of ICSI, corporate governance "is perhaps the only route which would enable Indian businessmen to cut through the maze of prevalent questionable practices, indefensible management attitudes to stakeholders and penetrable nondisclosures in their bid to integrate themselves with a far more demanding world order."

"Business does not fulfil its social responsibility by short-changing the customers, exploiting its labour, polluting the environment and then generating a surplus which it generally spends on adopting a remote village or erecting a statue. Business fulfils the social responsibility by doing the things it is in business to do and doing them well."[8]

Corporate Social Reporting

Several studies were made in the USA regarding publication of Social Reports by corporates and it was found that their social reports covered data relating to

---

8 Changing the Minset, Aga, Rohinton D. Aga, Tata McGraw-Hill, Delhi.

employment opportunities, environmental controls, community involvement and consumerism.

Considering India's socio-economic problems, eight major heads have been identified and recommended by experts, for the purpose of social reporting. These cover employment opportunities, foreign exchange transactions, energy conservation, research and development, contribution to government exchequer, social projects, environmental control and consumerism.

Creation of employment opportunities may be classified into opportunities in India and opportunities abroad. It is considered desirable to disclose foreign exchange transactions in view of the scanty foreign exchange reserves, or savings in foreign exchange. Energy purchased or generated and energy consumed per unit of standard product may be reported along with the consumption norm of the industry. The effect of research and development activities may be quantified in terms of cost saved/profit added. Contribution to Government exchequer by way of sales tax, income tax, excise, customs and other duties may be reported as an item of social benefits. Social projects such as the construction of roads, schools, hospitals, stadiums, etc., may be reported along with categories of beneficiaries and costs. It would be also important to report, at the same time, about the negative social effect caused by a corporate enterprise and these are concerned with the use of irreplaceable resources, nature of pollution caused, etc., and quantifying use of such resources. However, the cost involved for pollution control may be taken as an item of social benefit and reported accordingly.

Thus, the concept of social accounting involves, in monetary terms, the impact of objectives, policies and procedures of a commercial organization on different sections of society, compared to the benefits derived by the society.

6.2 SEBI SET TO ADOPT A VILLAGE IN MAHARASHTRA

Jalke, the dusty little village tucked away in the heart of rural Maharashtra in the district of Jalgaon, is about to have its fortunes turned with help from the country's biggest bank, the State Bank of India. Jalke with a population of 800 will soon be adopted by SBI as the first step towards the bank's endeavour of transforming it into a 'model village'. SBI will invest about Rs. 50 lakh initially, to set up power, water supply and other facilities for the villagers. The project is part of the bank's community service initiatives. The bank proposes to install a composite windmill along with solar energy and borewells. The bank proposes to get the villagers involved in the project, so that manpower costs could be saved in addition to maintenance not becoming a problem later. The bank will also teach the villages the techniques of rainwater harvesting by using simple bunds to store water from nearby canals. SBI has found that a large portion of the population is unemployed. It therefore proposes investment in vermiculture compost projects.

6.3 COMMUNITY SERVICE AWARD FOR ORCHID CHEMICALS AND PHARMACEUTICALS LTD.

The above Chennai based company received the annual Rotary Club of Madras award for environment and community service for 2003-04 in April 2004. The managing director of the company received the award on behalf of the company for being driven by a corporate philosophy that places people before products and profits. The 100 per cent export-oriented company makes antibiotics, particularly 'cephalosporins' which are used to treat infections caused by bacteria. The company has invested 414 million capital expenditure in environment friendly systems Orchid Limited Invested in technology to break down the effluents it produces by separating, healing and cooling and to convert them into useful or harmless waste. Ultimately water can be extracted from all liquid waste. Orchid Ltd recovers almost 100 per cent of the water used in its production processes. To minimise solid waste, the company has undertaken bio composting to produce manure, which has been tested and proved to be safe and effective. The company also works for community development through the Orchid Trust in seven villages around its plant at Alathur, close to Chennai. The trust also runs programmes on health, self-employment, capacity building and youth development.

PART - II

GENERAL REFERENCE AND CURRENT DEVELOPMENTS

General Reference

WHAT CONSTITUTES GOOD GOVERNANCE?

When there is chance of good governance? Independent directors have a Major role to play in promoting good corporate governance. In addition, if certain practical steps are taken to ensure the right composition of the board Adherence to standards and best practices, and accurate disclosure and reviews of audit plans, then there is a greater chance of good governance. In a seminar organised by the Bombay Chamber of Commerce and Industry (BCCI), it was brought out that global governance standards are driven by a system of accountability, checks and balances and the role of the management, the board and the shareholders in achieving greater shareholder value. The Joint Managing Director of Shook Lin & Bok, a Singapore law firm said, "adherence to governance standards is important to Regulators and exchanges because of competition for foreign portfolio investment and there is also evidence to suggest that investor behaviour is influenced by superior governance, resulting in better prices." He observed that the UK model stresses the role of directors, the directors' remuneration, relations with shareholders, accountability and audit, and institutional investors. Accordingly, there must be an effective board to l Lead and control the company, a separation of the Chairman and CEO posts, and a system of formal and transparent appointment/re-election, as well as supply of timely and appropriate information. Given that there has been much shareholder anxiety over CEO pay, the director's remuneration must also be sufficient and attractive and not excessive. And this should be linked to corporate and individual performance. For a really appropriate board composition, it must be made up of industry, financial, legal and other competencies, he said. "There must also be documentation of existing practices against governance principles, standards and best practices, compliance checklists and an accurate disclosure of existing governance, besides an annual review of market best practices." Some other speakers felt that corporate governance is usually a delicate balance between statutory compliance and the concept of fiduciary duties. The Chairman of Audit Committee, VSNL who expressed his view, felt that finally there must also be a mindset for obeying the law, because if legislation alone were enough, then India would be among the most reformed societies. There is a machinery to enforce the law, but the fundamentals are not being looked at closely; we are just introducing laws on top of laws.

CORPORATE GOVERNANCE PRACTICES

The enormous challenge of corporate governance in a highly disparate business environment, where corporate frauds thrive, can be best met through a "triple bottom line approach" according to the President of the London-based World Council for Corporate Governance (WCFCG). Dr. Madhav Mehra, the President, said that the three priorities for any corporate house are "people, planet (meaning the earth) and profits", in that order. He also favoured mandatory independent corporate governance ratings, which completely open up the company to all its stakeholders, including shareholders. On the prevailing situation in India, according to his assessment, there was much talk and too little by way of implementation. "The governance ratings now in vogue are grossly inadequate, as they reflect only what a corporate house wants its different stakeholders to know." Making a strong pitch for a larger crop of independent directors, especially in large Indian companies, as recommended by the Naresh Chandra Committee, he said the government should implement the panel suggestions without any further delay. Drawing a parallel with corporate governance practices in the developed world post-Enron, he said that the similar Derek Higgs report in the UK was implemented speedily despite certain hurdles. Prior to the Enron debacle, there was a tendency among corporates worldwide to whitewash the truth but all this has changed now as the "culture of concealment has been exposed". He visualised a much bigger role for government, especially for institutions like the Securities and Exchange Board of India, as greater Government–industry interaction was required. Governance-related issues have to be debated upfront, as this would be the major driver of all Indian corporates hoping for a Nasdaq or an LSE listing in the foreseeable future.

GLOBAL COMPACT FOR CORPORATES

FOUR years since the UN Chief floated the concept of 'Global Compact' for corporates, India figures among the top three nations with sizeable number of subscribers to it.

GC is meant to prod corporate conscience towards society and environment and till March this year, 46 public sector and 40from the private sector are now into the voluntary, value-based initiative of the ILO, according to Dr S.M. Dewan, DG, Standing conference of Public Sector Undertakings (Scope). As many as 13 are from the Tata Group.

Addressing a first Scope-ILO training programme for managers of PSUs, he said the concept mooted by Kofi Annan at the 1999 WEF makes CEOs to look beyond the company bottom-line and act fairly towards labour and society. Globalisation, he said, had caused regional imbalances and GC, which encompasses ILO-prescribed labour rights, and Rio environmental, concerns as good business ethics, can soften some of the harsh effects of a highly competitive world.

Of the 1,200 companies subscribing to GC so far, India, he said, is only after Spain with 118 GC practitioners and the Philippines with 90 of them.

Mr. Roy Chacko, ILO official from Geneva, said GC provoked new thinking that benefits the public. Companies need to write to ILO about their GC intent and show proof of its practice after a year.

According to Dr Rajen Malhotra, a Delhi-based ILO specialist on South Asia, GC is gaining relevance today. What started as ethical trading and sourcing practices in apparel, footwear, sports and toy industries is now getting extended to farm produce, auto, of, gas, biotech, FMCG.

SEBI CORPORATE GOVERNANCE NORMS SOON (MARCH 2004)

According to the Chairman of Securities and Exchange Board of India, it is not proposed to wait for the enactment of the Companies amendment Bill to issue the revised Clause 49 on Corporate governance. SEBI proposes to go ahead and address the dynamic issues relating to corporate governance through regulations. The NR Narayanamurthy committee has already heard the industry representations. The modified Clause 49 will be taken up by the SEBI Board soon. The amendments proposed aimed at strengthening the responsibilities of audit committees, improving the quality of financial disclosures, including those related to related party transactions and proceeds from initial public offerings, requiring boards to adopt formal code of conduct, whistle blower policy and improving disclosures related to compensation paid to non-executive directors.

All listed companies having a paid up share capital of Rs. 3 crore and above or net worth of Rs. 25 crore or more at any time in the history of the entity, were required to comply with the requirements of Clause 49. The earlier amendments had also stated that non-executive directors cannot have board representation more than nine years. Among the norms in the amended clause 49 that had got the corporate sector's goal was the one that envisaged that if a holding company is required to have 50 per cent independent directors, the same requirement would have to be complied with by the subsidiary company irrespective of its size and nature of business.

CORPORATE GOVERNANCE RATINGS

The benefit of corporate governance ratings (CGR) for the company, regulators and stakeholders, according to ICRA need to be advocated. However, according to the views of the Federation of Indian Chambers of Commerce and Industry, "companies should be allowed to weigh the pros and cons of the CGR model before adopting it. They are of the view that corporate governance norms should not be made mandatory. However, it should be recommendatory or voluntary in nature, left to the companies whether they want to adopt it or not." Industry sources are also concerned about the cost of compliance; According to them, as the company has to deal with so many disclosure norms under various provisions of the company law, if CGR is made mandatory it would eat into the profit margins of corporates.

Survey by ICRA: Companies such as ITC, Wipro, Godrej Consumer Products, PNB Gilts, ESSAP Ltd and Infosys Technologies Ltd., have gone ahead with such ratings. Some companies have opted for a rating that evaluates the Stakeholders value creation. ICRA had carried out a survey of 35 leading institutional investors and large brokerage houses during Oct.-Dec. 2003. An overwhelming majority felt that contrary to the apprehensions aired by the corporate sector, the current emphasis on corporate governance is desirable and will play a major role in making the capital markets a safer place for investors. Over 85 per cent of respondents felt that corporate governance is as important as quantifiable factors, such as the likely growth in earnings. The key variable in ICRA's rating methodology for corporate governance includes shareholding structure, governance structure and management process, board structure and process, stakeholders relationship, transparency and disclosure and financial discipline.

Should corporate governance ratings be banned? [1]

Debate: Madhav Mehra, President, World Council for Corporate Governance

- Two rating organisations in India–ICRA and CRISIL have developed well-thought out criteria for measuring corporate governance practices and value creation for all

[1] Business Standard dt. 14th April 2004.

stakeholders. These take into account ratings on wealth creation, wealth management, and wealth sharing and are based not only on data published in the public domain, but also detailed interviews with management and stakeholders.

- If there is one lesson that can be learnt from the corporate scandals at Enron, Worldcom, Global Crossing, Marconi, Equitable Life, Parmalat, Skandia, Vivendi and now Shell, it is to move away from box-ticking approach to corporate governance.
- Lynn Turner, Chief Accountant of SEC from 1998-2001, who was earlier a partner of Cooper & Lybrand, admitted in a TV interview, "All big Five accounting firms helped Wall Street investment banking firms to engineer hypothetical transactions to make companies look better than they actually were".

Unlike the UK, India is still grappling with reform on the appointment of Independent directors. A report submitted by Naresh Chandra Committee has been scuttled. The report that recommended at least 50 per cent directors to be independent, created the same stork as in the UK, but India did not have Patricia Hewitt to stem the revolt. The government has capitulated to these corporations and the report is collecting dust. Independent directors are the cornerstones of good corporate governance.

- To be meaningful ratings have to address the process and not the result. This is difficult to measure when we do not even have well defined criteria to measure them. Besides wealth creation, as measured by the market Capitalisation may be due to market effect and have nothing to do with Corporate governance practices.
- No law, rule or rating can be an effective measure. It is naïve to think that the rating can be an effective measure. It is naïve to think that the ratings can truly measure transparency, equity, accountability, integrity and responsibility—the five pillars of good corporate governance.
- Every CEO is in the mortal fear of quarterly results and lives from quarter to quarter. We have to educate investors that in an economy based on innovation there is no way companies can give a double digit growth every quarter, unless CEOs manage expectations and resort to earning manipulation.
- There is no doubt that the effort to popularise corporate governance rating has good intentions, but these intentions will be better served by directing all efforts on strengthening the fundamentals of corporate governance in India by getting the two important reports–Narayana Murthy's and Naresh Chandra Committee's implemented.
- The corporate governance rating is an opinion by an independent professional agency. The opinion is backed by adequate research and due diligence process carried out by competent professionals with appropriate skills, and reflects a dispassionate view.
- It takes into consideration aspects like ownership structure, management style, including board level issues, quality of financial reporting and disclosure practices, and sensitivity to the interests of different financial stakeholders. I firmly believe that all the stakeholders should have the right to obtain the benefit of an independent opinion on all the specific areas.

- Equity investors, in particular, may derive enough comfort in their decision-making process from such opinion on the corporate governance of an entity in which they are investing. The question is, why should these investors be deprived of this opinion?
- There are corporations that follow excellent corporate governance standards, which they need to communicate to the outside world. However, such claims by corporate entity, on its own, may not always be Credible and needs to be supported by verification by an independent body such as credit-rating agency.
- Credit rating agencies while assessing any rating make a comprehensive disclosure of the rationale behind such rating and also identify the deficiencies. This will enable an entity to improve on its level of governance by taking corrective measures. Rating agencies will carry out not only a rating but also monitoring of such ratings;
- A better opinion for the stakeholders would be to rely on an entity that would be prepared to deploy adequate resources to carry out the exercise, arrive at the judgment after a thorough analysis of all the objective and subjective issues through a process of collective consultation.

INFOSYS GETS FIRST S&P GOVERNANCE RATING

Standard and Poor (S&P) governance services assigned a corporate governance score of CGS-8.6 to Infosys Technologies (April 2004). This is the first instance of S&P assigning CGS to any Indian entity. Infosys has demonstrated strong standards of corporate governance. This score demonstrates that companies can create the right conditions for high standards of corporate governance both in developing as well as developed economies, said S&P's governance analyst. In a scale of 1 (low) to 10 (high), Infosys has scored nine for ownership structure and influence; 8.3 for financial stakeholder rights and relations; 9.2 for financial transparency and information disclosure; and 8.0 for board structure and process. Timing and access to disclosure is strong, given the company's compliance with the US Securities and Exchange Commission's regulations on fair disclosure. The lowest relative score was with Infosys board structure and process; however this is still assessed strong, given its success at bringing in a large number of outside directors in a relatively short amount of time.

Vision to Enable Public Enterprises to be Globally Competitive

According to Chairman Standing conference of Public Enterprises (SCOPE) a sustained empowerment of public sector enterprises will certainly result in a higher return on investment, a higher contribution to the exchequer, greater support to the overall economic growth and finally will lead to better products and services at competitive prices for end-user. He said that PSEs are poised to play a major role in accelerating the country's economic growth leading to a doubling of the per capita income by the year 2012. SCOPE, on its part had made substantial progress as an effective policy advocacy centre for the public sector.

Talking about the improved performance of the central PSEs, the SCOPE Chairman noted that between 1992-93 and 2001-02, the enterprises had posted an extremely impressive commercial performance. The return on investment of the PSEs had gone up from 11.4 per cent to 16.2 per cent. PSEs have also significantly increased the wealth of shareholders. As on March 31, 2002, on a total equity of central PSEs at Rs. 1,01,269 crore, the shareholders funds stood at Rs. 3,07,267 crore. Accounting for about 31 per cent of the revenue receipts of the government, the net profit of the PSEs stood at Rs. 26,045 crore, which meant an impressive return on investment about 16.2 per cent. SCOPE had also finalised its vision "to enable its member enterprises to be globally competitive in a market driven environment." Accordingly initiatives have been taken which also include efforts for further empowerment of PSEs, highlighting the perspectives of the public sector on issues pertaining to labour and human resources. RBI pulls up banks for not lending enough.

The Reserve Bank of India has pulled up banks once again for failing to lend enough. The RBI in its trends and progress report on the banking sector Has pointed out that banks are not passing the benefits of low interest rates to all credit markets. High reserve requirements and administered small savings interest rates are no longer impediments for a flexible rate regime. The rigidities in the system, the report says, emanate from low productivity in public sector banks and also the overhang of non-performing assets of the past.

The report cautions banks that ultimately the performance of banks depends on their ability to lend to industry. Banks should therefore concentrate on corporate governance, economic value added and technology up gradation. The report says bank's NPAs as a percentage of gross advances, as well as ndt NPAQs, fell in 2002 –03. In absolute terms, gross NPAs for commercial banks fell by Rs. 2,147 crore, while net NPAs dropped by about Rs. 1,800 crore. In the case of state-run banks, NPAs grew faster than recoveries.

Business Response to Environmental Concerns

At present business culture is largely driven by short-term profit and the stakeholders that generally hold the most influence are the providers of financial capital, the shareholders or owners of the business. For the purpose of greater environmental awareness, it is necessary to review the way the objectives are priortised to take account of the viewpoint of indirect stakeholders, This would ensure that the issue of sustainable development is brought on to the corporate agenda. For providing a greater level of corporate responsibility, should we use the laws and government regulations? Or should we decide voluntarily to act more responsibly towards general environment? The answer is said to be lying between the two.

The term corporate social responsibility encompasses a variety of subjects: Business ethics, corporate governance, business and the environment and corporate citizenship or business in the community. The country experienced the tragedy at Bhopal where the MNC Union Carbide had considered it appropriate or sufficient to accept lower standards of safety in a third world plant than would have been appropriate or permissible for a domestic plant in the United States; The following three types of organisations, may therefore be mentioned as models, which the business may exercise its choice to respond:

- *Social obligation*: where the organisation uses legal and economic criteria to control corporate behaviour; the strategy followed is reactive and it exhibits an exploitative strategy, giving in to environmental concerns only when it can obtain direct benefit. Profit is the primary objective

- *Social responsibility*: Under this choice, organisations try to go beyond the requirements prescribed by law and instead seeks to conform to the current values and norms of society. In this model, organisations become accountable to a range of stakeholders and in so far as it concerns profits, though it may be a dominant motive, it is not the only one.
- *Social responsiveness*: Through this model the organisation exhibits proactive strategy, actively seeking future social change. The business seeks to lead the field in terms of promoting a corporately responsible attitude.

IS GOOD GOVERNANCE CONFINED TO CORPORATE EXCELLENCE ONLY?

Good governance is not simply about corporate excellence. It's the key to economic and social transformation. The corporations of today are no longer sheer economic entities. These are the engines of economic and social transformation. Kenichi Ohmae argued in "The borderless world Power and Strategy in the Interlinked Economy that

"A Corporation is a social institution whose responsibilities extend far beyond the well being of its equity owners to giving security and a good life to its employees, dealers, customers, vendors and subcontractors. Their whole life hinges on the well being of the corporation."

Corporations are the powerhouses that generate employment, provide education and health care, and give sustenance to the society. Globalisation has given multinational overwhelming power at the expenses of democratically elected governments. Good governance needs to ensure that the corporations take into account the interests of all constituencies in which they operate. A business enterprise's corporate actions must be compatible with long term societal needs such as the quality of environment and welfare of local community."[2]

CORPORATE GOVERNANCE SYSTEMS

The UK compared with Germany and Japan.[3] Franks and Mayer (1990) have analysed differences in the rights attached to shareholding between countries. They argue that a key difference concerns the extent to which the claims to the residual are associated with rights to select and control managers. In the UK system these rights are integrated. Further, the principle of equality of shareholder status is supported by regulatory bodies. Small shareholders, for example, have proportional voting rights and the same access to information as those who hold larger stakes in a company. This has been an important consideration in the regulations governing takeovers established by the stock exchange. It has led to the undisclosed build up of large stakes in a company, and to a system which discourages acquisition of information which might make the recipient an insider. The very terminology is revealing. Shareholders in the UK system are expected, and to a degree encouraged, to be 'outsiders'. They are not part of the team.

---

2 Corporate governance, concept and dimensions, Snow White, 2003.

3 Capital markets and corporate governance, Clarendon Press, Oxford, 1994.

Institutional shareholders dominate the trade in shares in the UK. The managers of these funds must consider the interests of pensioners or others for whom they act as trustees.

The Japanese System

If shareholders in the UK are predominantly outsiders, those in Japan are largely insiders, having some kind of commercial contract with the company. Thus, although the structure of shareholding–three quarters institutions, one-quarter individuals–look very similar to that in the UK, the nature of institutional shareholding is very different.

The differences are of two sorts: the nature of the institutions and the nature of the obligations. The institutions are not independent pension funds and insurance companies with their own interests and obligations as described above. They are instead institutions such as banks who may have provided loan finance; supplying companies who may have a long-running association; or other companies linked by cross-shareholdings, who all may be part of a loosely structured keiretsu group. The second important feature of Japanese shareholding is that tradability of rights is more constrained than in the UK. It is estimated that nearly two-thirds of equity is held in the form of stable shareholding—antei kabunushi—which is distinct from interlocking shareholding–kabushiki mochiai—although the two may overlap. Stability arises from an implicit agreement to waive the exercise of control rights and not to sell shares to third parties, or at least to consult the firm whose shares are held if it is necessary to dispose of them. These obligations are implicit and do not entail shares never being sold.

However in practice it means that the most actively traded shares are those held by the household sector, the opposite of the situation in the U.K. Stable shareholding practices are designed to raise the transaction costs of transferring ownership and to ensure greater continuity of control. As a result, hostile takeovers in Japan are almost unknown.

The German System

In Germany, for instance, public companies are able to issue non-voting shares to an amount equal to that of all voting shares. Capital can thereby be raised, upto a point, by means of equity without affecting the control of the enterprise. It is also common in Germany for banks, which may hold a relatively small equity stake themselves, to exercise voting rights on behalf of other shareholders who deposit shares with them. Further the rights of German employees are embodied in the co-determination law. They are represented on supervisory boards and also on worker's councils relating to terms of employment and dismissal. Such employee rights constitute an attenuation of German shareholders' rights in comparison with those in the UK where employee involvement in corporate decision making is at the discretion of the management."

CORPORATE GOVERNANCE SYSTEMS WORLDWIDE

The functioning of corporate governance systems varies with different Socio-political cultures. It may be useful to keep track of these systems so that corporate entities can think of required improvements. The USA has accorded importance to the modern private corporation. The corporate form of organisation is taken as a bulwark of the free enterprise system. American society has placed an abiding faith in the system by giving property rights to individuals and corporations to generate dynamism and initiative for enterprise and industry. It has also devised and installed an elaborate legal framework for handling disputes. Supervisory mechanism by outside directors is strengthened with devices such as the audit and other committees.

The conflict of interests between owners and managers is sought to be tackled by providing profit related incentives, such as shares and stock options. The threat of losing corporate control is seen as preventing managements from settling down into an inefficient equilibrium, and therefore US has welcomed innovative methods like 'investment bankers' Bringing even the giant companies under the ambit of the market' for corporate control, if it is warranted. It has also taken resort to takeovers.

The system of corporate governance in Germany is much less driven by the stock market than that in the USA. It runs by consensus in the supervisory and management boards rather than by an all-important chief executive office as in the USA. The two-tier board in Germany institutionalises some checks and balances. Unlike in the USA, where banks cannot trade in securities, banks in Germany not only provide long-term finance but also hold stocks of companies. Banks also have positions on the top tier of the two-tiered board system. While the management board is responsible for running the company, the supervisory board is responsible for matters such as accounts, capital expenditure, acquisitions, closures etc.

Corporate governance in Japan is not focused on the board of directors of the company. The Japanese concept of obligation to company, country, and family is based on their willingness to follow a system of 'consensus'. The system's dynamism is derived from crossholdings and networks among companies in the group. The Ministry of International trade and Industry and Ministry of Finance provide them with useful information and impetus for strategizing their operations in the world markets. The German and Japanese models of corporate governance, despite their differences share certain important commonalities. Their distinctive features reveal the following: Banks and financial institutions have substantial stakes in the equity of companies, institutional investors view themselves as long-term investors, disclosure norms are not very stringent, checks on insider trading are not comprehensive, and emphasis on liquidity is not high. Takeovers are rare.

The Anglo American model carries some distinctive features; ownership of companies is more or less equally divided between individual shareholders and institutional shareholders; companies are typically run by professional managers; directors are rarely independent of management; institutional investor view themselves as portfolio investors; disclosure norms are comprehensive; the rules against insider trading and penalties for price manipulation are still, and there is fairly active market for corporate control that provides a credible threat of takeover to constant under-performance.

In India, the company boards generally comprise promoter directors, professional directors and institutionally nominated directors. Institutional investors have been supportive of promoters in general; individual shareholders have by and large been benign, tolerant and ignorant, and they are scattered and ill-organised. For electing the directors, though the majority rule voting system is followed, individual shareholders are not in a position to play a meaningful role in electing directors. In general, the Family-managed companies display greater entrepreneurial activity, they exercise unchallenged control and are able to garner personal enrichment at the expense of the company. The degree to which these aberrations occur depends on the level of integrity of the controlling groups.

CORPORATE GOVERNANCE AS A WAY OF LIFE

Delivering the fourth Palkhivala Memorial Lecture under the auspices of the Nani Palkhivala Foundation, Mr. YH Malegam said that issues involved in Corporate governance are no different from those involved in a 'functioning Democracy and hence proper governance of companies should be treated as a way of life. According to him, in the ultimate analysis, corporate governance involved issues such as efficient and honest handling of public assets handed over to managements, truthful communication to stakeholders, respecting the rights of individual shareholders and refraining from oppression of the minority shareholders by the majority. Thus corporate governance ought not to be considered involving mere compliance with the letter of the law but should be adopted as a way of life, he said. Mr. Malegam, who is Managing Partner of SB Bilimoria, a leading accounting and consulting firm, pointed out that the issue of corporate governance had arisen the world over in the wake of internal and external pressures on companies. Among internal pressures was the advice of financial analysts, which put fear in managements that unless they showed results in terms of profits and dividends, the companies would suffer by way of a fall in their share price in the market, fall in market capitalisation (namely, aggregate market value of shares) and erosion of the companies' ability to borrow. The wrongful response of managements by way of shoring up the companies' bottomlines through creative accounting (namely, showing not existing profits) led to unreliability of financial statements and sudden failure of companies. This in turn led to counter-pressures for corporate governance being exerted by institutional investors, who were increasingly dominating the capital deployed in companies and had ever larger stake in the proper functioning of companies. The institutional investors, including foreign institutional investors (FIIs) commanding huge funds, were so powerful that they could even force companies to follow the governance codes evolved by the FIIs themselves. Referring to the recommendations of various expert committees in the U.S. the U.K., Canada and the OECD (Organisation for Economic Cooperation and Development) on corporate governance, Mr. Malegam said India's recent initiatives included the reports of the Kumaramangalam Birla committee and the N.R. Narayana Murthy committee He said it was not enough to create top level structures such as independent directors and audit committees. The recommendation of expert committees to facilitate the process of 'whistle blowing' by employees should be implemented. Mechanism should be created to enable employees to alert top management and the board about the wrong doing within the organisation and for company wide communication about the availability of such a mechanism, besides ensuring that whistle blowers were not victimised. Failure of corporate governance affected not only the companies concerned, be it Enron or WorldCom or Parmalat, and their stakeholders but entire systems and economies. It undermined public confidence in institutions.

The South East Asian crisis of the Nineties too was the result of the absence of corporate governance in financial institutions and absence of mechanisms for whistle blowing. Corporate governance was equally important for family owned companies to free them from problems connected with succession, he added.

CORPORATE GOVERNANCE AND ACCOUNTABILITY

Some authors have defined corporate governance "as a system of checks and balances, both internal and external to companies, that ensures that companies discharge their accountability to all their stakeholders and act in a Socially responsible way in all areas of their business activity." The South African King Report (2002) however drew a distinction between accountability to shareholders and responsibility to stakeholders. The progressive approach to corporate governance adopted by the King report and its philosophy runs as follows:

"...Successful governance in the 21st century requires companies to adopt an inclusive and not an exclusive approach. The company must be open to institutional activism and there must be greater emphasis on the sustainable or non-financial aspects of its performance. Boards must apply the tests of fairness, accountability, responsibility and transparency to all acts or omissions and be accountable to the company but also responsive and responsible towards the company's identified stakeholders."[4]

There is emphasis on voluntary codes of practice which needs to be accompanied by an agenda of modernising company law; It is believed that a more inclusive system of corporate governance at a global level would be possible only through this method. The reform measures, it has been suggested, should not only pay attention to the financial aspects of corporate governance but also to the creation of a more ethical business environment.

Despite the wide range of different corporate governance systems around the world, there is gradual transformation of these systems. This change is due to worldwide agenda for corporate governance reform. Companies have started realising increasingly not just with shareholders' demands but also with the needs of a wide range of stakeholders. Company directors are discharging accountability to shareholding and non-shareholding stakeholders through the disclosure process and through stakeholder engagement programmes. There is a move away from a narrow agency theory view toward a broader, stakeholder-oriented view that embraces concepts of corporate social responsibility and sustainability.

It has been emphasised that institutional investors should no longer be passive, back-seat owners of companies but should discharge their responsibilities as shareholders. Investment institutions have also started realising that passive shareholding is not the route to shareholder wealth maximisation. Increasing shareholder activism, for example in the area of directors' remuneration, is a case of ethical activism. It should be recognised that institutional investors through portfolio investment are discharging an accountability first and foremost to their own clients but also to society as a whole; they need to act as socially responsible owners, satisfying the needs of a broad range of stakeholders as well as seeking maximum returns to investment for shareholders. If the recent scandals in the financial and corporate communities is to be avoided, they need to act as socially responsible owners.

---

[4] King Report, 2002, p.19.

Global Convergence

Another important issue for corporate governance is the extent to which harmonization in corporate governance standards will be achieved at an international level. Countries are moving toward a global convergence in corporate governance as well as toward some of the initiatives aimed at international harmonization of corporate governance, based on OECD (1999) Principles. At present, there is a danger of Anglo-Saxon model of corporate governance being granted onto corporate governance systems around the world. There is therefore the danger that countries with extremely different traditional styles of governance will be engulfed by a tide of market-oriented initiatives that may not be appropriate from their legal frameworks, economies and culture points of view. The governments and policy makers should carefully work out a model that would be sustainable over the long term.

An important question has also been raised as to whether we are really moving into a more accountable, socially responsible world. Companies have started embracing a broader approach to corporate governance by discharging accountability to a wider range of stakeholders. Institutional investors, worldwide have started encouraging corporate social responsibility through active socially responsible investment strategies of engagement and dialogue with their investee companies. Companies however need guidance on the type and form of information that their shareholders and other stakeholders require. Standardisation is also required for comparison and for accountability and decision-making purposes. Based on the Higgs Report, for one non-executive director in every listed company to assume the role of a senior independent director, who should represent shareholders' interests, it has been suggested, could be extended to embrace social responsibility. Such directors could take on the role of championing the interests of non-shareholding stakeholders, such as employees, local communities, environmental concerns. It may be a more direct and more effective means of furthering stakeholder accountability than the process of stakeholder engagement. Perhaps encouraging one of the non-executive directors to attend meetings between the company and various stakeholder groups would be an effective means of improving corporate accountability within a broader Corporate governance agenda.

RISK DISCLOSURE AND CORPORATE GOVERNANCE

Corporate risk disclosure is an important category of corporate disclosure obligations. It is linked to the general agenda for corporate governance reform and therefore there is now an increasing emphasis on corporate risk disclosure. The Turnull Report focused attention on this crucial aspect. The emphasis was on the reporting of internal control systems, for the purpose of corporate accountability and for the future success of business. The Cadbury Report (1992) also highlighted the relevance of risk disclosure to the corporate governance agenda by suggesting that validating the company as a going concern and improving the disclosure of internal control should lead to improvements in the communication links between investors and their investee companies. Improving information flows between companies and their shareholders represents one effective way of reducing information asymmetry; it lessens the agency problem inherent in the corporate governance agenda.

The Turnbull Perspective

The Turnbull report is based on the adoption of a risk-based approach to establishing a sound system of internal control and on reviewing its effectiveness. It especially relates to social, environmental and sustainable development risk issues. For identifying and managing the Risks, the following types of risks are relevant:

(i) **Supply chain risks:** These are suppliers based in countries that have

- human rights abuses;
- child-enforced labour concerns;
- living wage issues.

Suppliers that are high pollutants; using unsustainable production Technologies (e.g. Forestry,fisheries etc.); Involved with GMOs.

(ii) **Operational risks:** Companies operating in countries with: Human rights abuses; child and forced labour concerns; living wage Issues. Also: unsatisfactory employee satisfaction levels; potential to contaminate land; involvement with dangerous activities; level of noise/visual pollution; compliance with environmentally and socially regulated processes; location of sites (urban/rural);

(iii) **Product risks:** the use of unsustainable or hazardous raw material used in product composition; quantity and type of waste produced during production; end-of-life disposal methods; health and safety concerns related to product use; environmental effects from product use;

(iv) **General societal expectation:** Disclosure of environmental and social performance via a report; Certification to environmental and social standards; Statement of business principles.

The following are some of the statements that bring out the institutional investors' attitudes toward corporate risk disclosure practices:

- believing that increased corporate risk disclosure would help institutional invetors in their portfolio investment decisions
- the belief that increased risk disclosure would improve the corporate governance of investee companies
- the belief that financial risk information is more relevant to institutional investors than other risk information e.g. Product/service, compliance and environmental risks
- the blief that improvements in risk disclosure are essential to a company as a going concern
- the belief that the Operating and Financial Review (OFR) is the most appropriate vehicle for increased risk disclosure.

MODEL TO ASSESS AN EXEMPLARY BOARD

The following questionnaire re-produced from the article 'Performance Evaluation of the Board of Directors, Chartered Secretary September 2004, listing 22 questions may be referred. According to the article, if the answer is found to be "yes" to all the 22 questions, the concerned company can be termed as a company having an exemplary board.

It may be noted, as stated in the above article, the list of questions are not exhaustive and it provides only a model.

Sl. No.	*Question*	*Yes*	*No*
1.	Are there three or more outside directors for every insider?		
2.	Are the internal whole-time directors on the Board limited to the position of Managing Director, the Chief Operating Officer and the Chief Finance Officer?		
3.	Does the concerned internal directors routinely share information to concerned senior managers who are not represented on the board?		
	Is the board having the right size (8 to 15 members)?		
	Does the Audit Committee meet without the representatives *of* the management?		
6.	Does the audit committee routinely review "high-exposure" areas?		
7.	Does the board seek consultants' report relating to compensation payable to employees and directors?		
8.	Has the Board formed any, compensation committee with the courage to establish formulas for managerial remuneration for the directors based on long-term results -even if the formulas differ from industry norms?		
9.	Are the activities of senior management sufficiently contained to prevent the emergence of a "two tier" board?		
10.	Does non-executive or independent directors annually review succession plans, for senior management?		
11.	Does non-executive or independent directors formally evaluate the MD's strengths and performance every year?		
12.	Is there any nominating committee rather than the MD to direct the search for new board members and invite candidates in stand for election?		
13.	Is there a way for non-executive or independent directors to alter the meeting agenda, set by the MD?		
14.	Does the company help directors prepare for meetings by sending relevant routine information, as well as analyses of key agenda items, ahead of time?		
15.	Is there sufficient meeting time for thoughtful discussion in addition to management monologue?		
16.	Do the non-executive or independent directors meet without management at least once in a year?		
17.	Is the board actively involved in formulating long-range business strategy from the start of the planning cycle?		
18.	Does the board, select the new chief executive?		
19.	Is at least some of directors' pay to linked to corporate performance?		
20.	Is the performance of each of the directors reviewed on quarterly or half-yearly basis?		
21.	Are the directors who are no longer pulling their weight discouraged from standing for re-election?		
22.	Does the Board through MD take the right measures to build trust among directors?		

WHAT IS CORPORATE GOVERNANCE

In a narrow sense, corporate governance involves a set of relationship amongst the company's management, its board of directors, shareholders and other stakeholders. Corporate governance is concerned with aligning the interests of investors and managers and in ensuring the firms are run for the benefit of all classes of investors.

In a broader sense, however, good governance–the extent to which companies are run in an open an honest manner–creates overall confidence, enhance efficiency of international capital allocation, and contribute ultimately to the nations' overall wealth and welfare.

Why is Corporate Governance Important?

Corporate governance is important for the following reasons:

- It lays down the frame-work for creating long-term trust between companies and the external providers of capital;
- It improves strategic thinking at the top by inducting independent directors who bring a wealth of experience, and a host of new ideas;
- It rationalizes the management and monitoring of risk that a firm faces globally;
- It limits the liability of top management and directors, by carefully articulating the decision making process;
- It ensures the integrity of financial reports;
- And finally, it helps provide a degree of confidence that is necessary for the proper functioning of a market economy.

Should Governance be Concerned with Protecting the Interest of all Stakeholders or only one class of Stakeholder i.e. Shareholders?

As shareholders are residual claimants, in well performing capital and financial markets, whatever maximizes shareholder value should maximize corporate security and best satisfy the claims of creditors, employees, and society at large.

Moreover, in our country, there exist well defined laws to protect the interest of employees, and recently have considerably strengthened the rights of creditors.

How is Corporate Governance Regulated in India?

Listed companies have to comply with the provisions of Clause 49 of the listing agreement. In addition, all companies incorporated in India have to adhere to the corporate governance provisions of the Companies Act.

Who is an Independent Director?

As the name suggests, an independent director is a director who is not aligned with either the management or the promoters, and is capable of exercising independent judgment.

His key responsibility is to ensure that the management and the board takes decisions that are in the interests of all shareholders and do not favour any one class of shareholders.

In India, SEBI's Clause 49 has stipulated the conditions that an individual should meet to classify as an independent director.

Clause 49 seeks to ensure that individuals who have materially significant financial transactions with company or its promoters, directors, senior management; or are related to them; or have worked in the company in the recent past; or have a share holding of more than two per cent in the company are disallowed from becoming independent directors in that company.

Why are Independent Directors Important for Good Governance?

An active and involved board consisting of professional and truly independent directors plays an important role in creating trust between a company and its investors, and is the best guarantor of good corporate governance.

Competent and qualified independent directors play an important role in the stewardship and strategy formulation. Indian corporates that have appointed such directors have benefited from their guidance and inputs.

How many Independent Directors should there be in a listed company?

In a listed company, 50% of the board should consist of independent directors if the company has an executive chairman.

In case of a non-executive chairman, 1/3 of the board should consist of independent directors.

CORPORATE GOVERNANCE - ADDING VALUE TO STAKEHOLDERS

Corporate organizations have to function in far more organized manner and strive for enhancing the long-term value of the shareholders. Level of accountability to shareholders and the transparency of operations by disclosure through annual and other periodic reports are going to be much more than hitherto. The new norms of governance which are enshrined in various statutes compares well with that of international standards. The work of the professionals in practice will also be subject to review by an independent quality review board as recommended by Naresh Chandra Committee.

All those in-charge of governance should recognize the challenges that lie ahead in as much as companies will be subjected to more scrutiny will be made more accountable and may have to face heavier penalties for negligence on their part. Professionals, like Company Secretaries, Accountants and Auditors shall have to, work together more closely so as to help to restore confidence and trust in the companies they work for.

The Securities and Exchange Board of India has extensively revised Clause 49 of the Listing Agreement pertaining to Corporate Governance vide circular dated October 29, 2004. The major changes in Clause 49 include amendments/ additions to provisions relating to definition of independent directors, strengthening the responsibilities of audit committees, improving quality of financial disclosures including those pertaining to related party transactions and proceeds from public/ rights/preferential issues, requiring Boards to adopt formal code of conduct, CEO/CFO certification of financial statements and for improving disclosures to statutory authorities. Practising Company Secretaries have been given the recognition alongwith Auditors to certify compliance of conditions of Corporate Governance as stipulated in Clause 49.

Audit Committees have gained much prominence after a string of corporate failures in US, which highlighted the need for an independent supervision at the board level. The result is audit committee. As the name suggests, Audit Committee do serve the boards by providing qualitative impetus to correct the financial statement and thus save board's time and efforts. Both Audit Committee effectiveness and auditor's independence provide significant checks and balances on financial reporting process and enhance quality of financial reporting.

The directors are the custodian of the investments of shareholders and are duty bound to maximize their net worth. If any thing illegal or un-ethical is observed the concerned professional should be bold enough to prevent such happening. Of late, due to the repeated losses suffered by investors the ethics, code of conduct and principles of Corporate Governance have drawn the attention of professionals. Great responsibility is fastened on the shoulders of professionals like Company Secretaries to safe guard and protect the interest of the stakeholders by observing the secretarial standards.

In this backdrop, the Southern India Regional Council of the Institute of Company Secretaries of India is organizing a one day Seminar on CORPORATE GOVERNANCE–ADDING VALUE TO STAKEHOLDERS.

POST MEMBERSHIP QUALIFICATION – COURSE COVERAGE

Paper I Concept Framework of Corporate Governance

Objective and Scope: To provide an in-depth study of the Evolution and Development of Corporate Governance.

Detailed Contents:

- Evolution of Corporate Governance–Ancient and Modern Concept
- Concept of Corporate Governance
- Principles of Corporate Governance
- Beneficiaries of Corporate Governance
- Business Ethics vis-à-vis Corporate Governance
- Corporate Governance in various organizations
- Corporate Social Responsibilities and good corporate citizenship.

Paper II Corporate and Board Management

Objective and Scope: To provide a detailed insight into the concept, issues and practices that governs the corporate sector.

Detailed Contents:

- Corporate Business Ownership Structure
- Board of Directors–Role, Composition, Systems and Procedures
- Fiduciary relationship

- Types of Directors–Promoter/Nominee/Shareholder/Independent
- Rights, Duties and Responsibilities of Directors
- Training of Directors–need, objective methodology
- Executive Management Process
- Functional Committees of Board
- Rights and Relationship of Shareholders and other Stakeholders
- Investor servicing and investor protection measures
- Good Secretarial practices and Standards for corporate disclosure.

Paper III Legal and Regulatory Framework of Corporate Governance

Objective and Scope: To provide expert knowledge of the legal and regulatory framework in respect of corporate governance in India and aboard.

Detailed Contents:

- Need for Legislation of Corporate Governance
- Legislative Provisions of Corporate Governance in Companies Act 1956, SCRA 1956, Depositories Act 1996, Securities and Exchange Board of India Act 1992. Listing Agreement, Banking Regulation Act 1949 and Other Corporate Laws
- Legal Provisions relating to Investor Protection
- Legislative Framework of Corporate Governance in US, UK and other developed countries including CACG, OECD etc.
- Listing Requirements–Indian and International perspective
- MIS and Corporate Disclosure Requirements covering Accounting Standards and Secretarial Standards also.

Paper IV Board Committees and Role of Professionals

Objective and Scope: To provide expert knowledge on the functioning of Board Committees.

Detailed Contents:

- Board Committees–Audit Committee, Remuneration Committee, Shareholders Grievance Committee, other committees
- Need, Functions and Advantages of Committee Management
- Constitution and Scope of Board Committees
- Board Committees' Charter
- Terms of Reference and performance appraisals
- Attendance and participation in committee meetings
- Independence of Members of Board Committees
- Disclosures in Annual Report
- Role of Professionals in Board Committees
- Role of Company Secretaries in compliance of Corporate Governance.

Paper V Corporate Governance–Codes and Practices

Objective and Scope: To provide thorough knowledge of the global trends and developments so as to have an integrated view of the entire framework for corporate governance.

Detailed Contents:

- Major Expert Committees' Reports–India and Abroad
- Study of Codes of Corporate Governance
- Case Studies on Corporate Governance–Indian and overseas perspective
- Best Practices of Corporate Governance
- Value Creation through Corporate Governance
- Corporate Governance Ratings.

Dissertation/Project Report

Each examinee shall be required to work on a project touching upon any issue relating to Corporate Governance or of relevance to the cause of Corporate Governance under the guidance of a supervisor/guide appointed by ICSI-CCRT. CCRT shall act as a monitoring agency for dissertation. The dissertation/project report shall be submitted within a period of 12 months of admission to PMQ Course in Corporate Governance.

The examinee shall be issued certificate/diploma only after passing the exam and submission of dissertation/project report.

Members are invited to send their suggestions on the proposed course contents of the PMQ Course in Corporate Governance. Detailed format for suggestion under various heads is hosted on the Institute's website www.icsi.edu.

CORPORATE GOVERNANCE: INDIA

The NFCG has an online library of principles, codes, rules and regulations related to corporate governance. These relate to both the Indian as well as the international context. In addition, the online library will also contain original research papers commissioned by the foundation. The library resources are freely accessible.

- **Clause 49 (2004) (SEBI):** Listed companies in India (with paid-up capital of Rs. 3 crore and more) have to comply with the corporate governance related provisions of Clause 49 of the Listing Agreement of Stock Exchanges. Clause 49 has been prepared by the Securities and Exchange Board of India (SEBI).
- **1st National Conference on Corporate Governance Trends in India 18 October 2004, New Delhi:** Ministry of Company Affairs (MCA) and the Confederation of Indian Industry (CII) in partnership with the Institute of Company Secretaries of India (ICSI) and the Institute of Chartered Accountants of India (ICAI) has set up the National Foundation for Corporate Governance (NFCG).
- **Narayana Murthy Committee Report: Report of the SEBI Committee on Corporate Governance (2003):** The Committee was constituted by SEBI to review the performance of corporate governance in the country as well as to

determine the role of companies in responding to rumour and other price sensitive information circulating in the market in order to enhance the transparency and integrity of the market. The Committee submitted its report to SEBI in February 2003.

- **Recommendations of the Naresh Chandra Committee Report on Corporate Audit and Governance (2002):** Following the corporate scandals of the US, the Department of Company Affairs (DCA), Government of India set up the Naresh Chandra Committee to examine various corporate governance issues. Many recommendations of the report were incorporated in the Companies (Amendment) Bill 2003, which is currently being reviewed.
- **Kumar Mangalam Birla Committee on Corporate Governance (1999):** The Committee was set up by SEBI to promote and raise the standards of Corporate Governance. The Committee's terms of reference included suggesting suitable amendments to the listing agreement executed by the stock exchanges with the companies in order to enhance corporate governance standards of listed companies, drafting a code of corporate best practices; and suggest safeguards to be instituted within the companies to deal with insider information and insider trading. Several of the Committee's recommendations were incorporated in Clause 49 of the listing agreement of stock exchanges.
- **CII Code on Corporate Governance (1998):** The Confederation of Indian Industry (CII) published India's first comprehensive code on corporate governance (Desirable Corporate Governance: A Code) in 1998. This Code was well received by Corporate India and many of its recommendations became part of subsequent regulations.

Discussion Paper on Corporate Governance in India: NFCG (2004)

The National Foundation for Corporate Governance (NFCG) has prepared a Discussion Paper on Corporate Governance in India (Corporate Governance: Theory and Practices) for debate and discussion. The Discussion Paper examines the definition and importance of corporate governance as well as the importance of regulating corporate governance practices in the country. The Discussion Paper also traces the initiatives and regulations with regard to the evolution of corporate governance in the country and benchmarks the existing regulations and practices against the widely accepted and well-known OECD Principles of Corporate Governance.

The Paper identifies the future drivers of corporate governance in India and examines how, apart from regulations, the forces of competition and demand for low cost capital will provide the momentum for Indian companies striving to achieve higher standards of corporate governance. Finally, the Paper contains a chapter on the initiatives and activities that the NGCG proposes to undertake to promote good corporate governance practices in the country.

The Discussion Paper is being placed on the website for debate, discussion and feedback. Please e-mail your valuable comments and suggestions with regard to the Discussion Paper on nfcg@ciionline.org. Your comments will enable us to enrich and improve the contents of the Discussion Paper.

CORPORATE GOVERNANCE: INTERNATIONAL

The NFCG has an online library of principles, codes, rules and regulations related to corporate governance. These relate to both the Indian as well as the international context. In addition, the online library will also contain original research papers commissioned by the foundation. The library resources are freely accessible.

- **OECD Principles of Corporate Governance (2004):** The Principles are intended to assist governments in their efforts to evaluate and improve the legal, institutional and regulatory framework for corporate governance in their countries, and to provide guidance and suggestions for stock exchanges, investors, corporations, and other parties that have a role in the process of developing good corporate governance. The Principles focus on publicly traded companies, both financial and non-financial.
- **ASX Corporate Governance Council Report (2003):** On 15 August 2002, the ASX Corporate Governance Council was formed in Australia with the objective of developing and delivering an industry-wide, supportable and supported framework for corporate governance. In March 2003, the ASX Corporate Governance Council released "Principles of Good Corporate Governance and Best Practice Recommendations". Compliance with the recommendations was not mandatory, except for the recommendations dealing with Audit Committees, but from 2004 listed entities are required to report in their annual report on whether they have complied during the year the subject of the report, or if they have not, the reasons why not.
- **Higgs Report: Review of the role and effectiveness of non-executive directors (2003):** The report reviewed the role and effectiveness of non-executive directors in the UK. The Review further developed the UK framework of corporate governance, which commenced with the publication of the Cadbury report in 1992 and was taken forward by the Greenbury, Hampel and Turnbull reports.
- **The Combined Code on Corporate Governance (2003):** This UK based code supersedes and replaces the Combined Code issued by the Hampel Committee on Corporate Governance in June 1998. It is derived from a review of the role and effectiveness of non-executive directors by Derek Higgs and a review of audit committees by a group led by Sir Robert Smith.
- **Sarbanes Oaxley Act (2002):** Following the corporate governance scandals in the US, the Sarbanes Oaxley Act was enacted which brought about fundamental changes in virtually every area of corporate governance and particularly in auditor independence, conflict of interest, corporate responsibility and enhanced financial disclosures.
- **King Committee On Corporate Governance (2002):** The King Report on Corporate Governance for South Africa (the "King Report 2002") has been developed as an initiative of the Institute of Directors in Southern Africa. It represents a revision and update of the King Report first published in 1994, in an attempt to keep standards of corporate governance in South Africa in step with those in the rest of the world. All companies listed on the Johannesburg Stock Exchange have to comply with the provisions of the Report.

- **Blue Ribbon Report (1999):** Blue Ribbon Committee was set up by the Securities and Exchange Commission (SEC), US, in 1998. In February 1999, the Committee published the Report on Improving the Effectiveness of Corporate Audit Committees (the Blue Ribbon Report). The recommendations of the Blue Ribbon Committee were adopted and declared to be mandatory by the NYSE, the American Stock Exchange (Amex), Nasdaq and the American Institute of Certified Public Accountants (AICPA). The recommendations are not mandatory for foreign issuers: these are subject to their own national laws.
- **CalPERS' Global Governance Principles (1999):** With the goal of encouraging a continual debate on best governance practices globally, in 1997 CalPERS' Board adopted a set of Global Governance Principles. In late 1999, the CalPERS Investment Committee analyzed other newer global governance principles and with the goal of supporting a single set of global governance principles, the Investment Committee revised CalPERS' Global Governance Principles to parallel the International Corporate Governance Network's statement on Global Governance Principles. The International Corporate Governance Network (ICGN) was founded with the objective to facilitate international dialogue and thereby helping companies to compete more effectively. The ICGN welcomed the OECD Principles as a remarkable convergence on corporate governance common ground among diverse interests, practices and cultures. While the ICGN considered the OECD Principles the necessary bedrock of good corporate governance, it held that amplifications were required to give them sufficient force. Read More >>
- **Hampel Report (1998):** The Hampel Committee was constituted in UK in 1995. The task of this committee was to consolidate the recommendations of the Cadbury Report in 1992 (focusing on financial reporting) and the Greenbury Report in 1995 (focusing on directors' remuneration), and prepare a 'Combined Code' on corporate governance. The Code, published in 1998, was attached to the listing rules of the stock exchange with the requirement that in order to be listed, companies must either declare their adherence to its provisions or explain any deviation from them.
- **Cadbury Report-The Financial Aspects of Corporate Governance (1992):** The Cadbury Committee was set up in May 1991 by the Financial Reporting Council, the London Stock Exchange and the accountancy profession to address the financial aspects of corporate governance. The Committee's objective was to help to raise the standards of corporate governance and the level of confidence in financial reporting and auditing. The report reviewed the structure and responsibilities of boards of directors, rights and responsibilities of shareholders and the role of auditors. It also addressed a number of recommendations to the accountancy profession.

WHISTLEBLOWER POLICY[5]

Whistleblower Policy is an internal policy on access to audit committees. Elimination of unethical or improper practices is the responsibility of respective corporate promoters and management for which they have to put in place systems for efficient administration

---

5 Source: Corporate Governance Reporting – Best Practices.

and transparent transaction. Clause 49 of the Listing Agreement provides for the formulation of internal policy which extends to any level of employment and by virtue of which any personnel who observes an unethical or improper practices shall be able to approach the audit committee without necessarily informing their supervisors. Whistleblower Policy will afford protection to the Whistleblower from reprisals such as loss of employment, financial issues, harassment in the workplace etc. Company shall annually affirm that it has not denied any personnel access to the audit committee in respect of matters involving alleged misconduct and that it has provided protection to whistleblowers. Such affirmation shall form part of the Board report on Corporate Governance which is required to be prepared and submitted together with the annual report. The following format may be used for devising Whistleblower Policy of the company.

Model Whistleblower Policy

As a public company, the integrity in the financial matters of the "Company" and the accuracy of its financial information is paramount. The Company's financial information guides the decisions of the Board of Directors of the Company (Board). The stockholders of the Company and the financial markets rely on this information to make decisions. For these reasons, the Company must maintain a workplace where it can retain and treat all complaints concerning questionable accounting practices, internal accounting controls, or auditing matters (Questionable Accounting/Audit Matters), or concerning the reporting of fraudulent financial information to our shareholders, the Government or the financial markets. The employees should be able to raise these concerns free of any discrimination, retaliation or harassment.

The Company recognizes the value of transparency and accountability in its administrative and management practices. Therefore, it supports the making of disclosures that reveal serious misconduct, i.e., conduct which results in violation of law by the Company or in a substantial mismanagement of company resources, and if proven constitutes a criminal offence or reasonable grounds for dismissal of the person engaging in such conduct.

Therefore, it is the policy of the Company to encourage employees, when they reasonably believe that Questionable Accounting/Audit Matters, or the reporting of fraudulent financial information to our shareholders, the Government or the Financial markets and/or serious misconduct has occurred or are occurring, to report those, concerns to the Company's management (on an anonymous basis, if employees so desire) or to raise those concerns by sending e-mail to the Company's e-mail id for this purpose, on an anonymous basis, as described below.

All reports will be taken seriously and will be promptly investigated. The specific action taken in any particular case depends on the nature and gravity of the conduct or circumstances reported, and the quality of the information provided. Where Questionable Accounting/Audit Matters have occurred, or fraudulent financial information has been reported to our shareholders, the Government or the financial markets, or serious misconduct has occurred, those matters will be corrected and, if appropriate, the persons responsible will be disciplined.

In addition, the Company is committed to providing a work environment in which employees, when they reasonably believe that Questionable Accounting/Audit Matters have occurred, or that fraudulent financial information has been reported to our shareholders, the Government or the financial markets, or that serious misconduct has occurred, can raise those concerns free of discrimination, retaliation or harassment. Accordingly, the Company strictly prohibits discrimination, retaliation or harassment of any kind against any employee who based on the employee's reasonable belief that such conduct or practices have occurred or are occurring, reports that information.

Reporting and Investigation

If you have reason to believe that you have become aware of Questionable Accounting/Audit Matters, or the reporting of fraudulent financial information to our shareholders, the Government or the financial markets, or of serious misconduct, you must immediately report those facts to your immediate supervisor or to the corporate counsel. You may then be requested to document your report in writing. If you have reason to believe that both of those individuals are involved in these matters, you should report those facts to the Audit Committee of the Company's Board of Directors (the "Audit Committee"). You may also report your concerns anonymously by sending e-mail to the e-mail id or by sending an anonymous letter to the corporate counsel.

If you later believe that you have been subject to discrimination, retaliation or harassment for having made a report under this Policy, you must immediately report those facts to your immediate supervisor or the Corporate Counsel. If, for any reason, you do not feel comfortable discussing the matter with your immediate supervisor or the Corporate Counsel, IOU should bring the matter to the attention of the supervisor of your immediate supervisor, and if you are not comfortable with discussing the matter with any of those individuals, you should bring the matter to the attention of the Audit Committee. It is imperative that you bring the matter to the Company's attention promptly so that any concern of discrimination, retaliation or harassment can be investigated and addressed promptly and appropriately.

All complaints under this policy will be promptly and thoroughly investigated, and all information disclosed during the course of the investigation will remain confidential, except as necessary to conduct the investigation and take any remedial action, in accordance with applicable law. All employee and supervisors have a duty to corporate in the investigation of reports of Questionable Accounting/Audit Matters, or the reporting of fraudulent financial information, or of serious misconduct, or of discrimination, retaliation or harassment resulting from the reporting or investigation of such matters. In addition, an employee shall be subject to disciplinary action, including the termination of their employment, if the employee fails to co-operate in an investigation or deliberately provides false information during an investigation. If, at the conclusion of its investigation, the Company determines that a violation of policy has occurred, the Company will take effective remedial action commensurate with the severity of the offense. This action may include disciplinary action against the accused party, up to and including termination. Reasonable and necessary steps will also be taken to prevent any further violations of policy.

Discrimination, Retaliation or Harassment

The company strictly prohibits any discrimination, retaliation or harassment against any person who reports incidents of questionable accounting or auditing matters, or the reporting of fraudulent financial information, or of serious misconduct, based on the person's reasonable belief that such misconduct occurred. The Company also strictly prohibits any discrimination, retaliation or harassment against any person who participates in an investigation of complaints about questionable accounting or auditing matters, or of the reporting of fraudulent financial information, or of serious misconduct.

Any complaint that any managers, supervisors, or employees are involved in discrimination, retaliation or harassment related to the reporting or investigation of questionable accounting or auditing matters, or the reporting of fraudulent financial information, or of serious misconduct, shall be promptly and thoroughly investigated in accordance with the Company's investigation procedures If a complaint of discrimination, retaliation or harassment is substantiated appropriate disciplinary action, up to and including discharge, will be taken.

Retention of Documents

All documents related to the reporting, investigation and enforcement of this policy, as a result of a report of questionable accounting, internal accounting controls, or auditing matters, or the reporting of fraudulent financial information to our shareholders, the Government or the financial markets or of serious misconduct, or of the discrimination, retaliation or harassment of an employee that made such a report, shall be kept in accordance with the Company's record retention policy and applicable law.

Additional Enforcement Information

In addition to the Company's internal complaint procedure; employees should also be aware that certain law enforcement agencies are authorized to review questionable accounting or auditing matters, or potentially fraudulent reports of financial information. The Company's policies and practices have been developed as a guide to our legal and ethical responsibilities to achieve and maintain the highest business standards. Conduct that violates the Company's policies will be viewed *as* unacceptable under the terms of employment at the Company. Certain violations of the company's policies and practices could even subject the Company and any individual employees involved to civil and criminal penalties. Before issues or behaviour can rise to that level, employees are encouraged to report Questionable Accounting/Audit Matters, suspicion of fraudulent financial information, or serious misconduct, or discrimination, retaliation or harassment related to such reports. Nothing in this Policy is intended to prevent an employee from reporting information to the appropriate agency when the employee has reason to believe that the violation of a statute or regulation has occurred.

Modification in the Policy

The audit committee or the Board of Directors of the Company can modify this Policy unilaterally at any time without notice. Modification may be necessary, among other reasons, to maintain compliance with laws and regulations and/or accommodation organizational changes within the Company.

Acknowledgement and Agreement regarding the Whistleblower Policy[6]

This is to acknowledge that I have received a copy of the Company's Whistleblower Policy. 1 understand that, as a public company, the integrity of the financial information of the Company is paramount. I further understand that the Company is committed to a work environment free of discrimination, retaliation or harassment for employees who have raised concerns regarding questionable accounting, internal accounting controls, or auditing matters, or reporting of fraudulent financial information, or of serious misconduct and that the company specifically prohibits discrimination, retaliation or harassment whenever an employee makes a good faith report regarding such concerns. Accordingly, I specifically agree that to the extent I have concerns that I reasonably believe to be related to questionable accounting, accounting controls, auditing matters, or reporting of fraudulent financial information, or of serious misconduct, or which is otherwise in violation of the Company's policies, I will immediately report such conduct in accordance with the Company's Whistleblower Policy.

I understand and agree that to the extent I do not use the procedures outlined in the Whistleblower Policy, the Company and its officers and directors shall have the right to presume and rely on the fact that I have no knowledge or concern of any such information or conduct.

.... Employee's signature

.... Employee's Name

.... Employee's Number

.... Date

---

6 Please sign the acknowledgement form above and return it to Human Resources Department of the Company. This will let the Company know that you have received the Whistleblower Policy and are aware of the Company's commitment to a work environment free of discrimination, retaliation or harassment for reporting of questionable accounting, internal accounting coatreis, or auditing matters, or fraudulent financiai information, or serious misconduct as well as your obligations to report such information.

Current Developments

CONSTITUTIONAL VALIDITY OF SECURITISATION ACT

The Supreme Court has recently (April 2004) upheld the constitutional validity of the Securitisation Act thereby allowing banks and financial institutions to sell assets of defaulting borrowers that have been attached under the Act. However, the court quashed as unconstitutional the provision that required aggrieved borrowers to make an upfront deposit of 75 per cent of the dues claimed in case they preferred to go on appeal on action initiated against them. The Securitisation and Reconstruction of financial assets and Enforcement of Security Interests Act, 2002 was challenged on Grounds that it was loaded heavily in favour of lenders, giving little chance to the borrowers to explain their views once recovery process is initiated under the legislation. Leading the charge against the Act was Mardia Chemicals in its plea against notice served by ICICI Bank. The Government had, however, argued that the legislation would do bring financial discipline and reduce the burden of NPAs of banks and institutions. The Securitisation Act has also been made applicable to urban co-operative banks and housing finance companies. Top bankers said that the judgment would come as a major relief to the entire banking industry. "This would put tremendous pressure on the borrowers to repay. Fresh defaults would also be much less". The judgment would have a deep impact on the financial sector and would enable banks to extend loans at cheaper rates.

The court's decision on the validity of the Securitisatio Act would have a major impact on cases pending before the Board for Industrial and Financial Reconstruction (BIFR). The Act provides that if secured creditors representing three-fourths of the amount agree then they could seek abatement of the case pending before the BIFR once proceeding under the Securitisation Act starts. Bankers pointed out that that provision for abatement of BIF cases could be a major help since many companies had approached the Board only to seek it shelter to defer payments due to lenders.

ICRA Survey on Corporate Governance

The survey by rating firm ICRA says that capital market participants feel that insider trading, selective leak of price sensitive information and dubious Accounting practices are their biggest concerns from the corporate governance perspective. The survey, conducted among fund managers, brokers and institutional investors recently, says that unethical practices and inadequate concern for minority shareholders are also major worrying factors. Excessive promoter control on management, unrelated diversification and overreaching CEOs were also cited as concerns but ranked lower in the order of seriousness.

The survey says that a large majority of investors are willing to pay premium for the companies with good corporate governance practices. "Over 95 per cent of the respondents stated that they would be willing to pay a premium with good corporate governance practices. However, nearly 60 per cent of the respondents were not in a position to quantify the premium." The survey said that corporate governance practices are at least as important as other quantitative numbers such as financial numbers and growth prospects from the point of view of investment decision making. Investors look at corporate governance while investing in companies, as they feel confident about the integrity of the accounting numbers. Fund managers and brokers feel that the possibility of fraud is less and the interest of minority shareholders will be protected in companies with good corporate governance practice. About 40 percent of the respondents admitted to having invested in companies with questionable corporate governance practices in the past, in case the growth and earnings prospects appeared attractive. The capital market participants felt that segment reporting is also very important for ensuring, a high level of transparency and disclosure.

The survey said that the characteristics of good corporate governance include high level of transparency and disclosures, integrity of accounts strong and independent board of directors and active board committees.

RBI PULLS UP BANKS FOR NOT LENDING ENOUGH

The Reserve Bank of India has pulled up banks once again for failing to lend enough. The RBI in its trends and progress report on the banking sector has pointed out that banks are not passing the benefits of low interest rates to all credit markets. High reserve requirements and administered small savings interest rates are no longer impediments for a flexible rate regime. The rigidities in the system, the report says, emanate from low productivity in public sector banks and also the overhang of non-performing assets of the past.

The report cautions banks that ultimately the performance of banks depends on their ability to lend to industry. Banks should therefore concentrate on corporate governance, economic value added and technology upgradation. The report says bank's NPAs as a percentage of gross advances, as well as ndt NPAQs, fell in 2002–03. In absolute terms, gross NPAs for commercial banks fell by Rs. 2,147 crore, while net NPAs dropped by about Rs. 1,800 crore. In the case of state-run banks, NPAs grew faster than recoveries.

OVERALL RISK OF A BANK

A banks overall risk can be defined as the probability of failure to achieve an expected value and can be measured by the standard deviation of the value.[1]

The chart of check list for risk management compiled by Bank of Japan and quoted by RBI in the Report on Trend and Progress of Banking in India, 1996-97 which is quite comprehence is presented below:

VISION TO ENABLE PUBLIC ENTERPRISES TO BE GLOBALLY COMPETITIVE

According to Chairman Standing conference of Public Enterprises (SCOPE) 'a sustained empowerment of public sector enterprises will certainly result in a higher return on investment, a higher contribution to the exchequer, greater support to the overall economic growth and finally will lead to better products and services at competitive prices for end-user. He said that PSEs are poised to play a major role in accelerating the

---

1 Reserve Bank of India, Report of Trend and Progress of Banking in India, 1998-99, p. 99.

country's economic growth leading to a doubling of the per capita income by the year 2012. SCOPE, on its part had made substantial progress as an effective policy advocacy centre for the public sector.

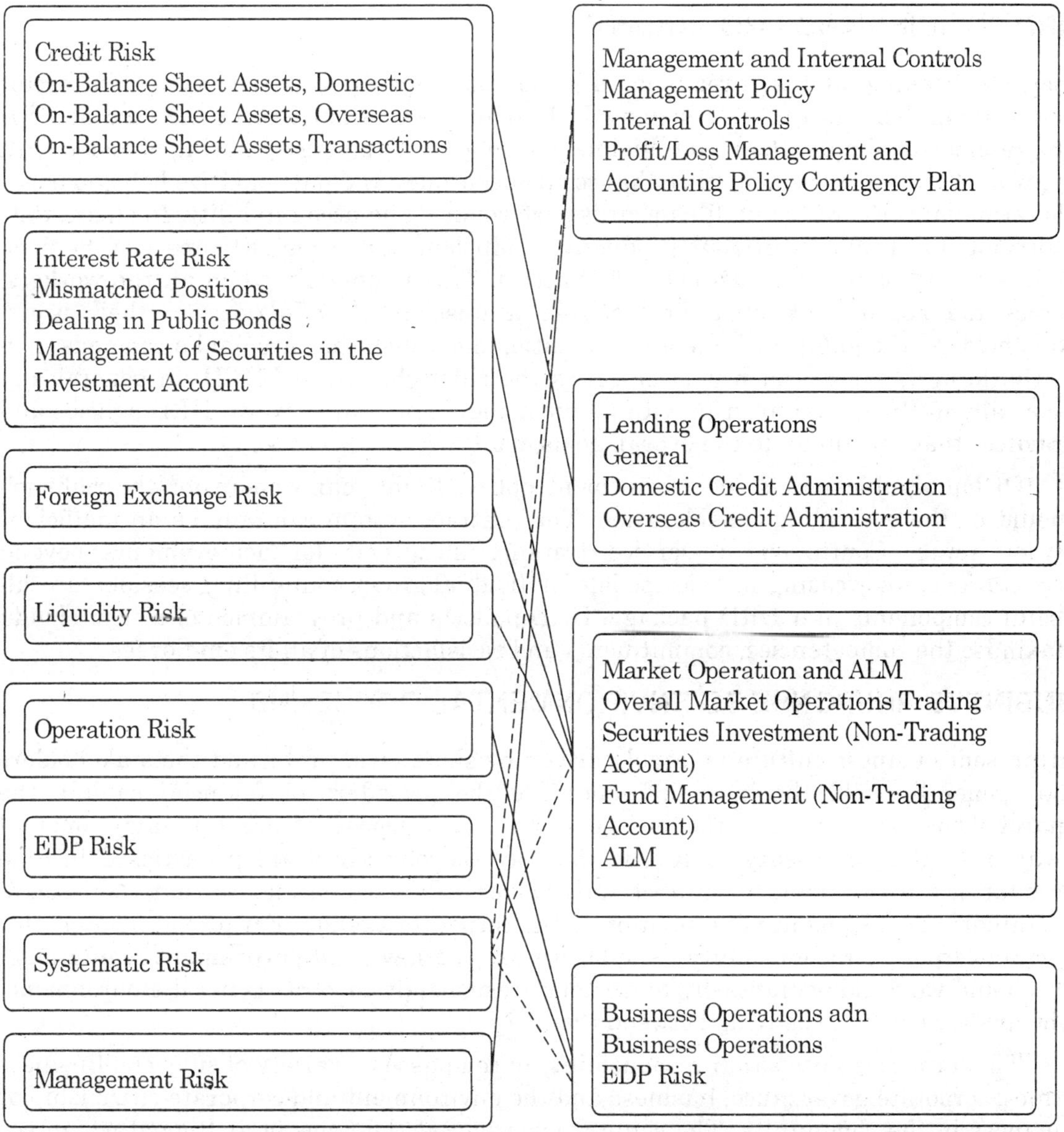

Talking about the improved performance of the central PSEs, the SCOPE Chairman noted that between 1992-93 and 2001-02, the enterprises had posted an extremely impressive commercial performance. The return on investment of the PSEs had gone up from 11.4 per cent to 16.2 per cent . PSEs have also significantly increased the wealth of shareholders. As on March 31, 2002, on a total equity of central PSEs at Rs. 1,01,269 crore, the sharehlders funds stood at Rs. 3,07,267 crore. Accounting for about 31 per cent of the revenue receipts of the government, the net profit of the PSEs stood at Rs. 26,045 crore, which meant an impressive return on investment about 16.2 per cent. SCOPE had also finalised its vision "to enable its member enterprises to be globally competitive in a market driven environment." Accordingly initiatives have been taken which also include efforts for further empowerment of PSEs, highlighting the perspectives of the public sector on issues pertaining to labour and human resources.

HRD POLICIES AND PROGRAMMES

"Setting, seeking and self-realising a vision is imperative for every public sector undertaking. This is the first step in PSU reform and should form the core of HRD programmes in simple, clear , intelligible and coherent language. Sharing of vision with the workers at all levels not only enhances transparency and participative behaviour but also stimulates the rank and file towards performance and accountability. In effect , they contribute to the appreciation of productivity, efficiency and competitiveness of the firm. To-day the watchword is customer satisfaction. This is possible when all the workers, across the board, look at their work as a mission, as a service to their users, stakeholders, the public at large and the nation, for which they are paid a compensation in the form of salary. Such a mind-set is the chief objective of HRD, in general and especially in PSUs that are run with public money. There are several HRD policies and practices that contribute to the overall goals of a PSU.

Of top significance is the recruitment policy. Right man/woman for the right job should be the overriding consideration. The contract system can only be an inefficient escape route. Continuous in-service training incentives for achievements beyond expectations, showcasing of role models, individual/group counselling sessions are all useful components of a HRD package. HRD policies and programmes of a firm should maximise the competencies, commitments and satisfactions of all its employees.

BUSINESS RESPONSE TO ENVIRONMENTAL CONCERNS

At present business culture is largely driven by short term profit and the stakeholders that generally hold the most influence are the providers of financial capital, the shareholders or owners of the business. For the purpose of greater environmental awareness, it is necessary to review the way the objectives are prioritiesed to take account of the viewpoint of indirect stakeholders, This would ensure that the issue of sustainable development is brought on to the corporate agenda. For providing a greater level of corporate responsibility , should we use the laws and government regulations? Or should we decide voluntarily to act more responsibly towards general environment? The answer is said to be lying between the two.

The term corporate social responsibility encompasses a variety of subjects: Business ethics, corporate governance, business and the environment and corporate citizenship or business in the community. The country experienced the tragedy at Bhopal where the MNC Union Carbide had considered it appropriate or sufficient to accept lower standards of safety in a third world plant than would have been appropriate or pemissible for a domestic plant in the United States; The following three types of organisations, may therefore be mentioned as models, which the business may exercise its choice to respond:

- *Social obligation*: where the organisation uses legal and economic criteria to control corporate behaviour; the strategy followed is reactive and it exhibits an exploitative strategy, giving in to environmental concerns only when it can obtain direct benefit. Profit is the primary objective

- *Social responsibility*: Under this choice, organisations try to go beyond the requirements prescribed by law and instead seeks to conform to the current values and norms of society. In this model, organisations become accountable to a range of stakeholders and in so far as it concerns profits, though it may be a dominant motive, it is not the only one.
- *Social responsiveness*: Through this model the organisation exhibits proactive strategy, actively seeking future social change. The business seeks to lead the field in terms of promoting a corporately responsible attitude.

WHISTLE BLOWER PROTECTION

In the United States, the Whistleblower Protection Act was passed in 1989 to prohbit Federal Government from retaliating against employees who blow the whistle against public sector misconduct. In the United Kingdom , protection to employees is provided in the form of the Public Interest Disclosure Act of 1998. In Australia, whistle blowing legislation has also been adopted both in the States and the Federal Government. A number of other countries including India are in the process of enacting the necessary legislation for the purpose. The corporate scandals in America have shook the shareholders confidence tremendously. Therefore the Sarbanes Oxley Act 2002 (SOX) was passed and the Act paved the way for effective corporate governance implementation. The Act has three major requirements:

1. The CEOs of publicly traded companies vouch for the veracity of the firm's published financial statements;
2. Corporate boards must have audit committees drawn from independent directors; and
3. Companies can no longer make loans to corporate directors. The Act goes on to spell out penalties for various levels of failure in corporate governance.

SOX attempts to provide fundamental mechanism to prevent the misdeeds that led to investor losses. These mechanisms are intended as best practices. The approach prescribed requirements on corporations to disclose various aspects and then let the market decide what importance is to be attached on such disclosures. Sarbanes-Oxley acknowledges the importance of stakeholder value. It strengthens the role of directors as representatives of stockholders and reinforces the role of management as stewards of the stockholders' interest. The Sarbanes-Oxley Act generally makes no distinction between US and non-US issuers. The Act does not provide any specific authority to exempt non-US issuers from its reach. The Act leaves it to the SEC to determine where and how to apply its provisions to foreign companies. Further, a significant aspect of the Sarbanes-Oxley is expanding the role and responsibilities of audit committee. It requires the audit committee to be responsible for the outside auditor relationship,including the responsibility for the appointment, compensation and oversight of a company's outside auditor. The Act requires the members of the audit committee be "independent" from company management. The SEC (the Securities and Exchange Commission) was directed by Sarbanes-Oxley to adopt final rules regarding "minimum standards of professional conduct" for attorneys. According to a new proposal of SEC, an attorney should disclose material violations of securities laws to the SEC. These proposals, one can understand, are as a result of recent revealations of corporate mismanagement, malfeasance and/or incompetence which all have undermined the world's financial markets.

Whistle blowers are insiders who go public, usually at great risk to their careers on matters such as corruption, malpractices in the organisations they are employed in etc. The need for legally protecting the whistleblowers in the country has been recognised only recently. The decision to empower the Central Vigilance Commission to act on the complaints of whistleblowers has been welcomed. This is treated as an interim measure, until such time as a full-fledged Whistleblowers Act is put in place. The current notification authorises CVC to act on any complaint of corruption or misuse of office against employees of the central government, or of a corporation, company, society or local authority under the control of the centre. It empowers the Commission to keep the identity of the complainant secret and if necessary, to protect him/her from being victimised. These steps for protecting whistleblowers was pitchforked to public attention by the Satyendra Dubey murder case. Satyendra Dubey, the civil engineer who worked for the National highways Authority of India, was murdered because he had complained about the rampant corruption and poor implementation of work in a section of the Golden Quadrilatertal. In the wake of these developments, a comprehensive legislation to protect whistleblowers has been urged and the emphasis runs as follows:[2]

"All legislation protecting whistleblowers is rooted in two vital rights—the public right to be informed and the whistleblower's right to be protected for acting justly. The legal protection is also recognition that there is a public good involved in the practice. The Government of India's notification covers only employees under its control but legislative protection must extend to the domain of State and local governments and of course, to the private sector. The U.K. legislation covers the private sector. Following the recent financial fiddles in corporate houses such as Enron and Worldcom, the US extended legal protection to whistleblowers in publicly traded companies. A comprehensive legislation on whistleblowing must provide legal immunity to those who complain in the public interest against both government and corporate transgressions."

CALPERS TO BE GUIDED BY CORPORATE GOVERNANCE

CalPERS (California Public Employees Retirement System) has been a warpath with many of the companies it Invests In, regarding practices, which it believes are against sound corporate governance. According to CalPERS spokesperson, CalPERS takes corporate governance into consideration as one of many factors when deciding whether to invest in a particular country's equity market. Thus its activism on adherence to corporate governance standards indicates that the Indian Investments would be restricted to stocks of very few companies.

In American companies that CalPERS invests in, it has a three-pronged strategy - promoting-effective shareholder participation In selection of management-nominated directors; proxy reform, especially for confidentiality, in collection, independence in tabulation and uniformity in the treatment of abstentions and non-votes; and setting

---

[2] Blowing the whistle, the Hindu dated May 3, 2004.

meaningful criteria for director qualifications, to be adopted publicly by the board of each company. CalPERS allocation of funds to emerging markets is expected to be $2 billion. The CalPERS spokesperson has said, "The manager's performance is a measure against an international benchmark in which the countries are weighed according to market capitalisation".

Recently, CalPERS demanded the resignation of Mr. Richard Grasso, Chairmen, New York Stock Exchange, on the basis of his $30 million pay package and substantial retirement benefits. Similarly it had voiced concern about Mr. Michael Eisner, Chairman and Chief Executive, Walt-Disney, before he was stripped of his chairmanship, Currently, CalPERS is voting against the re-election of directors of companies whose auditors also provide non-audit consultancy services.

RBI GOVERNOR ANNOUNCES ANNUAL POLICY STATEMENT FOR 2004-05

Dr. Y. Venugopal Reddy, Governor, RBI, in a meeting with Chief Executives, of major commercial banks today presented the annual policy Statement for 2004-05. The Statement follows the pattern already set in the previous years. Broadly, the Statement covered a review of macroeconomic and monetary developments with several analytical and structural issues concerning financial sector and monetary policy. It delineated and elaborated on various areas in which RBI has been taking measures from time to time and provided a focus on broad policies that are intended to be pursued for the year 2004-05, while retaining the flexibility to take specific measures promptly and effectively as the evolving circumstances warrant. He announced a number of measures for strengthening the financial system, improving the credit delivery mechanism and indicated measures addressing institutional improvements to support growth consistent with stability in a medium-term perspective. He also underscored the need to deepen the consultative process to achieve further social good.

Following are the highlights of the Annual Policy Statement for 2004-05:

Domestic Developments

- GDP growth for 2004-05 projected at 6.5-7.0 per cent.
- Assuming no significant supply shocks and appropriate management of liquidity, the inflation rate projected for policy purposes at around 5.0 per cent during 2004-05.
- Growth in reserve money and Money supply (M3) were higher during 2003-04 reflecting capital inflows; the expansionary impact of foreign currency assets, however, was neutralised to a large extent by substantial open market operation (OMO) including sustained repo operations under.
- Sustained pick-up in non-food credit since September; total flow of resources to the commercial sector was higher than last year.
- Government market borrowing programme in 2003-04 completed at a much lower cost; while noting reduction in fiscal deficit, need to step up capital expenditure stressed.
- Further reduction in interest rates in money and government securities markets observed in 2003-04.

- Public-sector banks have reduced their BPLR in the range of 25-100 basis points.
- RBI to continue with its policy of active liquidity management; Market Stabilisation Scheme (MSS), is an additional tool.

External Developments

- Global economic recovery has broadened and strengthened faster than expected despite some uncertainties.
- The exchange rate of the rupee appreciated vis-à-vis. US dollar but depreciated against the Euro, Pound sterling and Japanese yen in 2003-04.
- India's foreign exchange reserves increased by US $ 37.6 billion during fiscal 2003-04 and are at US $ 118.6 billion by May 7, 2004.
- India's exports in US dollar terms increased by 17.1 per cent white imports by 25.3 per cent; the current account expected to register surplus during 2003-04 for the third year in succession.
- Exchange rate management, as in the past, based on flexibility, without a fixed or pre-announced target, but with ability to intervene.
- The most distinguishing feature of the external sector during 2003-04 relates to the large capital flows with its inevitable implications for the conduct of domestic monetary policy and exchange rate management.

Overall Assessment

- Despite uncertainties, India's position among the top performers globally in terms of GDP growth is expected to continue during 2004-05.
- As regards prices, despite overhang of problems on account of oil prices and large domestic liquidity, price situation unlikely to cause concern to macro stability during 2004-05.
- Need to overcome the bottlenecks in flow of bank credit to agriculture and small and medium enterprises emphasised.
- Restructuring of rural banking sector stressed for enhancing the quality, purposiveness and reach of, banking in India.
- Whereas the Reserve Bank will continue to provide a policy environment that avoids excessive and destabilizing volatility as a public good, market participants were urged to take into account the portfolio risks arising from *any* unexpected developments and provide adequately for them.
- The outlook for the external sector accords comfort to the conduct of public policies.

Stance of Monetary Policy

- Monetary management during 2003-04 broadly in conformity with the stance of the policy set out for the year.
- Projected expansion of money supply (M3) at 14.0 per cent with credit growth by 16.0-16.5 per cent during 2004-05.

- Noticeable uncertainties including geopolitical risks impacting on international oil economy reckoned white designing the stance of monetary policy. As such, the inflationary situation needs to be watched closely and there could be no room for complacency on this count.
- The overall stance of monetary policy for 2004-05 will be:
  - *(i)* provision of adequate liquidity to meet credit growth and support investment and export demand while keeping a very close watch on the movements in the price level.
  - *(ii)* Consistent with the above, while continuing with status quo, RBI to pursue an interest rate environment that is conducive to maintaining momentum of growth and, macroeconomic and price stability.

Measures

- Bank Rate kept stable at 6.0 per cent.
- Repo Rate unchanged at 4.5 per cent.
- Revised LAF scheme operationalised.
- The entire export credit refinance was made available at reverse repo rate.
- Almost all banks have adopted the new system of BPLR and the rates are lower from their earlier PLRs.
- Banks are encouraged to align the pricing of credit to assessment of credit risk to improve credit delivery and credit culture.
- RBI accepted some recommendations of the interim Report of Vyas Committee for implementation, e.g., loans for storage facilities under priority sector, securitised agricultural loans as priority sector lending, waiving margin/security requirements for certain agricultural loans up to a limit, NPA norms for crops loans aligned to crop seasons.
- Development of mechanism for debt restructuring for medium enterprises on the lines of corporate debt restructuring.
- Definition of infrastructure lending broadened.
- Working Group constituted on Credit Enhancement by State Governments, for financing infrastructure.
- A Gold Card Scheme for creditworthy exporters drawn up.
- Various restructuring options being considered by the Government and other stakeholders for rationalising the structure of RRBs—Vyas Committee is also looking into restructuring of RRBs.
- Limit on the lending of non-bank participants in the call/ notice money market reduced to 45, percent effective June 26 2004.
- Automated value-free transfer of securities proposed between market participants and the CCIL under CBLO.
- RBI constituted Working Group to review the performance of negotiated dealing system (NDS).
- Clearing of OTC derivatives through CCIL being considered.

- CCIL to work out arrangement for settlement of trades in non-SLR debt instruments for NDS members.
- Discussion paper on Capital Indexed Bonds being put in public domain.
- The ECB limit already enhanced to US $ 500 million under the automatic route for investment in the real sector.
- Resident individuals already permitted to remit freely up to US $ 25,000 per calendar year.
- Indian corporates and partnership firms allowed to invest overseas upto 100 per cent of their net worth.
- Banks allowed to raise long-term bonds to finance infrastructure.
- The extant limit on unsecured exposures for banks withdrawn.
- Exposures on all public financial institutions (PFIs) to attract a risk weight of 100 per cent.
- Banks required to maintain capital charge for market risk in a phased manner.
- Banks to draw a road map for migration to Basel II.
- Banks to make higher provisioning according to the age of NPAs.
- Banks/Fls to provide credit information to CIBIL.
- Banks to fully adhere to the KYC policy for opening new accounts.
- Report of the Working Group on Financial Conglomerates is being put in public domain.
- Risk based' supervision extended to more banks.
- Fresh licences to UCBs only after a comprehensive policy.
- Report of the Working Group on Development Finance Institutions is being put in public domain.
- Technical Group to evaluate the regulatory and supervisory systems deployed by refinancing institutions (RFIs).
- Waiver of service charges on banks for electronic funds transfer and electronic clearing services.
- RBI sets up a Board for Payment and Settlement Systems.
- RBI expects most commercial banks to join the RTGS system by June 2004.
- A Working Group on Electronic Funds Transfer for Capital Market constituted.
- Single window services for all transactions in RBI cash department.
- Operationalisation of On-line Tax Accounting System by June 2004.
- Standing Committee on Procedures and Performance Audit on Public Services has submitted four Reports, being put in the public domain.
- The recommendations of the Advisory/Technical Groups on International Financial Standards and Codes are being pursued. [PIB Press Release dated 18.05.2004.]

Indian Boiler Reguations with amendments Launched in DIPP Website

The Department of Industrial Policy & Promotion, Ministry Commerce & Industry launched the Indian Boiler Regulations, 1950 with up to date amendments on the website (http:// dipp.nic.in) of the Department of IPP for use by the industry.

The Indian Boilers Act was enacted in 1923 to provide mainly for safety of life and property from the danger of explosion of boilers and for achieving uniformity in registration and inspection during operation and maintenance of boilers throughout the country.

The website will provide information relating to the Indian Boiler Regulations, the standards in respect of materials, design and construction, inspection and testing of boilers and boiler components for compliance by the manufacturers and users of boilers. These regulations are statutory in nature and are mandatory for the users of boilers in India. The regulations are framed by the Central Boilers Board and are being updated regularly by amending them in line with the fast changes in boiler technology throughout the world. With the hoisting of these regulations on the Internet, the user organisations will have access to latest regulations in design, fabrication, installation, inspection, testing and certification, commissioning, operation and registration of boilers for specific conditions of use in the industry and thermal power stations in India. [PIB Press Release dated 14.05.2004.]

Opening of Current Accounts by Banks – Need for Discipline

Please refer to our Circular DBOD.No.BC.136/09.08.001/992000 dated January 25, 2000 wherein we had advised, banks that at the time of opening of current accounts, they should insist on a declaration from the account-holder to the. effect that he is not enjoying any credit facility with any other bank or obtain a declaration giving particulars of credit facilities enjoyed by the intending customer with any other bank(s). Besides, in the letter case, the concerned lending bank(s) were required to be duly informed so that suitable precautionary measures are taken.

MALPRACTICES AND SCAMS IN THE MARKETS[3]

Besides the above glaring discouraging facts which stare at our faces, the following recent unfortunate events in the stock exchanges have also exposed the hollow ethics of many of the Indian Corporates:

(i) Rampant insider trading by the promoters in league with big market players

(ii) Massive price rigging/manipulation by the promoters in league with big market players prior to mergers/takeovers.

(iii) Gross misuse of Bank funds for clandestine stock market operations.

(iv) Criminally motivated investments in violation of laid down norms.

The above are duly corroborated by the following shocking facts:

- As per the Global Competitiveness Report 1999 published by the World Economic Forum India is ranked 52 out of 59 countries.
- More than half of the 5515 companies which raised resources from the capital markets through public issues before 1996, have not paid any dividend since 1996.
- The number of vanishing companies stands at 143 which have duped public money to the tune of Rs. 66861 crores.

3 Source: Corporate Governance, Concept and Dimensions, Snow White 2003.

- Non-performing assets of scheduled commercial banks approximately amounted to Rs. 75000 crores, as on 31st March, 2002.
- As per the Transparency International Corruption peroption Index 2000, India ranks 69 out of 70 countries.
- India has the dubious distinction of having had the largest number of scams since liberalisation was introduced in 1992 namely the Securities Scam of 1992, the CRB fraud of 1996, the vanishing companies in 1996-97, the scam of plantation companies in 1997-98,

Corporate Governance: Time for Real Action Begins

The boom of phoney IT companies in 1999-2000, the cyberspace scandal of 2001, NBFC's bankruptcy of 2000, Ketan Pareek scam of 2002, the rampant insider trading and price rigging in 2000-01 the Cooperative Banks Broker nexus to swindle the monies of the co-operative banks (popularly known as the home trade scam).

AREAS FOR EXCEL ENCE[4]

Our People

We share common challenge to serve customers, sell, and manage risk. We will succeed by approaching these responsibilities in a creative and ethical manner with a commitment to the communities we serve. We value team work and seek the true success that comes from collaboration.

Customer Service

We strive to provide a unique Citizens Service Experience every time we interact with a customer or colleague to set ourselves apart from our competitors and create value for our customers. We will exceed our customer's expectations by providing prompt, consistent and knowledgeable service in a friendly, caring and neighbourly fashion. The Citizens Service Experienv, most important when we have the opportunity to resolve a customer's problem. We will treat our customers and colleagues as we would like to be treated with courtesy and enthusiasm.

Sales Success

We know that financial success at Citizens will be determined by the sales effort of every one of us. Sales are not a passive exchange but an aggressive pursuit of a solution to a customer's needs and problems that we identify. Our sales approach will be creative, professional and informed while we build a reputation for predictability and integrity in all of our dealings with customers.

Risk Management

We recognize that virtually every aspect of our business involves a degree of risk. Our mission is to manage risk and prevent losses so that we can achieve our objectives. We

4 Source: Dynamic Directors, Allen Blake, Macmillan Business.

are all responsible for identifying and evaluating risk as well as knowing and appropriately exercising the policies that apply to our area.

People Management

We commit to provide the tools necessary to succeed at Citizens while consistently adding to the opportunities for our higher achievers. Key to this commitment is an evolving Performance Management System which communicates high standards, provides frequent feedback and rewards achievement fairly. We take great pride in our diversity and intend that nothing stand between us and success other than our own wills and skills.

Community Involvement

We seek to distinguish ourselves within banking and industry by our extraordinary commitment to community involvement and public service. Our financial contributions will be augmented by a spirit of volunteerism for each of us has a special responsibility for community service. Through our collective efforts we will improve the communities we are privileged to serve.

BOARD FOR PSU RECONSTRUCTION

In September 2004, the Prime Minister Manmohan Singh announced that a board for reconstruction of public enterprises would be set up to guide policy, on this sector, Addressing a conference of chief executives of public sector enterprises organised by the Department of Public Enterprises and the Standing conference of Public Enterprises (SCOPE), he said "Our government believes that the process of disinvestments should increase competition and not decrease it." Stressing that there should be a link between disinvestment and the provisioning of basic social goods, he said revenues generated through disinvestment would be used for designated social sector spending. Besides, public sector companies and nationalised banks would be encouraged to enter the capital market to raise resources and offer new avenues to retail investors, The proposed Board advise the Government on measures to be taken to restructure central PSEs. In this context, he called for a wider and more meaningful debate on the questions of making PSEs more efficient and competitive.

Social Commitment

On the burden of social development placed on PSEs, Dr. Manmohan Singh said it was an 'extraordinary challenge' faced by companies' required to fulfill the charter of social commitment and simultaneously meet the imperatives of managerial efficiency, He therefore felt if PSEs, continued to do well, even when asked to combine these two objectives, their performance needed to be commended. He said the Government would implement the recommendations of the TKA Nair committee report after they are duly examined.

Corporate Governance

On the need for good corporate governance, he said transparency and accountability were essential ingredients of any managerial system, especially with respect to PSEs where public money was involved He wanted-it to be debated, as to whether the instrument of a memorandum of understanding (MOU) between PSEs and the government has been an effective mechanism of ensuring operational autonomy and managerial accountability. The Prime Minister presented the MoU awards for excellence in performance to the top 10 PSUs-NTPC, BPCL, PFC, RINL, Hindustan Aeronautics, Indian Railway Finance Corporation, Bharat Electronics, HPCL, Hindustan Latex and PEC, for the year 2002-03, RITES was awarded in the smaller public enterprises category for scaling new heights.

BANKING CODE SET FOR OVERHAUL

The Indian bank's Association's code for Banking Practice is set to undergo a makeover; To be christened as the 'Model Code for Fair Business Practices', the new code of ethics aims at fostering healthy co-operation between banks and build a sound banker-customer relationship. The new Code, being revamped by the Indian Bank's Association, seeks to bring under one umbrella the principles governing inter-bank relationship, the industry-wide convention on application of Interest on deposit accounts and the Model Citizen's charter, which deals with minimum service commitments by banks their customers.

In the light of emphasis being placed on corporate governance and social responsibility in business, it is expected that banks' will conduct their operations based on the ethical principles of integrity, impartiality and transparency -and frame/execute business policies consistent with social responsibility, The new code aims to promote good banking practices by setting out the minimum standards to be followed by bank's employees, agents and other personnel in their dealings with customers. Besides it deals with the policies that need to be put in place to address the interest o all stakeholders In particular and the banking system in general. The code envisages that banks should win business based on merits of their products and services, even as their business policy is anchored in fairness and impartiality. Business courtesy that bank employees, agents and business associates extend to customers, both internal and external, should stand the scrutiny of propriety and not amount to unfair business practices/contravention of any law or regulation.

On the customer relationship front, banks have to ensure that customers have access to all the information about their products and the terms and conditions governing purchase and use. A minimum 30 days notice is to be given to customers in order to make any changes effective in the terms and conditions of the contracts entered with banks.

WIPRO LEADS IN INVESTOR RELATIONS

WIPRO has been ranked number one among technology companies for its investor relations function in Asia and across all industries in India by sell-side analysts in the latest Institutional Investor Asia Equities Market Report 2004. The Institutional investor Research group is the premier resource of information on equity research in every major market. CFO, Wipro Ltd., confirmed that this ranking is a reflection of the faith reposed by analysts and investors in Wipro's communication and disclosure standards and it also reflects the highest standards of corporate governance that WIPRO strive to maintain.

The report attempts to provide a definitive overview of performance excellence and important trends in the Asian equities market. There were 14 criteria on which the rankings were done. These included transparency, and quality of financial reporting and disclosure, access to senior management, helping understand the long-term company and industry direction, quality of on-going relationship and speed of response to queries.

WIPRO is in the company of Qantas Airlines (Australia) and Acer Inc from Taiwan in their respective countries. In the industry segment, WIPRO is in the company of Hyundai Motors, Taiwan Semiconductor Manufacturing Co Ltd., Acer and Qantas.

NORMS FOR PRIVATE DIRECTORS' APPOINTMENTS

The Reserve Bank of India has tightened norms for appointment of directors on the board of private sector banks through a process of internal checks and balances. In a circular addressed to the CMD and CEOs of private sector banks, RBI has stated that private banks should udertake due diligence to determine the suitability of the person for appointment/continuing to hold appointment as a director on the board. The due diligence must be based on qualification, expertise, track record, integrity and other 'fit and proper' criteria. Banks should obtain necessary information and declaration from the proposed/existing directors for the purpose.

RBI has asked the boards of the banks to costitute a nomination committee to scrutinise the declarations. It has also directed that due diligence should be undertaken by the banks at the time of appointment and renewal of appointment. Banks also have to obtain annually on March 31, a simple declaration that the information already provided has not undergone change and if there is any change, requisite details are furnished by the directors. The information includes the list of entities or banks that the director has interest in, details of any proceedings, or prosecution against him/her and whether the director, at any time, came to the adverse notice of a regulator, such as SEBI, IRDA, DCA. The Dr. Ganguly Group report had recommended that banks should require the directors to execute a covenant binding them to discharge their responsibilities to the best of their abilities, individually and collectively. The report had also recommended that due diligence of directors should be done based on their suitability for the post keeping in mind their qualifications, technical expertise, track record and integrity.

CORPORATES MUST CREATE TRUSTWORTHINESS

In his address at a function of FICCI, on the topic 'Management's crisis of legitimacy', Prof Sumantra Ghosal of the London Business School implored corporates to rectify the image that managements were acquiring globally and in India (November, 2003). "Worldwide people do not trust managements and corporate leaders and distrust is growing and not reducing," he said. A trustworthiness survey showed that managers were way down in the trustworthiness score. He felt that it was necessary for managers to be trusted and respected because there was a strong co-relation between economic prosperity of a nation and companies. He made a distinction between markets and companies and said that markets operate solely on self-interest, but companies have to grow, diversify and control their destinies, hence they should operate in collective interest and create new values. In the sphere of corporate governace, Mr Ghosal said that research has shown that there is no significant association between performance and the three prescriptions of corporate governance such as creating more independent directors, separating the role of Chairman and CEO in a company and giving stock options. He said even Enron followed these parameters. In his view it was time to look at a new intellectual agenda for management, where business leaders would reshape the models of economic growth by going beyond the myth of the market economy, revise the process of corporate governance by going beyond shareholder absolutism and rethink the concepts of strategy.

CORPORATE GOVERNANCE CENTRES

The Governing Council of National Foundation for Corporate Governance has recently approved the accreditation of six premier institutions on an ad-hoc basis as national centres for corporate governance. These Institutes are thc four Indian Institutes of management (IIMs of Ahmedabad, Bangalore, Kolkata and Lucknow) along with the Administrative College of India, Hyderabad and the Indian School of Business, Hyderabad. The National Foundation envisages setting up NCCG to provide training to directors and undertake research and advocacy in corporate governance.

The NFCG is a trust set up by the Government in association with the Confederation of Indian Industry, Institute of Chartered Accountants of India and Institute of Company Secretaries of India. The objectives of the setting up the NFCG are: discussing issues relating to corporate governance, sensitising corporate leaders on the importance of good corporate governance, self regulation and directorial responsibilities, and providing research and training in corporate governance. It was proposed to take further initiatives on research and case studies, which also included a model whistle blower's policy, a corporate governance policy for large institutional investors and a corporate governance audit after consultations with stakeholders.

The council also launched the Web site www.nfcgindia.org. NFCG will post a discussion paper on corporate governance on this site and invite feedback.

CENTRE ISSUES SPECIAL SECURITIES TO BAIL OUT IDBI

The Government on 29th September 2004 issued special securities for Rs 9,000 crore towards the creation of the 'Stressed Assets Stabilisation Fund to help-Industrial Development Bank of India tackle its problem of stressed amounts.' The amount will be invested in non-interest bearing special securities 0-20 year maturity with call option. The transaction is budget neutral for the Government. The amount realised by SASF on the recovery of dues will be paid to the Government annually. The Government will redeem bonds of an equivalent amount thus leaving IDBI with an equivalent amount of cash. There will be no net out-go from the government on account of the transaction.

IDBI becomes Deemed Banking Company

From October 1, 2004, IDBI, the erstwhile principal development financial institution with a four decadal multifaceted contribution towards catalysing industrialisation in the country, metamorphosed into a banking company. IDBI has become a deemed banking company and the new entity is to raise Rs. 5000 crores including foreign exchange resources of $300 million in the second half of current fiscal ending March ending 31, 2005. Other than merger of IDBI Bank with IDBI Ltd., it is also thinking about possible merger with other banks.

Transfer of NPA

The transformation into bank comes on the heels of the establishment of the Stressed Assets Stabilisation Fund (SASF), domiciled in a Special Purpose Vehicle set up by the Government in the form of an Asset Management Trust, to which stressed assets amounting to Rs. 9000 crores have been transferred. The Central Government has also accorded SASF the status of a 'financial institution', to enable it to access the Debt Recovery Tribunals for recovery' of debts.

KALAM SPELLS OUT SIX POINT MISSION FOR BANKS

The President, A.P.J. Abdul Kalam asked banks to play a bigger role, follow a mission –mode approach and help the country realise 7-8 per cent economic growth by doubling farm credit and developing ways to utilise the foreign exchange reserves in high yielding enterprises. Inaugurating "BANCON", the Bankers' conference jointly organised by Punjab National Bank and the Indian Bank's Association on 10th November, 2004, Dr. Kalam spelt out a six point mission for banks saying that the Development finance responsibility with its inherent risks was squarely and fully on the banking sector. The days of development financial institutions seem to be over. The current fashion is the Universal bank. Even the redoubtable IDBI has converted itself into a Universal Bank shedding the robe of a pure development Financial institution", he said urging the bankers to play a positive role to assist the Country to march towards development faster. As part of his mission, the President urged the banking sector to raise agricultural and agro-processing credit to Rs. 200,000 crores from the existing Rs 90,000 crores over the next three years. Besides facilitating infrastructure development. He said the banks should take it upon themselves to add to the $ 120 billion foreign exchange reserves by investing a portion of them in relatively higher yield enterprises.

The President said the banks should be more liberal in offering educational loans, which should be extended to non-technical education as well. The bank branches should adopt schools in rural areas and meet the infrastructure needs besides promoting quality education. His mission also envisaged banks coming forward to make provisions for 100 million quality dwelling units apart from innovatively funding. Three lakh sick small-scale units to enable them to adopt the latest technology and overcome the problems to becoming profitable.

Employment front. Even in meeting the challenges on the employment front , he said the banks could play a critical role. He suggested that the banks should take a lead to create and nurture five rural development projects similar to bio-fuel project so as to create additional employment for at least 10 million youth. He also asked the banks to allocate at least Rs. 10,000 crores for providing venture capital from the next financial year to innovative scientists and technologists working in all the three major sectors—agriculture, manufacturing and services—including information and communication technology based knowledge products and software development and software services.

Stressing that venture capital business had to increase in magnitude, particularly with hassle–free procedures, he said, "I have come across a European experience of a physics graduate turning into $100 million exclusive venture capital banker and leading to a establishment of $10 billion company." Dr. Kalam asked banks to provide concessional interest rate funding for creation of corporate hospitals, which could make available networked healthcare for the rural community through medical insurance on the Yeshaswini model followed by Karnataka and also attract medical tourists for cost effective treatmet through the country's quality doctors.

CORPORATES MUST CREATE TRUSTWORTHINESS

Prof Sumantra Ghosal of the London Business School who marked the occasion of Unveiling new logo of FICCI in the capital on 25th November, 2004, addressed on the subject of "Management's crisis of Legitimacy". He implored corporates to rectify the image that managements were acquiring globally and in India. "Worldwide people do not trust managements and corporate leaders and the distrust is growing, not reducing," he said quoting a trustworthiness survey that showed that managers were way down in the trustworthiness score. Putting the blame on the shoulders of management academicians, corporate managers and journalists, Mr Ghosal said that business academicians have created amoral practices of management, managers have made the practice unreasonable and journalists/consultants are guilty of making the practice of management heroic. Collectively, the three have promoted irresponsible management.

He felt that it was necessary for managers to be trusted and respected because there was a strong co-relation between economic prosperity of a nation and companies. He made a distinction between markets and companies and said that markets operate solely on self-interest, but companies have to grow, diversity and control their destinies, hence they should operate in collective interest and create new values. In the sphere of corporate governance, Mr. Ghoshal said that research has shown that there is no significant association between performance and the three prescriptions of corporate governance such as creating more independent directors, separating the role of chairman and CEO in a company and giving stock options. He said even Enron followed these parameters.

In his view it was time to look at a new intellectual agenda for management, where business leaders would reshape the models of economic growth by going beyond the myth of the market economy, revise the process of corporate governance by going beyond shareholder absolutism and rethink the concepts of strategy.

FROM RURAL POVERTY TO POTENTIAL MARKETS

The following re-production from the Chairman's speech (YC Deveshwar) at the 93rd Annual general meeting held on 30th July 2004 of ITC Ltd., may be noted. The material has particular relevance to the Chapter 6: Business ethics and social Responsibility and therefore may be usefully referred.

Nearly 87% of India's 640, 000 villages have population clusters of 2000 people or below. Despite a universe of roughly 3.6 million rural retail outlets, there is no active marketing or distribution in these small villages because of uneconomical "last mile" logistics. Nearly, 35% of India's villages are yet to be connected by roads. Rural teledensity is barely 1%. Apart from being geographically dispersed, these villages as economic units are too feeble to support the scale of investment required to upgrade last mile connectivity. A substantial proportion of the rural population subsists on less than $1 per day – less than half the subsidy provided to each head of cattle by the OECD.

Rural India accounts for about 60% of the country's household consumption expenditure. Yet, consumer research reveals that the propensity to consume for a rural wage earner is only half that of an urban wage earner for the same level of income. The lower propensity to spend arises from uncertainties the future holds in the absence of effective mechanisms to manage risk. Agriculture continues to be the predominant source of rural livelihood. A host of factors including small and fragmented farms, over dependence on monsoons, and lack of sophisticated inputs and knowledge traps the farmer in a vicious cycle of underdevelopment. The growth opportunity lies in building capacity to induce productivity led growth by providing cost effective last mile connectivity.

Your Company has nurtured deep linkages with rural India both as a buyer of agri commodities and as a seller of goods and services. ITC's e-Choupal model seeks to address the issues relating to last mile connectivity by leveraging IT to build capability at the grassroots through empowerment of the small farmer. This model seeks to enhance farm productivity and income by aligning output with market demand through connectivity. Its primary focus revolves around creating markets by helping raise incomes before servicing such markets commercially. Indeed these processes occur more or less simultaneously–a phenomenon that C K Prahalad so aptly refers to as "co-creation of value". Such an e-infrastructure can also serve as a powerful and effective delivery channel for a host of goods and services, including those related to farm practices, risk management, education and health. In effect, the e-Choupal is potentially an efficient delivery channel for rural development and an instrument for converting village populations into vibrant economic organizations.

Despite daunting implementation challenges, this initiative now comprises over 4100 installations covering nearly 25,000 villages and serving 2.4 million farmers. The World Business Award is an acknowledgment of your Company's abiding commitment to the rural value chain. To me, it also serves as a humbling reminder of the journey yet to be traversed, of the commitment to connect 100,000 villages in this decade, and is a celebration of a small beginning–the first step in a journey which will not end till every Indian farmer is reached.

BUSINESS ETHICS CAN ENHANCE BOTTOM LINES

According to Dipankar Gupta, who founded the consultancy's Business ethics and Integrity division of KPMG, corporate ethics does not mean standing on a pulpit, sermonising and taking the high moral ground. He believes that corporate ethics could have a substantial impact on the bottom line of a company and his latest book 'Ethics incorporated: Top priority and bottom line' states just that. When KPMG began its assignments, it did not have a clearly formulated idea of how to put business ethics to work other than a set of guidelines in which the company firmly believed. The company was convinced that if business ethics were to advance then it must be able to articulate itself in practice and show empirically verifiable deliverables. Mr. Gupta argues that there is no off-the-shelf module for corporate Ethics and that the best practice would be to try and integrate the company norms with its business policies and code of conduct. He believes that it would be wise for companies to emphasise the don't instead of stress on the do's and if rules such as these are demonstrated by the company's leadership, it would be all the more acceptable to employees and positively impact attrition rates. Mr. Gupta makes a case for the inextricable link between coporate governance and business ethics and how sans business ethics, corporate governance would "run the very risk of becoming a bloodless and ghostly apparition, far removed from its original condition of robust well-being." He also points out how it is possible for a less ethical company to reduce corporate governance to a mere paper exercise and outlines what is incorporated in corporate governance today and what it actually should be.

Though Gupta finds companies much more geared towards business ethics now than in the past, he feels the reason why ethics have not taken centrestage is because, unlike in the West, in India there is not enough pressure on companies to comply with shareholder wishes. "Shareholders and stakeholders are still afraid to question authority, are not demanding enough and have yet to shake off the hierarchical yoke," he says. But the fact that investors do not rock the boat does not mean that bottom lines can take the same indifference. Business ethics, reputation, and low employee turnover are all the impact of better business ethics and also have a substantial influence on the bottom line.

TATA STEEL TO PUSH FOR SOCIAL RESPONSIBILITY OF BUSINESSES

The Tata Iron and Steel Company (TISCO) will announce in the course of this year (2004) a policy framework whereby it will do business only with entities which show a commitment to corporate social responsibility. "We want to encourage our suppliers and customers to adopt social responsibility because business has an obligation to give something back to society", said B Muthuraman, Managing Director of TISCO, which is known for its committed budgets down the decades for community welfare beyond the confines of its own Employees.

Addressing the open session of the 168th Annual general meeting of the Madras Chamber of Commerce and Industry (MICCI), he disagreed with the proposition that the "business of business is business and adding to shareholder value" and that social welfare was beyond its purview. For businesses to be "sustainable in the long term", they had to commit themselves to social good, he said. The TISCO MD said his company was already the lowest cost producer of steel in the world, thanks to huge investments it made in modernisation in the post–1991 years and total involvement of the workforce upto the lowest level in evolving and implementing the company's vision. Further cost cuts would be possible only if externalities like infrastructure and rail freight improved. The steel industry the world over had performed poorly till the last three years or so, because of slump in demand with developed countries with limited population having crossed the stage of creation of infrastructure. The revival in the fortunes of steel at present was due to the demand shifting to countries like India, and China, which had both large programmes for building infrastructurte like roads and ports and huge populations that could sustain a rising domestic demand, he observed.

BASEL II NORMS TO IMPROVE BANK'S RISK MANAGEMENT SYSTEM

India's decision to implement Basel II norms from December 2006 will improve Bank's risk management system and provide them incentives for meeting the prudential norms, said the Basel Committee on Banking Supervision Chairman, Jamie Caruna. Mr. Caruna lauded the efforts of the Reserve Bank of India, which has set up a steering committee for the purpose, for sharing its views and data for the implementation of the norms with the bank for International Settlements. He said the framework was developed by the Basel committee on Banking Supervision and outlines various methods for banks to calculate the minimum regulatory capital for different types of risk. The committee recommended the less sophisticated approaches for credit and operational risk to be implemented by the end of 2006, with the most sophisticated techniques to be in place by year-end 2007. It allowed individual countries to determine their own commencement dates. "When to implement the Basel II norms is the national decision said Mr. Caruna at the bankers conference at New Delhi. The three part accord lays out guidelines for the minimum regulatory capital requirements, bank supervision and improved disclosure".

Under Basel II, mortgage lending to creditworthy borrowers will require less capital to be set aside, while riskier loans, such as those made to companies, will need more backing. He hoped that more than 100 countries would comply with the prudential norms. Mr. Caruna said Basel II would help in ensuring competition among the banks on the basis of their strengths and not countries. The focus of the new prudential norms was to have cooperation among supervisors to ensure stability and risk mitigation.

EMERGING GLOBAL TRENDS IN CORPORATE FINANCE

According to Bala Balachandran, J.L. Kellogg, distinguished professor in the Kellogg School of Management, U.S. Chief Financial Officers are well placed to become "chief risk managers" whose perspective and advice are crucial for the decision-making processes of the chief executive officer (CEO). The CFOs, with their potential for familiarity with "strategic choices of the business, core business processes and critical business issues" should become "internal consultants" to their company in indentifying and managing risks, Prof Balachandran said. Participating through video-conferencing in the India Financial Forum (TIFF) 2004, a two-day conference on "emerging global trends in corporate finance", organised by the Confederation of Indian Industry, Southern Region, he said the demanding provisions of Sec. 404 of the Sarbanes Oxley Act of the U.S. could be exploited by Indian companies as a "trigger mechanism" in identifying and managing risks related to technology, finance, political environment and the market. The advisor, Ashok Leyland (T Anantha Narayanan) suggested that corporate governance standards should be embraced by unlisted companies as also by NGOs (non-government organisations) through which companies often fulfilled their social responsibilities. The Managing Director of ICRA, which has undertaken corporate governance rating of Indian companies, said the fear of disclosure of confidential information considered crucial for their competitiveness in the marketplace dissuaded many companies from taking to governance rating. Multiplicity of regulatory agencies, too much of theorising and confusion between corporate governance and corporate social responsibility marked the emerging scenario. Rating helped companies to benefit from "regulatory tolerance" in case of suspected cases of misdemeanour, he said. Deepankar Gupta of Jawaharlal Nehru University said a code of conduct clearly defining what would not be allowed or countenanced would help corporates in working a system of grievance redressal. Internal ombudsman should be preferred to external ombudsmen. Corporate social responsibility should not 'degenerate into charity' but should be competence-driven and add value to the business by way of new experience and perspectives, he said. He suggested, for instance, that hotel companies could run old age homes or kitchen for the elderly, and a battery company could promote garbage clearance that it in turn promote recycling of waste.

MAKING PSUs WORK

In October 2004, the Government began a review of the functioning of Public Sector Undertakings (PSUs), with the Cabinet Committee on Economic affairs (CCEA) asking the heavy industries ministry for specific proposals on ten areas, including corporate governance, research and development and quality management. Finance Minister P. Chidambaram told reporters after the meeting that the proposal was aimed at undertaking financial and physical review of central PSUs. Chidambaram said the government had also approved the revision of provisions for liquidated or consequent damages due to time overrun for turnkey contracts. The move is aimed at ensuring timely implementation of projects, besides bringing more transparency in Contract documents. A decision on the Lokpal Bill to probe corruption in high offices was also deferred, as the CCEA felt more discussions were needed before a final view is taken on it.

The following are the ten areas, on which inputs have been sought on PSU's working:

- Greater functional autonomy for central PSUs
- Making PSU Boards more professionally oriented
- Devolution of financial powers
- Improving corporate governance
- Empowering Navratna and Miniratna PSUs
- Concentrating on MOU route for modernisation
- Increased focus on research and development and quality control
- Evolving an institutional mechanism for revival of sick PSUs
- Rationalisation of manpower
- Studying the efficiency of the purchase preference policy

KNOWLEDGE COMMISSION

The Prime Minister, Manmohan Singh announced the setting up of a National Knowledge Commission so that India becomes not only a knowledge producing society but also a knowledge sharing and knowledge-consuming society. (January 2005) Delivering his inaugural address at the CII Partnership summit at Kolkata, Dr. Singh said this was the only way to meet the challenges of globalisation. The commission's agenda would be shaped by a "knowledge pentagon with five action areas." These included increasing access to knowledge for public benefit, developing higher education concepts, rejuvenating science and technology institutions, enabling application of knowledge by industry to enhance manufacturing competitiveness and encouraging intensive use of knowledge based services by government for citizen's empowerment. He also said that Government have committed in the National Common Minimum Programme to boost private investment and encourage FDI particularly in infrastructure, high technology and exports. If Communist China can be the top investment destination in the world and if a left Government in West Bengal woos FDI aggressively, I see no reason why the UPA Government cannot make India an important FDI destination, he said. In this context, he said that India's response to offers of assistance was not shaped by false pride or chauvinism. "We are happy to be part of a global community and will seek international assistance for our reconstruction effort." The do-it-yourself mood of the nation was not an index of its isolationism. Rather, it reflected the countries resolve to turn adversity into an opportunity.

E-GOVERNANCE INITIATIVE BY MINISTRY OF COMPANY AFFAIRS

The Ministry of Company Affairs proposes to achieve paperless office through its e-governance initiatives and once the project gets completed in the next 15 months (from February 2005), accessing even financial and other information on closely-held companies would just be a mouse click away. Talking to media persons after launching the Rs 341-crore project awarded to a consortium of Tata controlled TCS-CMC, the Company Affairs Minister, Prem Chand Gupta, said that all documents filed by even the private companies, apart from the thousands of listed entities would be available on one's computer free of cost for initial three years and on payment thereafter. Christened as "MCA-21", the project would connect the Ministry and all its regional offices and the 22 registrars of companies across the country with a centralised system to provide on-line information to all the stakeholders including public, financial institutions and companies. "MAC-21 is a unique initiative of the Ministry of Company Affairs that will provide facility of e-filing of returns to the corporate sector with on line access to all information about companies, including that of the unlisted ones", Mr. Gupta said.

NEW POLICY FOR AN INTERNET DOMAIN NAME ANNOUNCED

With a view to bring about significant improvement in Indian Internet domain name registration system and to connect all Internet Service Providers (ISPs) in India to a National Internet Exchange the Government has announced the New Policy for the Internet domain name. Having made progress on this issue in the last few months, the Minister of Communications & Information Technology, Dayanidhi Moran has announced the new policy at a Press Conference held on 28.10.2004. Moran said while the Internet domain name registration system will focus greatly to proliferate the Internet, connecting all ISPs of the country to the National Internet Exchange is aimed to achieve efficient Internet traffic routing and cost reduction, thereby improving the quality of service for the Internet users in India. Today's announcement made by the Minister is in consonance with the Ten Point Programme for the Department of Information Technology (announced by him earlier. One of the focus areas of the Ten Point Agenda was to increase the PC penetration and thereby bring cyber connectivity to every citizen.

After an indepth review of the situation, the Government has decided to revamp the in Domain Name Registry in India to provide a greater thrust to its activities. The new policy for in Domain Nome registration covers the following main elements:

- Unlimited generic in registration will be offered of 2nd level of Domain Nome and also at the 3rd level in the globally popular zones of Domain registration, e.g., .co.in, .net.in and .org.in..
- Registrations will be carried out by Registrars to be appointed by the .in Registry through an open process of selection on the basis of transparent eligibility criteria.
- Registrations will be offered by the Registrars following a competitive pricing policy and best market practices. The minimum fee charged by the .in Registry will ho Rs. 250 and Rs. 500 per year for registrations of 3rd and 2nd levels respectively.
- The .in Registry will adopt Uniform Dispute Resolution Policy (UDRP), and will be assisted by a Dispute Resolution Committee to resolve disputes involving the Registry. It will also appoint Arbitrators to address disputes involving the Registrars and the registrants.
- The entire process of registration will be online and should be completed in less than 24 hours of the receipt of the request from a registrant.
- The in Registry will announce a 'Sunrise period' of 90 days to enable registered trademark owners, registered companies and owners of Intellectual property having a legitimate interest in protecting their brand to secure registration of their Domain Names after due verification.
- The zones for Government, Military and Educational Institutions will be reserved for exclusive use by the respective organizations. Registrations for these will be offered by NIC, an organization nominated by the Ministry of Defence, and ERNET, respectively.
- The in Registry will have the authority to deny or suspend any registration if it conflicts with the sovereign national interest or public order.
- The names of Constitutional Authorities, States/Union Territories and specific names used by the .in Registry will constitute the reserved category of names, which will not be available to the general public.

In India, .in is the allocated country code Top Level Domain (ccTLD). It is recognized that its all-round adoption by Indian residents, individuals, Government entities, public service organizations and businesses will help in establishing their Indian identity in the Internet space using a short and unique Domain Name. Internet Domain Names worldwide have assumed greater significance in recent times with the Internet increasingly being used as an effective medium for commerce, governance, education and communication. The system of registration of Internet Domain Names can facilitate the proliferation of Internet in a country. Many countries have, therefore, adopted liberal and market friendly policies to register large number of Domain Names under their country code, broadly consistent with globally accepted policy and procedures of Domain registration.

The number of .in Domain Names so far registered does not truly represent the penetration of information technology in India when compared with a large number of companies and public institutions engaged in the area of Information Technology (IT) and Information Technology enabled Services (ITeS). An overcautious registration policy and absence of contemporary processes and infrastructure for registration have so a hindered the growth of .in Domain. It is widely recognized that .in Domain Name has an untapped growth potential. A proactive policy for .in Domain proliferation can help establish .in as a globally recognized symbol of India's growth in the area of IT.

DIT, in association with the Internet Service Providers Association of India, has promoted National Internet Exchange of India (NIXI) as a Not-for-Profit Company under Section 25 of the Indian Companies Act, 1956 with an objective of facilitating improved Internet services in the country. In its operation, NIXI aims to ensure that the Internet traffic which originates within India and also has destination in India, remains within the country, resulting in improved traffic latency, reduced cost and better security. In order to address the problem of excessive cost of connectivity for smaller ISPs (Class B and C) operating in secondary cities, the Government is considering a proposal to set up, in partnership with the State Governments, and the ISPs as stake holders, the NIXI hubs in such cities.

As part of the implementation plan of NIXI, four Internet Exchange Nodes have been set up and operationalised at Noida (Delhi), Mumbai, Chennai and Kolkata in the premises of the Software Technology Parks of India. As many as 34 Internet Service Providers (ISPs), including major Class A ISPs, have joined these nodes as members. The number of ISPs joining the NIXI nodes is increasing in view of the demonstrated experience of improved traffic routing and savings in the usage cost of bandwidth.

NIXI has implemented a dynamic traffic routing and tariff policy for its members with effect from 1st July 2004. The policy is regularly reviewed by NIXI to ensure that the requirement of the members are addressed while ensuring that the objectives set for NIXI are met.

Recently, NIXI has also been entrusted with the responsibility of operating the .in Registry to implement the new policy framework for .in Domain Name by creating a .in Network Information Centre (INNIC). The synergy between NIXI and the INNIC is proposed to be established by ensuring that the Registrars selected by the .in Registry are from among or utilize the services of the Internet Service Providers connected to NIXI nodes.

The INNIC under NIXI will function as an autonomous body with the primary responsibility to maintain .in Domain and ensure its operational stability, reliability and security. It will implement the various elements of the new policy set out by the Government. [*PIB Press Release dated 28.10.2004*]

MANAGERIAL AUTONOMY FOR PUBLIC SECTOR BANKS

In a significant step in banking reforms, the Centre granted full managerial autonomy to pubic sector banks (PSBs). It demarcated the roles of the Government as owners, the Board of Directors of the banks and the executive management to separate the rights of the owners from the functional freedom of the management.

The relaxation enshrined in the United Progressive Alliance Government's Common Minimum Programme and coming just six days ahead of the new budget, is aimed at enabling the PSBs to have greater operational flexibility to transact business more efficiently.

This will enable them to compete more effectively with the private sector banks and function on "sound principles of corporate governance.

Henceforth, the PSB boards will enjoy the freedom to carry out their functions efficiently, subject to the statutory requirements, Government policy prescription and regulatory guidelines issued by the Reserve Bank of India from time to time.

Under the existing norms, the banks are required to follow the Government guidelines even on managerial and routine administrative issues. This, according to a Finance Ministry statement, is now being replaced by a frame work, under which all such issues are driven by policy prescriptions of the bank boards, along lines comparable with their global counterparts.

The PSBs will be allowed the freedom to pursue new lines of business as part of their overall business strategy.

They will also be permitted to make suitable acquisitions of companies or businesses. This includes both closure and/or merger of unviable branches, opening overseas offices, setting up subsidiaries as also exiting a particular line of business.

Human Resource Issue

The PSB boards will also be at liberty to decide on all human resource issues relating to the bank, including staffing pattern, recruitment, placement, transfer, training, promotions and pensions.

They will also be allowed to prescribe standards for categorization of branches based on the volume of business and other factors and fix norms for essential academic qualification standards and modalities of promotion/recruitment.

The boards will also be free to visits foreign countries to interact with investors, depositors and other stakeholders as well as lay down a policy of accountability and responsibility of bank officials.

Additional Autonomy

The Board of Directors of the stronger PSBs, with a capital adequacy ratio of nine per cent or more, net non-productive assets of less than four per cent, net profits over the last three years and minimum owned funds of Rs. 300 crores, will have additional autonomy to frame their own HR policies and procedures for recruitment, create additional posts of general managers, sanction differential pay linked to performance within the pay scales decided after negotiations, and decide the contribution to the staff welfare fund. All the PSBs will now function as if they were board-managed companies.

The liberalization comes close on the heels of the Government's decision to allow the PSBs to enter the market to raise fresh capital for meeting the Base II requirements, and thereby dilute the Centre's stake to the minimum majority level of 51 per cent.

CORPORATE SOCIAL RESPONSIBILITY, THE BPCL (BHARAT PETROLEUM CORPORATION LTD.) WAY

Under the Component Plan, BPCL has been adopting villages and initiating a series of activities towards sustainable development:

1. Infrastructure development like provision of tube wells/dug wells for drinking water and irrigation.
2. Construction of a multi purpose Community Centre to accommodate school (non-formal education)/Balwadi/Health Centre/Community centre.
3. Construction of sanitation block to promote hygiene.
4. Education support–provision of uniforms notebooks, stationery, teaching material, educational aids and sweaters.
5. Health care – Regular health check-up of villagers by doctors; provision of free medicines for minor ailments; guidance on family welfare and general health care; free medical dispensaries; cataract surgery and intra ocular lens treatment.
6. Adult education, modern farming practices, verterinary camps, cattle camps, distribution of smokeless chulhas/solar cookers/sewing machines etc.
7. Provision of altenate sources of energy like photo-voltaic solar energy base streetlights and lighting for village and Community Centre.
8. Provision of Biogas plant to avoid felling of forest wood.
9. Educationali Scholarships of Rs. 200/- to children from the economically backward classes for pursuing their studies, till they complete their education.
10. Aptitude testing and vocational guidance are conducted for higher secondary children through experienced psychologists
11. Vocational training on pisci-culture, beekeeping, goat-rearing poultry, bamboo artefacts, tailoring and sari weaving to women, and they display their work at exhibitions.
12. Creation of awareness on social issues and education, folklore is through colloquial songs, which grasp the attention of villagers.
13. "New Insights in Fishing" given, on new mechanisms in fishing and also to make and market products out of fish and other marine catches like crabs etc.
14. To give recognition to the excellent performance of the school as well as the student, the Bharat Petroleum Shield of Excellence is given to students, who are in the merit list in Std. X.

ARGUMENTS FOR AGAINST SOCIAL INVOLVEMENT OF BUSINESS

Arguments for Social Involvement of Business

1. Public needs have changed, leading to changed expectations. Business, it is suggested, received its charter from society and consequently has to respond to the needs of society.
2. The creation of a better social environment benefits both society and business.

Society gains through better neighborhoods and employment opportunities; business benefits from a better community, since the community is the source of its workforce and the consumer of its products and services.

3. Social involvement discourages government regulation and intervention. The result is greater freedom and more flexibility in decision making for business.
4. Business has a great deal of power that, it is reasoned, should be accompanied by an equal amount of responsibility.
5. Modern society is an interdependent system, and the internal activities of the enterprise have an impact on the external environment.
6. Social involvement may be in the interests of stockholders.
7. Problems can become profits. Items that may once have been considered waste (e.g., empty soft-drink cans) can be profitably used again.
8. Social involvement creates a favourable public image. As a result, the firm may attract customers, employees, and investors.
9. Business should try to solve the problems that other institutions have not been able to solve. After all, business has a history of coming up with novel ideas.
10. Business has the resources. Specifically, business should use the talents of its managers and specialists, as well as its capital resources, to solve some of society's problems.
11. It is better to prevent social problems through business involvement than to cure them. It may be easier to help the hard-core unemployed than to cope with social unrest.

Arguments against Social Involvement of Business

1. The primary task of business is to maximize profit by focusing strictly on economic activities. Social involvement could reduce economic efficiency.
2. In the final analysis, society must pay for the social involvement of business through higher prices. Social involvement would create excessive costs for business, which cannot commit its resources to social action.
3. Social involvement can create a weakened international balance-of-payment situation. The cost of social programs, the reasoning goes, would have to be added to the price of the product. Thus, socially involved companies selling in international markets would be at a disadvantage when competing with companies from other countries that do not have these social costs to bear.
4. Business has enough power, and additional social involvement would further increase its power and influence.
5. Businesspeople lack the social skills to deal with the problems of society. Their training and experience are with economic matters, and their skills may not be pertinent to social problems.
6. There is a lack of accountability of business to society. Unless accountability can be established, business should not get involved.
7. There is not full support for involvement in social actions. Consequently, disagreements among groups with different viewpoints will cause friction.

BUDGET FOR THE YEAR 2005-06

The budget for the fiscal year 2005-06 has been termed as a positive budget, with an, emphasis on rural development, education, job creation and infrastructure growth, thus paving the way for a higher growth rate of gross domestic product (GDP) over the medium to long term, The budget proposed a substantial tax reduction for lower-bracket taxpayers, thus potentially boosting domestic consumption, where consumer related sectors such as housing, consumer durables and the like have contributed significantly to incremental GDP growth over the past 2-3 years. The reduction in corporate income tax will also addto the profitability of the corporate sector, It was also predicted that interest rates and inflation would remain largely range-bound through calendar year 2005; equities to do well over the medium to long term, driven by strong macroeconomic fundamentals, robust corporate earnings growth, a sustained interest by FIIs and greater participation by domestic investors, After a record $8.5 billion net inflow from FIIs in calendar year 2004, equally sizeable net inflows for calendar year 2005 can be expected.

There are many positives for the capital markets, the most important being the commitment to develop the corporate debt markets. What stands out in the budget is the Finance Minister's progressive moves towards rationalisation of tax structure in both direct and indirect taxes, widening the tax base and simplification of processes for tax administration. These changes should result in greater tax-compliance and an increase in disposable income on an aggregate level and spur consumption spending by consumers, Rationalisation of personal income tax slabs along with scrapping the deductions under Section 88 and 80L and bringing all deductions under one overall ceiling of the new Section 80C with Rs. 1 lakh limit is a significant step forward. These measures will bring in long-term money into the capital market with greater participation by domestic retail investors as well. The budget continues with broad reforms that are necessary for propelling and sustaining Indian growth rate in the 8 per cent per annum range. The industry also has reacted to the budget favourably and accordingly the Union Budget 2005-06 is termed as "growth-oriented" "The proposals to enhance the competitiveness of manufacturing sector, reform of customs and excise duties are positive. The 'Bharat Nirman' is a constructive futurist plan was the commonly shared response of the captains of the Indian Industry, Describing it as a balanced budget focused on growth and social justice, they said that the fundamental aim of this Government seemed to further the reform process and foundation for it has been laid down.

The following highlights in respect of direct taxes, indirect taxes, reform measures and new proposals of the budget may be noted (*Source*: The Hindu dated March 1, 2005).

Direct Taxes

- Income between Rs. 1 lakh-1.5 lakhs to be taxed at 10%.
- 20% tax on income between Rs. 1.5 lakhs and Rs. 2.5 lakhs.
- 30% tax for income above Rs. 2.5 lakhs.
- Income up to Rs. 1.5 lakhs exempt for senior citizens.
- Tax exemption up to Rs. 1.25 lakhs for women.

- No rebate under section 88. Section 80 L goes.
- 30% tax on fringe benefits, conveyance, canteen expenses exempted.
- Corporate tax at 30%, surcharge at 10%.
- 10% surcharge on taxable income above Rs. 10 lakhs.
- Tax on cash withdrawals over Rs. 10, 000 a day.

Indirect Taxes

- Surcharge on tea goes, no excise on refined edible oil and vanaspati.
- 2% excise duty on branded jewellery.
- Excise duty on imitation jewellery cut to 8%.
- Excise duty on tyres, A/Cs, polyester filament yarn cut.
- Excise duty on mosaic tiles at 8%.
- Specific duty on cement clinkers and molasses up.
- Excise duty on non-farm tractors.
- Customs duty on select capital goods, parts cut.
- Customs duty on textile machinery import slashed.
- Hand-made matches fully exempted from excise duty.

Reform Measures

- RBI Act to be amended.
- Changes in Banking Regulation Act coming.
- Mutual funds to introduce Gold Exchange Traded Funds.
- New law to improve environment for SMEs.
- 108 items identified for dereservation.
- Farm procurement to be decentralized.
- Working group to vet new pricing for fertilizer.
- Move to make Mumbai a regional financial hub.
- Panel to suggest steps to popularize corporate bond market and securitisation.
- Reserve Bank prepares road map for foreign banks' presence.

New Proposals

- Backward Regions Grant Fund set up.
- Bharat Nirman to be a business plan.
- Package to nurse sick sugar mills back to health.
- Cluster approach to help handloom units.
- Capital subsidy for textile processing industry.
- Fellowships for SCs/STs to pursue M. Phil and Ph.D.

- New scheme to beef up farm marketing infrastructure.
- Greater role for NGOs in micro-finance field.
- Expert panel to examine price stabilization fund for plantation sector.
- RBI to study agency model for banks to provide agricultural credit.

FDI in mining, Retail Trade and Pension Sectors under Study

The Finance Minister, while refraining from making any announcements on liberalising foreign direct investments, indicated that the mining, retail trade and pension sectors were areas where proposals were under consideration, The Government proposes to come forward with suitable proposals. He referred to the fact that China had received $500 billion of investment since it opened its economy in 1980, of which $60 billion came during the calendar year 2004. "Our own experience has been that the automobile, software, telecommunication and electronic sectors have benefited from FDI and assimilated themselves into the global production' chain", he said, adding that there were opportunities also in other sectors like mining, trade and pensions.

Proposals Relating to the Financial Sector

The Finance Minister, articulating the recent policy measures contemplated for banking,, said that a roadmap for banking sector reforms would be unveiled by the Reserve Bank of India. For this, some legislative measures will be necessary. He also announced new legislative initiatives to make the statutory pre-emptions in banks-SLR and CRR-more flexible, This way thc RBI could impart greater liquidity to the market, With the time-bound changeover (by March 31, 2007) by Indian banks to the Basel II capital adequacy norms, the budget makes a reference to the tasks on-hand. The budget contemplates legislative and other measures to allow banks to issue preference shares which, under specified conditions, can be treated as regulatory capital under the new Basel norms, For better supervision of banks and their subsidiaries specific measures in line with the best international practice are proposed to be issued. As regards capital market, while the securities transactions tax has been marked up for certain categories, greater significance is attached to the measures intended to popularise derivatives and the bond market, FIIs will be permitted to bring in collateral when trading in derivatives, The Minister has promised to remove the legal ambiguities that have stood in the way of over-the-counter (OTC) derivatives becoming more popular. OTC derivatives are customised, risk mitigating instruments, popular in the developed markets, Legislative measures to expand the definition of securities to provide a legal framework for trading in securitised debt has been promised. An expert committee is proposed to be appointed to look into the corporate bond market in its entirety and suggest measures for popularising it. Further, with gold as the underlying asset mutual funds will be asked to market gold exchange traded bonds.

The following editorial comments may also be covered[5]. These summarise the reactions to the various budget proposals and provide an overall summary picture.

- The stimulus for industrial growth has been either selective for specific industries or has bee in the form of simplification and ratlonalisatlon of tax laws.

---

5 Source: The Hindu dated 1st March 2005.

- It would perhaps be an exaggeration to term the budget proposals a new deal for rural India, but the outlays for employment, education, health, and water supply for the rural areas have been stepped up substantially. The national rural employment guarantee scheme assuring 100 days of employment in a year for an adult member of every rural; family was the most far reaching of the programmes offered.
- Substantial reforms have been promised though in the area of agricultural credit to provide easier access for the farmers and other borrowers.
- In the area of taxes, the emphasis has been on rationalising the rates and the tax structures and bringing in a simpler and non-distorting regime with fewer slabs, lower rates and minimal exemptions.
- The move towards an East Asian level of customs tariffs continues, with the peak import duty cut from 20 to 15 per cent, and the duty on capital goods used in industries such as textiles, information technology and telecommunications reduced to encourage investment,
- Following the thrust of the Kelkar committee recommendations, the income tax rates have been reduced, with a marginal rate of 30 per cent and a surcharge of 10 per cent to apply beyond Rs 10 lakh, and the plethora of exemptions for savings replaced by a single consolidated exemption of Rs. 1 lakh.

The following are the Editorial comments from the Financial Express, dated March 1, 2005:

- Bharat Nirman; a scheme for building infrastructure, especially in the rural areas takes pride of place.
- Whether it is in operationalising the National Horticulture mission or in setting aside money for micro irrigation, flood management and erosion control, or announcing new improved schemes for farm insurance, including micro insurance, the budget is not short on new schemes.
- Emboldened by the higher than budgeted customs collection despite the reduction in duty effected over the years, peak customs duty has been cut to 15%, Better still, customs duties on capital goods and raw materials have been cut and inverted duty structures that militate against value addition corrected. Textiles, food processing, pharma, biotech and leather have come in for special treatment. Customs duty on machinery meant for these sectors have been drastically slashed, in some cases down to 5%, on the excise front, too, a fair amount of rartionalisation has been affected.
- Markets have already given the thumbs-up-the Sensex rose by a dizzying 144 points, to touch a new record of 6,714, Economies react slower. But we are sure it is only a matter of time before the Indian economy, too, cottons on to the intrinsic soundness of Budget 2005.

Select extracts from Budget Speech: Financial Sector and Capital market.

The incipient investment boom in infrastructure, industry (including housing), and services needs to be nurtured through further reforms in the financial sector including reforms in bank finance and debt and equity markets.

Banking

The banking sector presents a picture of paradoxes. There are many banks in India but none among the top twenty in the world. Our largest bank, the State Bank of India, ranks 82 in terms of business. It is universally acknowledged that the key drivers of the banking sector in the future will be Competition, Consolidation and Convergence. RBI has prepared a road map for banking sector reforms and will unveil the same. While most proposals will be implemented by the RBI on its own authority, some legislative changes would be required to be made.

I had promised that comprehensive Bill to amend the Banking Regulation Act, 1949 will be introduced in the Budget Session. In consultation with the RBI, I propose to introduce amendments to the Act.

- to remove the lower and upper bounds to the statutory liquidity ratio (SLR) and provide flexibility to RBI to prescribe prudential norms;
- to allow banking companies to issue preference shares, since preference share capital can be treated as regulatory capital under specified circumstances as per Basel norms;
- to introduce specific provisions to enable the consolidated supervision of banks and their subsidiaries by RBI in consonance with the international best practices in this regard;

I also propose to introduce amendments to the Reserve Bank of India Act, 1934.

- To remove the limits of the cash reserve ratio (CRR) to facilitate more flexible conduct of monetary policy; and
- To enable RBI to lend or borrow securities by way of repo, reverse repo or otherwise.

PFRDA

With increasing longevity, the problem of old-age income security can no longer be ignored. Government had announced a defined contribution pension scheme for newly recruited Central Government employees which would also be extended to the unorganized sector. I am happy to inform the House that seven State Governments– Andhra Pradesh, Chhatisgarh, Himachal Pradesh, Jharkhand, Manipur, Rajasthan and Tamil Nadu - have introduced similar schemes for their employees. Other States have also evinced interest. An Ordinance was promulgated on December 29, 2004 to set up a Pension Fund Regulatory and Development Authority (PFRDA). I propose to introduce a Bill to replace the Ordinance during this session.

Through the new scheme, it is proposed to offer a menu of investment choices to the subscriber and to provide a strong regulatory mechanism to ensure that the interests of subscribers are protected. I appeal to workers all over the country to join the new pension system.

Capital Market

The capital market has emerged as a major vehicle for converting savings into investment. It is also the preferred investment destination of foreign savings. The steps announced by me last July, and implemented, have strengthened the capital market. It is time for more measures and, hence, I propose to

- authorize Securities and Exchange Board of India (SEBI) to set up a National Institute of Securities Markets for teaching and training intermediaries in the securities markets and promoting research; and
- permit FIIs to submit appropriate collateral, in cash or otherwise, as prescribed by SEBI, when trading in derivatives on the domestic market.

While India's equity market has made progress, the corporate bond market still lags behind. In order to address this gap, I propose to –

- amend the definition of 'securities' under the Securities Contracts (Regulation) Act, 1956 so as to provide a legal framework for trading of securitized debt including mortgage backed debt; and
- appoint a high level Expert Committee on corporate bonds and securitization to look into the legal, regulatory, tax and market design issues in the development of the corporate bond market.

Over the Counter (OTC) Derivatives

Over the counter (OTC) derivatives play a crucial role in mitigating the risks of corporates, banks and other financial entities. There is, however, some ambiguity regarding the legality of OTC derivative contracts which has inhibited their growth. I, therefore, propose to take measures to provide for clear legal validity of such contracts.

Stamp Duty on Stock Exchange Corporation

The Securities Contracts (Regulation) Act, 1956, as amended recently, requires all stock exchanges to be corporatized and de-mutualized. Three stock exchanges are not yet corporatized. In order to facilitate their corporatization, I propose to grant a one-time exemption to them from stamp duty on the notional transfer of assets.

Stamp Duty on Commercial Paper

In order to create a level playing field for banks and non-bank entities to issue commercial paper, and to bring the Indian commercial paper market closer to international standard, I propose to rationalize the stamp duty so that it applies uniformly regardless of the issuing entity.

Mumbai-A Regional Financial Centre

When I look at the map of the world, I am struck by the strategic location of Mumbai. It lies almost midway between London and Tokyo, two nerve centers of world finance. Mumbai is also home to the National Stock Exchange (NSE) and the Bombay Stock Exchange (BSE) which now rank no. 3 and no. 5 among the stock exchanges of the world by the number of trades per year. In the last decade, we have built world class institutions on the securities markets and we now compare with the best in terms of technological sophistication, risk management and sound governance. I believe the time has come to begin work on making Mumbai a regional hub for finance. In consultation with the RBI, I propose to appoint a high powered Expert Committee to advise the Government on how to make Mumbai a regional financial centre.

Gold Units

Ten years ago we embarked on the process of ensuring that gold inflows are through the official channels alone. I believe that we are now in a position to introduce 'gold units'. and create a market for such units. I propose to ask SEBI to permit, in consultation with RBI, mutual funds to introduce Gold Exchange Traded Funds (GETFs) with gold as the underlying asset, in order to enable any household to buy and sell gold in units for as little as Rs. 100. Such units could be traded in the same manner as units of mutual funds.

BANKING SECTOR REFORMS

The Finance minister, noting that the Government attached the highest Importance to maintaining price stability, complimented the RBI for Its efforts In containing inflationary expectations during the current year Declaring that he was looking forward to a year of growth, low inflation and a benign Interest rate scenario, he said that he expected banks to become more competitive and efficient and thus lower their spreads that were still high, Welcoming the Finance Minister's various initiatives, particularly with regard to rural credit, the directors of RBI desired greater thrust on an appropriate interest rate environment, risk mitigation and warehouse receipt facilities in the context of their relevance to the large rural population. They hailed the minister's concern for preventing tax evasion and suggested various measures to encourage the "cheque habit" and widen the tax base, The RBI Governor specifically mentioned the budget announcements relating to the proposed amendments to the Banking Regulation Act and the Reserve Bank of India Act and noted that these would provide the basis for the next stage of banking sector reforms.

The Finance Minister has observed that competition, consolidation and convergence would be the key drivers of the banking sector in India and elsewhere. The roadmap for the banking sector unveiled by the RBI on budget day reconciles the often conflicting positions of the several players—the foreign banks, the domestic private banks and other stakeholders, In this connection, the following comments on the opening up the FDI route for the banking sector, may be usefully quoted: "For the banking sector, opening up FDI route connotes several issues. Infusing foreign capital has been thought of as a way to resurrect weak banks in the private sector. One new generation bank, the Centurion Bank was rescued by the infusion of foreign direct investment, Greater clarity on the FDI issue will obviously benefit foreign banks such as the HSBC that has been unable to pick up an additional stake in the UTI Bank, In short, mergers and acquisitions within the banking sector may become more common if foreign direct investment is allowed more easily."[6]

The road map for foreign banks: The roadmap visualises changes in two distinct phases, During the first phase beginning March 2005 and ending March 2009, foreign banks can establish wholly owned subsidiaries (WOS) or convert existing branches into WOS, Detailed guidelines have been issued by the RBT, They cover the eligibility criteria for the applicant foreign bank, ownership pattern, international ranking and capital adequacy (at least Rs. 300 crores).

---

6 Banking reform-a balancing act, the Hindu dated 7th March 2005

INTRODUCTION OF BANKING REGULATION (AMENDMENT) BILL, 2005

On 13th May, the Finance Minister introduced two major banking legislations in the Lok Sabha and the measure is expected to usher in major reforms in the financial sector. The long awaited Banking Regulation (Amendment) Bill, 2005 seeks to lift the existing 10 per cent ceiling on the voting rights of foreign banks irrespective of their equity holding in Indian banks. In effect, the legislation seeks to provide voting rights to foreign banks in proportion to their equity stake in the domestic banks, The Bill also provides that any person acquiring more than 5 per cent equity stake in an Indian bank will have to obtain the prior approval of the Reserve Bank of India.

The second legislation seeks to amend the Reserve Bank of India Act to provide, among other things, more operational flexibility to the central bank to fix the Statutory Liquidity Ratio (SLR) and the Cash Reserve Ratio (CRR) so as to make available more funds for productive growth. It also seeks to empower the RBI to deal in derivatives, lend or borrow securities, undertake repo or reverse repos and the other monetary instruments for checking excess or inadequate liquidity. Also, by making its regulatory powers more effective, the RBI is proposed to be given powers to order special audits of cooperative banks for more effective supervision in public interest. According to the statement of objects and reasons, the amendments to the Banking Regulation Act is to enable the RBI to specify acquisition of a minimum percentage of shares in a banking company, if considered necessary. The Bills immediately after introduction in the House, were referred to the Parliament Standing Committee on Finance.

CREDIT INFORMATION COMPANIES

A Bill to set up and regulate credit information companies received the approval of Parliament on 13th May, after the Lok Sabha cleared it on the assurance of finance Minister that the Government meant business in bringing down the non-performing assets (NPAs) of banks. The Credit Information Companies (Regulation) Bill provides legislative support to the business of credit information to equip banks to deal with NPAs by providing information regarding credit-worthiness of various categories of customers. The Minister, however, explained that the Bill was aimed at preventing accretion of NPAs and had nothing to do with the current NPAs. The Minister informed the House that the gross NPAs of banks had declined from Rs. 70,861 crores in 2002 to Rs. 64,786 crores in 2004.

RBI GUIDELINES FOR PRIVATE BANKS M&As

In May, the Reserve Bank of India has instructed banks to ensure that the decision on merger is approved by two-third majority of the total, board members and not those present alone, thus placing the onus on the boards of private sector banks in the event of mergers and acquisition among banks. It has also stated, "in view of the importance of the responsibility implicit in such merger decisions, it will be necessary that the directors, who participate in such meetings, are signatories to the Deeds of Covenants as recommended by the Ganguly Working Group on Corporate Governance".

The RBI has laid down guidelines for the process of merger proposal, determination of swap ratios, disclosures, the stages at which boards; will get involved in the merger process and norms of buying and selling of shares by the promoters before and during the process of merger. The guidelines cover two situations of mergers and amalgamations; an amalgamation of two banking companies and amalgamation of a non-banking finance company (NBFC) with a banking company. Further, where an NBFC is proposed to be amalgamated into a banking company, the banking company should obtain the approval of the RBI after the scheme of amalgamation is approved by its board but before it is submitted to the High Court for approval. The insider trading regulations stipulated by the Securities and Exchange Board of India will, be applicable for bank mergers and acquisitions.

DEFAULTS BY NIDHIS: EXPERT GROUP TO CURB INSTANCES OF DEFAULT

The Ministry of Company Affairs is planning to set up an expert group to examine any lacunae in the existing norms governing the nidhi companies or mutual benefit societies (MBS) and to suggest measures to curb instances of default by such entities. The move has been prompted by continuous instances of default by Nidhi companies or MBS, official sources said. The Government wants to take immediate steps to curb such defaults and if need be, it would like to further tighten the norms governing such entities, as it is mainly investors who are affected. Noting that Nidhi companies required improved regulatory framework to strengthen their functioning and also to instill confidence in the minds of the investors, the Ministry had notified necessary change in the norms in July 2001.

The notification prescribing the supervisory framework and prudential norms, on the pattern of NBFCs, were later revised in April 2002 at the instance of Chamber of Nidhis and Federation of Benefit Funds Despite stringent parameters set by the government, it continues to receive depositor complaints against the defaulting entities, including the Chennai-based RBF Nidhi, The Nidhis, which have defaulted, include Kuber Mutual Benefits Ltd., Trikone Mutual Benefits, Ican. Mutual Benefit and Alwarpet Benefit Fund. Further it has been brought to the MCA's notice that despite the CLB's orders, there, are instances of default by such entities.

PART – III

COMPANY LAW AND BOARD MANAGEMENT

Company Law and Company Precedents

DUTIES OF DIRECTORS

Duties of directors may be broadly divided under two heads and these are duties called as statutory duties and the other, duties of a general nature. Statutory duties are based on specific provisions included or provided in the Company law. First we may cover the general duties of directors followed by discussion on company law provisions. Directors stand in a fiduciary relationship to the company and they are agents and trustees in certain respects; they are also bound to exercise a reasonable degree of skill and care in the performance of their duties. The general duties of directors are

(a) Duty of good faith

(b) Duty of care

(c) Duty to attend board meetings

(d) Duty not to delegate and some other duties

(a) Duty of Good Faith

The directors must act in the best interest of the company. He should not make any secret profits. He should also not exploit to his own use the corporate opportunity (Cook v Veeks (1916) AC 554). Directors are not at liberty to sacrifice the interest of the company while ostensibly acting for the company.

(b) Duty of Care

A director must display care in the performance of work assigned to him. A director must exercise some degree of skill and diligence. However, directors are not liable for mere errors of judgment. They are required to take such care as is to be reasonably expected of them having regard to their knowledge and experience; if they act honestly for the benefit of the company, they discharge both their equitable and legal duty to the company. Company's articles cannot exclude the liability of directors for negligence, default, misfeasance, breach of duty or breach of trust (S.201).

(c) Duty to attend Board Meetings

A director should take care to attend meetings held from time to time and he should not fail to attend three consecutive meetings or all meetings for a period of three months, whichever is longer, without permission and if there is failure, his office shall automatically fall vacant.

(d) Duty not to Delegate

A director must perform his functions personally. However exceptions have been provided and he may delegate where permitted by the Companies Act or articles of the company and also having regard to the exigencies of business, certain functions may be delegated to other officials of the company.

Some of the other duties of directors include convening statutory, annual and extraordinary general meetings, to prepare and place at the annual general meeting a report on the company's affairs along with the-balance-sheet and profit and loss account; when there is a member's voluntary winding up, a declaration of solvency is required to be made.

Statutory Duties

(a) The following provisions may be mentioned:

(b) To file return of allotments vide section 75 of the Companies Act 1955, stating the specified particulars.

(c) Not to issue irredeemable preference shares or shares redeemable after 20 years (S.80)

(d) To disclose interest vide Sections 299-300. In respect of contracts with a director, Section 299 casts an obligation on a director to disclose the nature of his concern or interest, if any, at a meeing of the board of directors. A general notice to the board by a director, has also been provided vide S.299(3)(a), for disclosure of concern or interest in relation to any contract or arrangment.

(e) To disclose receipt from transfer of property vide Section 319. Any money received by directors from the transferee in connection with the transfer of the company's property or undertaking must be disclosed to the members and approved by the company in general meeting.

(f) To disclose receipt of compensation from transferee of shares vide Section 320. If the loss of office results from the transfer of all or any of the shares of the company, directors would not receive any compensation from the transferee unless the same has been approved by the company in general meeting before the transfer takes place.

(g) To authenticate and approve annual financial statement vide S.215, to appoint first auditor vide S.224 and to appoint cost auditor vide S.233B etc..

The above list is not an exhaustive list, listing all the statutory duties of the directors.

In general, a director individually and a board of directors as a whole must act in accordance with legal standards spelled out by the Government, vide provisions of the Companies Act 1956. It is therefore essential that each director has a working knowledge of the Act and should know when to seek competent legal advice. A director, in reality cannot know everything nor be totally expert in every facet of a business. While they have the duty to be very careful in determining the facts, directors can rely on management and Experts for Information they do not have and judgments about which they are not expert. Directors need to follow the laws and build records of what they have done to protect themselves from challenges that have the advantage of hindsight.

The duty of supervision deals with the effectiveness with which directors exercise their oversight responsibilities. The duty of supervision, in order to be discharged effectively demands that directors know about the operations of management and also know what they should do when there is an issue or problem requiring attention. In fulfilling this duty, the board must establish policies of ethics and disclosure that set the standards for behaviour of directors. The board must also ensure that there are internal controls in- place. It must establish policies addressing which decisions require board approval and what information the board should receive regularly. The duty of supervision also calls for regular meetings of the boards to discuss the performance of the organisation. A director has to develop his intuitive sense as this provides him the ability to sense what needs to be questioned and also to press for access to relevant information.

The following rules of guidance have been suggested as duty of care commandments and the board is likely to have met its duty of care, if it

- Engages experienced legal counsel to design and manage the governance process and maintain appropriate records of the proceedings.
- Does not rush important decisions; at least not unnecessarily.
- Gives board members adequate prior notice- of important business to be conducted at a meeting.
- Distributes major documents or position papers to board members well in advance of meetings.
- If possible, has one or more informational meetings.
- Provides board members with adequate information to make an informed decision; this may also include opinion of expert advisers, management analysis and recommendations.
- Does not submit to the pressures of a domineering Chief Executive Officer.

The problems with the duty of loyalty could be avoided if the following principles are followed:

- An interested director must fully disclose any conflict of interest end the basis for it and in advance of related discussions.
- The interested director must not unduly influence discussion of the transaction, may need to leave the discussion and should abstain from voting on the issue.
- The proposed issued must be resolved by a majority of the disinterested directors.

LIABILITIES OF DIRECTORS

The liabilities of directors may be discussed under the following heads:

(a) Liability to the company

(b) Liability to third parties

(c) Liabilitis for breach of statutory duties

(d) liability for acts of co-directors

(e) Criminal liability.

Liability to the Company

Liability to the company may arise from breach of fiduciary duty, ultra vires acts, negligence and malafide acts. Where a director acts dishonestly to the interest of the company, he will be liable for breach of fiduciary duty. The powers of directors are 'powers in trust' and should be exercised in the interest of the company and not in the interest of the directors or any section of members (Hogg v. Cramphorm Ltd., 1967 Ch.

254); Ultra vires acts: Directors should act within the parameters of the provisions of the Companies Act and Memorandum and articles of the company. They may be held personally liable if they act beyond their powers. For example, if directors pay dividends or interest out of capital, they will be liable to indemnify the company for any loss or damage suffered due to such act. Negligence. If directors fail to exercise reasonable care, skill and diligence, they shall be deemed to have acted negligently and consequently liable for any loss or damage resulting there from. However error of judgment will not be deemed as negligence. In the case of mala fide acts, as they are trustees for the moneys and property of the company, if they dishonestly exercise their powers they will be liable for breach of trust and may be required to make good the loss or damage suffered. Directors are also accountable for any secret profits. If there is misfeasance that is misconduct or willful misuse of powers, they may be held liable. If there is misappropriation of money or property, Court may order to repay the money or restore the property or pay compensation. Where there is violation of statutory provisions, it has been held that the discretionary powers of the court under S.633 cannot be exercised in favour of the defaulters.

Liability to Third Parties

Liabilities to third parties may be either on account of liability under the provisions of the Companies Act 1956 or Liability for breach of warranty of authority. In the first category, reference may be made to the provisions of s. 56 making directors personally liable for mis-statement of facts in a prospectus, irregular allotment (S.69) etc. In the case of breach of warranty, where the transactions are ultra wires the company or ultra wires the articles, directors may be proceeded against personally for any loss sustained by any third party.

Liability for Breach of Statutory Duties

The Companies Act 1956 imposes numerous statutory duties on the directors and default in compliance of these duties attract penal consequences. For example, every director who fails to comply with the provisions of sub-section (4) of section 299 (disclosure of concern or interest) shall be punishable with fine which may extend to Rs. 50,000.

Liability for Acts of Co-directors

The absence of a director from meeting of the board does not make him liable for the fraudulent act of a co-director on the ground that he ought to have discovered the fraud, except where he had the knowledge or he was a party to confirm that action (Dovey v. Cory (1901) AC 477.

Criminal Liability

In addition to civil liability under the Act or under the common law, directors may also incur criminal liability under common law as well as under the Companies Act and other statutes. Some of the provisions, which may be quoted are: S.58A (5) (failure to repay deposits), S.63 issuing a prospectus containing untrue statement, S.207 default in distributing dividends, S. 209(5) Non compliance with the requirement of maintenance of proper books of account etc.

Directors also incur personal liability in certain circumstances, such as where they contract in their own names, where they use the company's name incorrectly, where it is not clear whether it is the principal (the company) or the agent who is signing and where they exceed their authority, e.g. where they borrow in excess of the limits imposed upon them.

It may also be useful to trace the reasons as to how Directors get into trouble. Some of them are:

- **Tolerating legal violations:** All boards should avoid any violation of laws. The most culpable act of boards is to intentionally conspire to defraud creditors or other stakeholders; unintentional violations due to ignorance or lax oversight may be equally troublesome
- **Poor results:** A board's best defence is to deliver strong positive results. The goal must be to conduct itself so as to make the right decisions that in turn, deliver favourable results. There may be a number of causes for poor results and these may include poor leadership, personality conflicts that may prove disruptive for the entire group, ineffective board organisation and processes etc. A primary duty of a board is to keep itself fully informed about the affairs of the company.
- **Small or large perquisites:** that directors are apt to find personally convenient or attractive. While there is a tendency to emulate other companies with regard to such perks, boards must keep in mind the negative impressions such uses of the shareholders' funds may invoke.
- **Lawsuits can be initiated by individuals or by entities:** There can be class-action suits that seek some remedy by a group of individuals or entities with some mutual dispute with the company. The various types of suits are almost limitless and are varied; most companies indemnify or protect their directors and officers from personal liability that might be incurred in the process of carrying out their duties as directors (indemnification insurance). However illegal acts of the board and/or directors are not indemnified.

THE ROLE OF NON-EXECUTIVE DIRECTORS

From an agency theory perspective, the presence of non-executive directors on company boards is considered essential, as this can help to reduce notorious conflicts of interest between shareholders and company management. They perform a monitoring function by introducing an independent voice to the boardroom. For an effective board and for achieving the appropriate balance between outside and inside directors on boards, the role of non-executive directors has been stressed. The inside directors provide valuable information about the firm's activities, while outside directors may contribute both expertise and objectivity. With the addition of non-executive directors, a powerful governance mechanism is possible to be achieved. If we should refer to the Cadbury Report, it has recommended that the board of directors should include a minimum of three non-executive directors. It stipulated that non-executive directors should provide an independent view on corporate strategy, performance, resources, appointments and standards of conduct. Further several ways of ensuring the independence of non-executive directors have been suggested. With regard to fees payable to non-executive directors, the Cadbury Report preferred that a balance needed to be struck between recognising the value of the contribution made by non-executive directors and avoiding compromising their independence. Yet another way was to encourage the non-executive directors not to take part in share option schemes. A formal selection process also strengthened their independence.

The Higgs Report was published on 20 January 2003 and the report recommended that at least half of company's board of directors should be independent non-executive directors. The report also made a progressive recommendation that is giving encouragement and linkage to two essential corporate governance mechanisms, namely the role of non-executive directors and the role of institutional investors. According to the report, such linkage should be synergistic, as the combination of the two mechanisms should result in a much stronger monitoring instrument than when they function separately. There was a call in the report for modest pay rises for non-executive directors to reflect their growing range of responsibilities. There is substantial quantity of academic literature indicting that boards of directors perform an important corporate governance function and that non-executive directors act as necessary monitors of management. Without such monitoring function, it was considered to be more likely that inside executive directors would be able to manipulate their position by gaining complete control over their own remuneration packages and securing their jobs. There was also evidence to suggest that the turnover of chief executives was more strongly related to company performance in companies characterised by a majority of non-executive directors. In relation to hostile takeover bids, empirical evidence shows that boards with a significant independent contingent benefit shareholders in the bidding process. Evidence of a positive share price reaction to their appointment was also noticed.

In USA people are less and less inclined to become involved in companies as either inside or outside directors, given the potentially frightening repercussions from Sarbanes-Oxley. If non-executive directors are meant to bring impartiality into the boardroom, the question for legislators is the extent to which legal liability, including criminal sanctions, should attach to the role of non-executive directors. It would therefore be a significant disincentive to people considering a position as a non-executive director.

THE CORPORATE GOVERNANCE AUDIT

Is your company's board really equipped and empowered to govern? Use this diagnostic to determine the efficacy of your company's directors:

1. Does your board include...
   - *(a)* One external director for each internal director? 2
   - *(b)* Two external directors for each internal director? 5
   - *(c)* Three or more external directors for each internal director? 10
2. Does you board comprise...
   - *(a)* Directors who have experience only in your industry? 2
   - *(b)* Directors with experience in other related industries too? 5
   - *(c)* Directors with experience in related as well as unrelated industries 10
3. Is the agenda for your board...

	(a) Set by the CEO with inputs from internal directors?	2
	(b) Set by the CEO with inputs from all, directors?	5
	(c) Flexible and set in keeping with emerging requirements?	10
4.	Are the agenda and reading materials for your board circulated ...	
	(a) Two weeks prior to the meeting?	2
	(b) Three weeks prior to the meeting?	5
	(c) At least a month in advance?	10
5.	Is the typical board meeting...	
	(a) Structured so as to offer only token discussions of each issue?	2
	(b) Structured so as to ensure enough time for discussions?	5
	(c) Structured so as to always ensure time for free-wheeling exchanges?	10
6.	Is the nomination of a new board member handled ...	
	(a) By the CEO after getting inputs from all directors?	2
	(b) By a nominations committee with strong inputs from the CEO?	5
	(c) By a nonnations committee with inputs from all directors?	10
7.	Board members are replaced...	
	(a) When a director wishes to step down.	2
	(b) When one, or more, directors do not attend meetings	5
	(c) On the basis of a formal evaluation of directors	10
8.	Is the audit committee of the board...	
	(a) Involved in selecting the audit firm from a short-list?	2
	(b) Asked to recommend to the board which audit firm to use?	5
	(c) Asked to make its recommendations and to approve the choice?	10
9.	Does the audit committee establish its agenda...	
	(a) On the basis of the internal auditors' suggestions?	2
	(b) With complete freedom to choose its areas of investigation?	5
	(c) After setting priorities for systematic study of high-exposure areas?	10
10.	Does the compensation committee base its recommendations...	
	(a) Using inputs from the human resource department?	2
	(b) On the basis of historical trends and industry practices?	5
	(c) On pre-established standards and a formula-based reward system?	10

The Rating

20-33 Out of control. Your board is probably a liability.

35-70 Barely in control and things could get worse.

72-100 In control. Your board is an asset for your company.

Adapted from the Case for an Off Balance-Sheet Controller by R.F Lusch & M.G. Harvey, Sloan Management Review, Winter, 1994.

AUDIT COMMITTEES

Audit committees play a critical role in corporate governance. This committee of corporate boards has been drawing a critical eye of regulators, legislators and investors. When it is noticed that corporate giants plunge with startling speed to the brink of bankruptcy because of misleading, if not fraudulent, reporting of financial results, the business organisations as well as regulators have started seeking answers as how such shocking events were able to occur. Their investigations have led them paying attention to the constitution and functioning of audit committees. It was considered necessary that members of this committee must be wise, insightful and thorough in carrying out their duties. It was preferred that audit committees should be guided by sound guiding principles, such as having basic values of integrity and the expectation of legal compliance, forthright financial reporting and strong financial controls. A written charter, qualified and diligent members, members who can have direct, independent communications with both external and internal auditors and guarantee compliance with generally accepted accounting principles (GAAP) and also timely disclosure of all relevant information to the public were all considered to be the essential guiding principles.

Roles and Responsibilities

The roles and responsibilities of the audit committee should include the following:

- Ensuring that there is a well-defined, well-written, and well-communicated code of ethical standards and guidelines for acceptable behaviour, on which a climate of integrity is built and well established.
- Ensuring the adequacy of internal control policies, systems and practices that promote the effectiveness and efficiency of operations, reliability of financial reporting, and compliance with applicable laws and regulations.
- Selecting, evaluating and replacing the independent auditor subject to board and/or stockholder approval
- Reviewing in a timely manner all annual and interim financial statements; including the management's discussion and analysis, auditor's comments and suggestions, and any significant accounting or reporting issues.
- Reviewing the process of compliance with all laws and any legal matters that could have a significant impact on financial statements.
- Ensuring that business risks are identified and that appropriate actions are taken to monitor them and minimize exposure to them.

Section 292A of the Companies Act 1956

The above provision in the Companies Act requires every public company having paid up capital of not less than rupees five crore to constitute an audit committee as a committee of the board of directors. Sub-section (2) of Section 292A mandates that the audit committee shall act in accordance with terms of reference to be specified in writing by the board of directors. The audit committee is required to discuss periodically with the auditors about internal control system, the scope of audit and the observation of the auditors. The committee is statutorily required to review the half yearly and annual financial statements before submission to the Board and to ensure compliance of internal control systems in the company. The audit committee should hold periodic discussions with the auditors on the internal control systems, the scope of audit and observations of the auditors. The annual report of the company should disclose the composition of the audit committee. The committee's recommendations on 'financial management including audit report' have been made binding on the Board.

AUDIT AND CORPORATE GOVERNANCE

The external audit represents one of the important corporate governance checks and balances that help to monitor company management's activities. The audit increases transparency. The Cadbury Report also has emphasised that "The annual audit is one of the cornerstones of corporate governance".

The audit provides an external and objective check on the way in which financial statements have been prepared and presented. The audit function represents another important corporate governance mechanism that helps shareholders in their monitoring and control of company management. The audit makes disclosures more credible; it plays an important role in contract monitoring; the audited earnings numbers are also used for a number of purposes, such as bonus payments. In the case of Enron, failure of the audit function was one of the principal factors that contributed to the company's downfall. Therefore, the existence of an 'audit expectations gap' needs to be acknowledged. According to the Cadbury Report, it is important to bear in mind that the auditor's role is not to prepare the financial statements, nor to provide absolute assurance that the figures in the financial statements are correct, nor to provide a guarantee that the company will continue as a going concern, but the auditors have to state in the annual report that the financial statements show 'a' true and fair view rather than 'the' true and fair view. The Cadbury report stressed on the effectiveness and objectivity of the audit. Some of the ways which could ensure and meet these requirements are covered in the following paragraphs.

The Cadbury report pointed out that auditor independence could be compromised due to the close relationship that is inevitable between auditors and company managers; The report stated that "The central issue is to ensure that an appropriate relationship exists between the auditors and the management whose financial statements they are auditing." Establishing audit committees and developing effective accounting standards were suggested as the most apt means of ensuring this balance. Another problem raised in the Cadbury Report regarding the independence and effectiveness of the audit function involves the multiple services offered by auditors to their clients. Auditing companies offer consultancy services and IT services to the companies that they audit. The response to this is to prohibit auditors from offering other services in order to prevent their objectivity from being compromised through inevitable conflicts of interest. However, finally a weaker recommendation was made in the Cadbury report that companies should disclose full details of fees paid to audit firms for non-audit services. The Smith Report (2003) recommendations centre around passing responsibility for auditor independence on to the audit committee function.

The Smith Report emphasised the essential role the audit committee should play in ensuring the independence: and objectivity of the external auditor, as well as in monitoring company management. The report provided that the main role and responsibilities of audit committee should be to: monitor the integrity of companies' financial statements; review companies' internal financial control systems; monitor and review the effectiveness of companies' internal audit functions; make recommendations to the board In relation to the appointment of the external auditor and approve the remuneration and terms of engagement of the external auditor; monitor and review the independence, effectiveness and objectivity of the external auditor; and develop and implement policy on the engagement of the external' auditor to supply non-audit services. The Smith report also highlighted the -need for the audit committee to be proactive, raising issues of concern with directors. The report further stressed that all members of the audit committee should be independent, non-executive directors. Companies' annual report its should disclose detailed Information on the role and responsibilities of their audit committee and action taken by the audit committee in discharging those responsibilities (Smith Report, 2003, p.17).

There is lot of literature in accounting that exposes serious flaws in the current system but offering no serious alternative. It may not be possible to overthrow the status quo till a viable system is found to replace it. A lot of support to impose the alternative may also be necessary.

ENRON'S COLLAPSE

In this section the various factors that led to the collapse of Enron and how it has encouraged corporate governance reform worldwide have been considered and detailed.

In the year 2001 Enron became a household name. On 2 December 2001, one of the 10 largest companies in the USA, filed for the Chapter 11 bankruptcy (a type of court protection giving the company management time to make arrangements with their creditors). In the months that followed, more and more evidence emerged of corporate governance weaknesses and fraudulent activity. It was started to be realised that corporate governance failure and corporate collapse can happen in the strongest company. Investors, employees and creditors could be seduced by a company's reputation and success and can throw caution to the wind.

Enron, which was created in 1985, over a period of 16 years was transformed from relatively small concern, involved in gas pipelines and oil and gas exploration, to the world's largest energy trading company. Deregulation of the energy market in the USA had a far-reaching impact, allowing energy providers to diversify into other areas of the industry and become more competitive. By 1997 the company was selling $4 billion, which constituted almost a fifth of the North American wholesale market. In 1999 Enron's sales reached $40.1 billion. By 2000 the company's revenues reached over $100 billion. In February 2001 the company's stock market value was $60 billion. Enron became famous for its dexterity in handling Risk management derivatives, as well as for its abilities in the area of commodity trading derivatives. At the end of 1999,Enron launched its Internet-based trading platform, EnronOnline. Thus toward the end of its life, Enron had transformed itself from an energy company to a predominantly financial and energy trading company, trading financial derivatives as well as energy contracts and effectively running a gas pipeline on the side.

In 1998 queries were raised as to the permanency of Enron's success. Causes of concern were the different speeds of deregulation in different states in America and therefore the ability to achieve free competition in all of the states relatively quickly. It was also brought out that the company's management team was arrogant, over ambitious and even sycophantic. In 1997 Enron wrote off $537 million, mainly in order to settle a contract dispute over North Sea Gas. The company also became notorious for relying too heavily on non-recurring items such as asset sales, to reach its target of 15% annual growth in earnings. It seems that Enron's success in controlling the energy market came more from its dexterity in energy derivatives trading than its abilities in the core business. Toward end of October 2001, Moody's credit rating agency cut Enron's rating to barely above that of junk bond status. A severe lack of transparency in Enron's balance sheet meant that no one was aware of this and other off-balance-sheet liabilities until it was too late. The main accusations in class action Lawsuits covered fraud and material misstatement in the companies' financial reports. The company was also accused of insider trading. Enron's top executives sold over $1 billion of Enron shares to other investors. Even though Enron's annual reports indicated financial prosperity, it was clear that Enron's management knew a lot more than they were letting on, making hay while the sun shone. Thus there was information asymmetry and agency problems, with insider investors profiting from transactions.

What went wrong? Both the audit function and accounting function in Enron were fraudulent and opaque. Enron's collapse also had repercussions on the whole of the accounting and auditing profession, not just in the USA but worldwide. Examples of Enron's devious accounting abound. It transpired that the company's exaggerated focus on its EPS was certainly a factor in its eventual decline. The pressure on companies in the USA and elsewhere to increase their EPS year on year has been blamed for corporate short termism. It was also found to have removed substantial amounts of debt from its accounts by setting up a number of off-balance sheet entities; they were used to hide the company's liabilities from the balance sheet, in order to make the financial statements look much better than they really are. While the fall of Enron was the biggest corporate collapse ever, the downfall of Anderson the most significant death of an accounting firm ever.

It was also found that independent appointment of the company's auditors by the company's shareholders was frequently replaced by subjective appointment by company bosses, where the auditor is all too often beholden to the company's senior management. There were conflicts of interest arising from interwoven functions of audit and consultancy. Such conflicts of interest impinge on the corporate governance function. The Financial Accounting Standards Board (FASB) in the USA has been forced to consider its position on off-balance sheet financing, a subject that has troubled them for years. FASB is also reviewing its rules on how to account for special Purpose entities (financing vehicles), such as those created and used by Enron. The rule-based approach to accounting traditionally applied by the USA has also come under fire, as it provides companies with an incentive to comply with the letter but avoid the spirit of the rules. It has been commented that a more principles-based approach, as that adopted in the UK, would probably encourage companies to comply more in substance than in form. Reference may also be made to the Sarbanes-Oxley Act, brought in quickly in July 2002, which attempted to address accounting fraud through regulation. Chief executives and chief financial officers are now required to swear that to the best of their knowledge their latest annual reports and quarterly reports neither contain untrue statements, nor omit any material fact. The new legislation is intended to encourage directors to act ethically and monitor their own financial accounting practices and policies more carefully. Severe corporate governance problems emerge from the Enron's case. Unfettered power in the hand of the chief executive is an obvious problem and one that characterised Enron's management. Separation of the chairman and chief executive role is not common in the USA and its application in the USA would benefit American companies and also their shareholders. The function of the non-executive directors in Enron was weak, as they did not detect fraudulent accounting activities through their internal audit function. Overall, corporate governance in Enron was weak in almost all aspects. The non-executive directors were compromised by conflicts of interest. The internal audit committee did not perform its functions of internal control and of checking the external audit function. Both the financial director and the chief executive were prepared to produce fraudulent accounts for the company. Continuous updating of corporate governance codes of practice and systematic review of corporate governance checks and balances are necessary to avoid other Enrons in the future.

DIRECTOR'S REPORT (BOARD'S REPORT)

The purpose of the Directors' report is to assist in the interpretation of the financial statements and to provide non-financial information to users of the annual report. It provides the means and methods to understand the operations of a company and its internal and external working relationships. The principal activities of the company are outlined with a broad description of the areas of business activity to be read in conjunction with the segmental notes. The directors' report normally contains details of:

- principal activities;
    - the review of the business and likely future developments;
    - dividends;
    - research and development activity;
- differences between market and balance sheet value of property;
- directors and their relationship with the company;
- employment policy; supplier payment policy; environmental issues;
- political charitable contributions;
- major interests in the company's shares;
- post-balance sheet events;
- auditors;
- compliance with code of best practice.

The review of the business should give details of developments that are likely to affect future profitability, such as the launch of a new product, major capital investment programmes/planned acquisitions and disposals. Important or significant events that have occurred after the end of the financial year should also be mentioned. Operational and financial review provided adds to the amount of information available in the standard financial statements. Typically, the operational and financial review covers:

- significant political, economic and environmental factors;
- analysis of changing market conditions;
- turnover trends and market share;
- changes in turnover and margins;
- product development, new products
- acquisitions, disposals and closures;
- the impact of foreign exchange, interest and inflation rates.

The Accounting Standards Board, which was responsible for the introduction of operational and financial review to the UK, has advised that companies should use the medium of annual report not only for reporting good news but also to disclose principal risks and uncertainties in the main lines of business and how it was proposed to manage such risks. Companies should describe their policies and strategies for using any financial instruments and detail their activities concerning: interest rate risk; market price risk; currency risk; financial assets and liabilities held for trading; and hedging activities.

S.217 of the Companies Act provides that there shall be attached to every balance sheet laid before a company in general meeting, a report by its Board of directors, with respect to the following:

(a) the state of the company's affairs,

(b) the amounts, if any, which it proposes to carry to any reserves in such balance sheet,

(c) the amount, if any, which it recommends, should be paid by way of dividend,

(d) material changes and commitments, if any, affecting the financial position of the company which have occurred between the end of the financial year of the company to which the balance sheet relates and the date of the report.The report of the Board of directors forms part of the annual report of the company which is sent to every member;

Directors' Responsibility Statement: Companies (Amendment) Act, 2000 has introduced sub-section (2AA) in section 217 of the Act, requiring inclusion of 'Directors' Responsibility Statement in the Boards' Report. This amendment is because of the importance attached to the concept of 'Corporate Governance by the regulators in order to safeguard the interests of persons having stakes in the company. This statement shall indicate that:

(i) in the preparation of the annual accounts, the applicable accounting standards had been followed;

(ii) the directors had selected such accounting policies and applied them consistently and made judgments and estimates that are reasonable and prudent so as to give a true and fair view of the state of affairs of the company;

(iii) the directors have taken proper and sufficient care for the mintenance of adequate accounting records in accordance with the provision of the Companies

act for safeguarding the assets of the company and for preventing and detecting fraud and other irregularities;

(iv) the directors have prepared the annual accounts on a going concern basis.

Management Discussion and Analysis Report

The 'Management discussion and analysis' report forms part of Directors' Report or as an addition thereto forming part of the annual report to the shareholders. This report covers financial and operational performance, industry structure and developments, outlook, opportunities, threats and risks, internal control system and human resources.

Report on Corporate Governance

A separate section on 'corporate governance' in the annual report with a detailed compliance report on corporate governance is to be provided. Corporate compliance has been divided into two parts, namely mandatory requirements and non-mandatory requirements. Disclosures about the mandatory requirements is to cover brief statement on company's philosophy on code of governance, details regarding composition of the board, their attendance at board meetings, Audit committee and its composition, the scope of reference to the audit committee, Remuneration committee, other committees like shareholders/investors grievances committee, share transfer committee, general body meetings, insider trading, disclosures regarding conflict with the interest of the company, means of communication, general shareholder information such as listing in stock exchanges, Transfer agents, distribution and pattern of shareholding, dematerialisation of shares etc.

Corporate Report and User Groups

The present legal emphasis for providing financial information about a company in annual reports may be said to be biased towards the needs of shareholders and creditors and such emphasis is now taken to be a narrow interpretation of the needs of stakeholders. Company legislation has traditionally sought to protect the interests of shareholders and creditors; In the modern commercial environment, however, other broader user groups also require periodic information. Who are the other user groups? The list includes, apart from existing and potential shareholders and creditors, employees, analysts and advisers, business contacts and suppliers, Government and the general public. Employees may wish to know the level of profit for wage-bargaining purposes, while the Government may use the figure for taxation computations. The potential shareholders will require information to aid in the decision to acquire shares in that particular company. Such information should be comparable from company to company. The information required will relate to past profits and dividend levels which may give an indication of future returns. The annual report and accounts only provides a guide to past performance; the decision whether to hold, buy or sell a share very much depends on its current price relative to the expected future returns from any particular company when compared to similar returns at a comparable risk level. Long-term creditors will be considering the security of their loan to the company and the potential of the company to service the loans, that is, meet interest payments when they fall due and repay the loan at the due date. The greatest threat to such creditors is the failure of the company, as the limited liability may mean the loan is not repaid in full. The investment managers and analysts, reading the accounts and commenting upon the performance of any company aids the flow of information to less sophisticated stakeholders and therefore provides the market for shares with a sound information base upon which investors can make informal judgments. In many ways the summaries and comments in the financial press provide a more useful database for investors than the annual report and accounts themselves. Suppliers will be looking for continuing and increasing trade with the company, subject to the ability to pay, while customers will wish to be assured of the continuation of supply at existing levels or at increased levels if they wish to expand. The regulatory authorities and the government sector in general would want to ensure that the company is complying with current legislation, in the form of various taxes payable, contracts of employment, pollution control etc., The financial information produced by companies is used particularly for assessing taxation levels on company profits. In the above context, additional statements in the corporate report have been suggested, such as a statement of corporate objectives, a statement of future prospects, a statement of transactions in foreign currency, an employment report, a statement of value added etc. The general public (taxpayers, consumers, political groups, environmentalists etc.) also attach considerable importance to the discharge of social responsibilities, attitude to environmental policies and contribution to national wealth.

Chairman's Statement

Chairman's statement was originally developed, as a personal comment on the year by the chairman to shareholders and it is not constrained by legislation, auditing or accounting standards. Chairmen are free to make any comments and convey their views It is not unusual to find that their statements concentrate on good news rather than less positive aspects of the business. Some times they may turn out to be a sort of public relations statement or high on presentation but low on contents.

CONCEPT PAPER ON THE COMPANIES ACT

The Ministry of Company Affairs in its concept paper for a new Companies Act is proposing a slim legislation that would provide only a broad framework, thereby leaving its implementation through rules. The Companies Act, 1956 currently has more than 700 sections that corporate India has to comply with. The current trend among the regulators, especially those in the financial sector, is to mould the legislations in such a manner that most of the intended provisions are implemented through rules. The main advantage of such a route is that the regulatory response in certain instances need not wait for the legislation to be amended through Parliament. The concept paper is likely to incorporate the essential features of the existing Companies Act 1956, the salient features of the controversial Companies (Amendment) Bill, 2003 (which was withdrawn from Rajya Sabha) and the recommendations of the second report of the Naresh Chandra Committee.

According to the Minister for Company Affairs, the aim is to make compliance easier, remove redundant provisions and add greater flexibility in rule making. Government wants to improve compliance through simplification of laws, rather than just overburdening the corporates with greater regulations. The concept paper was released on 5 August 2004 and accordingly the ministry has sought to simplify the law and reduce the existing 781 sections to 287 sections, but also intends to place all procedures that were forming part of the existing law as part of rules. The concept paper proposals include ban on pyramidal corporate structures that would prohibit a subsidiary company from becoming a holding company. However, the only exception to this is that a subsidiary company can be a holding company of a body corporate incorporated outside India. It also suggests restrictions on the number of investment companies that can be floated by a company for holding investments. On the contentious issue of board composition, the concept paper has held that "every public company having paid-up capital or turnover of such amount as may be prescribed shall have a minimum of seven directors out of which not less tan three or such numbers as near to 50 per cent of the strength of the board, whichever is higher shall be independent directors." The Ministry intends to prescribe the attributes of an independent director through the rules for the proposed provision. The proposal on board composition and pyramidal structures are concepts that need debate, according to the Ministry and the Ministry is open to newer ideas on the same. Besides introducing the concept of consolidated balance sheet, it has also said that no Government approval would be required for any increase in payment of remuneration by way of commission to non-executive directors. Further, declaration of dividend out of reserves is proposed to be made self-regulatory–no Government approval will be required. The following highlights of the concept paper may be noted:

- Removal of redundant provisions
- Separate schedule for all penalties
- Auditor disqualification on non-audit services
- Appointment of Chief Accounts Officer being made mandatory
- Time limit for mandatory name change extended to 5 years
- ICAI suggestion on format of balance sheet adopted
- Streamlined provisions on related party transactions
- Functioning of Audit Committees to be administered through rules

The following may also be added:

- *Higher Fines for Violating Guidelines:* The concept paper has drawn out a separate schedule of penalties prescribing a fine upto Rs. 10 lakh and a maximum imprisonment of 2 years. The paper has linked the magnitude of fines to the gravity of offence. The protection of investors has received special attention. While the penalty for fraudulent inducement to invest has quadrupled from Rs. 1 lakh to Rs. 5 lakh with a floor of Rs. 50,000, the accompanying imprisonment has been reduced from 5 to 2 years. The failure to pay dividend would attract a Rs. 10 lakh penalty subject to a minimum of Rs. 1 lakh, along with imprisonment upto two years. Penalties for people impersonating as the owner of shares of the company has been fixed at a maximum of Rs. 5 lakh, subject to a minimum of Rs. 50,000 with an imprisonment of upto 2 years. Non-compliance with any provision relating to audit and auditors has been increased to Rs. 1 lakh subject to a minimum of Rs 10,000.
- *Disclosure Norms Tightened:* All directors in a new company will have to give an affidavit that they have not been convicted of any fraud or financial malpractice. In other words, the doors to the corporate world will be shut for businessmen

found guilty of siphoning of money of small investors. In order to check vanishing companies, the concept paper has also proposed to make the guidelines related to changing of names more stringent and accordingly companies are proposed to be barred for a period of five years from changing their names.

- Companies can look forward to greater flexibility in holding annual general meetings and board meetings with the government proposing to allow board meetings through video conferencing and also permitting AGMs on any day of the week.
- Issue of securities, capital and related matters, civil and criminal liability for mis-statement in prospectus and other related matters, issue of securities at premium or discount, allotment of shares and debentures, issue of certificate for securities and reduction of share capital will be prescribed by rules.
- Companies will have to appoint the chief accounts officer, who will be responsible for the matters relating to accounts and audit.
- The prohibition of performance of non-audit services by the auditor as recommended by the Naresh Chandra Committee will be prescribed by way of rules.
- The recommendations of the Naresh Chandra committee regarding independent directors have been accepted.
- Companies will have to self regulate transactions to related parties subject to an upper limit.
- Companies will be allowed to regulate the payment of managerial remuneration depending on the performance of the company, without the approval of the central government.
- Tribunal will have powers to give order on complaints made by any member regarding conduct of business prejudicial to public interest in a manner oppressive to any member or members.
- Modernisation of the offices of the registrars will be undertaken by allowing electronic filing of documents.

SARBANES-OXLEY ACT 2002 OF USA

The Sarbanes-Oxley Act (SOX Act) is a serious attempt to address all the issues associated with corporate failures to achieve quality governance and to restore investor's confidence. The following important provisions may be mentioned:

1. Establishment of Public Company Accounting Oversight Board, All accounting firms will have to register themselves with this board and submit among other details, particulars of fees received from Public company clients for audit and non-audit services etc., The board will conduct annual inspection of firms which audit more than 100 public companies and once in three years In other cases, the board will establish rules governing audit, quality control, ethics, independence and other standards. It can conduct investigations and disciplinary proceedings and can impose sanctions on auditors, The Board reports to SEC.
2. Audit committee. The SOX Act provides for a 'new improved' Audit committee, The audit committee is responsible for appointment, fixing of fees and oversight of the work of independent auditors, The committee is also responsible for

establishing, reviewing the procedures. for the receipt, treatment of accounts, internal control and audit complaints received by the company from the interestd or affected parties.

3. Prohibition of non-audit services, Under the Act, auditors are prohibited from providing non-audit services concurrently with audit/financial review services.
4. CEOs and Chief Finance officers are required to certify the reports filed with the Securities Exchange Commission.
5. The Act prohibits US and foreign companies with securities traded within US from making or arranging from third parties any type of personal loan to directors.
6. The attorneys dealing with the publicly traded companies are required to report evidence of material violation of securities law or breach of fiduciary duty or similar violations by the company or CEO.
7. The Act provides that brokers and dealers of securities should not retaliate or threaten to retaliate an analyst employed by the broker. or dealer for any adverse, negative or unfavourable research report on a public company.
8. The penalties prescribed under SOX Act for any wrong doings are very stiff.
9. The SOX Act provides for studies to be conducted by the Securities Exchange Commission or the Government Accounting office in the following areas: auditors rotation, off-balance sheet transactions, consolidation of accounting firms, role of credit rating agencies, SEC enforcement actions in the past five years, role of investment banks and financial advisers and 'Principle -based' accounting.

The provisions are expected to enhance accountability of directors, officers, auditors, security analysts and legal counsels involved in financial markets. It carries far-reaching implications for the audit profession. The Act does not distinguish between US and non-US issuers (companies) and it applies to all companies with a listing in the US.

VANISHING COMPANIES

So far, that is till January 2003, a joint committee of to DCA and the Securities and Exchange Board of India has identified 229 companies as 'vanishing companies' which tapped the capital market, collected funds from the public and subsequently became untraceable. Despite thorough investigation, some 69 companies are still out of reach-of this committee. According to sources in the case of these vanishing companies, the exact jurisdictional control of regulatory bodies was not clear. If there has been violation of the Company Law, the DCA is the regulator, In the case of violation of stock market norms, it is the SEBI and in the case of financial irregularity, it is the RBI which has to intervene. However with the setting up of the SF1O (the Serious Fraud Investigation office in the DCA), this multi-disciplinary body may eventually be handed over the task of investigating the frauds perpetuated on the public. The SF1O has been mandated to carry lout investigations into frauds which have inter-departmental or multi-disciplinary ramifications or which involve substantial public interest in terms of, number of people involved. Under both these criteria, the frauds perpetuated by the vanishing companies are covered. The investigations into the vanishing companies, which involve monies of ordinary people, have been slow till now.

Of the 229 companies identified, 63 were found to be regular in filing documents and 65 others started filing documents after action was initiated against them. Some 28 companies were found to be under liquidation, while two were seized by the State governments, Another two companies have been identified and asked to update documents. Still, some 69 companies remain against whom no action has been initiated.

Reference may be invited to the various provisions of the Companies (Amendment) Act 2003 and some the provisions are intended because of the "black sheep" and "vanishing companies" in the corporate sector. The Companies Act, vide Section 63, provides that every person who authorises the issue of a prospectus can be punished with imprisonment or a fine. However in practice, while the list of vanishing companies is long, hardly any prosecution has been launched against the major defaulters: Thousands of depositors have also been cheated of their fixed deposits. The various restrictions imposed by the RBI on non-banking companies, resulted in their collapse, Despite, S. 58A of the Companies Act, enabling action for failure to pay the depositors, an offence attracting imprisonment of upto five years and a fine, it has been reported that the Department has turned a Nelson's eye to such types of cases of default; Despite statutory provision vide S.628 of the Act, enabling action to be taken for false statements in documents or material omission, the relevant provisions have seldom been invoked. There are several cases of balance sheets containing false statements and misstatements in the prospectus. The solution suggested by Arvind P Datar may be noted here: "The solution lies in implementing the existing provisions. A strong message that defaulters will be prosecuted and punished quickly must be conveyed, Filing charge sheets or taking action months after the event makes a mockery of the entire proceedings. In fine, Companies Act, 1956 is fully equipped to deal with the 'black sheep' and vanishing companies, What is required is not an amendment to the Act but ~ Change in the mindset and attitude of the DCA," (Of black sheep and vanishing companies, the Hindu Business Line dated 19th August 2003).

VISION/MISSION STATEMENT OF BSES LIMITED

Vision

To be amongst the most admired and most trusted integrated utility companies in the world, delivering reliable and quality product and services to all customers at competitive costs, with international standards of customer care - thereby creating superior value for all stakeholders.

To set new benchmarks in standards of corporate performer and governance through the pursuit of operational and financial excellence, responsible citizenship, and profitable growth.

Mission

- To attain global best practices and become a world-class utility.
- To provide uninterrupted, affordable, quality, reliable and clean power, to millions of customers.
- To achieve excellence in service, quality, reliability, safety and customer care.
- To earn the trust and confidence of all customers and stakeholders, exceeding their expectations, and make the company a respected household name.

- To work with vigour, dedication and innovation, with total, customer satisfaction as the ultimate goal.
- To consistently achieve high growth with the highest levels of productivity.
- To be a technology driven, efficient and financially sound organization.
- To be a responsible corporate citizen nurturing human values and concern for society, the environment and above all, people.
- To contribute towards community development and nation building.

VISION AND MISSION STATEMENT OF INDIAN OIL CORPORATION LTD.

Vision

A major, diversified, transnational, integrated energy company, with national leadership and a strong environment conscience, playing a national role in oil security and public distribution.

Mission

- To achieve international standards of excellence in all aspects of energy and diversified business with focus on customer delight through value of products and services, and cost reduction.
- To maximize creation of wealth, value and satisfaction for the stakeholders.
- To attain leadership in developing, adopting and assimilating state-of-the-art technology for competitive advantage.
- To provide technology and services through sustained Research and Development.
- To foster a culture of participation and innovation for employee growth and contribution.
- To cultivate high standards of business ethics and Total Quality Management for a strong corporate identity and brand equity.
- To help enrich the quality of life of the community and preserve ecological balance and heritage through a strong environment conscience.

FORMAT FOR SECURING INFORMATION FROM NON-EXECUTIVE DIRECTORS REGARDING PECUNIARY RELATIONSHIP OR TRANSACTIONS MADE BY NON-EXECUTIVE DIRECTORS WITH THE COMPANY

To

The Board of Directors

……………….. Ltd.

Dear Sirs,

Pursuant to the provisions of Clause 49-VII(D) of the Listing Agreement, I give herein below the details of my pecuniary relationships/transactions with the company and the pecuniary benefit obtained by me out of or in relation to such relationships/transactions during the financial year ………..

S.No.	Nature of relationship/transactions	Amount (Rs.)
(1)	(2)	(3)

1. Remunerátion receieved from the company as a director (whether in the form of salary, commission, perquisites, fees for attending Board and other meetings or any expenditure made by the company in respect of the following:
   (a) providing any rent free accommodation or any other benefit or amenity in respect of accommodation free of charge;
   (b) providing any other benefit or amenity free of charge or at a concessional rate;
   (c) in respect of any obligation or service, which, but for such expenditure by the company would have been incurred by me;
   (d) to effect any insurance on the life of, or to provide any pension, annuity or gratuity for the undersigned or any of the persons such as his spouse or child.
2. Remuneration received for an office or place of profit held in the company (whether salary, commission, perquisite, fee for Board or any other meetings or any other).
3. Fees for rendering professional services to the company.
4. Commission or profit received or earned from goods or materials purchased from the company (whether for resale or otherwise).
5. Commission or profit received or earned from goods or materials sold to the company (whether for resale or otherwise).
6. Commission or profit received or earned/to be received or earned for rendering services to the company.
7. Any other remuneration/profit received or earned/monetary benefit obtained from the company (such as rent, sale of immovable property, free supply of foods/services/amenities/facilities by the company).
8. Any other

Signature ....
Full Name ....

Date ....
Place ....

DISCLOSURE OF DIRECTORS INTEREST IN TRANSACTIONS WITH THE COMPANY

Name of person/ orga-nization transac-ting with company	Name of related Director	Details of financial transac-tion	Detail of product/ Services involved	Total Amount involved in tran-sactions during the year	Amount involved as a % of total turn-over of the Company	Terms of credit, etc.	Trans-action rate	Market rate	Details of relevant share-holders/ CG permi-ssion u/s 297, if any	Remarks

ASSOCIATION OF DIRECTORS IN OTHER PUBLIC ISSUES IN LAST 10 YEAR

Name of Director	Name of Company with whose public issue Director was associated	Type of Industry	Date of appointment as Director in that company	Date of resignation/cessation, if any	Date of Public Issue						Current Status of such Company (Give details if delisted/ vanished)
					Type of security	Size of issue	Year of issue	Face value	Premium	Latest Market value	

DIRECTOR'S REMUNERATION FOR THE FINANCIAL YEAR

S.No.	Particulars	Name of directors			
		A	B	C	D
(1)	Remuneration • Salary • Contribution to PF & GPF • Benefits, perks/allowances • Bonuses • Stock Options • Pension • Sitting Fees • Leave Salary/encashment • Provision for gratuity				
(2)	Details of fixed component and performance linked incentives along with the performance criteria.				
(a)	Fixed component • Salary P.M. • Contribution to PF & GPF (presently 10% and 15% of salary) • Perks and other allowance (Ceiling of 90% salary)				
(b)	Performance linked incentives – Commission (Based on net profit for the year within the individual/overall ceiling for managerial remuneration from time to time) Minimum remuneration				
(c)	(In case of inadequacy of profits in any year as covered u/s 198/349 of the Act)				

(3)	Services contracts, Notice period Severance fees				
(4)	Stock option details, if any and whether the same has been issued at discount as well as the period over which accrued and over which exercisable				

Note: The performance criteria may be specified for each category of directors.

CONCEPT PAPER ON COMPANY LAW: APPROACH NOTE

Following the recommendations of the Company Low Committee known as the Bhaba Committee set up in 1950 the Companies Act, 1956, was enacted with the object to amend and consolidate the law relating to companies and certain other association by repealing the Companies Act, 1913. The Companies Act, 1956, has been amended as many as 24' times' since 1956. The major amendment to the Companies Act, 1956, was made after considering the recommendations of the Sachar Committee by enacting the Companies' Amendment Act, 1988. The next major amendment was mode by the Companies Amendment Act, 2002, consequent to the report of the high powered Eradi Committee. Looking at the proliferation and diversity of amendments which have been made to the Act, an attempt to recodify the law appears inevitable.

The previous' two attempts at making a comprehensive review of the existing law by introducing Companies Amendment Bill 1993 and 1997 failed as the assent of the, Parliament could not be received. The Ministry introduced the Companies (Amendment) Bill, 2003, containing important provisions in the arena of independence of auditors, relationship of auditors with the management of the company, independent directors with a view to improve the corporate governance practices in the corporate sector. Department examined the concerns expressed and the suggestions made by the industry associations, organizations and professionals and sought to introduce an amendment to the Amendment Bill. In the meanwhile, a decision was taken by the Government for preparation of a concept paper containing a model codified company law which would consolidate the existing provisions of the law. The following broad approach has been adopted while drafting the concept paper:

1. To bring the corporate law in consonance with the changes that have occurred in the economic development.
2. To delete the redundant provisions and to regroup the scattered provisions relating to specific subjects.
3. To condense, simplify and rationalize the provisions of company law.
4. To delink the procedural aspects from the substantive law.
5. To give an overview of the form of the re-codified companies Bill containing only 289 sections and a few schedules, in place of existing 781 sections and 15 schedules.

The concept paper as presented in the website contains XXV chapters. The chapters deal with the following:

(*i*) Chapter I-VII deal with formation of company and other organizational matters.

(ii) Chapter VIII-IX deal with Accounts and Audit.

(iii) ChapterX-XII deal with management of the company.

(iv) Chapter XIII contains powers of Central Government to carry out inspection and investigation of companies.

(v) Chapter XIV-XV relates to reorganization of companies by merger, amalgamation, etc.

(vi) Chapter XVI-XVIII deal with winding up the company.

(vii) Chapter XIX deals with other registerable entities.

(viii) Chapter XX deals with Producer Companies, a separate class of companies.

(ix) Chapter XXI to XXV deal with foreign companies, constitution of the Offices of the Registry of Companies and other miscellaneous provisions.

It is reiterated that the concept paper is only an approach to the introduction of a recodified bill in the Parliament. The concept paper has not been vetted by the Legislative Department, Ministry of Law.

The aim of this concept paper is only to provoke critical examination of the provisions contained in this concept paper by all chambers of commerce, business organizations, professional bodies, academicians and persons connected with corporate sector, directly or indirectly. The Ministry will feel rewarded if it stimulates widest possible public debate so that the bill as and when introduced in the Parliament will duly take into account the various points of view.

The Ministry invites suggestions and criticisms for improvement of the concept paper. After incorporating the valuable suggestions of the corporate sector, the Companies Bill will be framed for introduction in the Parliament. Once the concepts are frozen after public debate and completion of consultation process, necessary changes in rules and schedules will be proposed and finalized.

It will be appreciated if the suggestions are given, in a tabular form, against each clause. All suggestions must, however, reach the Department (by post or by e-mail at mca.conceptcolaw@sb.nic.in) latest by October, 31st 2004.

Notes on Chapters

Chapter I: Preliminary (Section 1 to 2)

This Chapter deals with the title "Date of Commencement of the Act" as well as the definitions.

Chapter II: Incorporation of Company and matters' incidental thereto (Sec. 3 to 16)

This Chapter deals with procedure for incorporation of companies, the liability of members and directors, types of companies, alteration of the type of company and change of name of the companies. The rules proposed to be prescribed under this chapter would cover the contents of the Memorandum and Articles of Association, being the charter of the company. The particulars furnished at the time of incorporation of companies, at present, are insufficient to clearly establish the identity of the promoters, especially in case of vanishing companies. It is proposed to strengthen the requirements of particulars at the time of incorporation of companies. The guideline for availability of name is also proposed to be prescribed by way of rules.

Chapter III: Issue of Securities, Capital and related matters (See. 17 to 32)

This Chapter deals with issue of prospectus, requirement of registration of prospectus with the Registrar, deemed prospectus, civil and criminal liability for misstatement in prospectus and other related matters. The contents of prospectus is contained in Schedule-II to the Bill. This Chapter also deals with further issue of capital, issue of securities at premium/discount, allotment of shares and debentures, issue of certificate for securities and reduction of share capital. The procedural part in respect of the above matters is proposed to be prescribed by way of rules.

Chapter IV: Public Deposits (Sec. 33)

This Chapter deals with invitation and acceptance of public deposits. While the protection of small depositors incorporated in the Act by Companies Amendment Act, 2000, is retained, the rigours of section 58AAA of 1956 Act is reduced by making only the offences relating to non-repayment of deposits as cognizable. The substantive part of the Companies (Acceptance of Deposits) Rules is proposed to be shifted to the Companies General Rules and Forms.

Chapter V: Registration of Charges (Sec. 34 to 36)

This Chapter deals with, registration of charges with the Registrar. The present procedure of condonation of delay in filing of charges with the Registrar by the Company Law Board/Central Government is proposed to be dispensed with by levying additional fee. Similarly, the Register of Charges maintained by the Registrars in Form No. 13 of Central Government Rules and Forms is proposed to be dispensed with. The existing Form-8, 10, 13 and 17 are proposed to be combined in a composite charge form, which will be available for inspection of the public. The time available with the company for filing charge documents is proposed to be increased to 60 days.

Chapter VI: Members meetings and resolution (Sec. 37 to 47)

This Chapter deals with maintenance of Register of Members, conduct of general meetings, rights of members, types of resolutions, enabling provisions for the companies to get the consent of the shareholders by postal ballot and maintenance of minutes of meetings. The requirement of holding statutory meeting by public companies has been done away with as it has become more of a formality than to serve any useful purpose. The existing restrictions in respect of conduct of Annual General Meetings on Sundays and public holidays is proposed to be removed in the Rules. The coverage of postal ballot is proposed to be enhanced to new businesses, as it will improve the participation of shareholders in the affairs of the company.

Chapter VII: Dividend, Investor Education and related matters (Sec. 48 to 50)

This Chapter deals with payment of dividend, transfer of unpaid dividend to Investors' Education and Protection Fund and prohibition' of payment of dividend out of capital. Transfer of Profits to Reserves before declaration of dividend and the method of arriving at the net profit for the purpose of declaration of dividend are proposed to be prescribed by way of rules. The unpaid dividend amount retained in the General Revenue Account of the Government of India under the existing section 205B is also proposed to be transferred to the Investors' Education and Protection Fund so that the shareholders' entitled to the unpaid dividend prior and, after the Companies Amendment Act, 1998, are placed on par.

Chapter VIII: Accounts (Sec. 51 to 55)

This Chapter deals with the books of accounts to be maintained by the company, the form and content of balance sheet, the manner of authentication of balance sheet and the contents of directors' report. The form of balance sheet recommended by the Institute of Chartered Accountants of India is adopted with some modifications as Schedule VI, This chapter, also requires companies to appoint the Chief Accounts Officer who will be responsible for the matters relating to accounts and audit.

Chapter IX: Matters relating to audit and auditors (Sec. 56 to 62)

This Chapter deals with appointment, powers, duties and liabilities of auditors. The recommendations of the Naresh Chandra Committee have been considered while formulating the provisions relating to appointment of auditors and constitution of the Audit Committee. The prohibition of performance of non-audit services by auditor as recommend by the said committee is proposed to be prescribed by way of rules. This chapter also deals with special audit and cost audit.

Chapter X: Matters relating to Directors, powers, functions, etc. (Sec. 63 to 71)

This Chapter deals with minimum and maximum number of directors, appointment of directors, retirement, disqualification, removal and vacation of office by directors; The recommendations of the Naresh Chandra Committee with reference to induction of independent directors have been included in the provisions of the Act. The attributes of an independent director, as recommended by the Naresh Chandra Committee are proposed to be prescribed by way of rules This chapter has attempted to consolidate the procedure for appointment of directors available in different sections of the present act.

Chapter XI: Meetings, powers of the Board and related party transactions (Sec. 72 to 81)

This Chapter deals with meetings, powers and 'restrictions of the board of directors including in respect of inter-corporate investments and loans. This Chapter also deals with the duties of the directors to the board with reference to disclosure of their interest in related party transactions. This Chapter attempts to consolidate the existing provisions of the Act in respect of transactions with related parties under a single section. At present certain types of transactions which are very significant in terms of the value of transactions are not covered by the provisions of the Act. The consolidated section covers almost all types of transactions which a company may enter into with the related parties. The rules proposed to be prescribed under this section will enable the companies to self-regulate the transactions to the related parties subject to an upper limit.

Chapter XII: Appointment of Managerial Personnel (Sec. 82 to 88)

This Chapter deals with appointment of managerial personnel, their remuneration and powers of Central Government to remove managerial personnel. No substantive changes have been made in the limits of remuneration payable to managerial personnel. The schedule to the Act dealing with appointment of managerial personnel has undergone some changes to enable the companies to self-regulate the payment of managerial remuneration depending on the performance of the company, without the approval of the Central Government.

Chapter XIII: Inspection and Investigation (Sec. 89 to 92)

This Chapter deals with the power of the Central Government to carry out inspection and investigation of companies.

Chapter XIV: Matters relating to Merger, Demerger, compromise and arrangement (Sec. 93 to 96)

This Chapter deals with procedure relating to proposals of compromise arrangement and the confirmation thereof by the National Company Law Tribunal. This Chapter deals with power of the company to acquire shares of dissenting shareholders in a scheme involving transfer of shares from one company to another.

Chapter XV: Oppression and Mismanagement (Sec. 97 to 100)

This Chapter deals with the power of the tribunal to give order on a complaint made by any member regarding conduct of business prejudicial to public interest or in a manner oppressive to any member or members. This chapter also deals with the power of Central Government to appoint directors to protect the public interest/shareholders. Miscellaneous provisions such as contribution of employees to the provident fund are also covered under this chapter.

Chapter XVI: National Company Law Tribunal (Sec. 101 to 122)

This Chapter deals with constitution of the National Company Low Tribunal, Appeal against order of the tribunal, constitution of the-Appellate Tribunal, legal representation before the tribunal and appeal against orders of the Appellate Tribunal.

Chapter XVII: Revival and Rehabilitation of Sick Industrial Companies (Sec. 123 to 132)

This Chapter deals with procedure for sick companies to make a reference to the Tribunal, order of enquiry by the tribunal to decide whether company has become sick, preparation and sanction of scheme, rehabilitation and consequences including winding up of sick companies.

Chapter XVIII: Corporate Winding up and Dissolution (Sec. 133 to 207)

This Chapter deals with provisions relating to corporate winding up and dissolution including voluntary winding up. Important amendments hove taken place in the Chapter on Winding up by The Companies Amendment Act, 2000, consequent to the report of the high powered Eradi Committee. The powers of the High Court in corporate winding up have been shifted to the National Company Law Tribunal though the provisions of the Act are yet to be implemented. In view of the above no major changes have been made except clubbing of various related provisions and shifting of procedural aspects to rules.

Chapter XIX: Organization capable of being register under this Act (Sec. 208-212)

This Chapter deals with the provisions to allow register under this Act certain companies, which were not registered under this Act but formed in pursuance of any Act of Parliament other than this Act or any other Indian Law. This could be allowed only if there is assent in writing of all members of the organization. In case the organization is to register as company limited by guarantee or an unlimited company the assent shall be along with an under taking from each member to contribute to the assets of company in case of its being wound up. After registration all provisions of this Act are to be applicable to such companies.

Chapter XX: Producer Companies (Sec. 213-233)

This Chapter deals with incorporation of producer companies, object for which producer company shall be incorporated and specific provisions applicable to producer companies. The contents of the memorandum, articles, object for which producer companies are incorporated and certain related matters are proposed to be shifted to rules. No substantial charges are made as the Act was passed by the Parliament only in the year 2000.

Chapter XXI: Companies incorporated outside India (Sec. 234-243)

This Chapter deals with the requirement of the companies incorporated outside India, but having a place of business in India, to register with the Registrar of Companies. At present the registration of the foreign companies is centralized with the Registrar of Companies, Delhi. Due to globalisation, more foreign companies have started places of business in India. Hence it is proposed to empower the other Registrars also to register the companies incorporated outside India subject to their jurisdiction over the place of business.

Chapter XXII: Registration Offices, Other Offices and fees (Sec. 244-250)

This Chapter deals with power of Central Government to constitute offices of the Registrars, appointment of Registrars, Regional Directors, Director General of Inspection and Investigation, duties of Registrars and fees payable at the time of filing of documents. The proposal to modernize the offices of Registrars by allowing electronic filing of documents has been taken into account while drafting this chapter.

Chapter XXIII: Information from companies and special types of companies (Sec. 251-256)

This Chapter deals with the power of Central Government to collect statistics and information from companies and power to exempt or modify applicability of certain provisions of the Act in respect of special types of companies.

Chapter XXIV: Offences and Penalties (Sec. 257-267)

At present penal provisions are provided in the section itself. It is proposed to shift the penalties to a separate schedule. The quantum of penalties is proposed to be rationalized keeping in view the principle that the penalty should be commensurate with the gravity of offences. It is also proposed to prescribe mandatory minimum penalty in case of public companies. The Chapter also deals with composition of offences under the Act.

Chapter XXV: Miscellaneous Provisions (Sec. 268 to 289)

This Chapter deals with miscellaneous provisions, power of Central Government to make rules, regulations, amend schedules and saving clauses. This Chapter also deals with the matters to be administered by Securities and Exchange Board of India in respect of listed companies and companies which propose to get listed in recognized stock exchanges.

INSIDER TRADING REGULATIONS

SEBI, in order to check the menace of 'insider trading' has framed regulations termed as 'SEBI (Insider trading) Regulations, 1992, as amended from time to time. Persons connected with a company usually have access to information which is not known to outsiders; this may relate to information about profits, proposed dividend, proposed bonus issue, rights issue, expansion plans, mergers, disposal of undertaking etc., The insider can take advantage of 'price sensitive information' as mentioned above. Insiders are persons who may be connected with a company and may be reasonably expected to have access to unpublished price sensitive information in respect of securities of a company. All directors of a company, senior officers of the company, including an auditor of the company, legal and professional advisers of the company, company under the same group, official or member of stock exchange, merchant banker to an issue of the company, employees of public financial company or SEBI or bankers of the company are all covered under the definition of 'insiders', if they have reasonable access to unpublished price sensitive information. SEBI, after investigation, is empowered to direct the insider not to deal in securities in a particular manner, prohibit the insider from disposing of the securities acquired in violation of regulations of insider trading and restrain the 'insider' to communicate or advise any person to deal in securities. The importance of the insider trading regulations could be appreciated from the following, "The smooth operation of the securities market and its healthy growth and development, depend to a large extent on the quality and integrity of the market. Such a market can alone inspire confidence in investors. Factors on which such confidence depend include, among others, that they will be protected against improper use of insider information. Inequitable and unfair practices such as insider trading, market manipulation and other security frauds affect the integrity, fairness and efficiency of the securities market, and impair the confidence of investors."[1]

SEBI insider trading regulations applies to all listed companies in India and all organisations associated with the securities market. It also applies to market intermediaries, as defined under Section 12 of the SEBI Act 1992.

Securities and Exchange Board of India (Insider trading) Regulations, 1992. Chapter l covers preliminary matters such as short title, commencement and definitions. Chapter II is the "charging" chapter and it is on prohibition on dealing, communicating or counseling on matters relating to insider trading. Chapter III is on investigation. The prohibition against insider trading is provided in Regulation 3 of the said Regulations and the regulation aims to prohibit the insider from breaching this duty to the company. Breach of this Duty necessarily involves on element of 'manipulation' or 'deceipt', and

---

1 Insider trading regulations, Chartered Secretary, August 2004.

the making of some secret profits or personal gain by the insider, Regulation 3 essentially provides for a 'disclose or abstain rule'.

Fiduciary duty, Since the insiders receive unpublished price sensitive information by virtue of their connection with the company and for corporate purposes only, such insiders owe a fiduciary duty to the company not to misuse or misappropriate such information for an unlawful purpose i.e. to make secret profits or personal gains for themselves (Chiarella v. US455 US 222).

Regulation 12 requires all listed companies and entities associated with securities market to frame code of conduct and code of internal procedures as per Modal Code prescribed under Schedule I to the Regulations. Listed companies shall abide by the Code of Corporate Disclosure Practices as specified In Schedule II to the regulations, Schedule II framed under regulation 12(2), bearing the heading Code of Corporate Disclosure Practices for Prevention of Insider trading is given below for reference.

Thus the aim of the SEBI regulations on the subject is to prevent insiders taking unfair advantage over other shareholders, by virtue of their position in the company and based on the confidential information available to them.

SCHEDULE II

[See under regulation 12(2)]

CODE OF CORPORATE DISCLOSURE PRACTICES FOR PREVENTION OF INSIDER TRADING

Corporate Disclosure Policy

To ensure timely and adequate disclosure of price sensitive information, the following norms shall be followed by listed companies:

Prompt Disclosure of Price Sensitive Information

(i) Price sensitive information shall be given by listed companies to stock exchanges and disseminated on a continuous and immediate basis.

(ii) Listed companies may also consider ways of supplementing information released to stock exchanges by improving Investor access to their public announcements.

Overseeing and Coordinating Disclosure

(i) Listed companies shall designate a senior official (such as compliance officer) to oversee corporate disclosure.

(ii) This official shall be responsible for ensuring that the company complies with continuous disclosure requirements. Overseeing and co-ordinating disclosure of price sensitive information to stock exchanges, analysts, shareholders and media and educating staff on disclosure policies and procedure.

(iii) Information disclosure/dissemination may normally be approved in advance by the official designated for the purpose.

(iv) If information is accidentally disclosed without prior approval, the person responsible may inform the designated officer immediately, even if the information is not considered price sensitive.

Responding to Market Rumours

(i) Listed companies shall have clearly laid down procedures for responding to any queries or requests for verification of market rumours by exchanges.

(ii) The official designated for corporate disclosure shall be responsible for deciding whether a public announcement is necessary for verifying or denying rumours and then making the disclosure.

Timely Reporting of Shareholdings/Ownership and Changes in Ownership

Disclosure of shareholdings/ownership by major shareholders and disclosure of changes in ownership as provided under any Regulations made under the Act and the listing agreement shall be made in a timely and adequate manner.

Disclosure/dissemination of Price Sensitive Information with special reference to Analysts, Institutional Investors

Listed companies should follow the guidelines given hereunder while dealing with analysts and institutional investors:

(i) *Only Public information to be provided*– Listed companies shall provide only public information to the analyst/research persons/large investors like institutions. Alternatively, the information given to the analyst should be simultaneously made public at the earliest.

(ii) *Recording of discussion* – In order to avoid misquoting or misrepresentation, it is desirable that at least two company representative be present at meetings with Analysts, brokers or Institutional Investors and discussion should preferably be recorded.

(iii) *Handling of unanticipated questions* – A listed company should be careful when dealing with analysts' questions that raise issues outside the intended scope of discussion. Unanticipated questions may be taken on notice and a considered response given later. If the answer includes price sensitive information, a public announcement should be made before responding.

(iv) *Simultaneous release of Information* – When a company organises meetings with analysts, the company shall make a press release or post relevant information on its website after every such meet. The company may also consider live webcasting of analyst meets.

Medium of Disclosure/Dissemination

(i) Disclosure/dissemination of information may be done through various media so as to achieve maximum reach and quick dissemination.

(ii) Corporates shall ensure that disclosure to stock exchanges is made promptly.

(iii) Corporates may also facilitate disclosure through the use of their dedicated Internet website.

(iv) Company websites may provide a means of giving investors a direct access to analyst briefing material, significant background information and questions and answers.

(v) The information filed by corporates with exchanges under continuous disclosure requirement may be made available on the company website.

Dissemination by Stock Exchanges

(i) The disclosures made to stock exchanges maybe disseminated by the exchanges to investors in a quick and efficient manner through the stock exchange network' as well as through stock exchange websites.

(ii) Information furnished by the companies under continuous disclosure requirements, should be published on the website of the exchange instantly.

(iii) Stock exchanges should make immediate arrangement for display of the information furnished by the companies instantly on the stock exchange website.

SEBI OMBUDSMAN REGULATIONS, 2003

The Securities and Exchange Board of India (SEBI) has set up a new institution called the "Ombudsman" for safeguarding the interests of investors. The office of ombudsman already exists in the banking and insurance sectors. The SEBI regulations have become effective from 21 August 2003. The concept of ombudsman, as explained in the following lines may be noted:

"The concept of ombudsman traces it roots to the branch of Administrative Law. It is a Scandinavian concept and a measure of imposing checks and balances on the functioning of public authorities. According to the Concise Oxford Dictionary, 7th Edition, Ombudsman means, "official appointed to investigate individual's complaints against public authorities." The term can therefore, be understood to mean an attorney or representative who investigates a complaint against the administration. The role of an ombudsman is in the nature of a watchdog on the administration. The SEBI ombudsman can be understood as an office (person) appointed to redress investors' complaints against a listed company and/or a capital market intermediary as defined in the SEBI Act."[2]

SEBI Regulation 11 deals with the general while regulation 12 deals with other powers and functions. The powers and functions include the following:

- To receive complain specified in regulation 13 against any intermediary or a listed company or both;
- To consider such complaints and facilitate resolution thereof by amicable settlement;
- To approve a friendly or amicable settlement of the dispute between the parties;
- To adjudicate such complaints in the event of a failure of settlement thereof by friendly or amicable settlement.

Regulation 14(3) stipulates certain conditions for the filing of a complaint before the ombudsman.

---

[2] SEBI Ombudsman Regulations, 2003: an analysis, Chartered Secretary February 2004.

Grievance Redressal

Chapter IV of the Regulations deals with the procedure for redressal of grievances. Regulation 13 provides that a person may lodge a complaint on any one or more of the following grounds either to the Board or to the Ombudsman concerned:

- non-receipt of refund orders, allotment letters in respect of a public issue of securities of companies or units of mutual funds or collective investment schemes;
- non-receipt of share certificates, unit certificates, debenture certificates, bonus shares;
- non-receipt of dividend by shareholders or unit holders;
- non-receipt of interest on debentures, redemption amount of debentures or interest on delayed payment of interest on debentures;
- non-receipt of interest on delayed refund of application monies;
- non-receipt of annual reports or statements pertaining to the portfolios;
- non-receipt of redemption amount from a mutual fund or returns from collective investment scheme;
- non-transfer of securities by an issuer company, mutual fund, collective investment management company or depository within the stipulated time;
- non-receipt of letter of offer or consideration in takeover or buy-back offer or delisting;
- non-receipt of statement of holding corporate benefits of any grievances in respect of corporate benefits, etc.
- any grievance in respect of public, rights or bonus issue of a listed company;
- any of the matters covered under section 55A of the Companies Act, 1956.
- any grievance in respect of issue or dealing in securities against an intermediary or a listed company.

From the above, it appears that a wide gamut of issues can form the ground for filing a complaint. Further, it may relate to companies, mutual funds, collective investment schemes and depositories.

Obligations of Listed Companies

It is necessary that every listed company and every intermediary shall display the name and address of the Ombudsman in its office premises in such manner and at such place as specified by SEBI, so that it is put to the notice of shareholders or investors or unit holders visiting the office premises of the listed company or the intermediary. In the offer documents or other agreements with clients, similar disclosure obligations has been prescribed.

Companies (Amendment) Bill, 2003 Withdrawn

On 21st October 2003, the Union Cabinet decided to withdraw the Companies (Amendment) Bill, 2003. A revised bill was proposed to be introduced and this bill is to take into account the concern raised by industry. The Bill that was introduced in May 2003 drew largely from the recommendations of the Naresh Chandra Committee on corporate audit and governance and the Joint Parliamentary Committee on stock market scam, besides left over items of the Companies Bill, 1997. The decision to pull the Bill out of Parliament has been taken due to numerous objections and suggestions received on it from industry associations, professionals, institutions and individuals.

SEBI AND CORPORATE GOVERNANCE MEASURES

SEBI appointed a committee on corporate governance in the year 1999. The committee's aim was to view corporate governance from the perspective of investors. The committee took note of various steps taken by SEBI for strengthening corporate governance like strengthening of disclosure norms for IPOs, inclusion of cash flow and funds flow statement in annual reports, declaration of quarterly reports, appointment of compliance officer for compliance with various rules and regulations, timely disclosure of price sensitive information etc., The committee identified three key constituents of corporate governance as the shareholders, the board of directors and the management. The committee recognised the three key aspects of corporate governance, namely accountability, transparency and equality of treatment for all stakeholders. The committee recommended inclusion of a separate section on corporate governance in the Annual Reports of companies, The recommendations made were of two categories, mandatory recommendations and non-mandatory recommendations, SEBI has taken steps to Implement the code of corporate governance by suitably modifying clause 49 of the listing agreement requiring companies to comply with the Corporate governance norms. The implementation schedule, in the case of listed entities having a paid up share capital of Rs. 3 crores and above or net worth of Rs. 25 crores or more, has been set as on or before 31st March 2004.

CLAUSE 49 OF THE LISTING AGREEMENT

Corporate governance in listed companies: Clause 49 of the listing agreement. The Securities and Exchange Board of India vide Circular No SEBI/CFD/DIL/CG/l/2004/ 12/10 dated October 29, 2004 has revised the existing Clause 49 of the Listing agreement directing all the stock exchanges to amend the listing agreement by replacing the existing Clause 49 of the listing agreement, The full text of the circular has been re-produced as APPENDIX to Chapter 2 Corporate Governance and compliance requirements, for necessary reference, In the following pages, Salient features/Difference between 2000/2001 regulations and 2004 regulations and gist of Disclosure and other obligations and Structure according to November 2004 regulations have been given.

Annexure I

Clause 49 – Corporate Governance.

Remarks/ Key Points to be noted

I. Board of Directors

(a) **Composition of Board:** Not less than 50 per cent of the board of directors should consist of non executive directors. If the chairman of the board is a non-executive director, at least one third of the board should consist of independent directors and in case he is an executive director, at least half of the board should comprise independent directors.

Definition of 'independent director' (non executive director) has been provided.

There is not much change in the above regulations when compared to earlier regulations.

(b) **Non executive directors' compensation and disclosures:** It has to be fixed by the Board and shall require previous approval of shareholders in general meeting. The resolution should specify the limits for the maximum number of stock options that can be granted.

(c) **Other provisions as to Board and committees:** Minimum information to be made available to the board. This is given in Annexure lA of the new regulations. New regulations as above require same information to be made available to the board as was prescribed earlier.

(d) **Code of conduct:** The Board shall lay down a code of conduct for all board members; there is the requirement to affirm compliance with the code on an annual basis.

II. Audit Committee

(a) Qualified and independent audit committee

(b) **Meeting of audit committee:** The committee should meet at least four times in a year and not more than four months shall elapse between two meetings. The earlier regulations prescribed at least thrice a year meeting/s.

(c) Powers of audit committee

(d) **Role of audit committee:** The role is also concerned with disclosure of related party transactions. According to explanation provided the term related party transactions is said to carry the same meaning as contained in the Accounting Standard 18 (ICAI).

There is also particular reference to Director's responsibility statement to be included in the Board's report in terms of clause (2AA) of section 217 of the Companies Act, 1956.

(e) Review of information by Audit committee: Mandatory review of information mentioned under this head such as management discussion and analysis of financial condition and results of operations etc., are additional responsibility of the audit committee.

III. Subsidiary Companies

These are additional new regulations in respect of subsidiary companies.

IV. Disclosures

(a) **Basis of related party transactions:** Summary form of transactions with related parties should be placed periodically before the audit committee.

(b) **Disclosure of accounting treatment:** There is reference to Corporate Governance Report.

(c) **Board disclosures – Risk management:** Procedures about the risk assessment and minimizaytion procedures required and these to be reviewed periodically; Board should be informed.

(d) **Proceeds from public issues, right issues, preferential issues etc.:** Audit committee responsibility has been specified, for taking necessary steps in this regard whenever required; disclosure obligations have also been prescribed; the statement has to be certified by the statutory auditors.

(e) **Remuneration of directors:** The remuneration paid to directors should be disclosed in the section in corporate governance in the annual report of the company. This includes details on stock options, pensions and criteria for payment to non executive directors. Various other disclosures reg: remuneration of directors as prescribed under this heading is also required to be made.

(f) **Management:** A management discussion and analysis report detailing industry structure and developments, opportunities and threats, segment wise or product wise performance, risks and concerns, market outlook etc., should be included in the directors' report of the annual report.

(g) **Shareholders:** Prescribed information is to be disclosed in case of appointment of new director or re-appointment of a director, quarterly results on company's website, a board committee for redressal of investor complaints (grievance committee), procedure for expediting process of share transfer have also been covered.

V. CEO/CFO Certification

CEO/CFO should certify to the board on matters prescribed, such as they have reviewed financial statements and the statements do not contain any materially untrue statement etc.

Various responsibilities have been cast on the CEO/CFO on different matters mentioned under the above heading.

VI. Report on Corporate Governance

There shall be a separate section on corporate governance in the Annual Reports of companies with a detailed compliance report on corporate governance.

List of items to be included in this report is give in Annexure – 1C and list of Non-mandatory requirements is give in Annexure 1D.

Annexure 1C is compulsory

There appears to be not much difference between the earlier regulations and the current one. However in Serial 7 Disclosures, there is reference to whistle blower policy and affirmation that no personnel has been denied access to the audit committee.

Reg: Non Mandatory Requirements (Annexure 1D)

Annexure 1D covers matters relating to the following:

1. The Board,
2. Remuneration committee
3. shareholder rights (including a half yearly declaration of financial performance, summary of significant events in last six months),

4. audit qualifications,
5. Training of board members,
6. mechanism for evaluating non executive board members (performance evaluation of non executive directors) and
7. Whistle blower policy, providing for a mechanism for employees to report to the management concerns about unethical behaviour of company's code of conduct or ethics policy.

Quarterly compliance report to the stock exchanges is required within 15 days from the close of the quarter as per the format given in annexure 1B (Annexure 1B: Format of Quarterly Compliance report on Corporate Governance). The obligation for the first report starts from the quarter ending June 30, 2005. Schedule of implementation starts from April 1, 2005.

General/Miscellaneous

According to other provisions as to board and committees, a director shall not be a member in more than 10 committees or act as chairman of more than five committees across all companies in which he is a director.

Application of funds, raised through a public offer must be reported on a quarterly basis to the audit committee, the report adds.

Vide Annexure 3 Non mandatory requirements (earlier regulations), section d deals with postal ballot; it lists some of the critical matters which should be decided by postal ballot; however these regulations have not been included in the new regulations relating to non mandatory requirements.

DATABASE FOR INDEPENDENT DIRECTORS

According to reports, the Government and industry are finalising a national panel of Independent directors, which will act as a database for companies looking for people to sit on their boards. The database is being prepared by the National Foundation for Corporate Governance (NFCG), which has the ministry of company affairs, Confederation of Indian Industry (CII), Institute of Chartered Accountants of India (ICAI) and Institute of Company Secretaries of India (ICSI) as its trustees. NFCG is finalising a committee of three-five eminent people who will vet the list of persons to be included in the database," said an industry source. NR Narayana Murthy, chief mentor of Infosys and vice chairman of NFCG would be on the committee, which was likely to be in place in three-four weeks, he added (the news is dated 3rd December 2004).

ICAI is finalising the guidelines and syllabus for a training programme of independent directors. The first two-day training programme will be in January and then taken to different cities, he added. In respect of ICSI, it proposes to put the directory of eminent professionals who could be approached for becoming independent directors on their web site. The concept paper on the new companies law currently being debated has further enlarged the universe of companies that need to have independent directors. It has proposed that every public company having paid up capital or turnover above prescribed limit will have to ensure that one half of the board comprises independent directors. NFCG was set up as a non-profit trust with a paid up capital of

Rs. 15 crore in October 2003 and it has now become active under the initiative of ministry of company affairs.

LAUNCH OF INDEPENDENT DIRECTORS DIALOGUE

The number of independent directors has been given importance recently and it may not be incorrect to say that this is because of the directive of the of the Securities and Exchange Board of India in the form of a revised Clause 49 for listed companies that comes into force from April 1, 05. According to the directive at least 50% of the board of directors should comprise of non-executive directors. In case the chairman of the board is a non-executive director, one-third of the board has to comprise of IDs; and if the chairman is an executive director, then the proportion of IDs goes up to half. According to Clause 49, the definition of an independent director has been made quite strict and this covers an array of situations. Therefore it is not surprising that some organisations have started to re-skill the pool of available potential IDs. From February 2005, the Independent Directors Dialogue, a joint initiative by consultant Ernst and Young and Mr. Goswami's CERG Advisory will be launched. IDD will include names of some prominent persons, such as Infosys's Mr. NR Narayana Murthy. The members will meet regularly and discuss a variety of issues related to corporate governance and the like. In addition, by March or April, IDD will begin an independent directors' training programme, with day long intensive courses. It has also been reported that another initiative has been taken up by the Chartered Accountant's Society and SP Jain Institute of Management and Research.

INDIAN CEOS: COMPETENCIES FOR SUCCESS

The Prime Minister, Manmohan Singh, asked industry leaders to emulate the Chinese economic model and promised to remove all the barriers to growth and create an environment to make Indian companies globally competitive. "Despite improved growth rates that we have achieved in the last 15 years, our share of world trade, our share of world gross domestic product, our share of world exports is much too small compared with our nation's potential and when we look at what a country like China has achieved in the last 20 years, I think that is the role model that we have to look at. We cannot be satisfied with status quo," Dr Singh said. He was delivering the inaugural address of the summit 'Indian CEOs–Competencies for success', organised jointly by the Public Enterprises Selection Board, the Bharat Petroleum Corporation Ltd., FICCI, CII and SCOPE. Exhorting Industry to achieve world class in the manufacturing and service sectors, Dr Singh said it was amazing to note how people of Indian origin did so well in other countries, particularly in the Silicon valley. "Our challenge is to reproduce in our own country these conditions so that our people don't have to go abroad to prove to the rest of the world that we Indians are second to none." Asserting that the best Indian CEOs did compare favourably with their international counterparts, and in some areas of management, they were even superior, Dr Singh said. "As in so many other things, in management too we seem to have high 'thinking capabilities but modest 'doing' capabilities. This is in some ways a national cultural trait, perhaps. That we are good at conceptualisation, at abstraction, at thinking, but not as good at execution, at implementation and at doing. Understanding this and recognising the problem is in itself a movement forward," he said.

PM for more autonomy to public sector CEOs: The Prime Minister advocated the need for greater functional autonomy to public sector CEOs while delivering the inaugural address of the summit 'Indian CEOs–Competencies for success" organised jointly by the Public enterprises selection Board and other organisations mentioned above. He said: "Many of our public sector enterprises (PSEs) have very talented and committed leaders. We must strengthen their hands so that they can provide effective leadership and manage public resources more efficiently. Our Government has made a clear commitment to empowering our PSEs and their managements. We already have given our commitment to help in the globalisation of lour 'navratnas', Especially of firms in strategic sectors like energy. Both the "navratnas" and the other PSEs require competent managerial leadership. They need to survive competition. Above all, they need this to grow and deliver on the promises they have made to their stakeholders. We cannot afford to waste public resources by allowing PSEs to function below par. They must be run efficiently and must be cost—effective if they are to serve the interests of the people." Dr Singh, however, said it was not the CEO alone who played an important role in any organisation. "I do believe that the real strength of any organisation lies in the commitment and capability of its many functionaries. The excessive focus on individuals is, in fact, antithetical to the spirit of democratic functioning. A true leader inspires by example so that others feel motivated to follow and do their assigned job to the best of their abilities. It is in this context that the management of human relations assumes great importance in the contemporary world," he said. "Citing the example of Korea's highly skilled workforce, Dr. Singh said India needed more centres of excellence as much as ordinary training institutions of high quality. India needs a revolution at all levels of knowledge and not just at the top of the pyramid." He released the monograph on the study of "Indian CEOs – Competencies for success."

SECURITIES AND EXCHANGE BOARD OF INDIA (EMPLOYEE STOCK OPTION SCHEME AND EMPLOYER STOCK PURCHASE SCHEME) GUIDELINES, 1999

The above guidelines have been issued by SEBI under Section 11 of the Securities and Exchange Board of India Act, 1992. Part A of the guidelines relate to ESOS meaning a scheme under which a company grants employee stock option. Part B of the guidelines relate to ESPS, meaning 'a scheme under which the company offers shares to employees as part of a public issue or otherwise'. The schedules provide guidelines on accounting policies for ESOS, accounting policies for ESPS, Disclosure document reg: statement of risks, Information required in the statement to be filed with stock exchange, etc.

SEBI vide their No. SEBUPMD/MBD/ESOP/2/2003/30/06 dated 30.6.2003 made some amendments to SEBI (Employee stock option scheme and employee stock purchase scheme) guidelines, 1999 and accordingly, the Board, after considering the recommendations of the Prof. J R Varma committee which reviewed the 1999 guidelines, approved certain modifications to be incorporated in captioned Guidelines. The amended guidelines are available in SEBI website, i.e. www.sebi.gov.in.

The above amendments include, inter alia, provisions of mandatory disclosures of employee compensation cost using fair value of ESOS/ESPS calculated on the basis of option pricing model and also the impact of the same on profits and EPS of the company, mandatory appointment of merchant banker, accounting treatment for ESOS/ ESPS administered through trust route, provisions to facilitate faster listing of shares arising out of exercise of ESOP, etc. Further, subsequent to the above amendments, SEBI received queries seeking clarifications. Therefore SEBI made further amendments to the said guidelines and clarified matters, vide Circular issued By SEBI vide No. SEBI/(-FV/DIIJÈSOP/3/2004/22/7 dated 22.07.2004.

According to the above guidelines, "employee stock option" means the option given to the whole time directors, officers or employees of a company which gives such directors, officers or employees, the benefit or right to purchase or subscribe at a future date, the securities offered by the company at pre-determined price. Further "employee stock purchase scheme (ESPS)" means a scheme under which the company offers shares to employees as part of a public issue or otherwise. The SEBI guidelines, further, provide as follows: Issue of stock options at a discount to the market price would be regarded as another form of employee compensation, ESOPS would not be covered by the pricing provisions of SEBI preferential allotment guidelines, shareholders should approve ESOS through a special resolution,' no restriction on the maximum number of shares to be issued to a single employee, the operation of the scheme would be under the direction of a compensation committee of the board, and stock option would be open to all permanent employees whether in India or abroad, The guidelines also prescribe disclosures in the Directors' report regarding total number of shares covered by the ESOP, pricing formula, options granted etc.

BUY BACK OF SECURITIES

Purchase of own shares by a company or what may be called buy back of securities is governed by the provisions of Sections 77, 77A, 77AA and 77B of the Companies Act. Section 77(l) provides that a company limited by shares or a company limited by guarantee having a share capital cannot buy its own shares. The Companies (Amendment) Act, 1999 vide sections 77A, 77AA and 77B however, allow companies to purchase their own shares or other securities subject to certain conditions. S.77A allows a company to buy its own shares or other specified securities out of its free reserves or the securities premium account, or the proceeds of any shares or other specified securities. The conditions prescribed provide that the buy back should be authorised by the articles, a special resolution in general meeting to be passed, the buy back should be limited to less than 25% of the paid up capital and free reserves of the company and the ratio of the debt owed by the company should not be more than twice the capital and its free reserves, only fully paid up shares being bought back and buy back of listed securities is also in accordance with stock exchange regulations. In the case of unlisted specified securities, separate guidelines have been laid down and these are required to be followed. Apart from the above and other conditions, the SEBI Guidelines stipulate as follows:

The SEBI (Buy back of securities) Regulations, 1998 make the regulations applicable to buy back of equity shares of a listed company on a stock exchange. The buy back may be made by any one of the following methods: from existing security holders on a proportionate basis through tender offer, from open market (book building/stock exchange) and from odd lot holders. Buy back through negotiated deals is not allowed and an insider shall not deal in securities on the basis of unpublished information relating to buy back of specified securities. A special resolution and public notice are also required. The regulations also detail the procedure for buy back through tender offer (Chapter III), buy back from the open market (Chapter IV) including through book building and also carry provisions for extinguishments of certificates. Chapter V of the regulations provide details of general obligations of the company as well as the obligations of merchant banker.

The major advantages of buy back of shares to investors, companies and the economy are claimed to be: Revival of the capital market, liquidity to dormant shares, restructuring of capital base by companies, increasing the earnings per share (EPS) and also providing an instrument to ward off hostile take over bids.

CORPORATE GOVERNANCE FROM THE ANNUAL REOPRT 2003-2004 OF (200-213) RELIANCE INDUSTRIES LTD.

Reliance is one of the pioneers in the country in implementing the best international practices of Corporate Governance. In recognition of this pioneering effort, the Institute of Company Secretaries of India has bestowed on the Company the National Award for Excellence in Corporate Governance for the year 2003.

Reliance's Corporate Governance Principles uphold its global standing at the forefront of corporate governance best practice. Reliance continues to review its corporate governance practices to ensure that they continue to reflect domestic and international developments to position itself to conform to the best corporate governance practices. It takes feedback into account in its periodic reviews of the guidelines to ensure their continuing relevance, effectiveness and responsiveness to the needs of local and international investors and all other stakeholders.

Principles

Reliance's corporate governance practices focus on the following main principles:

Recognising the Respective Roles and Responsibilities of Board and Management

To establish an effective mechanism for overseeing the affairs, keeping in view the Company's size, complexity, geographical operations and corporate tradition & culture, the Reliance's framework is designed to:

- enable the Board to provide strategic guidance for the Company and effective overseeing of the management;
- define the respective roles and responsibilities of senior executives and officers to ensure accountability; and
- ensure a balance of authority such that no single individual has unfettered powers.

Having a Board of Appropriate Composition, Size and Commitment to Adequately Discharge its Responsibilities and Duties

To ensure effectiveness of the Board, facilitating efficient discharge of duties and adding value in the context of the Company's circumstances, the Board periodically reviews its composition and size for ensuring a strong element of independence' and commitment. Accordingly the Board is structured in such a way that

- It has a proper understanding of, and competence to deal: with, the current and emerging issues of the business and the benefit of a variety of perspectives and skills.
- It has the appropriate mix of executive and non-executive directors ensuring Directors' commitment and time to participate in the affairs fully.
- It can effectively review and challenge the performance of management and exercise independent judgment.

The Directors are elected by the shareholders. However the Board plays an important role in the selection of candidates for shareholders' approval. Reliance s policy does not prescribe any term limit for Directors, as the term limits, while could help fresh ideas and view points, they have the disadvantage of losing the contribution of directors who over time have developed insight in to the Company and its affairs.

Independent Verification and Safeguarding Integrity of the Company's Financial Reporting

To ensure the truthful and factual presentation of the Company's financial position, the Company has put in place a structure of review and authorisation apart from strong internal audit process. For this purpose, the Board has also constituted an Audit Committee, which is charged with paying particular attention to the management processes supporting external reporting, the performance and objectivity of the internal audit function, and the performance and independence of the external auditors.

Timely and Balanced Disclosure of all Material Information Concerning the Company

To give investors an equal and timely access to material information, and to ensure that Company announcements are factual, balanced and in compliance with the applicable provisions of law, the Company has put in place a mechanism to ensure that:

- all investors have equal and timely access to material information concerning the Company–Including Its financial position, performance and governance.
- Company announcements are factual and presented in a clear and balanced way, disclosing both positive and negative information.

Highest importance to Investor Relations

To ensure long term shareholder value creation and to promote shareholder participation in corporate affairs, Reliance has established and maintained communication strategies, including a policy for, clarity in notices of meetings. Reliance also maintains its corporate website www.ril.com for convenient access by the shareholders to all material information about the Company. Reliance's endeavors are to empower its shareholders by:

- communicating effectively with them.
- giving them appropriate information about the Company.
- making it easy for them to participate in general meetings.

Sound System of Risk Management and Internal Control

To establish and maintain a system of risk management and internal control, the Company has set up a policy which includes a review of the risk management system, and maintenance of a risk profile (both financial and non-financial risks). Reliance has set up an effective internal audit function, independent of the external auditors, to review the effectiveness of the risk management system. Audit Committee of the Board oversees the risk management and internal control systems. This system is designed to:

- identify, assess, monitor and manage risks.
- inform investors of material changes to the Company's risk profile.

Fair Review, Active Encouragement and Management Effectiveness

To ensure consistent effectiveness of the overall management, the performance of the senior executives and officers is subject to review. This includes equipping individuals with the knowledge and information they need to discharge their responsibilities effectively, and reviewing individual and collective performance regularly. Performance evaluation process is fair and transparent and uses both measurable and qualitative indicators.

Efficient Exe utive Remuneration Policy

The Company has adopted a remuneration policy that attracts and maintains talented and motivated executives so as to encourage enhanced performance of the Company. The remuneration policy envisages a clear relationship between performance and remuneration, including the link between remuneration paid and the overall corporate performance.

Remuneration of managing and whole time directors is determined by the Remuneration Committee of Directors within the permissible limits under the applicable provisions of law and is approved by Shareholders. Non Executive Directors are paid sitting fees within the limits prescribed under law.

Corporate Ethics

Reliance has a defined policy framework for ethical business conduct by its personnel. The Ethics Policy sets forth, *inter alia*:

- Our Values and Commitments
- Our Code of Ethics
- Our Business Policies
- The Insider Trading Policy
- A detailed programme for Ethics Management at Reliance.

These policies support the consistent endeavour to enhance the reputation of the Company.

The *"Values and Commitments" policy document* states that Reliance believes that any business conduct can be ethical only when it rests on the nine core values of Honesty, Integrity. Respect, Fairness, Purposefulness, Trust, Responsibility, Citizenship and Caring.

These values are not to be lost sight of by anyone at Reliance under any circumstances irrespective of the goals that are intended to be achieved. To us, the means are as important as the ends.

In pursuit of these values outlined in the "Values and Commitments" policy document, we are committed to an ethical treatment of all our stakeholders–our employees, our customers, our environment, our shareholders, our lenders and other investors, our suppliers and the Government. A firm belief that every Reliance team member holds is that the other persons' interests count as much as their own.

The *"Code of Ethics" and the "Business Policies"* are in alignment with Reliance's Values and Commitments. The essence of these documents is that each employee should conduct the Company's business with integrity, in compliance with applicable laws, and in a manner that excludes considerations of personal advantage.

The "*Code of Ethics*" policy document contains the policy on the following:

- Conflict of Interest
- Payments and Gifting
- Receipt of Gifts
- Purchases through suppliers
- Appointment of full-time agents, consultants and representatives
- Political Contributions

The "*Business Policies" document* contains the policy on the following:

- Fair Market Practices
- Inside Information
- Financial Records and Accounting integrity
- External Communication
- Work Ethics
- Personal Conduct
- Health Safety and Environment
- Quality

The Insider Trading Policy: The "*Code of Conduct for Prevention of Insider Trading*" contains the policies prohibiting insider trading.

Programme for Ethics Management at Reliance: We have established an elaborate Ethics Management and Compliance Organisation/Process to underscore our commitment to ethical conduct throughout our Company. It is a key part of a vigorous corporate-wide effort to promote a positive and ethical work environment.

The Company's shares are listed on three Stock Exchanges in India and GDRs *are* listed on Luxembourg Stock Exchange. In accordance with Clause 49 of the listing agreement with the domestic stock exchanges and best practices followed internationally on Corporate Governance the details of compliance by the Company are as under:

1. **Company's philosophy on Code of Governance:** As discussed above, Reliance's philosophy on corporate governance envisages the attainment of the highest levels of transparency, accountability and equity, in all facets of its operations, and in all its interactions with its stakeholders, including shareholders, employees, the government and lenders. Reliance is committed to

achieving the highest international standards of corporate governance. Reliance believes that all its operations and actions must serve the underlying goal of enhancing overall shareholder value, over a sustained period of time:

2. **Board of Directors:** The Board of Directors consists of 12 directors, out of which 6 are independent directors. The composition of the Board and category of Directors is as follows:

Category	Name of the Directors
Promoter/ Executive Directors	M.D. Ambani *Chairman & Managing Director* A.D. Ambani *Vice Chairman & Managing Director* N.R. Meswani *Executive Director* H.R. Meswani *Executive Director*
Promoter Non-Executive Director	R.H. Ambani
Non-Promoter Executive Director	H.S. Kohli *Executive Director*
Independent Directors	M.L. Bhakta T.R.U. Pai Y.P. Trivedi U. Mahesh Rao* *(Nominee Director of GIC)* Dr. D.V. Kapur M.P. Modi S. Venkitaramanan

Ceased to be a Director with effect from 17th June, 2003 on the withdrawal of nomination by the General Insurance Corporation of India.

Brief Resume of the Directors being reappointed, nature of their expertise in specific functional areas and names of companies in which they hold directorship and the membership of the committees of the Board are furnished hereunder.

(a) **Shri M.L. Bhakta** is a Director of the Company since 27th September, 1977. He is a Senior Partner of Messrs Kanga & Company, a leading firm of Advocates and Solicitors in Mumbai. He has been in practice for over 40 years and has vast experience in the legal field and particularly on matters relating to corporate laws, banking and taxation. He is the legal advisor to leading foreign and Indian companies and banks. He has also been associated with a large number of Euro issues made by Indian companies. He was the Chairman of the Taxation Law Standing Committee of LAWASIA, an Association of Lawyers of Asia and Pacific which has its headquarters in Australia. He is a member of the, International Law Association, Indian Chapter Regional Branch, Mumbai, Nathdwara Temple Board, Nathdwara, Rajasthan and President of the Association of Hospitals, Mumbai. He is also

a Director in the following companies, viz. Gujarat Ambuja Cements Limited, Micro Inks Limited, The Indian Merchants'Chamber, Bombay, J.C. Bamford Excavators (India) Private Limited, JCB India Limited and JCB Construction Equipment Limited. He is the Chairman of the Remuneration Committee and the Shareholders'/Investors' Grievance Committee of the Company and Compensation & Remuneration Committee and Banking Matters Committee of Gujarat Ambuja Cements Limited. He is a member of the Audit Committees of Gujarat Ambuja Cements Limited, Micro Inks Limited and JCB India Limited.

(b) **Dr. D.V. Kapur** is a Director of the Company since 28th March, 2001. He is a Graduate with Honours in Electrical Engineering and is having vast experience in Power Sector, Engineering, Chemicals and Petrochemicals Industries. He served BHEL, a premier Indian public sector enterprise, in various positions. He was responsible for establishment of the Systems Oriented National Thermal Power Corporation (NTPC), a public sector enterprise of which he was the founder Chairman-cum-Managing Director. Under his leadership NTPC undertook and successfully implemented a series of 2000 MW power projects which today form the main stay of the Indian power sector For his contribution in building of NTPC, the World Bank Board of Directors.described him as a 'Model Manager'. He was Secretary to the Government of India in the Ministry of Power, Heavy Industry and Chemicals & Petrochemicals from 1980 to 1986. For the significant contributions made by him in the fields of Technology Management and Industrial Development. Jawaharlal Nehru Technological University conferred the degree of D.Sc. on him. He has also been associated with a number of national institutions as Chairman, Board of Governors, Indian Institute of Technology, Bombay; Chairman, National Productivity Council; Member, Atomic Energy Commission etc.

He is a Director on the Boards of a number of companies, viz. Reliance Power Limited, Jacobs H&G (P) Limited, GKN Driveline (India) Limited, Larsen Toubro Limited, Tata Chemicals Limited, Honda Sell Power Products Limited, Zenith Limited, DLF Power Limited, Drivetech Accessories Limited and Reliance Jamnagar Power Private Limited. He is the Chairman of the Audit Committee and Shareholders'/Investors' Relations Committee of Honda Seil Power Products Limited and the Audit Committee and the Chairman's Executive Committee of GKN Driveline (India) Limited and a Member of the Shareholders' Grievance Committee and Audit Committee of Larsen & Toubro Limited, the Audit Committee of Zenith Limited and the Remuneration Committee of the Company.

(c) **Shri M.P. Modi** is a Director of the Company since 28th March, 2001. He has held high positions in Government of India as Chairman of Telecom Commission, Secretary, Ministry of Coal and Special Secretary, Insurance. He has considerable management experience, particularly in the fields of energy, insurance, petrochemicals and telecom. At present he is a Director on the Boards of the following companies: ICICI Prudential Life Insurance Company Limited, Essar Shipping Limited and Mangalore Refinery & Petrochemicals

Limited. He is the Chairman of the Audit Committees of Mangalore Refinery & Petrochemicals Limited, ICICI Prudential Life Insurance Co. Limited and a Member of the Audit Committees of Esser Wiping Limited and the Company.

3. **Board Meetings its Committee Meetings and Procedures**

A. **Institutionalised decision making process:** With a view to institutionalise all corporate affairs and setting up systems and procedures for advance planning for matters requiring discussion/decisions by the Board, the Company has defined guidelines for the meetings of Board of Directors and Committees thereof. These Guidelines seek to systematize the decision making process at the meetings of Board/Committees, in an informed and most efficient manner.

B. **Scheduling and selection of Agenda Items for Board Meetings**

(a) The Company holds minimum of four Board Meetings in each year, which are pre-scheduled after the end of each financial quarter. Apart from the four prescheduled Board Meetings, additional Board Meetings are convened by giving appropriate notice at any time to address the specific needs of the Company. The Board may also approve permitted urgent matters by passing resolutions by circulation.

(b) The meetings are held at the Company's Office at 3rd Floor, "Reliance Centre", Walchand Hirachand Marg, Ballard Estate, Mumbai 400 038.

(c) All divisions/departments in the Company are encouraged to plan their functions well in advance, particularly with regard to matters requiring discussion/approval/decision in the Board/Committee Meetings. All such matters are communicated to the Company Secretary in advance so that the same could be included in the Agenda for the Board Meetings.

(d) The Board is given presentations covering Finance, Sales and Marketing, and the major business segments and operations of the Company, before taking on, record the results of the Company for the preceding financial quarter at each of the prescheduled Board Meeting. The Board's annual agenda Includes recommending dividend keeping in view the dividend policy, determining directors who shall retire by rotation and recommending appointment of Directors/Auditors, authentication of annual accounts and approving Directors' Report, long-term strategic plan for the Company and the principal issues that the Company expects to face in. the future. Board Meetings also note and review functions of its Committees.

(e) The Chairman of the Board and the Company Secretary in consultation with other concerned persons in the senior management, finalise the agenda papers for the Board Meetings.

C. **Board Material Distributed in Advance**

(a) Agenda papers are circulated to the Directors, in advance, in the defined Agenda format. All material information is incorporated in the Agenda Papers for facilitating meaningful and focussed discussions at the meeting. Where it is not practicable to attach any document to the Agenda, the same are placed on the table at the meeting with specific reference to this effect in the Agenda.

(*b*) In special and exceptional circumstances, additional or supplementary item(s) on the agenda are permitted. Sensitive subject matters may be discussed at the meeting without written material being circulated in advance or at the meeting.

D. **Recording minutes of proceedings at Board Meeting**

The Company Secretary records the minutes of the proceedings of each Board and Committee Meetings. Draft minutes are circulated to all the members of the Board for their comments. The minutes of proceedings of a meeting are entered in the Minutes Book within 30 days from the conclusion of the meeting.

E. **Post meeting follow up mechanism**

The Guidelines for Board and Committee meetings facilitate an effective post meeting follow-up, review and reporting process for the decisions taken by the Board and Committees.

F. **Compliance**

The Company Secretary while preparing, the agenda, notes on agenda, minutes etc. of the meeting(s), is responsible for and is required to ensure adherence to all the applicable provisions of law including the Companies Act, 1956 and the Secretarial Standards recommended by the Institute of Company Secretaries of India, New Delhi.

4. **Attendance of each Director at the Board meetings, last Annual General Meeting and Number of other Directorship and Chairmanship/ Membership of Committee of each Director in various companies:**

Name of the Director	Attendance, Particulars		No. of Directorships and committee memberships/chairmanship		
	Board Meetings	Last AGM	Other Directorships	Committee Memberships**	Committee Chairmanships**
M.D. Ambani	5	Present	6	1	–
A.D. Ambani,	5	Present	4	1	–
N.R. Meswanl	5	Present	1	1	–
H.R. Meswani\	5	Present	1	1	–
H.S. Kohli	4	Present	1	–	–
R.H. Ambani '	4	Present	8	–	1
M.L. Bhakta	5	Present	6	3	3
Y.P. Trivedi	4	Present	13	3	2
T.R.U. Pal	4	Present	5	2	–
U. Mahesh Rao*	2	Present	–	–	–
Dr. D.V. Kapur	5	Present	10	4	3
M.P. Modi	4	Present	3	2	2
S. Venkitaramanan'	5	Present	8	4	–

* Ceased to be a Director with effect from 17th June, 2003 on the withdrawal of nomination by the General Insurance Corporation of India.

** In accordance with Clause 49 of the Listing Agreement with the Stock Exchanges, membership/chairmanship of only the Audit Committee, Shareholders'/Investors' Grievance Committee and the Remuneration Committee of all the Public Limited Companies has been considered.

5. **Number of Board Meetings held and the dates on which held**

5 (Five) Board Meetings were held during the year, as against the, minimum requirement of 4 meetings, The dates on which the meetings held were as follows: 23rd April, 2003, 16th June, 2003, 31st July, 2003, 16th October, 2003, and 29th January, 2004. The Company has held at least, one meeting in every three months and the maximum time gap between any two meetings was not more than four months. None of the Directors of the Company was a member of more than ten Committees, nor was the Chairman of more than five Committees acros Companies in which he was a Director.

6. **Board Committees**

A. **Standing Committees**

The Company has the following standing Committees of the Board.

(i) Audit Committee

The Board of the Company has constituted an Audit Committee, comprising four independent, Non-Executive Directors viz. Shri Y.P. Trivedi, Chairman (having financial and accounting knowledge), Shri S. Venkitaramanan, Vice Chairman, Shri T.R.U. Pai and Shri M.P. Modi. The constitution of Audit Committee also meets with the requirements under Section 292A of the Companies Act, 1956.

The terms of reference stipulated by the Board to the Audit Committee are, as contained in Clause 49 of the Listing Agreement and Section 292A of the Companies Act, 1956, as follows:

(a) Oversight of the Company's financial reporting process and the disclosure of its financial information.

(b) Recommending the appointment and removal of external auditors, fixation of audit fee and also approval for payment for any other services.

(c) Reviewing with management the quarterly, half-yearly and annual financial statements before submission to the Board, focussing primarily on *(i)* any changes in accounting policies and practices, *(ii)* major accounting entries based on exercise of judgement by management, *(iii)* qualifications in draft audit report, *(iv)* significant adjustments arising out of audit, *(v)* the going concern assumption, *(vi)* compliance with accounting standards, *(vii)* compliance with Stock Exchange and legal requirements concerning financial statements and *(viii)* any related party transactions i.e. transactions of the Company of material nature, with promoters or the management, their subsidiaries or relatives etc. that may have potential conflict with the interests of Company at large.

(d) Reviewing with the management, external and internal auditors, the adequacy and compliance of internal control systems.

(e) Reviewing the adequacy of internal audit functions.

(f) Discussion with internal auditors any significant findings and follow up there on.

(g) Reviewing the findings of any Internal investigations by the internal auditors into matters where there is suspected fraud or irregularity or a

failure of internal control systems of a material nature and reporting the matter to the Board.

(h) Discussion with external auditors before the audit commences nature and scope of audit as well as have post-audit discussion to ascertain any area of concern.

(i) Reviewing the Company's financial and risk management policies.

(j) To look into the reasons for substantial defaults in the payment to the depositors, debentureholders, shareholders (in case of non payment of declared dividends) and creditors.

During the year, the Committee has met 5 times, as against the minimum requirement of 3 meetings. The head of finance function, head of internal audit and the representatives of the Statutory Auditors were invited to be present at the Audit Committee Meetings. The Cost Auditors appointed by the Company under Section 233B of the Companies Act, 1956 were also invited to attend the Audit Committee meetings.

Attendance of each Member at the Audit Committee meetings held during the year

Name of Member of Audit Committee	Attendance particulars
Shri Y.P. Trivedi Chairman	23rd April, 2003, 28th July, 2003, 16th October, 2003 and 29th January, 2004.
Shri S. Venkitaramanan, Vice Chairman*	23rd April, 2003, 28th July, 2003, 31st July, 2003. 16th October, 2003 and 29th January, 2004
Shri U.Mahesh Rao**	23rd April, 2003
Shri T.R.U Pai	23rd April, 2003, 28th July, 2003, 31st July, 2003 and 29th January, 2004
Shri M.P. Modi***	29th January, 2004

* Elected as Vice Chairman of the Audit Committee with effect from 28th July, 2003.

** Ceased to be a Director with effect from 17th June, 2003 on the withdrawal of nomination by the General Insurance Corporation of India.

*** Appointed as a Member of the Audit Committee with effect from 31st July, 2003.

(ii) Remuneration Committee

The Board of the Company has constituted a Remuneration Committee, comprising of 4 Independent, Non-Executive Directors viz. Shri M.L Bhakta, Chairman, Shri Y.P. Trivedi, Shri S. Venkitaramanan and Dr. D.V. Kapur.

The Remuneration Committee has been constituted to recommend/review the remuneration package of the Managing/Whole-time Directors, based on performance and 'defined criteria.

The remuneration policy is directed towards rewarding performance, based on review of achievements on a periodical basis. The remuneration policy is in consonance with the existing Industry practice.

During the year the Committee met once on 23rd April, 2003, and all the members of the Committee, who are independent non-executive directors, were present at the meeting.

Details of remuneration to Directors for the year

The aggregate value of salary and perquisites including commission paid for the year ended 31st March, 2004 to the Managing Directors/Whole time Directors is as follows: Shri M.D. Ambani, Chairman and Managing Director, Rs. 11.62 crore; Shri A.D. Ambani, Vice Chairman and Managing Director, As. 11.62 crore; Shri N.R. Meswani, Executive Director, Rs. 3.02 crore; Shri H.R. Meswani, Executive Director, Rs. 3.02 crore. The aggregate value of salary and perquisites paid to Shri H.S. Kohli, Executive Director was Rs. 0.18 crore. Besides this, all the Whole-time Directors were also entitled to Company's contribution to Provident Fund, Superannuation or, Annuity Fund, to the extent not taxable and Gratuity and encashment of leave at the end of tenure, as per the rules of the Company. The agreements with the above Directors are for a period of 5 years from the respective dates of appointments of the said directors and can be terminated by either party by giving three months' notice in writing.

The Company paid sitting fees to all the Non-Executive Directors at the rate of Rs. 5000/- upto 30th September, 2003 and pays at the rate of Rs. 20,000/- from 1st October 2003 for attending each meeting of the Board anctnr Committee thereof. The sitting fees paid for the year ended 31st March, 2004 to the Directors are as follows: Shri R.H. Ambani Rs. 50,000/-; Shri M.L. Bhakta Rs. 2,20,000/-; Shri Y.P. Trivedi Rs. 2,45,000/- Shri T.R.U. Pai Rs.70,000/-; Shri S. Venkitaramanan Rs. 1,15,000/-; Shri U. Mahesh Rao Rs. 20,000/-; Dr. D.V. Kapur Rs. 55,000/-; and Shri M.P. Modi Rs. 55,000/-.

The Company has paid Rs. 30,938/- as professional fees to Messrs Kanga & Company, a firm in which Shri M.L. Bhakta, Director of the Company, is a partner.

The Company has not granted any stock option to its directors.

(iii) Shareholders'/Investors' Grievance Committee.

The Board of the Company. has constituted a Shareholders'/Investors' Grievance. Committee, comprising of Shri: M. L. Bhakta, (Chairman), Shri Y.P. Trivedi, Shri M.D. Ambani-and Shri A. D. Ambani. The Committee, inter alias approves issue of duplicate certificates and oversees and reviews all matters connected with the securities transfers. The Committee also looks into redressal of shareholders' complaints like transfer of shares, non-receipt of balance sheet, non-receipt of declared dividends, etc. The Committee oversees the performance' of the Registrar and Transfer Agents, and recommend measures for overall improvement in-the' quality of investor services. The Board of Directors have delegated the power of approving transfer of securities to the Managing Directors and the Company Secretary. The Committee also monitors the implementation and compliance of the Company's Code of Conduct for prevention of Insider Trading in pursuance of SEBI (Prohibition of Insider Trading) Regulations, 1992.

Shri Vinod M. Ambani, President & Company Secretary, is the Compliance Officer for complying with the requirements of the Securities and Exchange Board of India (Prohibition of Insider Trading) Regulations, 1992 and Shri Surendra Pipara, Joint Company Secretary is the Compliance Officer for complying with the requirements of the Listing Agreement with the Stock Exchanges.

The total number of complaints received and replied to the satisfaction of shareholders during the year under review, was 20,483. Outstanding complaints as on 31st March, 2004 were Nil. 609 requests for transfers and 1521 requests for dematerialisation were pending for approval as on 31st March, 2004, which were approved and dealt with by 2nd April, 2004 and 3rd April, 2004 respectively.

(iv) Finance Committee

The Finance Committee makes recommendations to the Board relating to capital structure and the issuance of securities, reviews banking arrangements and cash management, and reviews and approves certain short-term and long-term investment transactions, etc. Finance Committee meets as and when the need to consider any matter assigned to it arises.

B. **Functional Committees**

The Board may, from time to time constitute one or more Functional Committees delegating powers and duties with respect to specific purposes. Meetings of such Committees will be held as and when the need for discussing the matter concerning the purpose arises. Time schedule for holding the meetings of such functional committee(s) shall be finalized in consultation with the Committee Members.

C. **Procedures at Committee Meetings**

Company's guidelines relating to Board Meetings are applicable to Committee Meetings as far may be practicable. Each Committee has the authority to engage outside experts, advisers and counsel to the extent it considers appropriate to assist the Committee in its work. Minutes of the proceedings of the each Committee Meeting are placed before the Board for its perusal and noting.

7. **General Body Meetings**

Location and time for last 3 Annual General Meetings were as follows:

Year	AGM	Location	Date	Time
2000-01	AGM	Sabhagar, 19 Marine Lines, Mumbai 400 020	15th June, 2001	11.00 a.m.
2001-02	AGM	Same as above	31st October, 2002	11.00 a.m.
2002-03	AGM	Same as above	16th June, 2003	11.00 a.m.

During the year ended 31st March, 2004, there have been no resolutions passed by the Company's shareholders through postal ballot. At the ensuing Annual General Meeting, there is no resolution proposed to be passed by, postal ballot.

8. ***(a)* Disclosures on materially significant related party transactions i.e. transactions of the Company of material nature, with Its promoters, the**

directors or the management, their subsidiaries or relatives, etc. that may have potential conflict with the interests of the Company at large.

None of the transactions with any of the related parties were in conflict with the interest of the Company.

(b) **Details of non-compliance by the Company, penalties, strictures imposed on the Company by Stock Exchanges or SEBI, or any statutory authority, on any matter related to capital markets, during the last three years.**

SEBI had imposed a monetary penalty of Rs. 4.75 lakhs on the Company for the alleged nondisclosure under Regulations 7(1) and (2) of the Securities and Exchange Board of India (Substantial Acquisition of Shares and Takeovers) Regulations, 1997 in respect of acquisition of shares of a listed Company in the year 2002-03. The Company has preferred an appeal to the Hon'ble Securities Appellate Tribunal against the said order of SEBI and the said appeal is pending.

9. **Means of communication**

Half-yearly report sent to each household of shareholders

Half yearly report for the half year ended 30th September, 2003 was duly sent to shareholders.

Quarterly results

The quarterly results were published in 'Financial Express' and 'Tarun Bharat', alongwith the official news release, and the detailed presentations made to the media, analysts, institutional investors, etc. were displayed on the corporate website, www.ril.com.

The Management Discussion and Analysis (MD&A) is a part of the annual report, and each quarterly official media release.

SEBI DEFERS IMPLEMENTATION OF CLAUSE 49

Bowing to demand from corporates, the Securities and Exchange Board of India (SEBI) today deferred implementation of Clause 49 of the listing agreement till December 31 to provide listed entities, including public sector companies, time to appoint adequate number of independent directors and comply with the norms.

The board discussed Clause 49 of the listing pact which was expected to come into effect from April 1 2005 to improve governance, the SEBI Chairman, M. Damodaran, told reporters after the board meeting.

It was felt; that the large number of listed entities would not be in a state of preparedness to comply with Clause 49 by March 31, 2005 and hence would be 'appropriate to defer implementation till 2005 end,' he said.

"During the next nine months it is expected that listed entities would identify adequate number of independent directors and equip them to work effectively on the company boards," he said. The objective of the Clause, 49 provisions is to improve quality of corporate governance at the board level, he added. Asked about any special concession for state-owned listed entities, the SEBI chief said this matter did not come up for discussion but they (PSUs) were not looked up on as special class and would have to comply with the provisions.

The government nominees are representatives of majority owner on the board of state-owned companies, he said.

On show cause notices to market participants for the May 17, 2004 crash, Mr. Damodaran said SEBI had issued 12 notices on charges of behaving in a manner inconsistent with what was expected of market intermediaries. He, however, declined to give the timeframe for completing probe and initiate action against those found guilty

NARESH CHANDRA COMMITTEE

Naresh Chandra Committee appointed by the Department of Company Affairs made recommendations, *inter-alia,* on the issues of corporate governance:

1. The auditors-company relationship, disqualification for audit assignments because of direct financial interest in audit clients, loans and guarantees and business relationships between the company and the audit firm.
2. List of prohibited non audited services prescribed.
3. Independence standard for consulting other entities that are affiliated for audited firms.
4. Compulsory audit partner rotation.
5. Disclosure of contingent liabilities by auditors.
6. Setting up of independent oversite boards for supervising the work of auditors.
7. Setting up an independent quality review board of auditors.
8. Independent director defined. Apart from following the criterion of family pecuniary business relationship, one should also not be director for more than three terms of three years and prescribed that not less than 50 percent of the board of directors should comprise independent directors.
9. Minimum boards size prescribed.
10. Provisions regarding the audit Committee and its powers.
11. SEBI not to exercise subordinate legislation. Special legislation exist.
12. Improving facilities in the DCA offices.
13. Setting up of a serious fraud office in the Department of Company Affairs.

INTERIM NEW YORK STOCK EXCHANGE CODE OF BUSINESS CONDUCT AND ETHICS FOR MEMBERS OF THE BOARD OF DIRECTORS

Introduction

The New York Stock Exchange Board of Directors (the "Board") has adopted the following Code of Business Conduct and Ethics for Members of the Board of Directors (the "Code"). Each director must comply with the letter and spirit of this Code. No code or policy can anticipate every situation that may arise. As the nation's leading public marketplace for corporate securities, the NYSE has an inviolable responsibility to insure that its activities are conducted in accordance with the highest standards of business and personal integrity. Accordingly, this Code is intended to serve as a set of guiding principles for directors. Directors must conduct themselves accordingly and seek to avoid even the appearance of improper behavior.

Directors encouraged to bring questions about particular circumstances that *may* involve one or more of the provisions of this Code to the attention of the Chair of. the Governance Committee, who may consult with inside or outside legal counsel as appropriate. Directors who also serve as officers or employees of the NYSE must also comply with the Officers' and Employees' Statement of Business Conduct and Ethics and Guidelines on Gifts and Entertainment.

1. Compliance with Laws, Rules and Regulations

Obeying the law, both in letter and in spirit, and behaving in a manner consistent with the NYSE's values is the foundation on which the NYSE's ethical standards are built. All directors are expected to conduct all their business and affairs in full compliance with applicable laws, rules and regulations, and shall encourage and promote such behavior for themselves, officers and employees.

2. Conflicts of Interest

Directors must avoid any conflicts of interest between the director and the NYSE. A "conflict of interest" exists when a director's personal or professional interest is adverse to or may appear to be adverse to the interests of the NYSE. Conflicts of interest may also arise when a director, or members of his or her family, or an organization with which the director is affiliated receives improper personal benefits as a result of his or her position as a director of the NYSE. Any situation that involves, or may involve, a conflict of interest with the NYSE, should be promptly disclosed to the Chair of the Governance Committee, who may consult with inside or outside legal counsel, as appropriate. The NYSE Constitution and certain NYSE Rules address specific conflicts of interest, and situations that involve the disqualification of a Director from participating in the consideration of a matter.

This document is labeled "Interim" as it remains subject to review and amendment by the NYSE's Board of Directors, upon the recommendation of the Special Committee on Governance of the NYSE. The Special Committee on Governance of the NYSE may make such a recommendation upon completion of its review of the NYSE's corporate governance.

See Article IV, Section 15 of the NYSE Constitution, and Rules 21 and 22 of the NYSE Rules.

3. Insider Trading

The securities laws impose severe sanctions upon any individual who uses "inside information" for his or her own benefit or discloses it to others for their use. Directors who have access to confidential information as a result of their Board service are not permitted to use or share that information for securities trading purposes or for any other purpose except the conduct of the NYSE's business. All non-public information about the NYSE should be considered confidential information. To use non-public information for personal *financial benefit or to "tip" others who might make an investment decision on the basis of* this information is not only unethical but also illegal.

4. Corporate Opportunities

Directors are prohibited from taking for themselves personally or' for the organizations with which they are affiliated opportunities that are discovered through the use of NYSE property, information or position without the consent of the Board of Directors. No director may use NYSE property, information, or position for improper personal gain. Directors owe a duty to the NYSE to advance its legitimate interests when the opportunity to do so arises.

5. Competitions and Fair Dealing

The NYSE adheres to a policy of fair dealing in all its activities. Directors shall endeavor to deal fairly with the NYSE's customers, suppliers, competitors and employees. No director should take unfair advantage of anyone through manipulation, concealment, abuse of privileged information, misrepresentation of material facts, or any other intentional unfair-dealing practice.

The purpose of business entertainment and gifts in a commercial setting is to create goodwill and sound working relationships, not to gain unfair advantage with customers. Directors and members of their immediate families may not accept gifts from persons or entities where any such gift is being made in order to influence the director's actions as a member of the Board, or where acceptance of the gifts could create the appearance of such influence.

6. Antitrust Laws

The NYSE believes that vigorous competition is in the best interest of the NYSE, its employees,; and the public. The antitrust laws were conceived and enacted to help preserve private enterprise capitalism in America by promoting fair and healthy competition. It is the firm policy of the NYSE to comply fully with the spirit and letter of these laws.

Essentially, the antitrust laws prohibit activities which constitute unreasonable restraint of trade, unfair trade practices and other anti-competitive practices which restrict or lessen competition, including:

- Creation of, or attempts to create, a monopoly;
- Agreements among competitors to increase, decrease or stabilize prices; to divide territories or markets; to allocate customers; to limit the quality of products; or to limit production; or
- Price discrimination and other predatory trade practices.

Any failure to comply with the antitrust laws can have grave consequences not only for the NYSE but for any Director who may be involved in a violation. Any Director having any question concerning compliance with the antitrust laws should seek the advice of the NYSE's Antitrust Compliance Officer in the Office of the General Counsel.

7. Confidentiality

Directors must maintain the confidentiality of confidential information entrusted to them by the NYSE or its customers, except when disclosure is required by law or regulation. Confidential information includes all non-public information that might be of use to competitors, or harmful to the NYSE or its members or listed companies, if disclosed. It also includes information that vendors, listed companies, prospects and members have entrusted to the NYSE.

8. Protection and Proper Use of NYSE Assets

Directors may not use NYSE assets, labor or information for personal use, unless approved by the Governance Committee, or as part of a compensation or expense reimbursement available to all directors.

9. Waivers of the Code of Business Conduct and Ethics

Any waiver of this Code may be made only by the Board and will be promptly publicly disclosed.

10. Reporting any Illegal or Unethical Behavior

Directors should promote ethical behavior and encourage an environment in which the NYSE encourages employees to talk to supervisors, managers or other appropriate personnel about observed illegal or unethical behavior and, when in doubt, about the best course of action in a particular situation. It is the policy of the NYSE not to allow retaliation for reports of misconduct by others made in good faith.

11. Enforcement of the Code of Business Conduct and Ethics

The Board shall determine appropriate actions to be taken in the event of violations of this Code. Such actions shall be reasonably designed to deter wrongdoing and to promote accountability for adherence to the Code. In determining what action is appropriate in a particular case, the Board shall take into account all relevant information, including the nature and severity of the violation, whether the violation appears to have been intentional or inadvertent, and whether the individual in question had been advised prior to the violation as to the proper course of action.

12. Annual Review

The Board shall review and reassess the adequacy of the Code annually and make any amendments to the Code that the Board deems appropriate.

MEASURING THE PERFORMA NCE OF ALTERNATIVE SYSTEMS OF CORPORATE GOVERNANCE

This article has explored the need for greater institutional investor involvement in corporate governance. In light of the fact that greater institutional involvement in corporate governance entails substantial costs and risks to institutions, the potential benefits from institutional investor involvement should be considered. One way of measuring these benefits is to measure how well the current system is performing. I suggest three ways for measuring the performance of a corporate governance system.

First, I propose measuring the private benefits of control by examining the relative share price performance of voting and non-voting shares in firms with a capital structure that includes both voting and non-voting stock.

Second, I propose looking at the willingness of firms to go public. Investors will not pay full value for firms with weak corporate governance because they will discount the price they pay for such firms by an amount sufficient to compensate them in the future for possible exploitation by management. This will, in turn, lead to a situation in which entrepreneurs refuse to sell their shares to the public because they can't receive an adequate price. Thus, where a corporate governance system is not performing well, there will be relative few public offerings.

Third and last, I argue that a good corporate governance system can be measured by the speed with which management is replaced for sustained poor performance. Systems with weak corporate governance systems won't replace management very often.

The purpose of this article has been to suggest some ways of measuring the performance of a corporate governance system. This seems superior to simply asserting that the U.S. system of corporate governance does not work. The article does not purport to fully test the performance of the U.S. system, although it does make some tentative observations. In particular, I find no evidence that the U.S. system is performing badly, and indeed, the U.S. system seems to be used as the benchmark for comparing the performance of rival systems.

It should be clear that none of the tests suggested in this article is meant to be used in isolation to measure the performance of a system of corporate governance. Rather, they should be used together, since shortcomings in one measurement can be compensated for by strengths in another. Finally, it goes without saying, I think, that the U.S.'s market-oriented system of corporate governance has been hurt in recent years by the wave of anti-takeover statutes and court decisions that are hampering the market for corporate control. One of the few salutary effects that institutional investors are having on U.S. corporate governance are their actions directed at lowering or removing some of these barriers.[3]

ACCOUNTING STANDARDS

On the above subject, the provisions of Sections 211 and 210A of the Companies Act, 1956 may be referred, The expression "accounting Standards" means the standards of accounting recommended by the ICAI Constituted under the Chartered Accountants Act, 1949, as may be prescribed by the Central Government in consultation with the National Advisory Committee on accounting standards established under S.210A of the Act, Further until the accounting standards are prescribed by the Central Government, the accounting standards specified by the ICAI shall Be deemed to be the accounting standards, The following may be noted:

(i) Where the profit and loss account and the balance sheet of a company do not comply with the accounting standards such company shall disclose in its profit and loss account and balance sheet the following: the deviation from the accounting standards; the reasons for such deviation; and the financial effect if any, arising due to such deviation,

(ii) Any of the requirements of the Act in this regard, may be modified by the Central, Government on the application of the company or with the consent of the board of the company,

---

3 Source: The Revolution in Corporation Finance, 4th Edition Blackwell Publishing, p.588.

(iii) If any person who is responsible for keeping proper books of account in terms of section 209, fails to take all reasonable steps to secure compliance with the requirements of law relating to the form and contents of the annual financial statements, he is liable for each offence to imprisonment terms and fine.

In the following pages, details of various accounting standards issued by ICAI (till March 2003) have been listed, along with a copy of Preface to the statement of accounting standards, issued by ICAI. The Preface covers the following matters: Formation of the accounting standards boards, scope and functions of accounting standards board, audited financial statements, scope of accounting standards, procedure for issuing accounting standards and compliance with accounting standards.

Till March, 2003, the ICAI had issued the following accounting standards

1. Disclosure of Accounting Policies (AS 1)–1-4-1991
2. Valuation of Inventories (AS 2)–1-4-1999.
3. Cash Flow Statements (AS 3)–1-4-2001 (is not a specified accounting standard in terms of section 211 of the Act)
4. Contingencies and Events occurring after the Balance Sheet Date (AS 4)–1-4-1995.
5. Net Profit or Loss for the period, prior period items and Changes in the Accounting Policies (AS 5)–1-4-1996
6. Depreciation Accounting (AS 6)–1-4-1995
7. Construction Contracts (AS 7)–1-4-2003.
8. Accounting for Research and Development (AS 8)–1-4-1991 (stands, withdrawn w.e.f. 1-4-2003)
9. Revenue Recognition (AS 9)–1-4-1991
10. Accounting for Fixed Assets (AS 10)–1-4-1991
11. Accounting for the Effects of changes in Foreign exchange Rates (AS 11) 1-4-1995
12. Accounting for Government Grants (AS 12)–1-4-1994
13. Accounting for Investments (AS 13)–1-4-1995
14. Accounting for.Amalgamations (AS 14)–1-4-1995
15. Accounting for Retirement Benefits in the Financial Statements of Employers 1-4-1995.
16. Borrowing costs (AS 16)–1-4-2000
17. Segment Reporting (AS 17)–1-4-2001
18. Related Party Disclosures (AS 18)–1.4-2001
19. Leases- (AS 19)–1.4-2001
20. Earnings per share (AS 20) 1-4-2001
21. Consolidated financial Statements (AS 21)–1-4-2001:
22. Accounting for Taxes on Income (AS 22)–1-4-2001 for Companies.
23. Accounting for vestments in Associates in Consolidated Financial Statements (AS 23)–1-4-2002 (applicable to companies, which prepare consolidated account)

24. Discontinuing operations, (AS24) 1-4-2004.
25. Interim financial reporting (AS25)–1-4-2002.
26. Intangible Assets (AS26)1-4-2003.
27. Financial Reporting of interests in Joint Ventures (AS-27) 1-4-2002.
28. Impairment of assets (AS-28) 1-4-2004.

Preface to the Statements of Accounting Standards

1. **Formation of the Accounting Standards Boards:** The Institute of Chartered Accountants of India, recognising the need to harmonise the diverse accounting policies and practices at present in use in India, constituted an Accounting Standards Board (ASB) on 21st April, 1977.

2. **Scope and Functions of Accounting Standards Board**

2.1 The main function of ASB is to formulate accounting standards so that such standards may be established by the Council of the Institute in India. While formulating the accounting standards, ASB will take into consideration the applicable laws, customs, usages and business environment.

2.2 The Institute is one of the Members of the International Accounting Standards Committee (IASC) and has agreed to support the objectives of IASC. While formulating the Accounting Standards, ASB will give due consideration to International Accounting Standards, issued by IASC and try to integrate them, to the extent possible, in the light of the considerations and practices prevailing in India.

2.3 The Accounting Standards will be issued under the authority of the Council. ASP has also been entrusted with the responsibility of propagating the Accounting Standards and of persuading the concerned parties to adopt them in the preparation and presentation of financial statements. ASB will issue guidance notes on the Accounting Standards and give clarifications on issues arising therefrom. ASB will also review the Accounting Standards at periodical intervals.

3. **Audited Financial Statements**

3.1 For discharging the above functions, ASB will keep in view the purposes and limitations of published financial statements and the attest function of the auditors. ASB will enumerate and describe the basic concept to which" accounting principles should be oriented and state the accounting principles to which the practices and procedures should conform.

3.2 ASB will clarify; the phrases commonly used in such financial statements and suggest improvements in the terminology wherever necessary. ASB will examine the various current alternative practices, in vogue and identify such alternatives which should be preferred.

3.3 The Institute will issue the Accounting Standards for use in the presentation of the general purpose financial statements issued to the public by such commercial, industrial or business enterprises as may be specified by the Institute from time to time and subject to the attest function of its members. The term "General Purpose Financial Statements" includes balance sheet, statement of profit and loss and other statements and explanatory notes which form part thereof, issued for the use of shareholders/members, creditors, employees and public at large. References to financial statements in this Preface and in the standards issued from time to time will be construed to refer to General Purpose Financial Statements.

3.4 Responsibility for the preparation of financial statements and for adequate disclosure is that of the management of the enterprise. The Auditor's responsibility is to form his opinion and report on such financial statements.

4. **Scope of Accounting Standards**

4.1 Efforts will be made to issue Accounting Standards which are in conformity with the provisions of the applicable laws, customs, usages and business environment of our country. However, if due to subsequent amendments in the law, a particular Accounting Standard is found to be not in conformity with such law, the provisions of the said law will prevail and the financial statements should be prepared in conformity with such law.

4.2 The Accounting Standards by their very nature cannot and do not override the local regulations which govern the preparation and presentation of financial statements in our country. However, the Institute will determine the extent of disclosure to be made in financial statements and the related Auditor's reports. Such disclosure may be by way of appropriate notes explaining the treatment of particular items. Such explanatory notes will be only in the nature of clarification and therefore, need not be treated as adverse comments on the related financial statements.

4.3 The, Accounting Standards are intended to apply only to items which are material. Any limitations with regard to the applicability of a specific Standard will be made clear by the Institute from time to time. The date from which a particular Standard will come into effect, as well as the class of enterprises to which it will apply, will also be specified by the Institute. However, no standard will have retroactive application, unless otherwise stated.

4.4 The Institute will use its best endeavours to persuade the Government, appropriate authorities, industrial and business community to adopt these Standards in order to achieve uniformity in the presentation of financial statements.

4.5 In carrying out the task of formulation of Accounting Standards, the intention is to concentrate on basic matters. The endeavour would be to confine Accounting Standards to essentials and not to make them so complex that they cannot be applied effectively and on a nation-wide basis. In the years to come, it is to be expected that Accounting Standards will undergo revision and a greater degree of sophistication may then be appropriate.

5. Procedure for Issuing Accounting Standards

Broadly, the following procedure will be adopted for formulating Accounting Standards:

5.1 ASB shall determine the broad areas in which Accounting Standards need to be formulated and the priority in regard to the selection thereof.

5.2 In the preparation of Accounting Standards, ASB will be assisted by Study Groups constituted to consider specific subjects. In the formation of Study Groups, provision will be made for wide' participation by the members of the Institute and others.

5.3 ASB will also hold a dialogue with the representatives of the Government, Public Sector Undertakings, Industry and other Organisations for ascertaining their views.

5.4 On the basis of the work of the Study Groups and the dialogue with the organisations referred to in 5.3 above, an exposure draft of the proposed standard will be prepared and issued for comments by members of the Institute and the public at large.

5.5 The draft of the proposed standard will include the following basic points:

5.5.1 A Statement of concepts and fundamental accounting principles relating to the Standard.

5.5.2 Definitions of the terms used in the Standard.

5.5.3 The manner in which the accounting principles have been applied for formulating the Standard.

5.5.4 The presentation and disclosure requirements in complying with the Standard.

5.5.5 Class of enterprises to which the Standard will apply.

5.5.6 Date from which the Standard will be effective.

5.6 After taking into consideration the comments received, the draft of the proposed Standard will be finalised by ASB and submitted to the Council of the Institute.

5.7 The Council of the Institute will consider the final draft of the proposed Standard, and if found necessary, modify the same in consultation with ASB. The Accounting Standard on the relevant subject will then be issued under the authority of the Council.

6. Compliance with the Accounting Standards

6.1 While discharging their attest functions, it will be the duty of the members of the Institute to ensure that the Accounting Standards are implemented in the presentation of financial statements covered by their audit reports. In the event of any deviation from the Standards, it will be also their duty to make adequate disclosures in their reports so that the users of such statements may be aware of such deviations.

6.2 In the initial years, the Standards will be recommendatory in character and the Institute will give wide publicity among the users and educate members about the utility of Accounting Standards and the need for compliance with the above disclosure requirements. Once awareness about these requirements is ensured, steps will he taken, in course of time, to enforce compliance with the accounting standards in the manner outlined in para 6.1 above.

6.3 The adoption of Accounting Standards in our country and disclosure of the extent to which they have not been observed will, over the years, have an important effect, with consequential improvement in the quality of presentation of financial statements.

TELE/VIDEO CONFERENCING

The Institute of Company Secretaries of India (ICSI), in the light of Companies (Amendment) Bill 2003 (since withdrawn), in a consultative paper on the issue of 'CD recording of board meetings' had suggested recording of minutes and proceedings in a hi-tech manner–through a CD recording. According to the proposals, the chairman of the meeting would be duly required to authenticate such a recording to avoid the possibility of tampering. The consultative paper, circulated by ICSI, it has been claimed would facilitate a practical legislative and procedural regime for conducing such meetings. The past President of ICSI, Shri Pavan Kumar Vijay, justifying the proposal has said, "the increasing globalisation of the world economy, international operations of business and formation of joint ventures necessitates a large number of directors, with varied experience in legal, financial and commercial matters; the resource of such persons can be more effectively utilised by encouraging the holding of board meetings through tele/video conferencing". "The increasing importance accorded to independent directors has led to a need to attract talent and expertise. The facility of conducting board meetings through this process will enable companies to reap the benefit of professional advice from experienced directors facilitate effective participation by directors and will also be cost Effective by saving time and money," he said.

The paper touches upon all the procedures involved in holding a board meeting and how a meeting through tele or video conferencing should be conducted. The paper also specifies the technology requirements. A practical legislative and procedural regime for such meetings may therefore be expected soon.

In the above context, the following issues/requirements may be mentioned:

- There should be amendment to the legislation which should permit conducting of meetings through this mode; the new provisions should declare that a meeting of a board of directors of a company may be conducted through audio. conferences and videoconferences provided that there is an electronic record within the meaning of section 4 of the Information and Technology Act, 2000. On the basis of the above, the company concerned also should make necessary arrangements including provisions in its articles of association.
- The concerned provisions in the Companies Act, such as the provisions of S.289 regarding passing of resolution by circulation and its compliance requirements should be taken care of. However, having regard to the provisions of Ss 292 and 372A, the annual accounts of a company should be approved at a meeting of the board and should not be approved by means of a resolution passed by circulation should be noted; similarly quarterly or half yearly financial results should be

approved only at a meeting of the Board or its committee and not by means of a resolution passed by circulation.

- Section 4 of the Information Technology Act; 2000 provides legal recognition to information or matter that is rendered in an electronic form and is accessible to be usable for a subsequent reference, The directors may be able to sign the resolutions thus submitted by circulation either by affixing their digital signatures or in the normal way on a hard copy.
- Further where the records are stored as electronic record by the company, protection through adequate firewalls, against intrusions into the company's computer is essential. Where the items of business concern matters like tax planning, competition, business plan such protection may be indispensable.
- The directors having regard to the above and various other matters may be required to determine the items of business that may be conducted through such meetings and what steps are necessary to ensure compliance with legal requirements.

SEBI (DISCLOSURE & INVESTOR PROTECTION) GUIDELINES, 2000

The above guidelines have been issued by the Securities and Exchange Board of India under Section 11 of the Securities and Exchange Board of India Act, 1992. A summary of its contents may be detailed: Chapter I Preliminary: Some important definitions have been provided, including in respect of 'abridged prospectus', 'book building', 'composite issues', 'depository', 'net worth', 'offer document', 'offer for sale', 'public issue' and 'rights issue'.

These guidelines are applicable to all public issues by listed and unlisted companies, all offers for sale and rights issues by listed companies. The words and expressions used but not defined in the guidelines, but defined in the Companies Act or in the Securities Contracts (Regulation) Act and/or the rules and regulations made thereunder, shall have the meanings respectively assigned to them in such Acts/rules.

Chapter II, Eligibility norms for companies issuing securities. This chapter deals with conditions for the issue of securities. Guidelines provide the filing of a draft prospectus with the board through an eligible banker, at 21 days prior to the filing of the prospectus with the RoC. The public issue of securities, can be made only if an application for the listing of those securities are made in the stock exchanges. This chapter also deals with public issue by unlisted companies. Further, in the case of public issue by listed companies, in the case of a listed company which does not fulfill the conditions given in the provision to clause 2.3-1, it shall be eligible to make a public issue only through a book-building process. In the case of public or rights issue of debt, instruments, credit rating from a credit rating agency should be obtained.

Chapter III deals with pricing by companies issuing securities. A listed company, whose equity shares are listed on a stock exchange, may freely price its equity shares, offered through a public or rights issue. Further, the issuer company can mention a price band of 20 per cent in the offer document filed, with the Board and its actual price can be determined at a later date before the filing of offer document with the RoCs.

Chapter IV deals with Promoters' contribution and lock-in requirements. In the case of public issued by an unlisted company, the promoters' contribution shall not be less than 20 per cent of the post-issue capital. Securities ineligible for the computation of promoters' contribution have been detailed. Para. 4.8 provides that promoters' participation in excess of the required minimum contribution is to be treated as a preferential allotment. In that case, the pricing provisions of guidelines on preferential allotment shall apply, if the issue price is lower than the said preferential allotment guidelines. According to para 4.9, promoters' contribution is to be brought in before a public issue opens. Part II of the guidelines deals with lock-in requirements.

Chapter V and Chapter VII deal with pre-issue and post-issue obligations.

Chapter VI deals with contents of the offer document, Section 1 dealing with the contents of the Prospectus and Section II dealing with the contents of an abridged prospectus.

In the case of a prospectus, the risk factors, lead merchant banker, issue opening date, credit rating, names of stock exchanges where listing is proposed, minimum subscription clause, filing of offer document, issue schedule, capital structure, terms of issue, objects of the issue, project cost, appraisal, deployment of funds, company management and project, stock market data, analysis of financial statements, basis of issue price, outstanding litigations and defaults including statutory and other information are required to be covered.

Chapter VIII deals with other issue requirements, while Chapter IX is concerned with guidelines on advertisement. Chapter X provides guidelines for the issue of dept instruments. Chapter XI deals with guidelines for book-building. Chapter XIA deals with guidelines on initial public offers through the stock exchange online system (e-IPO).

The following remaining chapters may be detailed:

Chapter XII	Guidelines for the issue of capital by designated financial institutions.
Chapter XIII	Guidelines for preferential issues.
Chapter XIV	Guidelines for OTCEI issues.
Chapter XV	Guidelines for Bonus issues.
Chapter XVI	Operational guideline
Chapter XVII	Miscellaneous.
Schedule I	Memorandum of Understanding (MoU) between the lead merchant banker to the issue and the issuer company.
Schedule II	*Inter se* allocation of responsibilities.
Schedule III	Format of due diligence certificate to be given by Lead Merchant bankers.

SEBI BOARD APPROVES MODIFICATIONS TO DISCLOSURE NORMS

The Board of Securities and Exchange Board of India today approved modifications to SEBI (Disclosure and Investor Protection) Guidelines, 2000. Announcing this here today SEBI chairman, Mr. D R Mehta, said initial public offerings (IPOs) of issue size up to five times the pre-issue net worth would be allowed only if the company had a track record of profitability and net worth as specified in the guidelines.

On the other entry norms Mr. Mehta said companies not having track record as specified in the guidelines would be eligible to make IPOs only through the book building route. In such a case, 60 per cent of the issue size would be allocated to 'qualified institutional buyers' (QlBs). If this does not happen, the issue would fail. IPOs of issue size more than five times the pre-issue net worth and public issues by listed companies of more than five times the pre-issue net worth would be allowed only through the book-building route. In such a case 60 per cent of the issue size would be allocated to QIBs. If the institutional subscription is not received the issue would fail.

The lock-in provisions applicable to initial public offerings have been rationalised to provide that the minimum promoters contribution of 20 per cent will be locked-in for three years as at present and the balance of the entire pre-IPO capital held by the promoters or others (except shares allotted to registered venture capital funds which will be subject to lock-in as per Venture Capital Guidelines) will be locked-in for one year from the date of allotment. The amount against promoters contribution brought in the form of cash either before or along with the issue shall be kept in a separate escrow account and released to the company with public issue proceeds. Notwithstanding the above, where the contribution has been brought prior to the issue and already deployed, a cash flow statement shall be given in the offer document disclosing the use of funds received against promoters' contribution.

It is also decided to lock-in the shares issued on preferential basis by a listed company to any person for one year from the date of its allotment except such preferential issues which involved share swap for acquisition. This will be over and above the 20 per cent of total capital of the company held by the promoter being subject to lock-in as stated in the guidelines. It has also been decided to strengthen the disclosure requirements in the notice convening the general meeting for the purpose of preferential allotment and also extend the present disclosure requirement of utilisation of public issue proceeds to preferential offers also.

The board has approved the introduction of carry forward system in the rolling settlement as proposed by the reconvened Prof. J R Varma committee. There will be both daily and weekly carry forward system with maturities 1, 2, 3, 4 and 5 days. However, Mr. Mehta did not give details of the timeframe to implement this. The SEBI board also approved the introduction of continuous net settlement (CNS) by exchanges.

The board also approved the following changes in the existing carry forward system under the weekly account period settlement:

1. Increase in the carry forward limit per broker from the existing limit of Rs. 20 crore to Rs. 40 crore. The margin up to the present limit of Rs. 20 crore will remain at the present level of 15 per cent and the incremental position will attract a minimum margin of 20 per cent. Further there will be scrip-wise broker-wise position limit, which presently will be Rs. 5 crore.
2. To continue the margin on carry forward trades on gross basis. The introduction of margin on gross basis in the cash market as well as the incorporation of client code will be considered separately by the Risk Management Group constituted by the SEBI.

3. To discontinue the present limit of 75 days for carrying forward trades and
4. To introduce specific eligibility criteria for scrips in the carry forward system both in the account period and rolling settlement as well as for scrips in the CNS.

SEBI (DIP) GUIDELINES

SEBI (Disclosure and Investor Protection) Guidelines, 2000, given in the Appendix may be referred. RMB (Compendium) Series Circular No. 1(1999-2000) dated 19 January 2000 gives, vide Annexure A, the gist of changes made in the guidelines relating to entry norms, lock-in-period and promoters' contribution, as part of a consolidated exercise.

Amendments to the SEBI (DIP) guidelines: Major amendments have been made on 14 August 2003, in the Disclosure and Investor Protection Guidelines, 2000. These have been made, based on the recommendations of various committees. The purpose of amendments, vide the SEBI circular dated 14 August 2003 are:

(i) To enhance the level of investors' protection,

(ii) To increase the transparency and efficiency of primary market,

(iii) To strengthen the disclosure and eligibility norms for issuer companies, and

(iv) To rationalise and simplify various operational procedures in the primary market so as to facilitate raising resources by the issuer companies.

The amendments have come into force with effect from 14 August 2003. These are applicable to all public issues, rights issues, offer for sales. The highlights of amendments are covered in the succeeding paragraphs.

SEBI has made it necessary for companies to have minimum net tangible assets of Rs. 3 crore to raise funds through public issues. In this way, SEBI feels that it would keep off fly-by-night operators from the market. The existing eligibility norms for issuers have been amended to help small- and medium-companies tap the primary market without exposing the public to undue risk. The amended norms are expected to improve the quality of the issuer companies. On the issue of price discovery through book building, the SEBI said companies could indicate a movable price band or a fixed floor price to make it realistic and immune from artificial demand. Similarly, it has made provisions for a green shoe option and an arrangement for allocating shares in excess of the shares included in the public issue. It would act as a price stabilisation tool helping to curb speculative forces that work immediately after listing, resulting in short-term volatility in post-listing prices.

The disclosures have been strengthened and the period between closure of the issue and listing/trading of shares have been shortened from 22 to 6 days for book built issues. The definition of QIBs has been widened to include insurance companies, provident funds and pension funds with a minimum corpus of Rs. 25 crore. The SEBI has said that willful defaulters would be barred from issuing debt instruments and hence, raising funds. Financial instruments by corporates would need an investment grade credit rating for making a debt issue. SEBI has also relaxed the existing provisions of promoter's contribution in the IPO of a debt issue. On the operational/procedural requirements in DIP norms, it said the validity period for SEBI's observation letter had been reduced from 356 days to 6 months. The amendments also incorporate the finance ministry's circular dated 23 April 2003 about the concept of the regional stock exchange being withdrawn. As a consequence, the company would have the freedom to choose any stock exchange as a designated stock exchange.

ISSUE OF BONUS SHARES AND PROTECTION OF INTEREST OF DEBENTURE HOLDERS

Every listed company desirous of issuing bonus shares must ensure that the bonus issue is not in lieu of dividends. It should also be ensured that no public/rights issue is made within 12 months prior to the bonus issue.

The proposal for the bonus issue must be implemented within six months from the date of approval of Board of Directors and the decision of bonus issue once taken cannot be changed. The guidelines require the bonus issue to be made out of free reserves built out of general profits or share premiums collected in cash only and reserves created by revaluation of fixed assets are not permitted to be capitalised. Proposed issue should not dilute the value or rights of holders of debentures, convertible fully or partly. No company, pending conversion of FCDs/PCDs is allowed to issue any bonus shares unless similar benefit is extended to holders of such FCDs/PCDs. The shares so reserved may be issued at the time of conversion of such debentures on the same terms on which bonus issues were made.

Protection of Interest of Debenture Holders

Companies can issue debentures for any purpose. However, issue of debentures by a company for financing acquisition of shares or for providing loans to any company belonging to the same group is not permitted. Issue of fully paid convertible debentures providing conversion within a period of 18 months can be made for acquisition of shares or for providing loans to companies belonging to the same group. Fully convertible debentures having a conversion period of more than 36 months are to be made optional with 'put' and 'call' option. Where the conversion of debentures (in part or whole) is to take place at or after 18 months from the date of allotment but before 36 months. conversion is to be made optional at the hands of the debenture holders.

Credit rating by the approved credit rating agency is compulsory in all public/rights issue of debt instruments whether fully convertible or partly convertible debentures or non-convertible debentures irrespective of their maturity or conversion period. In case of public/rights issue of debt instruments greater than or equal to Rs. 100 crore, credit rating from two different credit rating agencies is required to be obtained. Also, all the ratings so obtained whether accepted or unaccepted along with all the credit ratings obtained during the three years preceding the public or rights issue of debt instrument including convertible instrument is required to be disclosed in the offer document. Fresh credit rating is also required when debentures are sought to be rolled over. The time of conversion and the premium amount on conversion must be determined and disclosed in prospectus. However, issuer companies are free to determine the rate of interest on these FCDs.

The companies issuing debentures with a maturity of over 18 months are required to appoint debenture trustees and to create debenture redemption reserve (DRR) and in cases of partly convertible debentures the redemption reserve should be created to the extent of non-convertible portion. A moratorium period up to the date of commencement of commercial production can be provided for creation of Debenture Redemption Reserve in respect of debentures raised for project finance. However, creation of DRR is not necessary in case of infrastructure companies.

In case of rollover of the non-convertible portion of PCDs/NCDs. value of which exceeds Rs. 50 lakh with or without chance in interest rate, a compulsory option should he given to debenture holder, to redeem the debentures as per the terms of the offer documents, Rollover can be done only in case of those debenture holders who have given their consent and is obligatory for the company to obtain fresh credit rating within a period of six months before the due date of redemption of debentures and the credit rating so obtained must be communicated to the shareholders/debenture holders before the roll over and a fresh trust deed be executed and fresh security be created in respect of debentures rolled over.

The companies making debentures issue are required to file a certificate with SEBI, obtained from their bankers to the effect that the assets of the company on which security is to be created are free from encumbrances or the necessary permission to mortgage the assets have been obtained from the financial institutions or banks for second or *pari passu* charge where the assets are encumbered. The security should be created within six months from the date of issue of debentures. If for any reason the company is not able to create security within 12 months the company shall be liable to pay a penal interest 0.2 per cent to the debenture holders. If the said security is not created even after 18 months, meeting of the debenture holders shall be called within 21 days to explain the reasons thereof and time within which the security shall be created.

Companies may issue unsecured/subordinated debt instruments/obligations which are not public as per provisions of section 58A of the Companies Act, 1956 or such other notifications guidelines, circulars. etc. issued by Reserve Bank of India, Department of Company Affairs or other authorities. Such a issue should be subscribed by qualified institutional buyers or other investors who have given positive consent for subscribing to such unsecured/subordinated debt instruments/obligation.

Source: Student Company Secretary, April 2001.

NORMS FOR IDR ISSUES

Guidelines for overseas corporates to raise funds through the Indian capital markets are to be issued shortly. The Securities and Exchange Board of India is working on the operational aspects of the issue of Indian depository receipts (IDRs) by international companies. IDRs are instruments in the form of depository receipts created by the domestic depository in India against the underlying equity shares of the issuing international company.

The Department of Company Affairs (DCA) has notified the Companies (Issue of Indian Depository receipts) Rules 2004 and the rules pave the way for foreign companies to raise funds in India by means of issue of depository receipts against their underlying equity shares. Section 605A of the Companies Act gives power to the central government to make rules on the subject. The depository receipts would be listed on stock exchanges in India and would be freely transferable. The actual shares underlying IDRs would be held by an Overseas Custodian, which shall authorise the Indian depository to issue the IDRs.

The DCA had announced that foreign companies that have pre-issue paid up capital and free reserves of at least $ 100 million and an average turnover of $ 500 million during the three financial years preceding the issue would be allowed to participate,. in the Indian stock markets. The norms specify that the company should have been making profits for at least five years preceding the issue and should have declared dividend of not less than 10 per cent each year during this period. The issuing company should also have a pre-issue debt equity ratio of not more than 2:1.

An IDR issue needs to be approved by SEBI and an application in this regard has to be made a minimum of 90 days before the issue-opening date. The overseas company also has to file a due diligence report and a prospectus or letter of offer with SEBI and the ROC. Further the overseas company will have to obtain in-principle permission for listing on stock exchanges in India. The issue rules also elaborates the documents to be delivered by the merchant banker to the issue IDRs to SEBI and Registrar of Companies, New Delhi. The IDR norms also outline continuous disclosure requirements. The IDR rules specify that the repatriation of proceeds of the IDR issue would be subject to the prevalent exchange control regulations. Further Indian investors also need to consider the implications of investment in the IDRs/underlying equity shares.

GUIDELINES FOR PREFERENTIAL ISSUES

Chapter XIII of SEBI (Disclosure and Investor Protection) guidelines, 2000 provides the guidelines for preferential issues and the preferential, issue of following types are governed by these guidelines. Preferential issue of equity shares/fully convertible debentures (FCDs)/partly convertible debentures (PCDs) or any other financial instruments which would be converted into or exchanged with equity shares at a later date, by listed companies whose equity share capital is listed on any stock exchange, to any select group of persons under Section 81(1A) of the Companies Act, 1956, on private placement basis. The procedures for the purpose includes convening of board meeting to consider the proposal, convening of general meeting for passing a special resolution in terms of Section 81(1A) of the Companies Act, in case of acquisition of the voting share capital through preferential allotment, notifying the details to the stock exchanges where the shares are listed, where the acquisition exceeds 53.5% of the voting share capital of the company a report to the SEBI giving details of acquisition, acting upon the resolution within a period of three months of passing of the resolution, etc.

Pricing of the Issue

The issue of shares on a preferential basis can be made at a price not less than the higher of the following:

(i) the average of the weekly high and low of the closing prices of the related shares quoted on the stock exchange during the six months preceding the relevant date; or

(ii) the average of the weekly nigh and low of the closing prices of the related shares quoted on a stock exchange during the two weeks preceding the relevant date.

The relevant date, for the above purpose, means the date thirty days prior to the date on which the meeting of the shareholders is held. The explanatory statement to the notice for the shareholders meeting shall contain the objects of the issue through preferential offer, promoters intention to subscribe to the offer, shareholding pattern before and after the offer, proposed time within which the allotment shall be completed and the identity of the proposed allottees and the percentage of post preferential issue capital that may be held by them.

The instruments allotted on preferential basis to the promoter/promoter group shall be subject to lock in of three years from the date of their allotment. The locked in shares/instruments can be transferred to and amongst promoter/promoter group subject to continuation of 'lock' in the hands of transferees, for the remaining period.

Apart from making an application to the recognised stock exchange for listing of the issue, a certificate from Auditors is also required; the statutory auditor of the issuer company, in case of every issue of shares/warrants/FCDs/PCDs/or other financial instruments having conversion option, should certify that the issue of the said instruments is being made in accordance with the requirements contained in the SEBI guidelines. It is also obligatory to disclose in the balance sheet of the company, the purpose for which preferential issue proceeds have been utilised along with details of unutilised monies under separate need. The guidelines also provide that certain clauses of the guidelines shall not be applicable in respect of cases specified and these relate to allotment of further shares in pursuance to the merger and amalgamation scheme approved by the High Court, further allotment of shares on account of rehabilitation packages approved by BIFR, allotment of further shares to all India Public Financial Institutions in accordance with the provisions of loan agreements signed prior to 4th August 1994.

THE COMPETITION ACT 2002[4]

In June 2001, the government cleared the long awaited Competition Bill, thus bringing the country's corporate sector within the scope of internationally recognised rules and regulations to prevent abuse of dominance and anti-competitive practices. The legislation is to replace the out-dated Monopolies and Restrictive Trade Practices (MRTP) Act and meet the needs of industry in the liberalised environment. It lays down procedures for mergers and acquisitions which were virtually non-existent in the past and also provides for setting up a Competition Commission. The Competition Commission would replace the existing MRTP Commission. The MRTP Commission would be wound up as the areas relating to abuse of dominance would be handled by the Competition Commission, while other areas relating to unfair trade practices would be handled by the consumer courts.

The Competition law does not frown on mergers and monopolies, but only on the abuse of it. Anti-competitive practices include cartelisation, collusive bidding, bid rigging, territory sharing, restriction of supply and predatory pricing. Under the new provisions, entities entering into merger and acquisition (M&A) deals, irrespective of the value of their assets and turnover, need not inform the commission of the planned deal. However, they have the option to seek an advance ruling on whether the proposed merger could have an appreciable adverse impact on competition. According to the law

---

4 No. 12 of 2003. Received the assent of the President of India on 13 January 2003.

minister, the Commission would be vested with powers to scrutinise mergers and amalgamations, post deals, if it is left that the M&A has had appreciable adverse impact on the competition, that is, if there is distortion of fair play in the market or if the merged entity is found to be indulging in anti-competitive practices. The post-merger scrutiny would be subject to the merging entities crossing a prescribed threshold limit. The threshold limit for pre-notification has been fixed at a combined turnover of Rs. 3,000 crore for the merging entities and/or an asset base valued at Rs. 1,000 crore. The post-merger scrutiny could be taken up by the commission on the basis of the complaints received by it or suo moto. The threshold limits could be revised as and when warranted.

The Competition Act, 2002, which has since received the assent of the President of India, states that it is an Act to provide, keeping in view the economic development of the country, for the establishment of a Commission to prevent practices having adverse effect on competition, to promote and sustain competition in markets, to protect the interests of consumers and to ensure freedom of trade carried on by other participants in markets in India and for matters connected therewith. Chapter II of the Act makes provisions for prohibition of certain agreements, abuse of dominant position and regulation of combinations. According to Section 3 on anti-competitive agreements, no enterprise or association of enterprises or person or association of persons shall enter into any agreement in respect of production, supply, distribution, storage, acquisition or control of goods or provision of services, which causes or is likely to cause an appreciable adverse effect on competition within India and if any agreement is entered into in contravention, it shall be void. Apart from certain types of agreements referred to in sub-section (3), vide sub-section (4), any agreement amongst enterprises in respect of production, supply, distribution, storage, sale or price of, or trade in goods or provision of services, including tie-in arrangement, exclusive supply agreement, exclusive distribution agreement, refusal to deal and re-sale price maintenance shall be considered as an agreement contravening the provisions of sub-section (1) of Section 3, Anti-competitive agreements. While abuse of dominant position is governed by the provisions of Section 4, regulation of combinations is done vide Section 5 of the Act. Section 5 prescribes the assets value or turnover value in rupees/US dollars in respect of enterprises or the group as the case may be and such enterprises shall not enter into a combination which causes or is likely to cause an appreciable adverse effect on competition within the relevant market in India and such a combination shall be void.

Chapter IV of the Act provides for the duties, powers and functions of the Commission. Accordingly the Commission may inquire into any alleged contravention of the provisions contained in sub-section (1) of Section 3 or sub-section (1) of Section 4 either on its own motion or on receipt of complaints. The Commission, while determining whether an agreement has an appreciable adverse effect on competition under Section 3, shall have due regard to the undermentioned factors: creation of barriers to new entrants in the market, foreclosure of competition, driving existing competitors out of the market, accrual of benefit to consumers, improvements in production or distribution of goods or provision of services, and promotion of technical, scientific and economic development. Further while inquiring whether an enterprise enjoys a dominant position or not, factors like market share of the enterprise, size and resources of the enterprise, size and importance of the competitors, etc., would he given due regard.

The Act has faced some kind of criticism and accordingly, it is stated that assets or turnover should not be the criteria but market share in the industry in which the acquisition took place should be trigger point for the Competition Commission to step in. A large number of mergers and acquisitions would otherwise have to be referred to CCI.

FDl involving buyouts of Indian companies which is a potential sources for large amounts of FDI would also have to go to CCI. Though the reference is not mandatory, since CCI has the power to reverse mergers, no enterprise is likely to take the risk, it is claimed.

SECURITIES (AMENDMENT) BILL 2003

The above Bill (Bil! N(Y. 66 of 2003) has been introduced in the Lok Sabha on 18 August 2003 and it is intended to further amend the Securities Contracts (Regulation) Act 1956 and the Depositories Act 1996. According to the statement of objects and reasons, the 'following reasons have been given, `Although the Securities Contracts (Regulation) Act, 1956, aims to prevent undesirable transactions in securities by regulating the business of dealing therein, the existing mutual organizational structure of stock exchanges (except two exchanges), failed to address the conflict of interests on stock exchanges. The Joint committee on the stock market scam and matters relating thereto, recommended that the process of corporatisation and demutualisation of exchanges should be expedited. It also underlined the necessity for early implementation of corporatisation and demutualisation of stock exchanges.' Therefore, it is proposed to make necessary amendments in the Act mentioned above for the structural transformation of stock exchanges from a mutual organizational form to a demutualised form. The proposal involves that the representation of brokers in board of directors of stock exchanges is either not permitted at all, or is kept to a minimum. Demutualisation separates ownership, voting rights and management from the right of access of trading; The bill defines corporatisation and demutualisation, limits the organizational form to a corporate entity, specifies the procedure for corporatisation and demutualisation, restricts the voting right of brokers as shareholders, etc. Demutualisation means converting such mutual non-profit body into a corporate body where management and trading activities are segregated. Corporatisation means that the stock exchange should be organized as a company. The definition of 'securities' would be enlarged to cover underlying indices, rates, etc., that are not securities. It is also proposed to amend the Depositories Act 1996 to provide for appeals from the orders of the Securities Appellate Tribunal under that Act to the Supreme Court on the lines of the SEBI Act, 1992. Further, delisting of security is presently governed by SEBI guidelines that lack statutory force. Statutory provisions have now been proposed in the Act (SCRA) for delisting. Some important provisions have also been made for the protection of investors, such as non-attachment and no seizure of assets of investors lying with intermediaries. Necessary powers to SEBI to issue directions to stock exchanges, listed companies, etc., have also been covered.

The Lok Sabha approved the Securities Laws (Amendment) Bill 2004 to provide for the corporatisation and demutualisation of all the recognised stock exchanges. Finance Minister P Chidambaram said that retail investors were the 'driving force' of any stock market and the proposed legislation would encourage their increased participation.

TAKEOVER REGULATIONS 1997

- The principles of fairness and transparency have been followed by SEBI while providing the regulatory framework; protection of minority shareholders, providing equal opportunity to all shareholders, protecting the interests of investors and advancing capital market development are some of the other principles. A takeover attempt is made when a would be acquirer sees value and has the means to capitalise on the discount of the pricing inefficiency. The basic objective of any type of takeover is obtaining management control of a company. The Regulations envisage acquisitions for change in control of management, consolidation of holdings and substantial acquisitions. The legal course for takeover is obtaining sanction from SEBI in respect of offer document and government approval under Sections 108A and 372 of the Companies Act, 1956.
- *Consolidation of holdings/creeping acquisition*: Acquisition of shares which enable the shareholders having more than 15 per cent and less than 75 per cent to acquire shares up to the creeping limit of 5 per cent during a 12 month period without change in control; or acquire more than 75 per cent without resulting in change in control.
- *Public announcement*: An acquirer who picks up shares or voting rights exceeding 15 per cent of the equity of the target company must come out with a public announcement to acquire shares in the company. The contents of public announcement of the offer is prescribed in the SEBI regulations; the public announcement by acquirer primarily discloses the intention to acquire a of 20 per cent shares of target company from existing shareholders by means of an open offer. The disclosures in the announcement include the offer price, number of shares to be acquired from the public, identity of acquirer, purpose of acquisition, future plans of acquirer, change in control if any and the period within which all the formalities pertaining to the offer would be completed. It is mandatory to make a public offer when the threshold limits are crossed; Public announcement offer is triggered when the acquirer picks up a stake of 15 per cent in any company and also, when there is a change in control. A merchant banker of Category I is to be appointed before a public announcement and he is expected to ensure that the offer document contains all the relevant information and also ensure full accuracy thereof.
- *The bidding strategy*: It should consider the composition of shareholders of the defending company, the maximum price to offer, the approach to the defending board of directors and the action to be initiated if the bid is opposed. The last published accounts may provide an analysis of shareholders in terms of private shareholders, institutions and family holdings.
- *Preferential allotment not exempt under new Code* (12 September 2002): The new *code* notified by SEBI brings preferential allotment under the scope of takeover *code*. Although the Bhagwati Panel suggested the retention of the exemption, any acquisition of over 15 per cent in a company through preferential allotment will trigger an automatic open offer for another 20 per cent.

- *Exemption from takeover regulations*: Transfer of shares through mergers amalgamation and overseas mergers that cause a change in control in an Indian subsidiary are exempted from the takeover code.
- *Determination of minimum offer price in open offer*: MOP is the highest of : 1. The negotiated price under the agreement entered into by the acquirers which triggered the open offer; 2. Highest price paid by acquirer for any acquisitions including by way of public or rights issue during 20 week period prior to the date *public* announcement; 3. Price paid by acquirer under a preferential allotment made to him during 12 months up to closure offer; and 4. The acquirers offering shareholders either the average of the past 26 weeks price or the 2 week average price whichever is higher.
- *Duties of merchant banker*: Before announcement of offer, it has to be ensured that the acquirer can implement the offer, escrow account is opened, funds to fulfill obligations under the offer are in place and public announcement is made in terms of the regulations. Draft public announcement and letter of offer should he filed with SEBI, target company and stock exchange. The public announcement and letter of offer should be true, fair and adequate. The draft letter of offer should be accompanied by the due diligence certificate. A final report to SEBI is to be sent within 45 days of the closure of the offer.
- *The general obligations of a target company*: The board of target company without approval of general body of shareholders, cannot sell, transfer, encumber or dispose off *assets* issue any authorised but unissued securities carrying voting rights and enter into material contracts. The target company also should not appoint a director till the date of certification of merchant banker or allow anyone connected with the acquirer to participate in any matter relating to the offer. They can, however, send their biased comments and recommendations on the offer to the shareholders.

Reference may be invited to the Notification dated 30th December, 2004 notifying Securities and Exchange Board of India (Substantial acquisition of shares and takeovers) (Second Amendment) Regulations, 2004, Accordingly, various amendments have been effected as under:

1. The definition of "promoter" has been amended (Regulation 2, in sub regulation (I), substitution of clause (h)
2. Clause (j), the meaning of 'public shareholding' has been changed
3. In regulation 3 in sub regulation (1) in clause (e) in sub clause (iii) after the proviso, Explanation has been inserted (as to what the promoter means)
4. In regulation 7, in sub-regulation (1), after the words "fourteen per cent" the words "or fifty four per cent or seventy four per cent" has been inserted,
5. In respect of regulations 10, 11, 20 and 21 amendments have been effected, as reproduced below:

    (a) after clause (k), the following shall be inserted, namely,

    "(ka) acquisition of shares in terms of guidelines or regulations regarding delisting of securities specified or framed by the Board".

(*b*) after sub-regulation (1) the following sub-regulation shall be inserted, namely:

"(1A) The benefit of availing exemption under the relevant clauses of sub-regulation (1), shall be subject to compliance with requirement specified in subregulation (2A) of regulation 11."

6. In regulation 7, in sub-regulation (1), after the words "fourteen per cent." the words "or fifty four percent or seventy four per cent" shall be inserted;

7. In regulation 10, the following proviso shall be inserted, namely.

"Provided that no acquirer shall acquire shares or voting rights, through market purchases and preferential allotment pursuant to a resolution passed under section 81 of the Companies Act, 1956 or any other applicable law, which (taken together with shares or voting rights, if any, held by him or by persons acting in concert with him), entitle such acquirer to exercise more than fifty five per cent. of the voting rights in the company;

Provided further that if the acquirer has acquired shares or voting rights through such market purchases or preferential allotment beyond fifty five per cent of the voting rights in the company, he shall forthwith disinvest the shares, acquired in excess of fifty five per cent, and shall be liable for action under these Regulations and the Act.

Explanation: In case of acquisition through preferential allotment the limit of fifty five per cent voting rights as provided under this regulation shall be reckoned with reference to the increased share capital pursuant to such preferential allotment."

8. In regulation 11,

(*a*) in sub-regulation (1), for the figure and words "75 per cent." the words and figure "fifty five per cent (55%)" shall be substituted;

(*b*) for sub-regulation (2), the following shall be substituted, namely –

"(2) An acquirer, who together with persons acting in concert with him has acquired, in accordance with the provisions of law, fifty five per cent (55%) or more but less than seventy five per cent (75%) of the shares or voting rights in a target company, may acquire either by himself or through persons acting in concert with him any additional share or voting right, only if he makes a public announcement to acquire shares or voting rights in accordance with these regulations:

Provided that no acquirer shall acquire shares or voting rights, through market purchases and preferential allotment pursuant to a resolution passed under section 81 of the Companies Act, 1956 or any other applicable law, which (taken together with shares or voting rights, if any, held by him or by persons acting in concert with him), entitle such acquirer to exercise more

Provided further that if the acquirer has acquired shares or voting rights through such market purchases or preferential allotment beyond fifty five per cent of the voting rights in the company, he shall forthwith disinvest the shares acquired in excess of fifty five per cent and shall be liable for action under these regulations and the Act.

Explanation: In case of acquisition through preferential allotment the limit of fifty five per cent voting rights as provided under sub - regulation (ii) shall be reckoned with reference to the increased share capital pursuant to such preferential allotment."

(c) after sub-regulation (2), the following shall be inserted, namely–

"(2A) Unless otherwise provided in these regulations, an acquirer, who seeks to acquire any shares or voting rights whereby the public shareholding in the target company may be reduced to a level below the limit specified in the Listing Agreement with the stock exchange for the purpose of listing on continuous basis, may acquire such shares or voting rights, only in accordance with the of guidelines or regulations regarding delisting of securities specified by the Board:

Provided that, the provisions of this sub-regulation shall not apply in case of acquisition by virtue of global arrangement which may result in indirect acquisition of shares or voting rights or control of the target company."

9. in regulation 20, in sub-regulation (7), after the proviso, the following shall be inserted, namely–

"Provided further that the shares or voting rights so acquired taken together with the acquisition under the public offer and shares or voting rights, if any, held by him or by persons acting in concert with him, do not result in public shareholding in the target company being reduced to a level below the limit in the Listing Agreement with the stock exchange for the purpose of listing on continuous basis."

10. In regulation 21,

(a) in sub-regulation (1), the following proviso shall be inserted, namely–

"Provided that where any public offer is made in pursuance of sub-regulation (2) of regulation 11, such public offer shall be for such percentage of voting capital of the target company so that the acquisition does not result in the public shareholding in such company being reduced to a level below the limit specified in the Listing Agreement with the stock exchange for the purpose of listing on continuous basis."

(b) after sub-regulation (1), the following sub-regulation shall be inserted, namely–

"(2) Where an acquirer acquires more than fifty five per cent. (55%) shares or voting rights in the target company through an agreement or memorandum of understanding and the public offer made under regulation 10 or sub-regulation (1) of regulation 11 to acquire minimum percentage of voting capital as specified in sub regulation (1) of regulation 21 results in public shareholding being reduced to a level below the limit specified in the Listing Agreement with the stock exchange for the purpose of listing on continuous basis, the acquirer shall acquire only such number of shares under the agreement or the memorandum of understanding so as to maintain the minimum specified public shareholding in the target company;"

(c) for sub-regulation (3), the following shall be substituted, namely–

"(3) If consequent to the public offer made in pursuance of global arrangement referred to in proviso to sub regulation (2A) of regulation 11, the public shareholding falls to a level below the limit specified in the Listing Agreement with the stock exchange for the purpose of listing on continuous basis, the acquirer shall undertake to raise the level of public shareholding to the levels specified for continuous listing specified in the Listing Agreement with the stock exchange, within a period of twelve months from the date of closure of the public offer, by

(i) issue of new shares by the company in compliance with the provisions of the Companies Act, 1956 and the Securities and Exchange Board of India (Disclosure and Investor Protection) Guidelines, 2000; or

(ii) disinvestment through an offer for sale in compliance with the provisions of the Companies Act, 1956 and the Securities and Exchange Board of India (Disclosure and Investor Protection) Guidelines, 2000, of such number of shares held by him so as to satisfy the listing requirements; or

(iii) sale of his holdings through the stock exchange.

Provided that in case of acquisition of shares or voting rights or control in a target company where the public shareholding is below the limit specified for the purpose of listing on continuous basis in terms of the Listing Agreement with the stock exchange, the acquirer shall undertake to raise the level of public shareholding to the levels specified for continuous listing in terms of the listing conditions specified in the Listing Agreement with the stock exchange, within the period specified under the Listing Agreement."

11. in regulation 45, in sub-regulation 6, after clause (c), the following shall be inserted, namely–

"*(d)* directions under section 11(4) of the Act.

IRANI PANEL REPORT ON COMPANY LAW

The Irani committee has submitted its report to the Company Affairs Minister, Mr. Prem Chand Gupta, on May 31, 2005 and some of the key recommendations of the committee are listed here.

- **One third of listed companies board should comprise independent directors:** Taking a position that is at variance with that of the Securities and Exchanges Board of India, the committee has recommended that one-third of the board of a listed company should comprise independent directors. SEBI, vide clause 49 of the listing agreement, had mandated that at least 50 per cent of the board of a listed company comprise independent directors. The committee has now laid down guidelines on what independent directors should be doing on company boards to look after the interest of the minority shareholders.

- **Pyramidal structure for corporates should stay:** The committee has also suggested that corporates should be allowed to maintain pyramidal corporate structures. According to the committee, this would be in the interest of the corporate sector, especially when many companies are making acquisitions abroad.

- **Concept of single person company mooted:** The committee has also mooted the concept of single person company.

- **Harmonisation of committee's recommendations with Clause 49 Requirements and a new Company Law:** While recommending for a new company law, the committee has recommended that the Ministry of Company Affairs should sort out the harmonization issue with SEBI before December 31. The committee has not gone into the issue of regulatory overlap. The committee, at one level, had as its central theme simplification of existing corporate law, the Companies Act 1956 with its 658 sections (and 15 schedules) is to be pruned to around 300 sections. If the committee has its way, the new legislation will lay down only core principles, leaving procedural details to be decided by changes in rules. The idea is to ensure flexibility.
- **Shareholders should have larger say than Government:** The main thrust of the committee's recommendations were to give full liberty to the shareholders and owners of the company to operate in a transparent manner. The committee has suggested a number of areas where shareholders could take the final decision and the government need not have a role, e.g. Director's remuneration.
- **According to another significant recommendation:** The non-executive directors and independent directors should not be punished for day-to-day actions of the company that have not been brought to their notice.
- **Exit route for shareholders:** The panel moots one-time buyback by delisted companies. A one-time buyback offer for shareholders of a delisted company has been mooted to provide an exit route for shareholders who had not taken part in the delisting exercise. The committee has suggested that any company that opted to delist its shares must be required to come up with a buyback offer within three years of delisting. The committee has recommended that the Government should prescribe appropriate valuation rules for such a buyback.

To protect the rights of minority shareholders and also for investor protection, the committee has also suggested that the new company law should recognize principles such as 'class actions' and 'derivative actions'. Derivative actions are brought about by shareholders (on behalf of the company) against directors, management or other shareholders for a failure by the management. A class action is where on shareholder on behalf of one or more of the shareholders of the same kind are allowed by courts on the grounds of same locus stand it allows a group of individuals with a claim against a company or an individual to join together as plaintiffs in a single suit.

The panel has made out a case for introducing the concept of 'deemed approval' in cases where different regulations do not intimate their comments on time. The committee being concerned with procedural delays, has proposed statutory recognistion for contractual mergers and acquisitions; it has also proposed a concept of electronic registry. Mergers among associated companies, private companies or companies where no public interest is involved, should be allowed through a less stringent framework, the report said.

- **Better cover for whistle blowers:** The committee has said that the company law should recognize the "whistle blower concept" to enable individuals to expose offences by companies. It has also said that the law should provide for lifting the corporate veil to reach a promoter or a shareholder where it is proven that a fraud may have been committed with the knowledge of the promoter/shareholder or at their instance.

- **The Irani committee, to give fillip to entrepreneurship, has also some other key recommendations as follows:** no cap on number of subsidiaries, directors, limited liability partnership to be allowed, companies can issue loans to directors, companies can issue perpetual/longer duration preference shares, Nidhi companies to come under RBI regulation, Financials to be signed by MD, CEO, CFO, Company Secretary and a new liquidation regime with test for insolvency.

Bill on new company law in monsoon session: The Government plans to introduce a Bill to replace the existing company law during the monsoon session of Parliament. According to the Company Affairs Minister, the target is to have a new Companies Act in place by the end of the year. The new look company law should be compact, simple, easy to understand and easy to enforce. After receiving Dr. JJ Irani committee report, the minister expressed his desire that the corporate sector should be freed from the bureaucratic hassles. The Ministry of Company Affairs is accordingly to prepare a Bill to re-codify the company law after consultation with law and other ministries.

Selected portions from Dr. Irani committee report, in so far as it concerns Corporate Governance, have been included in the succeeding pages.

IRANI COMMITTEE ON CORPORATE GOVERNANCE — EXTRACTS

1. The Board of Directors has to exercise strategic oversight over business opeations while directly measuring and rewarding management's performance. Simultaneously the Board has to ensure compliance with the legal framework, integrity of financial accounting and reporting systems and credibility in the eyes of the stakeholders through proper and timely disclosures.

2. Board's responsibilities inherently demand the exercise of judgment. Therefore the Board necessarily has to be vested with a reasonable level of discretion. While corporate governance may comprise of both legal and behavoral norms, no written set of rules or laws can contemplate every situation that a director or the board collectively may find itself in. Besides, existence of written norms in itself cannot prevent a director from abusing his position while going through the motions of proper deliberation prescribed by written norms. Therefore behavioural norms that include informed and deliberative decision making, division of authority, monitoring of management and even handed performance of duties owned to the company as well as the shareholders are equally important.

3. However in a situation where companies have grown in size and have large public interest potential, it is important to prescribe an appropriate basic framework that needs to be complied with by all companies without sacrificing the basic requirement of allowing exercise of discretion and business judgment in the interest of the company and the stakeholders. The liability of compliance has to be seen in context of the common law framework prevalent in the country along with a wide variety of ownership structures including family run or controlled or otherwise closely held companies.

Board of Directors

1. Obligation to constitute of Board of Directors:

   (a) The Board of Directors of a company is central to its decision making and governance proces. Its liability to ensure compliance with the law underpins the corporate governance structure in a company, the aspirations of the promoters and the rights of stakeholders, all of which get articulated through the actions of the Board. There should be an obligation on the part of a Company to constitute and maintain a Board of Directors as per the provisions of the law and to disclose particulars of the Directors so appointed in the public domain through statutory filing of information.

   (b) Such obligation should extend to the accuracy of the information and its being update regularly as well as on occurrence of specific events such as appointment, resignation, removal or any change in prescribed particulars of Directors.

LIST OF INDEPENDENT DIRECTORS

The National Foundation for Corporate Governance (NFCG) has recently (June 2005) has asked the apex chambers and professional bodies to prepare a list of independent directors so that a database is ready by November 15 to enable India Inc for meeting the Securities and Exchange Board of India deadline of December 31, 2005. From January 1, 2006, the revised clause 49 regulations come into effect, which require companies to have specified number of independent directors on the company boards. According to the Secretary, the Ministry of Company Affairs, there is a need to create a database of such individuals, who could fulfil the criteria of becoming independent directors. The Secretary stressed that the initiative was only to catalyse the preparatory phase towards creation of such a database. It has been reported that there is a requirement of 3,000 to 4000 independent directors for about 6,000 companies and therefore various industry bodies have been advised to draw up a list of such persons.

SERIOUS FRAUDS OFFICE ALLOWED TO FILE COMPLAINTS UNDER IPC

The Ministry of Company Affairs has given more teeth to the Serious Frauds investigation office (SFIO) and it has allowed it to file complaints under the Indian Penal Code (IPC). This should enable the SFIO to move swiftly for successful prosecution of quality. According to the sources., in addition to initiating prosecutions for violations under the Companies Act, the SIFIO can now file private complains under the IPC. The investigation reports in certain cases like that of Vatsa Corporation and Daewoo Motors India revealed that prosecution under IPC was required. To file such cases, the SIFO required an authorization and hence the above move.

The JJ Irani committee on company law has also recommended that the SFIO be strengthened further while retaining its multi-disciplinary character.

Some of the important cases with the SFIO are those against the Usha group and its directors, DSQ Software Ltd. Mardia Chemicals Ltd., the Ketan Parekh group, Adam Comsof Ltd., Soundcraft Industries Ltd., and Kolar Biotech Ltd.

Board Management

BOARD'S ROLE

- Directors have collective responsibility in law as a board of directors for the affairs of the organisation;
- They share their legal responsibilities equally.
- They must see that the company obeys the law and regulations that Circumscribe its activities
- The board has full and ultimate responsibility for the well being of the company, its affairs, its actions and those of its employees.
- The directors act as stewards of the company on behalf of shareholders.
- Directors owe fiduciary duties to the company, meaning they are required to act in good faith in its best interests, not misapply their powers etc.
- The board must ensure that the company survives and prospers.
- Directors shape the destiny of the organisation, ensure its ongoing financial performance and safeguard its interests and reputation.
- The activities undertaken by directors should generally be forward looking and long-term oriented.
- Prosperity is also ensured through active interaction with other parties/ Stakeholders.

STANDARDS FOR THE BOARD

The following 'standards for the board' as set out by the Institute of Directors, London (1999) may be mentioned:

- The board must be simultaneously be entrepreneurial and drive the business forward while keeping it under prudent control.
- The board is required to be sufficiently knowledgeable about the workings of the company to be answerable for its actions, yet to be above to stand back from the day-to-day management of the company and retain an objective, long-term view.
- The board must be sensitive to the pressures of short-term issues and yet be informed about broader, long-term trends.
- The board must be knowledgeable about 'local' issues and yet be aware of potential or actual non-local, increasingly international, competitive and other influences.
- The board is expected to be focused upon the commercial needs of its business while acting responsibly towards its employees, business partners and society as a whole.

As already noted the directors have a collective legal responsibility to act in the best interests of the company at all times, within regulatory, legal and ethical constraints. Their judgments would naturally be conditioned by what the shareholders expect. The

Chairman helps the company to realise the overall purpose and discharge its responsibilities in the best interests of the company; he should guard against any tendency /actions, which may be for gratifying his personal wishes/interests.

CODE OF PROFESSIONAL CONDUCT FOR DIRECTORS

Directors should see directorship as a discrete profession. They are required to successfully apply a range of knowledge and to conduct themselves in a pertinently professional manner. The Institute of Directors, has laid down for Chartered Directors, a Code of Conduct, which all directors should comply. This code has 12 Articles. The 12 articles reproduced below, stipulate that a director shall:

- Exercise leadership, enterprise and judgment in directing the company so as to achieve its continuing prosperity and act in the best interests of the company as a whole.
- Follow the standards of good practice set out in the Institute's 'Good Practice for Directors – Standards for the Board' and act accordingly and diligently.
- Serve the legitimate interests of the company's shareholders.
- Exercise responsibilities to employees, customers, suppliers and other relevant stakeholders, including the wider community.
- Comply with relevant laws, regulations and codes of practice, refrain from anti-competitive practices, and honour obligations and commitments.
- At all times have a duty to respect the truth and act honestly in business dealings and in the exercise of all responsibilities as a director?
- Avoid conflict between personal interests, or interests of any associated Company or person, and his or her duties to the company.
- Not make improper use of information acquired as a director or disclose, or allow to be disclosed, information confidential to the company.
- Not recklessly or maliciously injure the professional reputation of another director and not engage in any practice detrimental to the reputation and interests of the profession of director.
- Ensure that he or she keeps abreast of current good practice in directing.
- Set high personal standards by keeping aware of and adhering to this code, both in spirit and in the letter, and promoting it to other directors.
- Apply the principles of this code appropriately when acting as a director of a non-commercial organisation.

CEO'S JOB DESCRIPTION

The CEO is the link in the chain of command that connects the board to the rest of management. The Board delegates to this one person the authority to manage everyone else in the operating structure. CEO becomes accountable for what is done with the delegated executive authority. All operational achievements, conduct, decisions and situations are on that person's head. Survival of companies depend on the ability of CEO (also Called as President, General Manager, Managing Director or the like) to adjust quickly to sudden marketplace shifts. Global competition, rapidly changing business environment, customer demand for quick turnarounds, quicker decisions demanded by the environment all these factors justify maximum CEO empowerment.

The CEOs job is to see that the company achieves the ends the board has established and avoids the unacceptable means the board has identified. In "How to run a company' CEOs look at their role from different angles: handling change (mergers, turning around companies, disappearing markets etc.); working with boards; achieving operational success and pursuing strategy; and communicating with the outside world. The key task of any CEO is to keep his board well informed, balancing overview with insights on markets, strategy and even failures. By constantly seeking advice on how to tackle certain issues, the CEO gains the respect of the board and their approval and constructive criticism. A business needs a central governing organ and this is provided by the office of CEO; similarly the business needs a central organ of review and appraisal and this is provided by the organ called 'board'.

Let us see how the chief executive functions or operates.

- The chief executive thinks through the business the company is in. He develops and sets over-all objectives. He communicates the objectives and the decisions to his management people; he educates his managers in seeing the business as a whole; he measures performance and results against the objectives. He reviews and revises objectives as conditions demand.
- He coordinates the product businesses within the company and the various functional managers. He also arbitrates conflicts within the group and either prevents or settles personality clashes.
- He takes the responsibility for capital expenditure planning and for raising capital. He negotiates and decides on bank loans, new stock issues,
- Issue of bonds etc. He also recommends dividend policy to the board. He is concerned with relations with stockholders; he answers questions at the annual general meeting. He must be available to the security analysts of institutional investors; he must also see financial writers of newspapers and business magazines.
- The agenda for the board meetings is another major responsibility; he Presents reports there and answers questions. He must relay board decisions to managers. In addition he has a host of public-relations duties.
- The chief executive's job of tomorrow will include understanding a host of new basic tools; these tools will include the techniques of analysing and anticipating the future; these may cover tools like 'operations research', 'information theory' and 'symbolic logic' etc.

Thus the chief executive job demands and requires not only a 'front man', 'a thought man' and 'a man of action' but, in addition, a first rate analyst and synthesizer.

The conclusion, as drawn by Peter F Drucker (The Practice of Management) runs as follows: " There is only one conclusion: the Chief Executive job in every business (except perhaps the very smallest) cannot properly be organised as the job of one man. It must be the job of a team of several men acting together." If the enterprise is to prosper and

succe...
compete...

What are ... ities of an organisation are required to be performed by a fit? The question b... parameters that makes a CEO to succeed or to be a best role of CEOs in the ... ant in the context of understanding the changing development of an active bo... siness scandals and the dot com bust. The

Any guidance that CEOs ... eously become important and to quote[1]: unenviable) a CEO's job is today. B... itical considering how insecure (and companies in the US removed their CEOs. ... and 2001, 57% of the 367 largest company's stock price within 19 months, or step ... s expect their CEOs to raise the Act on corporate governance and strictures from ... d there is the Sarbanes-Oxley Nasdaq, all keeping a close watch on the CEO's performa... York Stock Exchange and an active board" ... ugh the development of

Thus the role a CEO has to play in the context of constant ... strategy, such as the one when either the market suddenly collapses or ...es in business erodes as in the case of pharmaceutical companies (because of product pa... the market approaching in 2005), the critical aspect of a CEO's role becomes clear; Tak... regime into account the experience and history of CEOs in Corporate America and elsewhere, the ...t and know how to manage companies and their day-to-day issues successfully has to be learnt by CEOs and perhaps the record of the best of CEOs may provide the required helpline/guidance.

Some more 'help line' may be mentioned.

How well the job of a CEO is organised or disorganised?

Many CEOs/Executive directors are prone to let outside pressures and immediate emergencies dictate their day and the utilisation of their efforts and energies. In this context the following advise (re-produced material) [2]may be noted:

"Yet even the chief executive who lets outward pressures manage him is better than some. At least he spends his time on activities that are part of the chief executive's job (albeit the lesser part). Much worse is the chief executive who wastes his time running a function instead of the business: the president who entertains customers when he should be working on the financial policy, the president who corrects details in engineering drawings and neglects a crying problem of malorganisation; the president who personally checks the expense account of every salesman, etc., These men not only fail to accomplish their work; they also prevent the operating manager whose job they are doing from accomplishing his. And the number of chief executives who thus cling to the functional work in which they came up and with which they are familiar is uncomfortably large."

The CEOs should also be aware of the pitfalls and dangers of 'kitchen cabinets' and to quote (ibid as above):

---

1 Helpline for CEOs, Business world 9 February 2004: review of the book 'How to run a company' by Dennis C Carey & Marie Caroline Von Weichs.

2 The Practice of management, Peter F Drucker, Chapter: Chief Executive and Board.

"Even worse is the growth of 'kitchen cabinets'. ... his job, the chief surrounds himself with a motley staff of personal ... ellaneous assistants, analysts, a 'control section' and so forth. None ... clearly defined duties. None have clear responsibility. But all have ... the boss and are credited through out the organisation with myste... They undercut the authority of operating managers, duplicate their w... them off from easy communication with the chief executive. They are th... es of malorganisation – 'government by crony'. Yet the one-man chief exe... his kitchen cabinet. Not being allowed to organise a proper team, he ha... do with errand boys, private secretaries, chief clerks and favourites into wh... critical control of the basic decisions increasingly drifts."

How then the Chief ... utive's team be Organised?

The first requi... is that it should be a 'team' rather a 'committee'. There would be no collective ... ponsibility. Each member would have assigned areas of work and he makes fin... decisions, owning responsibility for the same. To clarify, while deliberations are held ... jointly, decisions are taken individually.

THE BOARD-CEO RELATIONSHIP AND THE RELATIONSHIP BETWEEN THE CHAIR AND THE CEO: HOW IT SHOULD BE?

On the first question, the following may be noted:

"The Board's accountability to owners is constant; the board is a permanent authority. Board leadership therefore should be constantly and consistently applied. It does not exist to help management, to duplicate management, or to fill in weaknesses of management. Proper governance exists to exercise an ongoing authority, establishing values that drive the company through all its known and yet to be known challenges. Management's job is to apply those values to the company's operations in a world of shifting conditions, opportunities and threats. Although the board's authority is clearly superior to the CEO's authority, in practice there is considerable partnership. The CEO has a vested interest in ensuring that the board's decisions are wise ones, for the board and the CEO will have to live by them and be evaluated according to them, not just today but every day for the foreseeable future." *Source*: Corporate Boards That Create Value.

If we take up, answering the second question, the following may clarify the Position:

"The proper relationship between the chair and the CEO also must be clear. The Chair and the CEO are both charged by the board with considerable authority and obligations for leadership. The two roles are not hierarchically related, for each works directly for the board. The CEO does not report to the chair but to the board; the chair has no authority over the CEO. If this is not true, the chair is in effect the CEO, regardless of titles". (*Source:* Corporate boards that create value.)

The Chair's job is to see that the board gets its job done. The CEO's job is to see to it that management gets its job done. Both the chairman and the chief executive need to have the capacity to lead, but leadership of the board is not the same as the leadership required to turn the board's decisions into action. Given that the board's job is to define the purpose of the company and how it is to be achieved, the chairman needs to have strategic sense, the ability to analyse competitive environment etc., He has to assume the responsibility for the long-term survival of the enterprise. The chief executive, on the other hand, in carrying out the board's strategy, should above all have the ability to make the right things happen. Perhaps, occasionally one person can be excellent both at strategy and also at putting strategy into effect. But the role difference is profound and it is impossible to discharge both duties properly at the same time. If one man tries to do both jobs, one of them is likely to go by default.

The separation of the two roles acts as a check and a balance. Chairman is responsible for ensuring that their boards take into account the interest of the shareholders and that they carry out their supervisory functions conscientiously. Chairmen, where is also the chief executive, have to be scrupulously clear in their own minds when are acting as the one and when as the other, as they move between the two roles.

Whether the Board is an organ of action?

According to Peter F Drucker, "the board cannot and must not be the governing organ that the law considers it to be. It is an organ of review, of appraisal, of appeal. Only in crisis does it become an organ of action—and then only to remove existing executives that have failed, or to replace executives who have resigned, retired or died. Once the replacement has been made, the Board again becomes an organ of review."

The erosion of the board of directors is not an accident but rooted in profound causes. Some of these are: the much publicized divorce of ownership from control which makes it absurd that the business enterprise be directed by the representatives of the shareholders; the complexity of modern business operations; the difficulty of finding good men with the time to sit on boards and to take their membership seriously.

BOARD FUNCTIONS

The real functions which the board has to discharge broadly comprise: approving the decision what the company's business is and what it should be, according final approval to the objectives the company has set for itself and the measurement it has developed to judge its progress towards these objectives, looking critically at the profit planning of the company, its capital-investment policy, expenditures budget, final judicial function relating to organisation problems, successfully utilising the strengths of people and neutralising their weaknesses, development of future managers, rewarding managers, strengthening the organisation etc. Yet it should be detached from operations. It must view the company as a whole. It has to ensure that the working executives do not dominate the board. The board, in order to be stronger and effective, should genuinely be an 'outside' board

To summarise the main functions of the board are:

- To define the company's purpose;
- To agree strategies and plans for achieving that purpose;
- To establish the company's policies;
- To appoint the chief executive;

- To monitor and assess the performance of the executive team; To assess their own performance.

The distinction between direction and management may also be noted. As it is crucial. Direction is the task of the Board and management is the task of the executives. The board should have a formal schedule of matters Specifically reserved for its decision. It is the job of the board to ensure that the aims of the enterprise are clear, that they are kept upto date and that they are backed by the commitment of those who are charged with carrying them out. The Board provides the company with a sense of vision as well as a sense of direction. The board is also responsible for the strategy of the business and for agreeing the operating plans and targets required to turn the stategy into action . Thus, in the above context, to sum up, the chair's job is to see that the board gets its job done (as charged or as set out by the board) and the CEOs job is to see that the management gets its job done (as charged or as set out by the board).

ESSENTIAL TASKS OF CHAIRMAN

The following may be mentioned:

- providing leadership to the board ;
- taking responsibility for the board's composition and development ;
- ensuring proper information for the board ;
- planning and conducting board meetings effectively;
- getting all the directors involved in the board's work;
- ensuring the board focuses on its key tasks ;
- engaging the board in assessing and improving its performance;
- overseeing the induction and development of directors ;
- supporting the chief executive/managing director.

Qualities

It is desirable that the chairman possesses the following qualities in order to perform his essential tasks with required competence:

- capability to take a wider view than confined by their background or discipline
- political astuteness and sensitivity
- good interpersonal skills
- ability to listen and to communicate ideas, concepts and facts succinctly and emphatically
- financial awareness and numeracy
- business competence
- good judgment, commonsense, diplomacy
- strength of character, courage, integrity and wisdom
- relevant experience, special knowledge and skills.

Why Leadership is Important?

Leaders show the way in organisations. As listed above while clear vision, sound judgment, knowledge and passion are qualities essential for successful leaders, there are other essential traits that define good leadership. A few of them, found to be helpful, may be mentioned:

- **Ethics:** Leadership is built on trust; their conduct inspires the confidence of the people they lead.
- **Knowledge:** Knowledge helps develop perspective. It removes biases and provides an agenda for the future.
- **The ability to listen:** it is well known; few only really listen, especially when they are at the top. The list provided includes their colleagues, collaborators, markets and constituencies, and finally even to themselves; this prescription is only if they wish to stay on course to success.
- **Decisiveness:** Leaders must rely on their intuition while making key decisions.
- **Communication:** The power to inform and persuade is critical for winning the hearts and minds of employees.
- **Exemplication:** They must be where they are expected to be, leading although; thus a leader must focus on 'having' values as well as 'creating' value; he would ensure that the organization offers a liberal atmosphere for people to work in. His success ultimately lies in how successfully he empowers individuals and taps their strengths. While cohesive organisational and individual goals are the key to success, he needs to effectively use technology to match the organisation's goals and needs. Thus leadership qualities, may be for different kinds/applications, are needed both in the case of CEO and the chairman.

BOARD MEETINGS: SOME GUIDELINES

- Any influence the chairman wants to have on the outcome of any matter, it should be done with subtlety and care.
- It may be unwise to try to persuade the board to chairman's point of view At a meeting where there is obvious overwhelming opposition to it; only On highly important issues or those affecting fundamental matters. The chairman should marshall his energies to influence decisions.
- As the meeting progresses, he should briefly introduce each topic. Thereafter the responsibility for opening a discussion/making a presentation passes to the person concerned.
- The chairman should keep control of the discussions; to save time and arguments, when necessary he may ask questions to clarify matters.
- He should facilitate communication at board meetings; possible Miscommunication should be prevented.
- If most members are looking languid, a break may be called to re-energise everyone.

- If the board is split on deciding an important issue, it may be preferable To defer decision for more consultation/information, rather than put it to Vote;
- Real credibility and support may be able to be achieved only if the Whole board can feel committed to them.
- As each item is concluded, state what the conclusion is and there should be consensus for the same.
- The chairman should try to finish on time; if need be he should defer some matters to a later meeting. Other points on' rules of engagement: three minutes is enough time to make a point; verbally supported visual presentations should be limited to five minutes; going off the topic should be prevented; if technical terms are used, it should be understandable by all; it would be inappropriate to demonstrate superior intellect, knowledge or excellence. Executive directors should not be inhibited from expressing alternative views; brevity is a virtue; speak slowly and economically; never repeat what is in writing; be positive and constructive.

COMPANY DIRECTION: PROGRAMME OF COURSES FOR DIRECTORS

It comprises the following areas and the directors are expected to be familiar with them:[3]

- The role of company director and the board: The crucial differences between direction, ownership and management and the legal framework within which directors operate. Corporate governance issues. The Board's purpose, tasks, functions, structure and mode of effective operation
- Strategic business direction. The issues and processes involved in formulating, implementing and controlling the company's corporate Strategies.
- Basic principles and practice of finance and accounting. Basic knowledge of accounting, financial language and concepts, and relevant financial tools and techniques.
- Human resource direction. The importance of employing the right
- People with the right skills and encouraging their commitment, involvement and contribution.
- Effective marketing strategies. The vital role of successful marketing strategies in creating customer value and improving a company's market Performance and how they should be devised, implemented and controlled.
- Improving business performance. How added value is created and the determining factors in enhancing the performance of a business.
- Organising for tomorrow how the board of a modern company anticipates and responds to a changing business environment and provide appropriate leadership.

Variety as well as depth of experience will enrich the board. While relevant knowledge in itself is necessary to the board's work, experience enhances the understanding, analysis and application of that knowledge.

---

3 *Source*: Chairing the Board John Harpre Kogan Page 2000.

The ICSI is also considering a post membership qualification course on Corporate Governance and the proposed course covers the following key areas: Conceptual framework of corporate governance, principles, Business ethics, CG in various organisations and corporate social responsibilities.

Corporate and Board Management: Ownership structure, role, composition, systems and procedures types of directors, Rights, duties and responsibilities of directors, training of directors, executive management process, functional committees, shareholder relations, investor servicing, corporate disclosure; Legal and regulatory framework of corporate governance: corporate governance legislations, Listing requirements, MIS and corporate disclosure requirements, accounting and secretarial standards, Board committees and role of professionals, Corporate governance codes and practices and Project Report.

Developing Individual Directors

- Distance learning, video and audio recordings
- Open and in-house courses, seminars and workshops Conferences
- Individual and group counseling, personal coaching and mentoring
- Information and opinion from colleagues and acquaintances
- Working on other boards as non-executive director on the job experience
- Books, journals and newspapers, Membership of professional bodies/management associations and also membership of local reputed libraries.

Non-Executive Directors' Contribution

How can a non-executive director, add value to strategy discussion? The director concerned has to prepare well, reads specific supporting information for the strategy review. The six point checklist is as follows:

1. What simply is the current strategy and is it working?
2. What are the key drivers to achieve long-term advantage?
3. What are the significant changes driven by external circumstances including the market place that have implications for the business?
4. What resources and skills are needed? Does the company have them?
5. What results do the shareholders need and does the strategy deliver them?
6. Is there a resultant need to change the core work or processes of the company?

DIRECTORS' PROFESSIONAL ATTRIBUTES

1. Decision Making

- *Critical faculty*: Probes the facts, challenges assumptions, identifies the (dis) advantages of proposals, provides counter arguments, ensures discussions are penetrating.
- *Decisiveness*: Shows a readiness to take decisions and take action. Is able to make up his or her mind.

- *Judgement*: Makes sensible decisions or recommendations by weighing evidence. Considers reasonable assumptions, the ethical dimension and factual information.

2. Communication

- *Listening skills*: Listens dispassionately, intently and carefully so that key points are recalled and taken into account, questioning when necessary to ensure understanding.
- *Openness*: Is frank and open when communicating. Willing to admit errors and shortcomings.
- *Presentation skills*: Conveys ideas, images and words in a way that shows empathy with the audience.
- *Responsiveness*: *Is* able to invite and accept feedback.
- *Verbal fluency*: Speaks clearly, audibly and has good diction. Is concise, avoids jargon and tailors content to the audience's needs.
- *Written communication skills*: Written matter is readily intelligible; ideas, information and opinions are conveyed accurately, clearly and concisely.

3. Interaction with Others

- *Confidence*: Is aware of own strengths and weaknesses. Is assured when dealing with others. Able to take charge of a situation when appropriate.
- *Coordination skills*: Adopts appropriate interpersonal styles and methods in guiding the board towards task accomplishment. Fosters cooperation and effective teamwork.
- *Flexibility*: Adopts a flexible (but not compliant) style when interacting with others. Takes their views into account and changes position when appropriate.
- *Integrity*: Is truthful and trustworthy and can be relied upon to keep his or her word. Does not have double standards and does not compromise on ethical and legal matters.
- *Learning ability*: Seeks and acquires new knowledge and skills from multiple sources, including board experience.
- *Motivation*: Inspires others to achieve goals by ensuring a clear understanding of what needs to be achieved and by showing commitment, enthusiasm, encouragement and support.
- *Persuasiveness*: Persuades others to give their agreement and commitment; in face of conflict, uses personal influence to achieve consensus and/or agreement.
- *Presence*: Makes a strong positive impression on first meeting. Has authority and credibility, establishes rapport quickly.
- *Sensitivity*: Shows an understanding of the feelings and needs of others, and a vjllingness to provide personal support or to take other actions as appropriate.

4. Analyses and the Use of Information

- *Consciousness of detail*: Insists that sufficiently detailed and reliable information be taken account of and reported as necessary.

- *Eclecticism*: Systematically seeks all possible relevant information from a variety of sources.
- *Numeracy*: Assimilates numerical and statistical information accurately, understands its derivation and makes sensible, sound interpretations.
- *Problem recognition*: Identifies problems' and identifies possible or actual causes.

5. Strategic Perception

- *Change-orientation*: Alert and responsive to the need for change. Encourages new initiatives and the implementation of new policies, structures and practices.
- *Creativity*: Generates and recognizes imaginative solutions and innovations.
- *Foresight*: Is able to imagine possible future states and characteristics of the company in a future environment.
- *Organizational awareness*: Is aware of the company's strengths and weaknesses and of the likely impact of the board's decisions upon them.
- *Perspective*: Rises above the immediate problem or situation and sees the wider issues and implications. Is able to relate disparate facts and see all relevant relationships.
- *Strategic awareness*: Is aware of the various factors that determine the company's opportunities and threats (for example, shareholder, stakeholder, market, technological, environmental and regulatory factors).

6. Achievement of Results (Business Competence)

- *Business acumen*: Has the ability to identify opportunities to increase the company's business advantage.
- *Delegation skills*: Distinguishes between what should be done by others or by him or herself. Allocates decision-making or other tasks to appropriate colleagues and subordinates.
- *Drive*: Shows energy, vitality and commitment.
- *Exemplar*: Sets challenging but achievable goals and standards of performance for self and others.
- *Resilience*: Maintains composure and effectiveness in the face of adversity, setbacks, opposition or unfairness.
- *Risk acceptance*: Is prepared to take action that involves calculated risk in order to achieve a desired benefit or advantage.
- *Tenacity*: Stays with a position or plan of action until the desired objectives are achieved or require adaptation.

THE ROLE OF BOARD COMMITTEES

A committee is an almost widely used organisational device. The board committees are no exception. The object and utility of various committees vary and some of the typical committees are: budget committee, works committee (welfare, safety, social activities), executive committee, financial committee, planning committee, operations committee and audit committee. The help of committees is generally taken for resolving problems which require more knowledge, expertise, experience and judgment; some of these may be for taking major financial and capital investment policy decisions, business planning and coordination etc In the case of companies, the board being the highest organ it may appoint committees for different purposes: such as allotment policy, approval of transfer of shares, financial committee etc. While appointing committees, the powers and authority should be carefully defined. The provisions of the Companies Act, such as S.292 of the Companies Act should be complied with as some of the powers under this section can be exercised only by means of resolutions passed at a meeting of the board. Three important things should be taken into account: committees should be set up properly, there should be a good chairman and the members should be able to participate effectively.

Sound principles for Board committees: It is very important that board wholeness is not jeopardised or short-circuited. Committees can play a useful part in governance as long as they never substitute for the full Board's decision-making authority and never get between the board and management. Using committees can save the full board's time; however, boards should take care that such use does not fragment governance into committee fiefdoms. It should also be noted that directors who are not on a given committee, are not relieved of their overall accountability. The importance of not short-circuiting the board has been underlined in the following words: "Board committees are subsets of the board as a whole. Therefore, by definition, they pose a potential threat to the board's wholeness and its ability to speak with one voice. When a board committee makes a decision that should belong to the whole board, the rest of the board has been disenfranchised. When part of the board has been disenfranchised, the board as a body has been disenfranchised. When the board as a body has been disenfranchised, the owners represented by the board have been disenfranchised. Consequently, as useful as committees can be, it is important to use them in such a way that board wholeness is not jeopardised or short-circuited." Board committees function under the control of the board and not management, the full board is not relieved of its ultimate accountability, and board committees are meant to help the board with some part of the governance and are never meant to help or advise management.

Some important committees may be mentioned:

Executive committee: They are frequently established to make decisions in the board's absence. However, any system that creates a real board within the full board does not bode well for total board accountability.

Audit committee: Mandatory requirements have been prescribed in the case of audit committee and for the purpose; clause 49-II (A) of the listing agreement may be referred. Under the listing agreement prescriptions, audit committee has a critical role to play in ensuring the integrity of financial management of the company. The clause stipulates that the board shall set up a qualified and independent audit committee. Clause 49 applies to all listed companies. It may be important to mention that the Naresh Chandra committee has recommended that audit committees of all listed companies as well as unlisted public companies with a paid up share capital and free reserves of Rs. 10 crore and above, or turnover of Rs. 50 crore and above, should consist exclusively of independent directors.

Compensation and remuneration committees: For the purpose of determining the company's policy on specific remuneration packages for executive directors including pension rights and any compensation payment, remuneration committee is appointed. The remuneration of non-executive directors is decided by the board. Compensation and benefit committee usually determines pay package for subordinate executives and other staff of the company. Monitoring and research role is undertaken by these committees and the options and implications of various approaches in the matter of director compensation are weighed in the best interest of all concerned.

In addition, there may be nominations committee and advisory committee. A nomination committee researches possible criteria for new directors. The appointment of new directors who meet the criteria decided on by the board is said to add value to the full board's role.

The following extracts from 'If you are bored of meetings, read this' [4] is relevant and to quote, "When properly utilised, meetings are actually time savers," No kidding. "Good meetings provide opportunities to improve execution by accelerating decision making and eliminating the need to revisit issues again and again." A subtle and enormous benefit of good meetings is to reduce 'unnecessary repetitive motion and communication in the organisation'. Else, you would have 'sneaker time'—the 'underestimated black hole' in corporate milieu – the time your executives waste by roaming the halls, reading e-mails, leaving voice mail, all to "clarify issues that should have been made clear during a meeting in the first place". Worth reading in your next meeting.

CHECKLIST OF TOPICS FOR BOARD AGENDAS

- the company's objectives, vision, mission and goals;
- strategies and strategic plans;
- annual budgets;
- regular reviews of performance against budgets and plans;
- any matter that would have a material effect on the company's financial position, liabilities, future strategy or reputation;
- major capital projects in excess of (x value);
- capital expenditure in excess of budgets;
- changes to the company's capital structure;
- significant changes in accounting, risk management, capital and treasury policies and practices, including foreign exchange exposures;
- significant changes to the company's financial and management control systems;
- capital expenditure, disposals, acquisitions and joint ventures above the authority levels delegated to the chief executive/MD;
- the establishment and annual review of such delegated authority levels;

---

4 *Source*: The Hindu Business Line dt. April 12, 2004 (Book referred to DEATH by Meeting Patrick Lencioni).

- contracts not in the ordinary course of business and material contracts in the ordinary course of business;
- net borrowings in excess of peak budgeted or forecasted levels;
- dividends to shareholders;
- financial statements, including interim and Annual Reports and Accounts;
- circulars and prospectus to shareholders, including listing arrangements and those convening general meetings, except circulars of a routine nature;
- review of auditor's letter of recommendations;
- changes to the Memorandum and Articles of Association;
- reappointment or change of auditors;
- approval of audit fee;
- approval of auditor's engagement letter and scope of audit;
- the issue of ordinary and preference shares;
- share option schemes;
- appointment and removal of directors and company secretary, including those of subsidiaries;
- powers, roles and duties delegated to individual directors, including the chairman, chief executive/MD and finance director;
- remuneration and terms of appointment of directors and senior executives, including bonus arrangements, share options, pensions and contracts of employment;
- terms of reference and membership of board committees;
- material changes in pension scheme rules;
- liability insurance arrangements for directors and officers of the company.

BOARD STYLES

The CHAIRMAN of the board inevitably has an effect on the way that the board goes about its business. Board styles vary enormously. Figure on the next page shows some of these, depending on the extent of the directors' concern for their interpersonal relationships at board level, on the one hand, and their tough-minded concern for the work of the board, on the other.

- **The rubber-stamp board** shows little concern either for the tasks of the board or the interpersonal relationships among the directors. Examples of such boards can be found in the "letter-box" companies registered in many offshore tax havens. The meetings of the board are a formality. Indeed, they are often minuted without them actually taking place. The boards of some private CLOSELY HELD COMPANIES also treat their BOARD MEETINGS as a formality; perhaps because one individual is dominant and takes the decisions, or because the key players see each other frequently and decisions are taken in the management context.

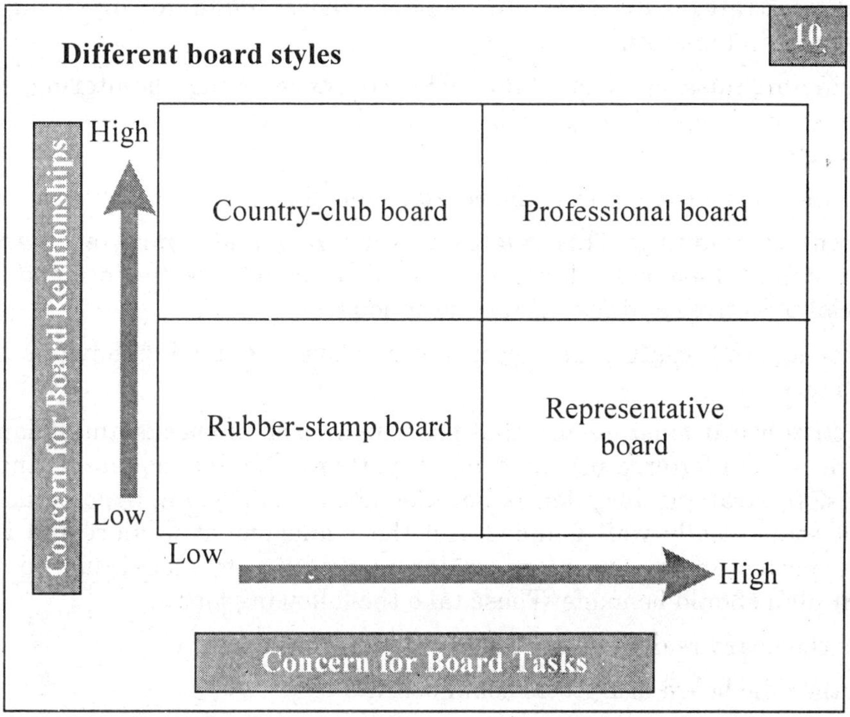

- **The country-club board,** in contrast, is very concerned with interpersonal relations at board level and the issues before the board may take second place. The boards of some old-established companies, which have been successful in the past, fit this model. There is likely to be a great deal of ritual about board meetings. The boardroom will be beautifully furnished, complete with sepia pictures of previous chairmen. Legends and myths surround board affairs. Meetings always follow the same pattern. Following the long-established traditions is revered. Innovation is discouraged.
- **The Representative Board** places more emphasis on the tasks of the board than it does on board relations. Frequently, this type of board has directors representing different SHAREHOLDERS or STAKEHOLDERS. The board is more like a parliament of diverse interests. Issues can easily become politicised. Board discussions can be adversarial. The basis and balance of power is important.
- **The professional board** adopts a style that shows a proper concern for both the board's tasks and its interpersonal relationships. A board with a successful professional style will have sound leadership from the chair. There will be tough-minded discussion among the members combined with a mutual understanding and respect for each other.

PERFORMANCE OF DIRECTORS: HOW TO MONITOR AND ASSESS THEIR PERFORMANCE?

For assessing the board performance, one has to concede that it may have to be on the basis of the main board responsibilities, which the board has chosen for itself. These normally cover the following:

- Providing strategic direction and values: these relate to approving corporate philosophy and mission
- Ensuring organisational capability: This covers selecting, monitoring, evaluating, compensating, replacing the CEO and other senior executives, thus ensuring management succession.

  It also includes ensuring that the board is effective.
- Approval of planning: This relates to reviewing and approving management's strategic and business plans; it may also include reviewing and approving financial objectives and material transactions
- Monitoring and control of performance: Covers ethical behaviour and Legal compliance

An effective board must ensure that there is no lack of checks and balances in the system, there is no unfettered power to anybody, there is no inadequate financial control and supervision, strategic direction is not distrubed by pursuing opportunistic thrusts that are not strategically well founded and the management is alert and is upto the standards expected of it; Questions which contribute or add value to the board development plan should be made; These take the following forms:

(i) Does the board really add sufficient value to the company?

(ii) Whether the board is a professional board?

(iii) Does the board work well together in its present configuration?

(iv) Whether the board is competent to direct the company in the future, given the objectives, challenges and opportunities?

(v) Whether the current size of the board is appropriate?

(vi) Whether the balance between executive and non executive directors the most appropriate?

(vii) Are sufficient non-executive directors genuinely independent of the company?

(viii) Is there separate chairman and chief executive/MD?

(ix) Is there succession plan for the board?

Evaluation of the board is the responsibility of the chairman and it is carried out by the whole board. Efficiently functioning boards will review their practices and outcomes on an ongoing basis, making changes where necessary. There should be a dynamic informal evaluation process. In order to test the effectiveness of the board and for the purpose of improvements, the following checklist of questions would help:

- Whether the board has devoted significant/sufficient time and serious thought to the company's long-term objectives and the strategic options open to it?
- Whether the board has reached formal conclusions on what may be referred to as 'corporate philosophy' and whether it has explicit statements of policy on value system, ethical and social responsibilities?
- Whether the board periodically undertakes periodical review of the organisational structure of the company?

- Whether the board routinely receives all the information it needed to ensure that it is in effective control of the company and its management?
- Whether the board ensures that the MD presents his annual plans and budgets for review and approval? Whether the actual results achieved are evaluated against plans and budgets?
- Whether the board takes major decisions and whether it had adequate Time and knowledge for those decisions or it is in effect, obliged to rubber stamp decisions already taken or commitments already made and/or whether it often finds itself overtaken by events?

CEO Evaluation

CEO evaluation is one of the more important duties undertaken by the board. The process should be positive and it should provide the CEO and the board with a better understanding of how the organisation is performing in relation to the implementation of strategies. The evaluation may be done on the basis of the following guidelines:

- Standards should be set through the CEO's work contract, annual work plan and quantitative performance standards. A set of standards and quantifiable objectives are essential; the performance evaluation may also be on the basis of financial ratios, human resource factors and where possible, data from comparable companies.
- Functional standards: This is a subjective area of evaluation, since it involves how the CEO should perform; the board may identify five to ten criteria that it considers essential to the performance of the CEO's role; the optimum performance levels should be defined and the range of possible performance levels of CEO should be specified, to measure against the set standards. Functional standards are set by each board on an organisation—specific basis.
- Conducting the evaluation: the board should meet without the CEO to discuss and reach agreement on its assessment of the CEO against the quantitiative criteria that has been set as above; Behavioural issues should also be discussed. The focus should be positive and should be on what needs to be done and how that can be achieved (rather than accusations as to why something was not done).

PART – IV

EXPERT COMMITTEE REPORTS AND CORPORATE GOVERNANCE AWARDS

Expert Committee Reports

DESIRABLE CORPORATE GOVERNANCE – A CODE BY CII

In 1996, CII took a special initiative on Corporate Governance-the first institutional initiative in Indian industry. The objective was to develop and promote a code for Corporate Governance to be adopted and followed by Indian companies, be these in the Private Sector, the Public Sector, Banks or Financial Institutions, all of which are corporate entities.

A National Task Force was set up with Mr. Rahul Bajaj, Past President, CII and Chairman & Managing Director, Bajaj Auto Limited, as the Chairman and including members from industry, the legal profession, media and academia.

This Task Force presented the draft guidelines and code for Corporate Governance in April 1997 at the National Conference and Annual Session of CII This draft was then publicly debated in Workshops and Seminars and a number of suggestions were received for the consideration of the Task Force. Reviewing these suggestions, and the developments which have taken place in India and abroad, the Task Force finalised the Desirable Corporate Governance Code.

Recommendation 1

There is no need to adopt the German system of two-tier boards to ensure desirable corporate governance. A single board, if it performs well, can maximize long term shareholder value just as well as two or multi-tiered board. Equally, there is nothing to suggest that a two-tier board, *per se*, is the panacea to all corporate problems.

However, the full board should meet a minimum of six times a year, preferably at an interval of two months, and each meeting should have agenda items that require at least half a day's discussion.

It has been proved time and again in the USA, Great Britain, Germany and many other OECD countries that the quality of the board–and, hence, corporate governance – improves with the induction of outside professionals as non-executive directors. As a recent article put it:

Obviously not all well governed companies do well in the market place. Nor do the badly governed ones always sink. But even the best performers risk stumbling some day if they lack strong and independent boards of directors.

Recommendation 2

Any listed company with a turnover of Rs. 100 crores and above should have professionally competent, independent, non-executive directors, who should constitute:

1. **atleast 30 per cent of the board if the Chairman of the company is a non-executive director, or**
2. **atleast 50 per cent of the board if the Chairman and Managing Director is the same person.**

Getting the right type of professionals on the board is only one way of ensuring diligence. It has to be buttressed by the concept of limitation: one cannot hold non-executive directorships in a plethora of companies, and yet be expected to discharge one's obligations and duties. This yields the third recommendation.

Recommendation 3

No single person should hold directorships in more than 10 listed companies.

As of now, section 275 of the Companies Act allows a person to hold up to 20 directorships. *The Report of the Working Group on the Companies Act (February* 1997) has kept the number unchanged. It is felt that with 20 directorships it would be extremely difficult for an individual to make an effective contribution and ensure good governance, and yet discharge his fiduciary responsibilities towards all.

Recommendation 4

For non-executive directors to play a material role in corporate decision making and maximising long term shareholder value, they need to

1. **become active participants in boards, not passive advisors;**
2. **have clearly defined responsibilities within the board such as the Audit Committee; and**
3. **Know how to read a balance sheet, profit and loss account cash flow statements and financial ratios and have some knowledge of various company laws. This, of course, excludes those who are invited to join boards as experts in other fields such as science and technology.**

The brings one to remuneration of nonexecutive directors receive a sitting fee which cannot exceed Rs. 2,000 per meeting. The Working Group on the Companies Act has recommended that this limit should be raised to Rs. 5,000. Although this is better than Rs. 2,000, it is hardly sufficient to induce serious effort by the non-executive directors.

Recommendation 5

To secure better effort from non-executive directors companies should

1. **Pay a commission over and above the sitting fees for the use of the professional inputs. The present commission of 1% of net profits (if the company has a managing director), or 3% (if there is no managing director) is sufficient.**
2. **Consider offering stock options, so as to relate rewards to performance. Commissions are rewards on current profits. Stock options are rewards contingent upon future appreciation of corporate value. An appropriate mix of the two can align a non-executive director towards keeping an eye on short-term profits as well as longer term shareholder value.**

The above recommendation can be easily achieved without the necessity any formal issued remuneration committee of the board. To ensure that non-executive directors properly discharge their fiduciary obligations, it is, however, necessary to give a record of their attendance to the shareholders.

Recommendation 6

While re-appointing members of the board, companies should give the attendance record of the concerned directors. If a director has not been present (absent with or without leave) for 50 per cent or more meetings, then this should be explicitly stated in the resolution that is put to vote. As a general practice, one should not reappoint any director who has not had the time to attend even one half of the meetings.

Recommendation 7

Key information that must be reported to, and placed before, the board must contain:

1. **Annual operating plans and budgets, together with up-dated long term plans.**
2. **Capital budgets, manpower and overhead budgets.**
3. **Quarterly results for the company as a whole and its operating divisions or business segments.**
4. **Internal audit reports, including cases of theft and dishonesty of a material nature.**
5. **Show cause, demand and prosecution notices received from revenue authorities which are considered to be materially important (Material nature if any exposure that exceeds 1 per cent of the company's net worth).**
6. **Fatal or serious accidents, dangerous occurrences, and any effluent or pollution problems.**
7. **Default in payment of interest or non-payment of the principal on any public deposit and/or to any secured creditor or financial institution.**
8. **Defaults such as non-payment of inter-corporate deposits by or the company, or materially substantial non-payment for goods sold by the company.**
9. **Any issue which involves possible public or product liability claims of a substantial nature, including any judgment or order which may have either passed strictures on the conduct of the company, or taken an adverse view regarding another enterprise that can have negative implication for the company.**
10. **Details of any joint venture or collaboration agreement.**
11. **Transactions that involve substantial payment towards goodwill, brand equity, or intellectual property.**
12. **Recruitment and remuneration of senior officers just below the board level, including appointment or removal of the Chief Financial Officer and the Company Secretary.**
13. **Labour problems and their proposed solutions.**
14. **Quarterly details of foreign exchange exposure and the steps taken by management to limit the risks of adverse exchange rate movement, if material.**

Recommendation 8

1. **Listed companies with either a turnover of over Rs. 100 crores or a paid-up-capital of Rs. 2 crores should set up Audit Committees within two years.**
2. **Audit Committees should consist of at least three members, all drawn from a company's non-executive directors, who should have adequate knowledge of finance, accounts and basic elements of company law.**
3. **To be effective, the Audit Committees should have clearly defined Terms of Reference and it's members must be willing to spend more time on the company's work *vis-à-vis* other non-executive director.**
4. **Audit Committees should assist the board in fulfilling its functions relating to corporate accounting and reporting practices, financial and accounting controls, and financial statements and proposals that accompany the public issue of any security – and thus provide effective supervision of the financial reporting process.**
5. **Audit Committees should periodically interact with the statutory auditors and the internal auditors to ascertain the quality and veracity of the company's accounts as well as the capability of the auditors themselves.**
6. **For Audit Committees to discharge their fiduciary responsibilities with due diligence, it must be incumbent upon management to ensure that members of the committee have full access to financial data of the company, its subsidiary and associated companies, including data on contingent liabilities, debt exposure, current liabilities, loans and investments.**
7. **By the fiscal year 1998-99, listed companies satisfying criterion (1) should have in place a strong internal audit department, or an external auditor to do internal audits: without this, any Audit Committee will be toothless.**

Recommendation 9

Under "Additional Shareholder's Information", listed companies should give data on:

1. **High and low monthly averages of share prices in a major S... Exchange where the company is listed for the reporting year.**
2. **Greater detail on business segments, up to 10% of turnover, giving share in sales revenue, review of operations, analysis of markets and future prospects.**

The Working Group on the Companies Act has recommended that consolidation should be operational, not mandatory. There were two reasons: *(i)* that the Income-tax Department does not accept the concept of group accounts for tax purposes–and the *Report of/the Working Group on the Income-tax Act* does not suggest any difference, and *(ii)* the public sector term lending inst...tion do not allow leveraging on the basis of group assets. Thus:

Recommendation 10

1. **Consolidation of Group Accounts should be optional and subject to:**
   (*a*) **The FIs allowing companies to leverage on the basis of the group's assets, and**
   (*b*) **The income tax Department using the group concept in assessing corporate income tax.**
2. **If a company chooses to voluntarily consolidate, it should not be necessary to annex the accounts of its subsidiary companies under Section 212 of the Companies Act.**
3. **However, if a company consolidates, then the definition of "group" should include the parent company and its subsidiaries (where the reporting company owns over 50% of voting stake).**

Recommendation 11

Major Indian stock exchange should gradually insist upon a compliance certificate, signed by the CEO and the CFO, which clearly states that:

1. **The management is responsible for the preparation, integrity and fair presentation of the financial statements and other information in the Annual Report, and which also suggest that the company will continue in business in the course of the following year.**
2. **The accounting policies and principles conform to standard practice, and where they do not, full disclosure has been made of any material departures.**
3. **The board has overseen the company's system of internal accounting and administrative controls systems either directly or through its Audit Committee (for companies with a turnover of Rs. 100 crores or paid-up-capital of Rs. 20 crores).**

Recommendation 12

For all companies with paid-up capital of Rs. 20 crores or more, the quality and quantity of disclosure that accompanies a GDR issue should be the norms for any domestic issue.

Recommendation 13

Government must allow far greater funding to the corporate sector against the security of shares and other paper.

When this is in place, the takeover code should be modified to reflect international norms. Once takeover finance is easily available to Indian entrepreneurs, the trigger should increase to 20%, and the minimum bid should reflect at least a 51%, takeover.

Recommendation 14

It would be desirable for FIs as pure creditors to re-write their covenants to eliminate having nominee directors except:

(*a*) in the event of serious and systematic debt default; and

(*b*) in case of the debtor company not providing six-monthly or quarterly operational data to the concerned FI(s).

Today, credit rating is compulsory for any corporate debt issue. But, as in the case of primary equity issues, the quality of information given to the Indian investing public is still well below what is disclosed in many other developed countries. Given below are some suggestions.

Recommendation 15

1. If any company goes to more than one credit rating agency, then it must divulge in the prospectus and issue document the rating of all the agencies that did such an exercise.
2. It is not enough to state the ratings. These must be given in a tabular format that shows where the company stands relative to higher and lower ranking. It makes considerable difference to an investor to know whether and rating agency or agencies placed the company in the top slots or in the middle or in the bottom.

Recommendation 16

Companies that default on fixed deposits should not be permitted to:

(*a*) accept further deposits and make intercorporate loans or investments until the default is made good; and

(*b*) declare dividends until the default is made good.

Recommendation 17

Reduction in the number of companies where there are nominee directors. It has been argued by FIs that there are too many companies where they are on the board, and too few competent officers to do the task properly. So, in the first instance, FIs should take a policy decisions to withdraw from boards of companies where their individual shareholding is 5 per cent or less, or total FI holding is under 10 per cent.

Concluding Remarks

A code of corporate governance cannot be static. It must be reviewed. Therefore, CII *must review this report after sometime, preferably within the next five years.* Having said this, the report focuses on two more issues: (*i*) What does one mean by a "code" of corporate governance? (*ii*) A vision of things to come in the next few years, and its implications for corporate governance.

Simply put, corporate governance refers to *an economic, legal and institutional environment that* allows companies to diversify, grow, restructure and exit, and do everything necessary to maximize long term shareholder value. Thus, non-executive directors and disclosures are parts, and not the whole, of corporate governance. To most international experts on the subject, corporate governance is an interplay between companies, shareholders, creditors, capital markets, financial sector institutions and company law. Hence, a code of corporate governance must attempt to address all these issues. This report, therefore, does constitute a code of corporate governance; and it consciously goes beyond the duty of boards and non-executive directors. Moreover, this code of corporate governance-despite its possible lacunae will not become a reality with a stroke of a magic wand. It is a fairly substantive and radical code; it will therefore have its detractors; and putting it into effect will be a long haul.

Nevertheless, it is vital for the well bring of corporate India. To appreciate this, it is useful to take a peep at the vision of the near future. It is a vision that will almost certainly come to bear, and shall, willy-nilly, shape tomorrow's corporate governance.

REPORT OF THE TASK FORCE ON CORPORATE EXCELLENCE THROUGH GOVENANCE

1. Objective of this Document and Definition

1.1 The objective of this document is to communicate the updated Code of Conduct "Code" of the Company to the employees. It is intended to serve as a guideline to corporate and individual behaviour in the conduct of business and the discharge of duties of all concerned.

1.2 The Code is fundamentally a set of principles and values expected to be maintained by the Company and its employees.

2. Applicability

2.1 The Code shall apply to all employees irrespective of level, across all units and offices.

2.2 Whenever any aspect of this Code is covered under any Act or Law, the more stringent of the respective provisions shall apply unless the law expressly forbids it. If any aspect is covered by any Act or Law but this Code is silent on the same, the provisions of the Act or Law shall apply.

2.3 The Board of Directors of the Company shall be the final internal authority as far as any interpretation of the Code or its applicability/violation and consequential actions are concerned.

2.4 The Code may be expanded and/or improved upon from time to time.

3. Corporate Governance

3.1 The Company is committed to adopting, besides any of its obligations under relevant laws or regulations, the best relevant practices for Corporate Governance.

3.2 The Audit Committee shall oversee the effectiveness of the audit and internal audit tasks, to assist the Board in providing useful supervision of the overall financial reporting process.

(*a*) Due emphasis shall be laid on the audit/internal audit process, as necessary to safeguard the interests of shareholders. Every employee must extend his full co-operation to the Auditors and ensure that all information as may be required by them is made available. The Audit Committee may also have propriety audit conducted from time to time.

3.3 A Remuneration and Evaluation Committee, including a majority of non-executive Directors, shall oversee the evaluation, compensation and promotion process to uphold transparency therein.

3.4 All employees shall ensure that they take adequate steps to completely familiarize themselves in depth with all laws, legal and procedural requirements relating to operations within their scope of work, as they shall be accountable for their compliance.

4. Quality of Goods, Services and Dealings

4.1 The Company and its employees are committed to building and maintaining long term and mutually beneficial relations with all our customers and stakeholders, by consistently providing high quality goods and services, through equitable conduct and by upholding the value of our commitments.

4.2 The Company and its employees shall ensure that due courtesy, consideration and promptness are exercised in communication and inter-personal dealings not limited to suppliers, agents, dealers, financial bodies, banks and shareholders or depositors.

4.3 The employees should exhibit such professional, fair and courteous values in dealings and behaviour that reputable third parties chooses to deal with the company time and again.

5. Conflict of Interest

5.1 Conflict of interest is a wide term (implying wider definition and implication commensurate with seniority of the employee) which calls for examples rather than definition.

5.2 For purposes of a limited illustration only, a Conflict of Interest can be said to have arisen or exist between an employee and the Company in circumstances when:

(a) Causing harm or financial loss to the Company due to any act(s), including obvious negligence or willful neglect of duty, non co-operation of the employee directly or through a third party or his abetting such action by another employee;

(b) Disclosure of any information (including, but not limited to competitive information) considered prejudicial to the Company's interest;

(c) Entering directly or indirectly into any form of relationship or association (with or without financial benefits or remuneration) with a direct competitor of the Company or a supplier or sub-contractor of the Company;

(d) Abetting of any third party to influence or effect supplies or services, either directly or indirectly, to the Company at prejudiced terms or at terms other than at arms' length;

(e) Operating/commencing or proposing to operate a business in direct conflict/competition with the business of the Company;

(f) Undertaking any business or professional activity in contravention of the guidelines herein, while in the employ of the Company;

(g) Utilizing Company's resources, financial or otherwise, to support personal, financial or business interest (or of a relative/associate) or promoting financial or business interest of any other employee; or

(h) Formal prosecution or legal sentence awarded at any time by a relevant competent or judicial authority for a serious misdemeanor (such as any criminal offence or morale turpitude, etc).

Executive Summary

A major contributory to corporate excellence is good corporate governance. In well developed, competitive and globalised economies, there is strong evidence to suggest that corporations well known for their high standards of transparency, accountability, professionalism, social responsiveness, corporate citizenry, and ethical business practices, in short, for good corporate governance, are also those which deliver excellent returns to their shareholders and are admired by their stakeholders and society at large. In the short decade that India has grappled with the challenges posed, and capitalized on the opportunities offered by a liberalizing economic environment, there are already shining examples of corporations achieving business excellence concurrently with, or perhaps more appropriately, because of the excellent standards of corporate governance that they have set for themselves. Further maturation of the market place is likely to recognize and reward such corporations in greater measure in the decades ahead.

Role and Responsibilities of Corporate Boards and Directors

The role of the corporate board of directors as stewards of their shareholders and stakeholders has internationally gained significant ground in recent decades. Successive corporate failures and other disasters have strengthened the demand for more transparency and accountability on the part of corporations. In the discharge of these onerous responsibilities, the corporate board has come to be regarded as the principal arbiter, ensuring on the one hand that executive management competently and through legitimate means creates wealth, and on the other, that such created wealth is equitably distributed to all shareholders after meeting the due aspirations of and obligations to other stakeholders. This requirement applies equally to cases of extreme separation of operational control from share ownership and those with dominant shareholders in charge of executive management as is the case in several developing countries. Hence the perceived need for the board to be independent of the executive, which position is sought to be achieved by infusion of a majority of competent non-executive directors with no material pecuniary relationships with the corporation or its opinion makers. **The Task Force recommendation in this field calls for a greater role and influence for non-executive *independent* directors, a tighter delineation of independence criteria and minimization of interest-conflict potential, and some stringent punitive punishments for executive directors of companies failing to comply with listing and other requirements.** Legal validation of electronic conferencing and other such measures to facilitate greater board participation, and attendance/participation by a majority of *independent* directors as a statutory quorum requirement for board meetings are further measures recommended. The position and status of nominee directors have also been addressed in the recommendations.

Centre for Corporate Excellence

Given the imperatives of improving standards of corporate governance to enhance the competitive capabilities of Indian corporations on the one hand, and on the other of providing institutionalised support for actualizing the desired goals in this direction,

there is a pressing need to set up an independent autonomous Centre for Corporate Excellence that would function as a knowledge portal and repository in this field. The Task Force has recommended the constitution of such a Centre with three broad functions, Research and Studies, Education Promotion and Development, and Accreditation with respect to matters bearing upon corporate governance and excellence.

Classification of Recommendation and Implementation

Recommendation of the Task Force have been grouped a *essential*, to be introduced immediately by legislation, and *desirable*, that can be left to the discretion of the companies and their shareholders in their wisdom. A model *governance code* incorporating both the essential and desirable measures has been recommended to be drafted and included as a Table in the Companies Act, to be adopted at the option of the companies. Given the challenges of managing change, the **Task Force has recommended phased implementation of the essential measures, depending upon the size and capabilities of the companies on the one hand and on the other, the requirements of the market place.**

Internationally, a growing school of influential thinkers advocate that corporate governance measures should be more by self discipline and market forces, rather than by legislation and regulation. This of course is unexceptionable and deserves full support. **The Task Force is however convinced that the level of non-legislative and non-regulatory intervention is a function of the maturity of the market and the economy. Until acceptable levels of such maturity and market influence are reached, it may be necessary to support self discipline and self regulation with appropriate legislative and regulatory support with a provision for review after three years.** However, emphasis continue to be on self regulation. The desire for self-regulation should be enhanced by a recognition of the advantages of good governance in improving the company's credibility and market acceptance.

The earlier reluctance to adopt self regulatory measures was partly due to the licence and permit system which reduced the effect of competitive forces. With competition now becoming a powerful force in the market there should be increased recognition of the advantages of good corporate governance. The recognition should be supported by education, promotion and propagation.

REPORT OF THE SEBI COMMITTEE ON CORPORATE GOVERNANCE (FEBRUARY 8, 2003)

The issues discussed by the Committee primarily related to audit committees, audit reports, independent directors, related parties, risk management, directorships and director compensation, codes of conduct and financial disclosures. The Committee's recommendations in the final report were selected based on parameters including their relative importance, fairness, accountability, transparency, ease of implementation, verifiability and enforceability. The key mandatory recommendations focus on strengthening the responsibilities of audit committees; improving the quality of financial disclosures, including those related to related party transactions and proceeds from initial public offerings; requiring corporate executive boards to assess and disclose business risks in the annual reports of companies; introducing responsibilities on boards to adopt formal codes of conduct; the position of nominee directors; and stock holder approval and improved disclosures related to compensation paid to non-executive directors. Non-mandatory recommendations include moving to a regime where corporate financial statements are not qualified; instituting a system of training of board members; and the evaluation of performance of board members. The Committee believes that these recommendations codify certain standards of "good" governance into specific requirements, since certain corporate responsibilities are too important to be left to loose concepts of fiduciary responsibility. When implemented through SEBI's regulatory framework, they will strengthen existing governance practices and also provide a strong incentive to avoid corporate failures. Some people have legitimately asked whether the costs of governance reforms are too high. In this context, it should be noted that the failure to implement good Governance procedures has a cost beyond mere regulatory problems. Companies that do not employ meaningful governance procedures will have to pay a significant risk premium when competing for scarce capital in today's public markets. The Committee would like to thank Mr. G.N. Bajpai, Chairman of SEBI and Mr. Pratip Kar, Executive Director, SEBI for their support. In addition, the Committee would like to thank Mr. P.K. Bindlish, General Manager, Mr. Manoj Kumar, Assistant General Manager and other staff at SEBI along with Mr. Sumanth Cidambi of Progeon Limited, who assisted in the preparation of this report.

N.R. Narayana Murthy Chairman Committee on Corporate Governance, SEBI Mumbai.

Corporate governance is a key element in improving the economic efficiency of a firm. Good corporate governance also helps ensure that corporations take into account the interests of a wide range of constituencies, as well as of the communities within which they operate. Further, it ensures that their Boards are accountable to the shareholders. This, in turn, helps assure that corporations operate for the benefit of society as a whole. While large profits can be made taking advantage of the asymmetry between stakeholders in the short run, balancing the interests of all stakeholders alone will ensure survival and growth in the long run. This includes, for instance, taking into account societal concerns about labour and the environment.

Studies of corporate governance practices across several countries conducted by the Asian Development Bank (2000), International Monetary Fund (1999), Organization for Economic Cooperation and Development ("OECD") (1999) and the World Bank (1999) reveal that there is not single model of good corporate governance. This is recognized by the OECD Code. The OECD Code also recognizes that different legal systems, institutional frameworks and traditions across countries have led to the development of a range of different approaches to corporate governance. Common to all good corporate governance regimes, however, is a high degree of priority placed on the interests of shareholders, who place their trust in corporations to use their investment funds wisely and effectively. In addition, best managed corporations also recognize that business ethics and corporate awareness of the environmental and societal interest of the communities within which they operate, can have an impact on the reputation and long-term performance of corporations.

Mandatory Recommendation

1. Audit committees of publicly listed companies should be required to review the following information mandatorily:
   - *(a)* Financial statements and draft audit report, including quarterly/half-yearly financial information;
   - *(b)* Management discussion and analysis of financial condition and results of operations;
   - *(c)* Reports relating to compliance with laws and to risk management;
   - *(d)* Management letters/letters of internal control weaknesses issued by statutory/internal auditors; and
   - *(e)* Records of related party transactions.
2. In case a company has followed a treatment different from that prescribed in an accounting standard, management should justify why they believe such alternative treatment is more representative of the underlying business transaction. Management should also clearly explain the alternative accounting treatment in the footnotes to the financial statements.
3. A statement of all transactions with related parties including their bases should be placed before the independent audit committee for formal approval/ratification. If any transaction is not on an arm's length basis, management should provide an explanation to the audit committee justifying the same.
4. The term "related party" shall have the same meaning as contained in Accounting Standard 18, *Related Party Transactions*, issued by the Institute of Chartered Accountants of India.
5. Procedures should be in place to inform Board members about the risk assessment and minimization procedures. These procedures should be periodically reviewed to ensure that executive management controls risk through means of a properly defined framework.

   Management should place a report before the entire Board of Directors every quarter documenting the business risks faced by the company, measures to address and minimize such risks, and any limitations to the risk taking capacity of the corporation. This document should be formally approved by the Board.
6. Companies raising money through an Initial Public Offering ("IPO") should disclose to the Audit Committee, the uses/applications of funds by major category (capital expenditure, sales and marketing, working capital, etc.) on a quarterly basis. On an annual basis, the company shall prepare a statement of funds utilized for purposes other than those stated in the offer document/prospectus. This statement should be certified by the independent auditors of the company. The audit committee should make appropriate recommendations to the Board to take up steps in this matter.

7. It should be obligatory for the Board of a company to lay down the code of conduct for all Board members and senior management of a company. This code of conduct shall be posted on the website of the company.

All Board members and senior management personnel shall affirm compliance with the code on an annual basis. The annual report of the company shall contain a declaration to this effect signed off by the CEO and COO.

Explanation – For this purpose, the term "senior management" shall mean personnel of the company who are members of the management/ operating council (i.e. core management team excluding Board of Directors). Normally, this would comprise all members of management one level below the executive directors.

8. All compensation paid to non-executive directors may be fixed by the Board of Directors and should be approved by shareholders in general meeting. Limits should be set for the maximum number of stock options that can be granted to non-executive directors in any financial year and in aggregate. The stock options granted to the non-executive directors shall vest after a period of at least one year from the date such non-executive directors have retired from the Board of the Company.

Companies should publish their compensation philosophy and statement of entitled compensation in respect of non-executive directors in their annual report. Alternatively, this may be put up on the company's website and reference drawn thereto in the annual report.

Companies should disclose on an annual basis, details of shares held by non-executive directors, including on an "if-converted" basis.

Non-executive directors should be required to disclose their stock holding (both own or held by/for other persons on a beneficial basis) in the listed company in which they are proposed to be appointed as directors, prior to the appointment. These details should accompany their notice of appointment.

9. The term "independent director" is defined as a non-executive director of the company who:

(a) Apart from receiving director remuneration, does not have any material pecuniary relationships or transactions with the company, its promoters, its senior management or its holding company, its subsidiaries and associated companies;

(b) Is not related to promoters or management at the board level or at one level below the board;

(c) Has not been an executive of the company in the immediately proceeding three financial year;

(d) Is not a partner or an executive of the statutory audit firm or the internal audit firm that is associated with the company, and has not been a partner or an executive of any such firm for the last three

years. This will also apply to legal firm(s) and consulting firm(s) that have a material association with the entity;

(e) **Is not a supplier, service provider or customer of the company. This should include lessor-lessee type relationships also; and**

(f) **Is not a substantial shareholder of the company, i.e. owning two percent or more of the block of voting shares.**

The considerations as regards remuneration paid to an independent director shall be the same as those applied to a non-executive director.

10. Companies shall annually affirm that they have not denied any personnel access to the audit committee of the company (in respect of matters involving alleged misconduct) and that they have provided protection to "whistle blowers" from unfair termination and other unfair or prejudicial employment practices.

The appointment, removal and terms of remuneration of the chief internal auditor must be subject to review by the Audit Committee.

Such affirmation shall form a part of the Board report on Corporate Governance that is required to be prepared and submitted together with the annual report.

11. The provisions relating to the composition of the Board of Directors of the holding company should be made applicable to the composition fo the Board of Directors of subsidiary companies.

At least one independent director on the Board of Directors of the parent company shall be a director on the Board of Directors of the subsidiary company.

The Audit Committee of the parent company shall also review of the financial statements, in particular the investments made by the subsidiary company.

The minutes of the Board meetings of the subsidiary company shall be placed for review at the Board meeting of the parent company.

The Board report of the parent company should state that they have reviewed the affairs of the subsidiary company also.

The Committee noted that evaluation of Board members is in a germane stage in India. It is necessary to have a robust process in place for such evaluation. It is also necessary to ensure continuity of top leadership, including CEO succession planning. However, the Committee believes that this should be a recommendatory nature at first, before becoming a mandatory requirement. This will help companies develop robust processes for Board evaluation. This may be made mandatory after a period of 4-5 years.

Corporate Governance Ratings

1. It was suggested that corporate governance practices followed by companies should be rated using rating models. It was also suggested that companies should be rated based on parameters of wealth generation, maintenance and sharing, as well as on corporate governance.

2. The Committee deliberated and noted that corporate governance ratings are desirable, as this will provide a process of independent appraisal. Certain rating agencies have begun work in this area; however, the process is still in a development phase and may need to be evolved based on future experience.
3. The Committee is therefore of the view that for the time being, it should not be mandatory for companies to be rated on corporate governance parameters. However, it should be left to the management of companies to decide whether they want to be rated or not, on corporate governance.

Implementation and Way Forward

The Committee noted that the recommendations contained in this Report can be implemented by means of an amendment to the Listing Agreement, with changes made to the existing clause 49.

RBI'S REPORT OF THE CONSULTATIVE GROUP OF DIRECTORS OF BANKS/FINANCIAL INSTITUTIONS

Executive Summary

1. The Consultative Group of Directors of banks and financial institutions was set up by the Reserve Bank to review the supervisory role of Boards of banks and financial institutions and to obtain feedback on the functioning of the Boards *vis-à-vis* compliance, transparency, disclosures, audit committees etc. and make recommendations for making the role of Boards of Directors more effective with a view to minimizing risks and over-exposure.
2. The Group has produced a list of recommendations after a comprehensive review of the existing legal framework governing constitution of the Boards of banks and financial institutions, interaction with various interested groups, organizations, etc. benchmarked its recommendations with international best practices as enunciated by the Basel Committee on Banking Supervision, as well as of other committees and advisory bodies, to the extent applicable in the Indian environment.
3. Due diligence of the directors of all banks—be they in public or private sector, should be done in regard to their suitability for the post by way of qualifications and technical expertise. Involvement of Nomination Committee of the Board in such an exercise should be seriously considered as a formal process.
4. The Government while nominating directors on the Boards of public sector banks should be guided by certain broad "fit and proper" norms for the Directors. The criteria suggested by the BIS may be suitably adopted for considering "fit and proper" test for bank directors.
5. For assessing integrity and suitability, factors such as criminal records, financial position, civil actions undertaken to pursue personal debts, refusal of admission to, or expulsion from professional bodies, sanctions applied by regulators or similar bodies, and previous questionable business practices, etc. should be considered.
6. The appointment/nomination of independent/non-executive directors to the Boards of banks (both public sector and private sector) should be from a pool of

professional and talented people to be prepared and maintained by Reserve Bank of India. Any deviation from this procedure by any bank should be with the prior approval of RBI.

7. In the present context of banking becoming more complex and knowledge-based, there is an urgent need for making the Boards of banks more contemporarily professional by inducting technical and specially qualified individuals.
8. While continuing regulation based representation of sectors like agriculture, SSI, cooperation, etc. efforts should be aimed at combining it with the need-based representation of skills such as marketing, technology & systems, risk management, strategic planning, treasury operations, credit recovery, etc. Further, the Boards of banks should also have representation in the areas such as finance, information technology, human resources development, economics and persons with good track record of experience in managing/advising industrial enterprises.
9. The independent/non-executive directors should raise in the meetings of the Board, critical questions relating to business strategy, including loans & recovery policy, housekeeping and internal control systems, record of exposure to various sectors/industries by way of both credit and investment, risk management systems, internal audit, accounting policy, senior management development, other important aspects of the functioning of the bank and investor relations. The good corporate governance in banks will be sustained by a knowledgeable, skilful and well informed Board of Directors with a proper blend of expertise/professionalism, independence and involvement.
10. In the case of private sector banks where promoter directors may act in concert, the independent/non-executive directors should provide effective checks and balances ensuring that the bank does not build up exposures to entities connected with the promoters or their associates. The independent/non-executive directors should provide effective checks and balances particularly, in widely held and closely controlled banking organisations.
11. Directors on the boards of NBFCs may be permitted to become Independent/ non-executive directors on the boards of banks, subject to certain conditions.
12. Every Director should be given a brief on the functioning of the bank, before his appointment/induction, covering various aspects of structure/functioning of the bank.
13. The Board should formulate policies relating to credit dispensation, particularly in regard to exposure to various productive sectors, geographical areas, investments, exposures to sensitive sectors such as capital market, strategies for recovery of loans and status of progress with respect to investments, risk management, etc.
14. The directors could be made more responsible to their organisation by exposing them to need-based training programmes/seminars/workshops to acquaint them with emerging developments/challenges facing the banking sector. Reserve Bank as the Regulator, could take the initiative to organizing such seminars.
15. The whole-time directors should have sufficiently long tenure to enable them to leave a mark of their leadership and business acumen on the bank's performance.
16. Reserve Bank may bring out an updated charter indicating clear-cut, specific

guidelines on the role expected and the responsibilities of the individual directors.

17. As a step towards effective corporate governance, it would be desirable to take an undertaking from every director to the effect that they have gone through the guidelines defining the role and responsibilities of directors, and understood what is expected of them and enter into a covenant to discharge their responsibilities to the best of their abilities, individually and collectively.

18. The existing level of remuneration paid (by way of sitting fees, etc.) to directors of banks and financial institutions is grossly inadequate, by contemporary standards, to attract qualified professional people to their boards, and expect them to discharge their duties as per the mutually agreed covenants. In order to attract quality professionals, the level of remuneration payable to the directors should be commensurate with the time required to be devoted to the bank's work as well as to signal the appropriateness of remuneration to the quality of inputs expected from a member. The remuneration of the directors may also include the form of stock option.

19. It would be desirable to separate the office of Chairman and Managing Director in respect of large sized public sector banks. This functional separation will bring about more focus on strategy and vision as also the needed thrust in the operational functioning of the top management of the bank.

20. The statutory prohibition under section 20 of the Banking Regulation Act, 1949 on lending to companies in which the director is interested, severely constricts availability of quality professional directors on to the Boards of banks. Internationally, however, banks are permitted to extend credit facilities to companies in which the directors are interested subject to full disclosure and appropriate covenants. This would require a change in the existing legal framework. We need to move towards this goal.

21. The information furnished to the Board should be wholesome, complete and adequate to take meaningful decisions. A distinction needs to be made between statutory items and strategic issues in order to make the material for directors 'manageable'. The manner in which the Board proceedings are recorded and followed up in public sector banks leaves much scope for improvement. The Reviews dealing with various performance areas could be put up to the Supervisory Committee of Board and a summary of each such review could be put up to the Main Board. The Board's focus should be devoted more on strategy issues, risk profile, internal control systems, overall performance of the bank, etc.

22. The procedure followed for recording of the minutes of the boards meetings in banks and financial institutions should be uniform and formalised. Banks and financial institutions may adopt two methods for recording the proceedings *viz., a* summary of key observations and a more detailed recording of the proceedings. In every meeting, the board should review the status of the action taken on the points arising from earlier meetings and till action is completed to its satisfaction; the pending items should continue to be put up before the board.

23. It would be desirable if the exposures of a bank to stockbrokers and market-makers as a group, as also exposures other sensitive sectors, viz., real estate etc. are reported to the Board regularly. The disclosures in respect of the progress made in putting in place a progressive risk management system, the risk

management policy, strategy followed by the bank, exposures to related entities, the asset classification of such landings/investments etc. conformity with Corporate Governance Standards etc., be made by banks to the Board of Directors at regular intervals as prescribed.

24. All banks should consider appointing qualified Company Secretary as the Secretary to the Board and have a Compliance Officer (reporting to the Secretary) for monitoring and reporting compliance with various regulatory/accounting requirements.
25. There could be a Supervisory Committee of the Board in all banks, be they public or private sector, which will work on collective trust and at the same time, without diluting the overall responsibility of the Board. Their role and responsibilities could include monitoring of the exposures (credit and investment) review of the adequacy of risk management process & upgradation thereof, internal control systems and ensuring compliance with the statutory/regulatory framework.
26. The Audit Committee should, ideally be constituted with independent/non-executive directors and the Executive Director should only be a permanent invitee. However, in respect of public sector banks, the existing arrangement of including the Executive Director and nominee directors of Government and RBI in the Audit Committee may continue.
27. The Chairman of Audit Committee need not be confined to the Chartered accountant procession but can be a person with knowledge on 'finance' or 'banking' so as to provide directions and guidance to the Audit Committee, since the Committee not only looks at accounting issues, but also the overall management of the bank.
28. It is desirable to have a Nomination Committee for appointing independent/non-executive directors of banks. In the context of a number of public sector banks issuing capital to the public, Nomination Committee of the Board may be formed for nomination of directors, representing shareholders.
29. With a view to building up credibility among the investor class, the Group recommends that a Committee of the Board may be set up to look into the grievances of investors and shareholders, with the Company Secretary as a nodal point.
30. The formation and operationalisation of the Risk Management Committees in pursuance of the guidelines issued by the RBI should be speeded up and their role further strengthened.
31. The banks could be asked to come up with a strategy and plan for implementation of the governance standards recommended and submit progress of implementation, for review after twelve months and thereafter half yearly or annually as deemed appropriate.

SEBI COMMITTEE ON CORPORATE GOVERNANCE – GUIDELINES TC TO INDIAN COMMERCIAL BANKS LISTED IN STOCK EXCHANGES (DBOD NO.BC.112 /08.138.001/2001-02 DT.4.06.2002)

1. As you are aware, the Securities and Exchange Board of India (SEBI) had cnstituted a Committee on Corporate Governance and circulated the recommendations to all stock exchanges for implementation by listed entities as

part of the listing agreement vide SEBI's circular SMDRP/Policy/CIR-10/ 2000 dated February 21, 2000. However it had at that time exempted body corporates such as public and private sector banks, financial institutions, insurance companies and those incorporated under separate statute. SEBI has now suggested to RBI to consider issuing appropriate guidelines to banks and financial institutions so as to ensure that all listed companies would have uniform standards of corporate governance. As requested by SEBI, it has now been proposed that the SEBI Committee's guidelines may be taken up for adoption by those commercial banks listed in stock exchanges so that they can harmonize their existing corporate governance requirements with the requirements of SEBI, wherever considered appropriate.

2. On a review by RBI of the existing corporate governance requirements in banks;, it is observed that many of the recommendations in regard to the following stand implemented in banks and may not require further action towards implementation in respect of these guidelines for the present.

   (a) Optimum combination of executive and non-executive directors in the Board.

   (b) Pecuniary relationship or transactions of the non-executive directors vis-a-vis the bank.

   (c) Independent Audit Committees, their constitution, chairmanship, power, roles, responsibilities, conduct, of business, etc.

   (d) Remuneration of Directors (in case of private sector banks).

   (e) Periodicity/number of board meetings.

   (f) Disclosure by management to the board about the conflict of interest.

   (g) Information to shareholders regarding appointment/re-appointment of directors, display of quarterly results/presentation to analysts on the web-site.

   (h) Maintenance of office by non-executive Chairman.

   (i) Reviewing with the management by the Audit Committee of the board the annual financial statements before submission to the Board, focusing primarily on:

   - Any changes in accounting policies and practices,
   - Major accounting entries based on exercise of judgement by management,
   - Qualifications in draft audit report,
   - Significant adjustments arising out of audit, compliance with accounting standards,
   - Compliance with stock exchange and legal requirements concerning financial statements, and
   - The going concern assumption.

3. The Audit Committee of the board may look into the reasons for default in payment to depositors, debenture holders, shareholders (non-payment of dividends) and creditors, wherever there are any cases of defaults in payment. SEBI Committee's recommendations on other additional functions to be entrusted to the Audit Committee may be complied with by the listed banks as per listing agreement.

4. As regards the appointment and removal of external auditors, the practice followed in banks is more stringent than that recommended by the Committee and hence will continue. Further, fixation of audit fee and also approval of payment for any other services are already subject to the instructions of RBI. As regards recommendation for obtaining a certificate from auditors regarding compliance of conditionss of Corporate Governance, it may be stated that the compliance of banks with RBI instructions is already being verified by the statutory auditors. Therefore, a separate certificate from the auditors is not considered necessary.

5. With a view to further improving the Corporate Governance standards in banks, the following measures are now recommended for implementation.

   (a) In the interest of the shareholders, the private sector banks and public sector banks which have issued shares to the public may form committees on the same lines as listed companies under the Chairmanship of a non-executive director to look into redressal of shareholders' complaints.

   (b) All listed banks may provide un-audited financial results on half yearly basis to their shareholders with summary of significant developments.

6. A brief summary of the SEBI Committee's recommendations on Corporate Governance as applicable to banks is enclosed for ready reference. Full text of recommendations of the Committee which form part of a detailed circular issued by SEBI to the stock exchanges on February 21, 2000 can be had by access to SEBI's website, www.sebi.gov.in/circulars/2000.

7. Please acknowledge receipt.

Yours faithfully,

(M.R. Srinivasan)
Chief General Manager

Annexure

Summary of the important Recommendations of the SEBI's Committee on Corporate Governance

The Securities and Exchange Board of India (SEBI) had constituted a Committee on Corporate Governance and circulated the recommendations to all stock exchanges for implementation by listed entities as part of the listing agreement vide SEBI's circular SMDRP/Policy/CIR-10/2000 dated February 21, 2000. . Full text of recommendations of the Committee which form part of the above circular can be had by access to SEBI's website. www.sebi.gov.in/circulars/2000. A summary of the important recommendations of the SEBI Committee as applicable to banks is furnished here under:

1.1 All pecuniary relationship or transactions of the non-executive directors should be disclosed in the annual report.

1.2 The Committee is of the view that non-executive directors help bring an independent judgement to bear on board's deliberations, especially on issues of strategy, performance, management of conflicts and standards of conduct. The

Committee therefore lays emphasis on the calibre of the non-executive directors, especially of the independent directors.

1.3 The Committee is of the view that it is important that an adequate compensation package be given to the non-executive independent directors so that these positions become sufficiently financially attractive to attract talent and that the non-executive directors are sufficiently compensated for undertaking this work.

1.4 The Committee recommends that the board of a company have an optimum combination of executive and non-executive directors with not less than fifty per cent of the board comprising the non-executive directors. The number of independent directors depends on the nature of the chairman of the board. In case a company has a non-executive chairman, at least half of board should be independent (Mandatory recommendation).

2.1 The Committee recommends that when a nominee of the institutions is appointed as a director of the company, he should have the same responsibility, be subject to the same discipline and be accountable to the shareholders in the same manner as any other director of the company. In particular, if he reports to any department of the Institutions on the affairs of the company, the institution should ensure that there exist Chinese walls between such department and other department which may be dealing in the shares of the company in the stock market.

3.1 The Committee recommends that a non-executive Chairman should be entitled to maintain a Chairman's office at the company's expense and also allowed reimbursement of expenses incurred in performance of his duties. This will enable him to discharge the responsibilities effectively.

4.1 The Committee recommends that a qualified and independent audit committee should be set up by the board of a company (Mandatory recommendation).

4.2 The Committee recommends that—

- the audit committee should have a minimum of three members, all being non-executive directors, with the majority being independent and with at least one director having financial and accounting knowledge;
- the chairman of the committee should be an independent director;
- the chairman should be present at the Annual General Meeting to answer shareholder queries;
- the audit committee should invite such of the executives, as it considers appropriate (and particularly the head of the finance function) to be present at the meetings of the Committee but on occasions it may also meet without the presence of any executives of the company. The finance director and head of internal audit and when required, a representative of the external auditor should be present as invitees for the meetings of the audit committee;
- the Company Secretary should act as the secretary to the committee.

4.3 The Committee recommends that the audit committee should meet at least thrice a year. One meeting must be held before finalisation of annual accounts and one necessarily every six months (Mandatory recommendation).

4.4 The quorum should be either two members or one-third of the members of the audit committee, whichever is higher and there should be a minimum of two independent directors (Mandatory recommendation).

4.5 Being a committee of the board, the audit committee derives its powers from the authorization of the board. The Committee recommends that such powers should include powers

1. To investigate any activity within its terms of reference.
2. To seek information from any employee.
3. To obtain outside legal or other professional advice.
4. To secure attendance of outsiders with relevant expertise, if it considers necessary.

4.6 As the audit committee acts as the bridge between the board, the statutory auditors and internal auditors, the Committee recommends that its role should include the following:

- Oversight of the company's financial reporting process and the disclosure of its financial information to ensure that the statement is correct, sufficient and credible.
- Recommending the appointment and removal of the external auditor, fixation of audit fee and also approval for payment for any other service.
- Reviewing with management the annual financial statements before submission to the board, focusing primarily on
  - ➢ Any changes in accounting policies and practices.
  - ➢ Major accounting entries based on exercise of judgement by management.
  - ➢ Qualifications in draft audit report.
  - ➢ Significant adjustment arising out of audit.
  - ➢ The going concern assumption.
  - ➢ Compliance with accounting standards.
  - ➢ Compliance with stock exchange and legal requirements concerning financial institutions.
  - ➢ Any related party transactions i.e. transactions of the company of material nature, with promoters or the management, their subsidiaries or relatives, etc., that may have potential conflict with the interests of company at large.
- Reviewing with the management, external and internal auditors, the adequacy of internal control systems.
- Reviewing the adequacy of the internal audit function, including the structure of the internal audit department, staffing and seniority of the officials heading the department, reporting structure, coverage and frequency of internal audit.

- Discussion with the internal auditors of any significant findings and follow-up thereon.
- Reviewing the findings of any internal investigations by the internal auditors into matters where there is suspected fraud or irregularity or a failure of internal control systems of a material nature and reporting the matter to the board.
- Discussion with external auditors, before the audit commences, of the nature and scope of audit. Also post-audit discussion to ascertain any area of concern.
- Reviewing the company's financial and risk management policies.
- Looking into the reasons for substantial defaults in the payments to the depositors, debenture holders, shareholders (in case of non-payment of declare dividends) and creditors.

This is a mandatory recommendation.

5.1 The Committee recommends that the board should set up a remuneration committee to determine on their behalf and on behalf of the shareholders with agreed terms of reference, the company's policy on specific remuneration packages for executive directors including pension rights and any compensation payment.

6.1 The Committee therefore recommends that board meetings should be held at least four times in a year, with a maximum time gap of four months between any two meetings. The minimum information should be available to the board (Mandatory recommendation).

6.2 The committee recommends that a director should not be a member in more than 10 committees or act as Chairman of more than five committees across all companies in which he is a director. Furthermore, it is a mandatory annual requirement for every director to inform the company about the committee positions he occupies in other companies and notify changes as and when they take place (Mandatory recommendation).

7.1 The recommendations contained in this section pertain to accounting standards on consolidation, segment reporting, disclosure and treatment of related party transactions and deferred taxation. The Committee recommended that the Institute of Chartered Accountants of India issue accounting standards on these areas expeditiously.

8.1 As a part of the disclosure related to Management, the Committee recommends that as part of the directors' report or as an addition thereto, a Management Discussion and Analysis report should form part of the annual report to the shareholders (Mandatory recommendation).

8.2 The committee recommends that disclosures be made by management to the board relating to all material financial and commercial transactions, where they have personal interest, that may have a potential conflict with the interest of the company at large (for e.g. dealing in company shares, commercial dealings with bodies which have shareholding of management and their relatives etc. (Mandatory recommendation).

9.1 The Committee recommends that in case of the appointment of a new director or re-appointment of a director the shareholders must be provided with the following information

- A brief resume of the director;
- Nature of his expertise in specific financial areas; and
- Names of the companies in which the person also holds the directorship and the membership of Committees of the board.

This is a mandatory recommendation.

9.2 The Committee recommends that information like quarterly results, presentation made by companies to analysts may be put on company's website or may be sent in such a form so as to enable the stock exchange on which the company is listed to put it on its own website (Mandatory recommendation).

9.3 The Committee recommends that the half-yearly declaration of financial performance including summary of the significant events in last six months, should be sent to each household of shareholders.

9.4 The Committee recommends that a board committee under the chairmanship of a non-executive director should be formed to specifically look into the redressing of shareholder complaints like transfer of shares, non-receipt of balance sheet, non-receipt of declared, dividends etc. The Committee believes that the formation of such a committee will help focus the attention of the company on shareholders' grievances and sensitize the management to redressal of their grievances (Mandatory recommendation).

9.5 The Committee further recommends that to expedite the process of share transfers the board of the company should delegate the power, of share transfer to an officer, or a committee or to the registrar and share transfer agents. The delegated authority should attend to share transfer formalities at least once in a fortnight (Mandatory recommendation).

10. The Committee recommends that there should be a separate section on Corporate Governance in the annual reports of companies, with a detailed compliance report on Corporate Governance. Non-compliance of any mandatory recommendation with reasons thereof and the extent to which the non-mandatory recommendation have been adopted should be specifically highlighted. This will enable the shareholders and the security to assess for themselves the standards of corporate governance followed by a company (Mandatory recommendation).

Corporate Governance Awards for Excellence in Corporate Governance

FIRST ICSI NATIONAL AWARD FOR EXCELLENCE IN CORPORATE GOVERNANCE: 2001

Realising that effective corporate governance is indispensable to resilient and vibrant corporates to make corporates more responsive to follow internationally accepted norms of corporate governance and to promote excellent governance practices, the ICSI organized ICSI National Award for Excellence in Corporate Governance function on November 19 2001. For eliciting required information from eligible companies, following questionnaire was sent to eligible participating companies:

Kindly fill in the following questionnaire on the basis of the facts and figures of your company. It is assured that the data provided by you shall be used only for rating and evaluating Corporate Governance Practices of your company for the "ICSI National Award for Excellence in Corporate Governance". The data furnished and the identity of the respondent will be kept confidential.

Instruction to be fill in the questionnaire:

(*a*) Please make ✓ mark in boxes for selection of your options.

(*b*) Please attach extra annexures/sheets for answering any question and if needed mention the question number in additional sheets.

(*c*) If you require any clarification while filling up the questionnaire please contact ICSI.

Questionnaire

1. Company's Name: ____________________

2. Group: ☐ BSE Group A ☐ S&P CNX Nifty ☐ Both

3. Which sector does the company belong to?

   ☐ PSU ☐ Private ☐ Joint ☐ MNC

4. Industry to which company belongs:

   ☐ Banking ☐ Cement ☐ Engineering ☐ IT ☐ Steel

   ☐ Pharmaceuticals ☐ Telecommunication ☐ Petrochemicals

   ☐ Diversified ☐ Any other Please specify ____________________

5. Web-site address: ____________________

6. Correspondence address and E-mail Id

   (*a*) Corporate/Head Office:

   (*b*) Registered Office:

   (*c*) Company Secretary Office:

(d) Investor Service Centre:

7. Financial year ending on
8. Last AGM of the Company held on
9. Dates of Board Meetings, held during the last Financial Year
10. Have you provided information in your Annual Report, like e-mail, phone number, addresses of corporate office and registered office to stakeholders to enable them to contact the company?

Yes/No

11. What is the Mission and Vision Statement of the company?
12. Capital structure of the company:

S. No.	Particulars	Amount (Rs. in lakes)	Promoters (%)	Public (%)	Others (%)
(i)	Total Paid up Capital				
(ii)	Net Worth				

- Please indicate amount of revaluation reserves, if any, included in the networth.

Amount: Rs.

13. Composition of Board of Directors

S. No.	Particulars	As on		
		30-9-2000	31-3-2001	30-9-2001
(i)	Total No. of Directors as on	Yes/No		
(ii)	No. of Executive Directors			
(iii)	No. of Non-Exe. Directors			
(iv)	No. of Independent Directors			
(v)	No. of Institutional Nominee Directors			
(vi)	Whether Chairman is a Non-Executive Director			

14. (a) Particulars of the Board of directors during the last Financial Year ended on:(Please furnish as annexure)

Sr. No.	Name of the Directors	Desig-nation	Age (yrs)	Educational/ Professional Qualifications	Sharehold-ing in the Company(%) (as On last AGM)	Remuneration paid during FY2000-01			
						Sitting Fees	Salary & Perks	Commission/ Others	Total =
	(a)	(b)	(c)	(d)	(e)	(fl		(h)	(f+g+h)
(i)									
(ii)									
(iii)									

(i) Designations such as Chairman, CMD, Executive Director, M.D., Whole time director. Nominee director, Ind + Independent Director- HRD, finance, Marketing, projects, etc.

(ii) Qualifications like: Academic: Graduate, Post Graduate.

(iii) Professional: CA, CS, CWA, LL.B.,-M.B.A., B.E., MBBS and others.

14. *(b)* Number of female directors

15. Detail of directors' membership on the Board and Board Committees of the other Companies as on 31st March 2001:

Sr. No.	Name of Director (as mentioned at col. (a) of Ques. No. 14)	Name of Directorship(s) held in other companies (specify category wise)				No. of Membership in Board Committees of other Companies		
		As an Executive	As a Non-executive	As an Independent	Total	As a Chairman	As a Member	Total
	(a)	*(b)*	*(c)*	*(d)*	*(e)*	*(f)*	*(g)*	*(h)*
(i)								
(ii)								
(iii)								
(iv)								
(v)								
(vi)								
(vii)								
(viii)								
(ix)								
(x)								
(xi)								
(xii)								
(xiii)								
(xiv)								
(xv)								

16. Attendance record of directors for the FY 2000-01

Sr. No.	Name of Directors (as mentioned at col. (a) of Question No. 10)	Category of Directorship in the Company (ED/NED /IND)	No. of Board Meetings Held Attended		Last AGM of the company attended	No. of Membership held in Board Committees of the Company		Attendance record of Board Committee Meetings(%)					
						As a Chairman	Only as a Member	Audit Committee		Shareholders' Grievances Committee (i)		Remuneration Committee (i)	
								Held	Attended	Held	Attended	Held	Attended
			(c)	(d)	(e)	(f)	(g)						
(i)													
(ii)													
(iii)													

(ED = Executive, NED = Non-executive Director, IND = Independent Director)

(If a director is not in the board committees then specify "NA" against his name)

17. *(a)* Please specify the details regarding the Board Committees during the FY 2000-01:

Sr. No.	Name of Committees	Name of the Chairman of the Committee	Composition of the Committee (membership including Chairman)				Frequency of Meeting in a year	Terms of Reference of the Committee in brief
	(a)	*(b)*	*(c)*	*(d)*	*(e)*	*(f)*	*(g)*	*(h)*
(i)	Audit							
(ii)	Remuneration							
(iii)	Shareholders' Grievance							
(iv)	Other Committees							

17. *(b)* How and to what extent the terms of reference of the Audit Committee have been implemented viz., adequacy of internal control system and adequacy of internal audit function, etc.?

18. *(a)* Is there any Employee Stock Option Plan of Company? Yes/No

If yes, please specify the following:

- Category of employees/directors covered and eligibility criteria
- Rate of discount
- Vesting period

(b) Details of shares in the past against Employee Stock Option Scheme

19. Are there Disclosures made in respect of the following. Please tick against the items disclosed:

(i) Disclosure of pecuniary relationship of Non-Executive Directors with Company ☐

(ii) Disclosure of pecuniary relationship of other Executive Directors with Company ☐

20. Please tick against the items included in Management Discussion and analysis Report of the Company:

Contents:

(a) Industry structure and developments. ☐

(b) Opportunities and threats. ☐

(c) Segment wise or product wise performance ☐

(d) Outlook ☐

(e) Risks and concern ☐

(f) Internal controls and their adequacy ☐

(g) Discussion on financial performance with respect to operational Performance ☐

(h) Development in Human Resources/Industrial Relations front, including number of people employed. ☐

21. Please specify, if any, statutory Non-compliances, Penalties, during the last three years.

22. Has the Company provided details of Directors appointed/Re-appointed in any of the following forms:

    ☐ Resume

    ☐ Expertise

    ☐ Companies in which directorship(s) held

    ☐ Others, if any

23. What are the Means of Communication with the Shareholders :

    Half yearly Report to individual shareholders ☐

    Quarterly Results to individual shareholders ☐

    Monthly Report to individual shareholders ☐

    Publication in Newspapers ☐

    Website display ☐

    Official news releases on website ☐

    Analysis presentation on website ☐

    Annual Report

    – Date of completion of dispatch ☐

    – Date of AGM ☐

    – Mode of Dispatch ☐

    – Other means to communicate with shareholders. (Please elaborate) ☐

24. Has the Company formed a Board Committee for redressal of shareholders' grievances and has also appointed a Compliance Officer? If yes, please specify the following details:

    – Name of the Chairman of Board Committee

    – Name, designation and qualification of Compliance Officer

    – No. of Complaints received and their broad category nature

    (*a*) Categories of Complaints

Nature of Complaint	No. of Complaint	Complaints solved (%)	Average time taken (Days)	Complaints pending (%)
Delay in transfer of shares				
Delay in Demat of shares				
Non-receipt of dividend/interest				
Non-receipt of annual Report				
Replacement of Lost/Stolen Share certificates				
Others				

(b) Complaint as to Transfers and Demat

Particulars	Average time taken (Days)	Pending		% of Total Transfers/Demat Requests
		Date	No.	
Transfers				
Demat				

25. Is the following general information provided to the shareholders? Please only tick against the information supplied.
    - Stock Code ☐
    - Market price data H/L and trading volume during each month in the last financial year ☐
    - Performance in Comparison to broad based indices such as BSE, Sensex, CRISIL, Indices, etc. ☐
    - Registrar and transfer agents ☐
    - Share transfer system ☐
    - Distribution of shareholding ☐

26. Please provide following share information:

A.

Particulars	Total Equity (Rs.)	% of total Equity	No. of Shareholders	% of total no. of Shareholders
Physical				
Demat				
Total				

B.

Year	Dividend % (including interim Dividend)	Bonus Ratio (if any)	No. of Shares	Buy-Back Price (Avg.)
2000-2001				
1999-2000				
1998-1999				
1997-1998				
1996-1997				

PART B

1. Initiatives taken and monetary contributions made by the Company on any of the following aspects:
    - Environmental Protection Measures
    - Human Resource Valuation
    - Contribution to Society
2. Whether the Company has voluntarily obtained Secretarial Compliance Report and annexured the same with the Board's Report?

3. How has your company achieved excellence through implementation of Corporate Governance Practices during the financial year ended March 2001?

   Please specify in each of the following areas

   (a) Transparency

   (b) Accountability towards shareholders, Government, creditors, society.

   (c) Disclosure.

   (d) Compliance.

   (e) Any innovative idea introduced by the company in this regard?

4. Whether the company appointed the small share holder director? Specify

5. Whether company has conducted any survey etc. to know the level of shareholders satisfaction? If yes, what was the response and who has the company tried to improve shareholder services?

6. Is the company circulating any newsletter/other communication to its shareholders and other stakeholders? If yes, specify:

   (a) Periodicity of publication

   (b) Number of copies circulated, also provide a latest copy of the same.

7. Whether the company has been ISO 9000 certified or has been certified for any other equivalent norms?

8. Is your company preparing and publishing accounts as per US/IAS GAAP norms?

9. Please mention whether award(s), if any, won by your company?

10. Any other major initiatives towards achieving excellence in Corporate Governance not mandatory required.

    Please specify the name of a person to be contacted for further information, in case of need:

    Name:

    Ph No: e-mail Id:

    (of the Company) e-mail ID:

    (of the Contact Person)

Signature. ....

Name ....

Designation. ....

Date: ....

Place:...........

A jury of eminent persons, under the Chairmanship of Hon'ble Justice Shri M N Venkatachaliah, former Chief Justice of India, selected the Companies and personalities for conferring the awards.

The then Vice President of India late Shri Krishan Kant, bestowed the awards on following companies:

1. , Infosys Technologies Limited as the "Best Governed Company".
2. BSES Limited as the second "Best Governed Company".
3. In recognition of the services rendered for grwoth of economy and for translating excellence in Corporate Governance into Reality, Lifetime Achievement Awards were conferred on late Rai Bahadur Shri Mohan Singh Oberoi, Chairman, Oberoi Group of Industries, and Shri Verghese Kurien, Chairman Emeritus, National Dairy Development Board.

The Winners were presented citation and trophy. The text of citation is reproduced below:

Infosys Technologies Limited

Chairman & CEO

Shri N R Narayananmurthy

Set up in 1981, Infosys is committed to good corporate governance and has benchmarked itself *vis-à-vis* the global best practices.

Infosys makes fullest possible disclosure of information to its shareholders about the performance of the company as a trustee of its shareholders.

Infosys ensures objectivity and independent decision-making by its Board by appointing independent directors on its various board-committees.

Infosys is one of the first Indian companies to adopt US GAAP besides Indian GAAP reporting with retard to its financial reporting.

Infosys believes in pursuing high quality standards in all aspects of its business including deliverables to the customer, human resource management and investor relations.

Infosys has abundantly rewarded its shareholders from its excellent financial performance.

Infosys is committed to fulfilling its social obligations and is actively involved in providing educational facilities to the rural poor and to the underprivileged.

Infosys has taken steps aimed at preserving and promoting Indian arts and culture.

Infosys is imbued with the principles of fairness, honesty, transparency and ethical dealings with all its stakeholders.

BSES Limited

Chairman & MD

Shri R V Shahi

BSES with its lineage going back to 1929 has been among the select few companies to take early initiatives to excel in its governance practices and thereby promoting corporate fairness, transparency and accountability.

BSES Board has the professional freedom to guide and provide direction to the company and different committees assist the Board to effectively perform its tasks.

BSES is committed to perform its activities in the most ethical and transparent manner and has formulated a Code of Ethical Practices for its employees to avoid any conflict of interests in discharging their duties.

BSES has consistently earned high returns, increased its net worth and enhanced its shareholders' wealth.

BSES believes in sustainable development and aims at preservation and protection of environment in all its activities.

BSES takes initiatives in promoting community development through various schemes in health care and education and providing relief to those affected by natural calamities.

BSES regards its human resources as the most precious asset and undertakes several measures for employee welfare including conferment of awards on deserving employees.

BSES has endeavoured to set a model in corporate governance for other service sector companies to emulate.

Dr. Verghese Kurien

Chairman Emeritus

National Dairy Development Board

Born on November 26, 1921 in Kerala, Dr Verghese Kurien chose Anand in Khaira District of Gujarat to be his Karmabhoomi where he gave practical shape to his ideals of the cooperative movement in the field of dairy development and extending its reach from a small taluk of Gujarat to every nook and corner of India.

Dr. Verghese Kurien pioneered Operation Flood and literally made rivers of milk run in India, transforming the lives of millions of small farmers and their families to become self-reliant.

Dr. Kurien with core values of integrity, devotion and commitment provided professional leadership by building the National Dairy Development Board (NDDB) and enabled it to successfully implement Operation Flood to the advantage of the consumers and the producers.

Dr. Verghese Kurien through his insight has drawn the active participation of village cooperatives to submerge the artificial distinction of caste and religion and has brought about equality between men and women and has established that they can build their own destiny.

Dr. Verghese Kurien's successful experiments in the field of dairy cooperatives have led to emulation of this model in sectors other than dairy farming like oilseeds, fruits, vegetables, horticulture and salt making.

Dr. Verghese Kurien is an institution epitomizing leadership, vision and all those qualities needed for bringing about meaningful and sustainable development.

Rai Bahadur Mohan Singh Oberoi

Chairman,

The Oberoi Group

Rai Bahadur Mohan Singh Oberoi, born on August 15, 1898, with an humble beginning rose to become an internationally renowned hotelier by dint of his sheer hardwork, dedication and initiative.

Rai Bahadur Mohan Singh Oberoi has the rare quality of facing and overcoming the overwhelming odds and shaping them into success stories.

Shri Oberoi has several firsts to his credit including the setting up of the first Five Star International Hotel in India and being the First Indian to tie up with international chain of hotels.

Shri Oberoi, in order to provide quality professional training in hospitality management has set up a hotel management school of international standard.

Shri Oberoi, a firm believer in women's development was among the first to employ women in his hotel chains.

Shri Oberoi, with his vision and mission has converted many dilapidated palaces, historical monuments and buildings into world renowned hotels.

Shri Oberoi, despite all his illustrious achievements, still maintains his unique humility and humanitarian values on various issues.

In the year 2002-2003

(i) In the year 2002, The Institute published a referencer on "Corporate Governance and Directors' duties and responsibilities".

(ii) In the year 2002, The Institute issued (SS-2) Secretarial Standard on "General Meetings"

(iii) In the year 2002, The Institute issued "Guidance Note on Meetings of Board of Directors", "Guidance Note on General Meetings", "Guidance Note on Passing of Resolutions by Postal Ballot".

(iv) In the year 2002, 34th Foundation Day lecture on the theme "Corporate Citizenship- Vision for the future" was organized. Keynote address was delivered by Shri Vinod Dhall, IAS, Secretary, Department of Company Affairs, Government of India.

SECOND ICSI NATIONAL AWARD FOR EXCELLENCE IN CORPORATE GOVERNANCE' FUNCTION

The Institute is dedicated to developing professionals with specialized training in the areas of corporate governance and management to serve the interests of all stakeholders and contribute to the public good. As a step towards it, on December 31, 2002, the Institute organized Second "ICSI National Award for Excellence in Corporate Governance".

A jury of eminent persons, under the Chairmanship of Hon'ble Justice Shri M N Venkatachaliah, former Chief Justice of India, selected following two Companies for conferring the awards in recognition of displaying their commitment to adhere to the norms of corporate governance and honouring following personality for Translating Excellence in Corporate Governance into Reality:

The Vice President of India Shri Bhairon Singh Shekhawat, bestowed the awards on following companies:

1. Dr. Reddy's Laboratories Ltd. (DRL); and
2. Tata Iron and Steel Company Ltd.

In addition to it, the Jury selected following Public Sector Company for conferring the Award.

3. IBP Co. Ltd.

ICSI Life Time Achievement Award for translating excellence in Corporate governance into Reality was conferred upon Dr. Yusuf Khwaja Hamied, Chairman and Managing Director, CIPLA Ltd.

Evaluation and Selection Methodology

The selection and evaluation methodologies were scientifically defined. The Companies were evaluated broadly on the following parameters:

1. Board Independence;
2. Board Systems and procedures;
3. Transparency and disclosures, Investor Relations and Services and Compliances;
4. Shareholders' value enhancement and stakeholders' claims; and
5. Social Responsibility.

For eliciting required information from the eligible Listed Companies, the Institute also developed an objective type Questionnaire. The Questionnaire was so devised that the answers were evaluated on the basis of options ticked and software was also designed to assign marks against the ticked options without human intervention. Thus, a scientific approach was followed to evaluate performance of companies and give weighted marks to them. The list of top Companies securing highest marks was then placed before the Jury to decide the winners.

For eliciting desired information, two Questionnaires were designed by the Institute and sent to eligible companies. Text of the Questionnaires is as follows:

Questionnaire 1 – For Rating and Evaluating Corporate Governance Practices

1. Name of the Company:
2. Correspondence Address:

(a)	Corporate Office:	Address	
		Telephone	Fax No.
		E-mail	
(b)	Registered Office:	Address	
		Telephone	Fax No.
		E-mail	
(c)	Investor Service: Centre	Address	
		Telephone	Fax No.
		E-mail	
(d)	Company Secretary:	Address	
		Telephone	Fax No.
		E-mail	
(e)	Web site Address:		

3. Year of incorporation
4. Listing on Stock Exchange (Please tick the relevant)

   BSE NSE Foreign Stock Exchange ....

   DSE CSE Regional SE ....
5. Stock Exchange Code
6. ISIN Number
7. Sector to which the company belongs (Please tick the relevant)

   PSU ☐ Private ☐ Joint ☐ MNC ☐
8. Industry to which the company belongs

   Banking ☐ Cement Engineering ☐ IT ☐ Steel ☐
   Pharmaceuticals ☐ Telecommunications ☐ Petrochemicals ☐
   Diversified ☐ Any Other, Please specify ....
9. ISO Certification, if any
10. Has the company won any award for implementation of Corporate Governance? If so, please name the award

Board and Management Structure

Independence of Directors

Total No. of Directors: ....

	Nature of Relationship of Directors	Number of Directors
1.	Employed with the company in the last five years.	
2.	Employed with the subsidiary(ies) of the company in the past five years	
3.	Association with another company which has significant business relationship with the company in which the incumbent is a director.	
4.	Acceptance of compensation either from the company or any of its subsidiaries other than compensation for the board.	
5.	Membership of the immediate family of an executive of the company.	
6.	An employee of the company to which the director belongs, sits on the compensation committee of another company in which the director is employed as an executive	
7.	Consultancy/Advisory or personal service contract with the company, its executive officers or affiliates.	

1.1 Is the Chairman Executive?

- Yes
- No

If chairman is Executive then please enter the following details

(a) Does 50% or more of the board consist of Independent directors?

- Yes
- No

If Chairman is Non Executive then please enter the following details

(b) Does 1/3rd of board consist of Independent directors?

- Yes
- No

1.2 Please indicate the proportion of Independent Directors to total number of Directors?

- Upto 49%
- 50-59%
- 60-69%
- 70-79%
- 80-89%
- 90% and above

1.3 Please indicate the percentage of directors holding directorships in more than 15 other public companies?

- 100%
- 90-99%
- 80-89%
- 70-79%
- 60-69%
- 50-59%
- 40-49%
- 30-39%
- 20-29%
- 10-19%
- Less than 10%

1.4 Whether the office of Chairman and Chief Executive Officer is held by different people?

- Yes
- No

Board Committees

Particulars of Board Committees

Name Date Major Decisions Attendance (%)

2.1 Which of the following Board Committees exist in the company?

- Audit Committee
- Remuneration Committee
- Shareholders Committee

- Nomination Committee
- Any Committee other than specified above.

2.2 Whether Chairman of all board committees is an independent nonexecutive director?

- Yes
- No

Board Systems & Procedures Particulars of Board Meetings

Date Purpose Attendance (%)

3.1.1 How many times did the Board of Directors meet during the last Financial year?

- Less than 4
- Equal to 4
- 5-8
- 9 or more

3.1.2 Was the interval between any of the two-board meeting more than three months on any occasion?

- Yes
- No

3.2 Please indicate the average percentage of board members who have *been* present in the board meetings as also the board committee meetings in the last financial year.

(A) Board Meetings:

- 0-40% Attendance
- 41%- 49%
- 50%-74%
- 75% or more

(B) Board Committees Meetings

- 0-40% Attendance
- 41%- 49%
- 50%-74%
- 75% or more

3.3 Agenda and information about Board Meetings is normally circulated to the members of the board

- Over a fortnight in advance of the meeting
- A week before the meeting
- Less than one week before the meeting
- Just before start of meeting

3.4 Please specify if following was circulated to the board members at board meeting(s) (Please tick the relevant)

- Only Agenda is circulated.
- Agenda alongwith prescribed information (as per listing agreement) is circulated.
- Agenda alongwith prescribed information (as per listing agreement) and relevant information for the period.
- Agenda alongwith prescribed information (as per listing agreement) and relevant information and any information sought by the Director.

3.5 Please specify whether any director of the company was re-appointed even if he/she remained absent in fifty percent or more of the board meetings held during the last financial year?

- Yes
- No

3.6 Who is the Compliance Officer of the company?

Company Secretary

Any other official (Please specify designation and qualifications)

TRANSPARENCY AND DISCLOSURES

4.1 Which of the following disclosures (as per Clause 49 of the listing agreement) were made to the shareholders in the Annual Report? (Please tick the relevant)

- Date, time and venue of AGM
- Financial Calendar
- Dates of Book Closures
- Dividends payment date
- Listing on Stock Exchanges
- Stock Code
- Market Price Data for each Month of last financial year
- Performance in comparison to broad based indices
- Registrar and Transfer Agent-Address, Phone, Fax, e-mail
- Share transfer system/Dematerialisation and liquidity
- Distribution of Shareholding
- Categories of Shareholding in the format specified in clause 35 of the listing agreement.
- Top ten shareholders of the Company.
- Change in Equity Capital during the financial year
- Outstanding GDRS/ADR/Warrants
- Convertibles, conversion date and likely impact on Equity
- Plant location
- Address for correspondence

- General Body Meetings
- Details of last three AGMs-Date, time and place
- Special Resolutions put through postal Ballot in the last financial year and details of voting pattern
- Material and financial transactions by Management where they have personal interest that may have potential conflict with the interest of the company
- Non-compliance by company or penalties imposed or/and strictures passed on the company by the stock exchange/SEBI/Statutory Authorities on any matter during the last three financial years.
- Industry Structure and Developments
- Opportunities and Threats
- Outlook
- Material Developments in Human Resources and Industrial Relations front, including number of people employed
- Risks and Concerns
- Internal Control and their adequacies
- Discussion of Financial performance with respect to operational performance
- Product disclosure about segment-wise information-financial as well as operating details.
- Details on developments like R&D, restructuring
- Reporting on conciliation of accounts with GAAP (if applicable) or other Indian accounting standards
- Means of communication adopted by the company and particularly whether the company maintains website to keep the shareholders informed of important financial and operational details

4.2 Which of the following elements of remuneration package of board members was disclosed in the annual report?

- All elements of salary, benefits, bonus, stock option, pension (*Le.* variable and not performance linked)
- Details of fixed component and performance linked incentive alongwith performance criteria.
- Service contracts, notice period severance fees
- Stock option details *e.g.* whether issued at discount, period over which accrued and over which exercisable.

4.3 Were the following disclosures made as regards the directors proposed to be appointed/re-appointed?

- Brief Resume of the person
- Nature of expertise in specific functional area
- Names of companies in which he holds directorship and committees membership.

4.4 Did the company enter into any transaction of material nature with promoters, directors, relatives or subsidiaries that might have potential conflict of interest during the last financial year?

- Yes
- No

4.5 Does the company pay a commission to the non-executive directors over and above the sitting fees for the use of professional inputs from them ?

- Yes
- No

4.6 Does the company maintain record of trading in company's shares by BOD/Senior Management?

- Yes
- No

4.7 In the last financial year, has the company made/given any investments, loans or advances to any group companies (subsidiaries/affiliates)?

- Yes
- No

4.8 In the last financial year, has the company received any investments, loans or advances from any group companies (subsidiaries/affiliates)?

- Yes
- No

4.9 Does the company have an Employee Stock Option Plan?

- Yes
- No

4.10 Does the company follows the Secretarial Standards issued by the ICSI?

- Yes
- No

Investor Relations

5.1 Does the company have an investor grievance cell?

- Yes
- No

5.2 Please indicate the percentage complaints of shareholders grievances/complaints resolved to the satisfaction of shareholders out of total received during last financial year

- Total Complaints pending in beginning of the year
- Total Complaints received during the year
- Total Complaints resolved during the year

5.3 Please specify the average time taken in resolving the shareholders grievances during last financial year (Please tick the relevant).

- 21 days or more
- 11-20 days
- 7-10 days
- Less than 7 days

6.1 Please mention the percentage of dividend, and bonus given by the company in the last seven years.

Year	% of Dividend	Ratio of Bonus
1 (Current Year)		
2 (Previous Year)		
3		
4		
5		
6		
7		

6.1.1 What is the EVA (Economic Value Added) of the company in the past three years?

6.1.2 On the basis of EVA, which of the following categories does the company belong to?

- Non Existent/Declining Trend in EVA in the past three financial years
- Between 10-20% growth in EVA in the past three financial years
- Between 20%-30% growth in EVA in the past three financial years
- More than 30% growth in EVA in the past three financial years

(*) Economic Value Added measures the profitability of the company after taking into account the cost of all capital including equity. It is the post tax return on capital employed minus the cost of capital employed. The companies earning higher returns than cost of capital are considered to create value i.e.

EVA = Post Tax Return on Capital Employed–Cost of Capital Employed.

6.1.3 Does the Company have an internal audit department?

- Yes
- No

Stakeholders Claims Satisfaction

7.1 Please indicate which of the following have been undertaken by the company towards discharge of social obligation during the last year (Please tick the relevant).

- Community development/Social Welfare
- Promoting the Interests of disadvantaged and impaired sections of society
- In the Interest of Women Development
- Sports Promotion
- Employment Generation

- Promotion of Educational facilities

7.2 Which of the following activities have been undertaken by the company during the last year?

- Employee Training/Training for board Members
- Housing schemes for employees/Financing of Employees Houses
- Education/Scholarship of Employee's Children
- Employee Representation in Management/Employee Grievance Redressal Machinery or Arrangement

7.3 Has the company conducted Environment Audit?

- Yes
- No

7.4 Does the company conduct Social Audit for large-scale projects?

- Yes
- No

8 Any other information relating to good corporate governance which the Company deems fit to be considered.

Second "ICSI National Award for Excellence in Corporate Governance" Supplementary Information

Board Management and Structure

1. Board ethics and conduct

(a) Is there any formal written code of conduct for directors?

- Yes
- No

(if yes, please provide us with a copy of the same)

(b) Is there any formal policy for succession planning at senior levels of management?

- Yes
- No

(if yes, please provide us with a copy of the same)

(c) Is there any written code/policy to prevent insider trading in the company?

- Yes
- No

(if yes, please provide us with a copy of the same)

(d) Is there any policy of conducting structured training programmes for directors?

- Yes
- No

TRANSPARENCY AND DISCLOSURES

Loans

2. Are there any cases in drt's or courts or any proceedings under the new securitisation act?
   - Yes
   - No

Risk Management

3. Please specify if the company has any formal risk management policy in place relating to:
   (a) Business/profits risks
   (b) Financial risks
   (c) Legal/statutory risks
   (d) Internal process risks
   (please tick the relevant)
4. Sustainability of the company
   (a) In the last three years, has the company acquired/sold another company or is any transaction entered into by the company involving substantial payment made or substantial payment received towards goodwill, brand equity or intellectual property rights ?
   - Yes
   - No

   (b) In the last financial year, is there any major foreign joint venture or collaboration agreement entered into by the company which has resulted in a major technology transfer from another country?
   - Yes
   - No

   (if possible, please provide the details of the same)

   (c) In continuation of question *(b)* above, please specify if, as a result of collabration, your company is the sole licencee in the world ?
   - Yes
   - No
5. Investment in subsidiary companies
   (a) what is the level of subsidiaries of the company?
   - One-tier
   - Two-tier
   - Three-tier

   (b) What is the amount of loans and investments made in group companies vis-à-vis. the funds borrowed by the company?

- less than 10%
- 11%-30%
- 31%-50%
- more than 50%

(if possible, please give the figures in absolute terms also)

Shareholders' Claims Satisfaction

6. Is there any independent professional observer at AGMS/EGM?
   - Yes
   - No

Resolution moved by shareholders

7. Please specify if any resolution is moved by minority shareholders holding more than 10% or 1000 shareholders, whichever is less, at the last AGM/EGM? If yes, please inform
   - Number of Shareholders involved in moving the resolution
   - Result of the resolution
   - Approved
   - Dropped
8. Funds utilisation

   (a) Is the share application money in other companies more than Rs. 1 crore lying for more than 3 months pending allotment?
   - Yes
   - No

   (b) Has the company written off/waived any amount which is (more than 5% of outstanding amount at the end of year) due to the company?
   - Yes
   - No

Auditors' Details

9. Are the company auditors conducting audit of accounts of subsidiary companies?
   - Yes
   - No

Unclaimed dividend

10. Please specify the proportion of amount of unclaimed dividend to the amount of total dividend as on 31/03/2002
    - Less than 5%
    - 5%-10%
    - more than 10%

11. Technological advancements

(*a*) What is the percentage (as %age of turnover) of expenditure incurred towards research and development in the last financial year?

- Less than 5%
- 5%-10%
- 11%-20%
- more than 20%

12. Shareholders' value enhancement

(*a*) What is the financial parameters used by compnay to evaluate financial performance

- Economic value added
- Cash value added
- Any other method

(*b*) If any investor has invested shares worth Rs. 100000 on the date of investment mentioned below, please specify the value of shares after adjusting the benefits of bonus, dividend, rights and splitting (as on 21/03/2002) in the following format

Amount of investment	Invested date	Market price (as on 31/03/2002)	Appreciation (in percentage)
100000	01/04/1992 (10 Years)		
100000	01/04/1997 (5 Years)		
100000	01/04/1999 (3 Years)		
100000	01/04/2001 (1 Years)		

Other Stakeholders Claims

13. If the company has to adhere to pollution control/environment laws, are all the complicances of environmental bodies undertaken by the company?

- Yes
- No

14. Miscellaneous

(*a*) Is there any written policy for adequate representation of women at the top level of the company?

- Yes
- No

(if yes, please provide us with a copy of the same)

(*b*) When the information is provided in real time by the company *i.e.* price sensitive information to be made available to stock exchanges on real time basis, what is the actual time taken?

- less than 15 minutes of the board meeting
- 15-30 minutes of the board meeting

- more than 30 minutes of the board meeting
- one day or more after the board meeting

Following is the text of citations presented to the winners of second award:

Dr. Reddy's Laboratories Ltd.

DRL has excelled in all the important dimensions of Corporate Governance.

It has shown high performance in the relevant parameters of sales growth, profitability, EVA and shareholder value.

Its potential future performance is underlined by a strong R&D pipeline of new chemical entities, drugs and delivery systems.

It has been pursuing a vision of a strong base in speciality segments, and a mission of a discovery-led global pharmaceutical company.

DRL has combined technical excellence with professional management. It has been rated as the top employer in the pharma sector.

It has the necessary recruitment, training, compensation and employee welfare schemes to attract and retain talent.

It has an empowered board, with independent directors, committees, systems and processes for good corporate governance.

Its accounts and reporting satisfy both the US and the Indian GAAP requirements.

The company's social contributions are channeled through the Dr. Reddy's Foundation.

It brings health care and education to poor children, youth and women. It has attracted support from national and international NGO's. The company aims to go beyond philanthropy, to catalyse sustainable development.

The winners were presented citation and trophy. The text of citations is reproduced below:

IBP Co. Ltd.

IBP has excelled in all the important dimensions of Corporate Governance.

It has shown sustained, high performance in petroleum products marketing and distribution, profits, high dividends and market capitalisation.

It has earned the "Excellent" rating, under the system of Memorandum of Understanding, with the Government of India, for ten consecutive years.

IBP has combined the strengths of its origin as a foreign oil company, with those of an autonomous PSU.

It has maintained and updated its professional management culture, systems and practices.

The thrust of its Human Resource Policy is to develop its people into "Achievers", than even just "Performers".

IBP has combined high business performance with a significant contribution towards environmental conservation and upgradation, as well as schemes for the welfare of the weaker sections of society, in the areas of its operation, especially the North East.

Following its selection for disinvestment, as part of the evolving policies of successive Governments of India, IBP has restructured its board, created and effectively utilised the various committees, reporting, control and corporate governance requirements.

TISCO

TISCO has delivered sustained high performance in an old economy, cyclical, commodity industry.

It has emerged as the lowest cost steel producer in the world.

It has reinforced its survival prospects by adopting risk management policies and practices.

It has also developed a corporate sustainability management system.

It has along record, of dividends, and capital appreciation.

TISCO is reputed for ethical dealing's with customers, government and business partners.

Its commitment to business ethics has been as strong as its passion for steel marking. It has an Ethics Officer, reporting to the Board. The practice of values is reinforced by a written contract with every TISCO executive to follow the code of conduct.

TISCO has been a role model in employee relations. The long tradition of employee loyalty and belonging has enabled TISCO to restructure, including rightsizing the labour force, to survive the global recession, over-capacity, competition and survival threats in the steel industry.

TISCO has been known not only for legal compliance, but for being ahead of the law, in good practices. It had pioneered social audit in the country, being the first to volunteer for it, two decades ago. It has shown concern for ecology and environment in its mines and factories, and the upkeep of the town of Jamshedpur.

It has also taken significant steps to preserve and revive tribal culture, customs and arts.

TISCO has had professional management and an empowered board of directors for long.

In line with modern trends and regulatory requirements, it has institutionalised corporate governance systems and processes, to discharge its accountability, both within the Tata Group and to all external stakeholders.

ICSI LIFE TIME ACHIEVEMENT AWARD FOR TRANSLATING CORPORATE GOVERNANCE INTO REALITY

DR. Y K HAMIED

Dr. Y K Hamied has provided outstanding leadership to Cipla on several important dimensions of Corporate Governance.

During his tenures as Managing Director, 1972 to 1989 and as Chairman and MD, 1989 to date, a total of three decades, the company has shown high growth. The sales have risen from Rs. 1.5 crores in 1972 to 1300 crores. It is one of the highly valued Indian pharma companies.

Dr. Hamied has also personified the mission of Cipla. It had been inspired by a visit of Mahatma Gandhi to the firm in 1939. Beginning with self-reliance, it has flowered into strengthening indigenous capability, R&D, moving up the value chain, from bulk drugs to formulations, exports and an Indian MNC.

Dr. Hamied has further strengthened professionalism in Cipla. He himself is a role model of the "professionalised entrepreneur" At the young: age of 21, he obtained the Masters Degree, followed by KD, in Organic Chemistry, from the Cambridge University, U.K. at 24, in 1960.

He is an unusual combination off a reputed; scientist, astute; businessman; and institution builder. Dr. Hamied has also demonstrated his national, concerns in many ways. He has been on the Governing Body of the CSIR.

He has collaborated closely with several national laboratories and institutions.

He has been active in the formation of Indian Drug Manufacturers' Association in 1961 and the cooperation with government in continuously evolving the regulatory framework, keeping in mind India's needs and global competitive opportunities and compulsions. Above all, Dr. Hamied has excelled in the area of corporate social responsibility.

He is a global pioneer in the development of drugs for AIDS and making them available at highly affordable prices, all over the world, including Africa and India. In this endeavour, he and Cipla have faced serious legal and business risks; and have conquered them.

PROCEEDINGS OF THE ICSI NATIONAL AWARD FOR EXCELLENCE IN CORPORATE GOVERNANCE, 2003

Award Function

The ICSI National Awards for Excellence in Corporate Governance were conferred by L K Advani, Hon'ble Deputy Prime Minister of India on December 15, 2003 at Vigyan Bhawan in the gracious presence of Justice M N Venkatachaliah, Chairman of the Jury and former Chief Justice of India, M K Sardana, Secretary, Department of Company Affairs, G N Bajpai, Chairman, SEBI, members of he Jury, Past Presidents and Council Members of the Institute. The function was also graced by a large number of members and students of the Institute, Government officials, professionals, industrialists, intellectuals and media.

G N Bajpai, Chairman SEBI said that the Corporate Governance was not only a National issue, but on international issue, because the impact of poor Corporate Governance can become apparent too quickly in the form of corporate scandals, corruption, capital flight, etc. He opined that Corporate Governance thus makes a business sense. In this context, he referred to a research conducted by McKinsey which surveyed around two hundred fund managers across continent and revealed that those companies which have good corporate governance, command an additional premium on their equities. Therefore, it makes a good business sense for the entrepreneurs to have good corporate governance, observed Bajpai. He referred to another study conducted by CLSA for Asia which revealed that the market returns have been negative in the year 2002 but those companies which have good Corporate Governance outperformed others in 2002. Bajpai stressed that it makes a good investment sense, to participate in those Companies, which have good Corporate Governance standards.

Speaking about the sources referred to for evaluation of the companies, Gangopadhyay informed that they included directors reports, auditors' reports, directors' reports on corporate governance, management discussion and analysis report, balance sheet and profit and loss accounts including notes to the account, questionnaire designed by the Institute, website of the respective corporates, the important inputs about the corporates available in press and media, assessment of corporates based on internal research and analysis and industry norms and investors' perception.

Hon'ble L.K. Advani, Deputy Prime Minister of India bestowed the ICSI National Awards for Excellence in Corporate Governance for the year 2003 on two companies in private sector and one company in public sector.

In private sector Awards were conferred on:

- Housing Development Finance Corporation Limited
- Reliance Industries Limited

In public sector Award was conferred on

- Oil and Natural Gas Corporation Limited

The Life Time Achievement Award for the year, 2003 for Translating Excellence in Corproate Governance into Reality was conferred on Ratan N Tata, Chairman, Tata Group. R Krishan Kumar, Director, Tata Sons received the Award on behalf of Ratan Tata.

Today ethics, morality, accountability and transparency are equally applicable to political governance, as they are to corporate governance, said Advani. In this context he referred to an essay of Acharya Vinoba Bhave and explained that there are three types of people–one who only gives and takes from the society only a bare minimum they are called Saints; two they give to the society in proportion of what they expect from the society, they are called businessmen; and third category which only takes and gives nothing to the society, they are called thieves. So in whatever activities we are in - be it corporate sector, politics, education or medicine, there are people with all these characteristics explained Advani and observed that it is our *duty* to encourage honesty, accountability, transparency, excellence and punish the wrong doers.

PROCEEDINGS OF THE ICSI NATIONAL AWARD FOR EXCELLENCE IN CORPORATE GOVERNANCE, 2004

Award Function

The ICSI National Awards for Excellence in Corporate Governance were conferred by Prem Chand Gupta, Hon'ble Minister of State for Company Affairs (Independent Charge) on December 15, 2004 at Vigyan Bhawan in the gracious presence of Justice B N Kirpal, former Chief Justice of India and Chairman of the Jury, Komal Anand, Secretary, Ministry of Company Affairs, Members of the Jury, Past Presidents and

Council Members of the Institute. The function was also graced by a large number of members and students of the Institute, Government officials, professionals, industrialists, intellectuals and media.

Prem Chand Gupta, Hon'ble Minister of State for Company Affairs (I/C) bestowed the ICSI National Awards for Excellence in Corporate Governance, 2004 on the two companies in private sector and one company in public sector.

In private sector Awards were conferred on –

- Hero Honda Motors Limited
- Wipro Limited

In public sector Awards was conferred on –

- Tamil Nadu Newsprint and Papers Limited

The Life Time Achievement Award for Translating Excellence in Corporate Governance into Reality was conferred on Keshub Mahindra, Chairman, Mahindra & Mahindra Limited in recognition to his remarkable contribution to the corporate sector.

Prem Chand Gupta Hon'ble Minister of State for Company 'Affairs while addressing the gathering commended the efforts; made by the Institute towards making the excellence in corporate governance a benchmark for companies in India and explained that the corporate governance is about disclosures and disclosure to all in the same manner and at the same time. It is not about lowering risk it is about disclosing risks. It is about disclosing above board dealings between the owners, managers, and the company. It is about implementing publicly stated strategies.

Further elaborating the concept of corporate governance, Prem Chand Gupta explained that corporate governance, as a system comprises two parts, one which is set by the general law of the land and the other a set of principles which the business community should impose on itself as a code of good corporate practices. The modern knowledge has opened new frontiers for capitalizing on innovations for corporate governance, observed Prem Chand Gupta and said that new ideas will not come out of rules and regulations alone but by the desire of all the stakeholders to try out new ethical standards and practices of corporate governance.

Lauding the efforts being made by the ICSI) in promoting good a governance, Minister expressed that efforts of the institute in adjudging the best governed company after evaluating its value creation, openness, governing body's record of compliances, scrutiny of shareholders risk, and ethical history, is a step in the right direction for setting standards of corporate excellence. While concluding, Minister said that ICSI has given a lead and there is need to sincerely make the flag of corporate governance fly high in the high seas of corporate world.

The Ministry of Company Affairs has set up a National Foundation for Corporate Governance in partnership with CII, ICAI and ICSI with the objective of deliberating on the issues relating to good corporate governance, sensitizing the corporate leaders on the importance of good corporate governance, self-regulation and also providing research and training in the field of corporate governance.

Earlier Mahesh Anant Athavale, then president, the ICSI while delivering the welcome address said that good corporate governance is not a matter of prescription, rather it should come from within. It is the manifestation of self discipline and business as well as professional ethics imbibed in Vedic literature and ancient teachings. Ethical behaviour is not an output of code of ethics or code of conduct, observed President and explained that it is a human activity, shaped on the daily basis by the existing organisational and social framework. While a lot has been done in the field of corporate governance there is need to advance it to the centre stage of corporate operations, added President and concluded that in order to bring it to the centre stage there is need to have an unambiguous yardstick, which can be used to measure and monitor the progress in the path of the corporate governance.

BEST BANK OF THE YEAR: BEST BANK 2003

The following extracts from the panel discussion: A rising Star, Business India November 24 – December 7, 2003 may be highlighted:

"Business India was among the first to start honouring the Best Bank of the year. In the five years since, we have fine-tuned the process to go far beyond numbers to qualitative parameters.

This year too Business India put together a distinguished panel of experts drawn from various disciplines."

"This exercise led to an initial shortlist of 15. The contenders: HDFC Bank, Citibank, State Bank of India, Bank of Baroda (BOB), Punjab National Bank, ING Vysya, ICICI Bank, UTI bank, Oriental Bank of Commerce (OBC), Corporation Bank, Andhra bank, UCO bank, HSBC, and Standard Chartered. Citi was eliminate because it won the award last year."

"A significant change that has taken place among banks is in customer orientation the industry is also looking at other markets – like the rural market, for instance. Another important parameter was endurance. The other parameter the panelists discussed was the basic role of a bank: that of allocating capital efficiently. They also decided to include shareholder value as one of tie criteria. Some other parameters were run through quickly to arrive at a shortlist. They included: customer service, reach; endurance; allocation of capital; shareholder value; number of employees; risk management; business ethics and asset quality.

While technology as a parameter was seen to be criticas, it was also recognised that most PSBs were in the process of putting their technology platform in place. These parameters were then fine-tuned to return on equity, diversity, growth, service-orientation, and management quality. This eliminated five contenders – UTI bank, BOB, Corporation bank, ING Vysya and UCO bank. "The final short list included HDFC bank, ICICI bank, Oriental bank of commerce, and State Bank of India. The panel's choice was clear. SBI was changing, but not adequately or quickly, given the changing face of the industry. On the other hand, despite huge challenges, OBC had been able to drive change aggressively, take its people along, and change from a predominantly north Indian bank and a slow mover to a nimble-footed and responsive entity. With no naysayers left, Oriental bank of commerce was crow end Business India's Best bank for 2003."

For details reg: A new orientation: Oriental bank of Commerce is a simple bank which conceals a huge success story please refer Business India Nov. 24–Dec. 7, 2003, p.64.

(*Source:* Business India Nov. 24 – Dec. 7, 2003).

THE ECONOMIC TIMES AWARDS 2003

The Economic Times announced the awards for the year 2003 (The Economic Times, dated 17th September 2003) and accordingly, the awards Go to Kumar Birla, Deepak Parekh, Ranbaxy, I-flex, Ela Bhatt, Amar Bose, Cafe Coffee day, Group Godrej. The highlights in the form of extracts may be mentioned:

"If in the past we have stretched the parameters of the ET awards for corporate excellence to reflect the changes in the pattern of India's socio-economic fabric, including corporate social responsibility, politics and governance, this year the patterns changed again."

The Economic Times Awards jury was chaired by NR Narayana Murthy, Chairman of Infosys.

"The final decision however was entirely in the hands of the jury. So no-more suspense, here is the eight the jury plicked to claim the title as the best of the brightest in India Inc for 02-03:

- Deepak Parekh of HDFC. At 57, the youngest ever to receive the ET Awards for Lifetime Achievement, following the likes of Dhirubhai Ambani and Verghese Kurien;
- Kumar Mangalam Birla, chairman of AV Birla Group, At 36, the youngest ever to be ET's Business Leader of the Year;
- As Company of the year, we give you Ranbaxy, India's pharmaceutical pioneer;
- As Emerging Company of the year, presenting I-flex Solution, whose banking software product has been tried and tech-ted around the globe;
- For Entrepreneur of the year, meet VG Siddhartha for creating a national brand and lifestyle chain Cafe Coffee Day from a commodity business;
- The winder for the Businesswoman of the year is Ela Bhatt, for creating the mamnoth business network that is SEWA;
- In the newest category, introduced this year, for Global Indian of the Year, the award goes to Amar Gopal Bose, the legendary creator of the world's greatest sound systems;
- The Godrej Group emerges as the corporate Citizen of the year, for its long and proven contribution to the social sector.
- For the applause, fast forward to October at the Oberoi, Mumbai, when over 300 CEOs and dignitaries will gather to salute the winning teams.

Here is a brief methodology on how the shortlists were prepared for Company of the year and emerging company of the year.

- For the company of the year and emerging company of the year, we first arranged all companies in descending order of market capitalization as on July 15, 2003. Companies above the cut-off level of Rs. 500 crore-market capitalization on that day were selected for the initial shortlist of Company of the year. This list was further whittled down to companies with revenue of Rs. 250 crore and above in FY03. Companies with less than six years of operating/listed history were also disqualified from company of the year category to remove any bias towards companies that have grown fast because of their low base.

- For Emerging Company of the year, we selected companies with a market cap above Rs. 100 crore as on July 15, 2003.

Once the two lists with Top 100 companies in each category was shortlisted, they were then ranked on various criteria. They were sorted on the basis of:

(i) Increase in market capitalisation over the 12-month period on the date of calculation.

(ii) Increase in revenues in 2002-02 over 2001-02.

(iii) Increase in profit after tax in 2002-03 over 2001-02.

(iv) Return on net work (RONW), as a measure of return on shareholder funds;

(v) Compunded annual growth in earling per share (EPS) over the past three years;

(vi) Price-earning ratio;

(vii) Market capitalisation as on July 15, 2003.

(viii) Sales for the latest finanical year;

(ix) Profit after tax for the latest financial year.

These companies were then sorted in descending order on each of these parameters–that is, companies with highest PAT growth were on top of the list. Ranks were than assigned to each of the companies in ascending order–that is, companies at the top got ranked one, two, three, etc. So for each parameter, a table of ranks was generated. An important point here is that the ranking method assumes that all factors have equal weightage. A weighted average method was not adopted because that could have given rise to a debate on the relative weightages to assign to various parameters.

Once the ranks were assigned, the sum of ranks for each company across different parameters was added up, leading up to a composite ranking for each company. For example, if Company X was ranked 4, 3, 2, 6, 3, 2, and 5 across the seven parameters used in this methodology, then the composite ranking would be a sum of all the ranking (25 in this case).

The company with the lowest composite ranking was then considered Number One. The lowest 20 composite ranking in Company of the year category, and likewise for Emerging Company of the year, were then shortlisted for the final selection. The ET editorial board then further culled the shortlist to the final 15 after debating the merits of each case and after rigid due diligence.

The shortlists for Business Leader of the year, Businesswoman of the year and Entrepreneur of the year were admittedly more subjective ones. The performance of each nominee's company or companies–and the perception of the stock market–was definitely a major factor. But in certain cases, we went beyond market cap and profit to look at persons who have brought about paradigm shifts in their businesses. Some of the choices might be considered mavericks or even controversial. The persons in question may not be universally liked or respected, but by their aggression and daring they have changed the rules of the game, thought and acted in global terms, stood traditionally–accepted mindsets on their head, and shaken up the industry or environment in which they operate.

It may be mentioned here that an extensive polling exercise was carried out among readers. ET printed ads with the nominations for the Company of the year, Emerging company of the year, Business Leader of the year, Businesswoman of the year and Entrepreneur of the year. An overwhelming number of readers responded with their choices. A reputed market survey agency was also appointed to conduct a poll among 180 CEOs across the country.

ET Awards for Corporate Excellence–Ranbaxy Labs Company of the Year

The company's strengths are:

- Ranbaxy has earned a name for itself in the US as an upcoming generic company;
- It has a robust marketing network in the US for generic products, through which the company has gained market share from innovator companies within a short time;
- It has proved its brand building abilities in the Indian market;
- It has NDDS research skills. The company's areas of weakness include: The anti-infective segment forms 62% of Ranbaxy's sales. World over, this is a low growth segment and mature in India unlike chronic segments like cardiovascular;
- In spite of exports forming a high proportion, Ranbaxy's profitability is less than companies like DRL and Sun Pharma;
- The genetic business from which Ranbaxy gets most of its revenues is intensely competitive, which could render a high level of volatility to the performance of the company.

ET Awards for Corporate Excellence– i-flex Solutions–Emerging Company

The company's strengths are:

- High exposure to the product segment helps the company attain higher profitability. The product segment ha prevented the erosion of margins in an era when the entire industry is seeing margin pressure.
- i-flex is a zero-debt company, which is an indication of its financial muscle. All investments in subsidiaries, JVs and infrastructure are financed from internal accruals.
- i-flex has partnered with several companies for knowledge infusion and support. Totally, the company has 30 partners in 50 countries. Relationships are also built with platform vendors and system integrators like Oracle and HP Consulting. These partners have expedited the geographical expansion of i-flex.
- A presence in 95 countries gives the company the advantage of being in sync with the latest trends and requirements. This helps in adopting a proactive stance towards building features in its products as well as enhancing its service quality.

Among the challenges that the company faces are:

- In the past, i-flex ventured into the various facets of banking. Currently, almost all banking needs have been covered by Microbanker, Flexcube, and its business intelligence product, Reveleus. Hence, in the future, growth will be limited in terms of new product design.
- Even though the services segment contributes to just 34% of total turnover, it is not insignificant. The lowering of billing rates would continue to pull down the company's margins.
- The global backlash, which has adversely affected the top management of i-flex in the past, could spring up again.
- Heightening competition calls for an increase in sales and marketing expenditure. The sales and marketing expenses of the company have jumped by 45% over the last year. If this kind of increase continues for long, it would drain profitability.

THE ECONOMIC TIMES AWARDS FOR CORPORATE EXCELLENCE 2004

The following material is based on The Economic Times issues dated 11th October 2004 and 18th October 2004 reports on the subject/selected excerpts from the same.

Picking the Best of the Brightest.

"ET awards are not about competing for a prize, they are not about the best a d the rest, They are for the best of the brightest, After all, each of our nominees have already conquered their own spaces and stand tall above the rest, The award is recognition for those who exemplify the spirit of excellence in India Inc. As former juror and Bharti Televentures chairman Sunil Mittel puts it last year". It is the one award every young Indian CEO aspires to.

Meet the men and woman who make the ET Awards the ultimate seal of approval of India Inc, MR Narayenaa Murthy, Chairman-of the Jury, Deepak Parekh, unrivalled senior statesman of Indian finance. Rahul Bajaj, equally unrivalled elder statesman of the Indian manufacturing Shenkar Acharya former chief economic edvissor to the government, who has advised three different finance ministers. Venu-Srinivasan, chairman of TVS Motor and a pillar of the business revolution in the south.

What the awards seek to:

- Honour the best and brightest, the men, women and organisations that have made a fundamental different to the way business is done.
- Recognise the contribution of those who have helped create a Corporate India that can look ahead with confidence and can dare to dream big.
- Set benchmarks in excellence for others to emulate, and help drive global standards in quality and competitiveness.
- Salute the super achievers, not only because they created wealth, but also because they, in their own way, have had a beneficial Impact on society at large.

ET AWARDS The Jury, the Verdict, the Chosen

- Business Leader of the Year – AZIM PREMJI, Chairman, Wipro Technologies.
- Businesswoman of the Year – Kiran Mazumdar Shaw, CMD, Biocon.

- Lifetime Achievement award – Rahul Bajaj, CMD, Bajaj Auto.
- Global Indian – CK Prahalad.
- Company of the year – Tata Motors.
- Emerging company of the year – Bharti Televentures.
- Entrepreneur of the year – CK Ranganathan CMD CavinKare.
- Corporate Citizen – HDFC.

For more details, please refer to pages 13 to 16, The Economic Times Bangalore, dated 18th October 2004.

CORPORATE GOVERNANCE AND DEVELOPMENT: WHY IT MATTERS, GN BAJPAI[1]

Corporate governance and growth

- Neither market nor state alone can ensure a high rate of economic advancement . They need to focus on the areas of their respective core competence for an economy to perform well. The state should provide basic support services such law and order, a conductive legal environment, a decent supervisory and regulatory infrastructure, a reliable accounting system, a vibrant securities market etc.
- If the securities market is efficient, it can penalise the badly governed companies and reward the better governed companies. Hence not only the corporate governance standards need to improve, but also efficiency and efficacy of securities market need to improve so that the resources are directed to the deserving companies which can rally boost economic performance. The securities market cannot make best allocation of resources if the standards of corporate governance are not followed in letter and spirit.
- The securities market facilitates the internationalisation of an economy by linking it with the rest of the world. This linkage assists through the inflow of capital in the form of portfolio investment. Moreover, a strong domestic stock market performance forms the basis of well performing Domestic corporate to raise capital in the international market.
- Globalisation represents the movement of the four elements of the economy across the national borders and thanks to the information technology this can happen *very* fast. The first element is physical capital in terms of plant and machinery. The second one is financial capital markets and in the form of foreign direct investment. The third is the technology and the fourth is labour.
- Virtually all developing, transition and emerging market economies take the challenge head on as they realise that the standards of corporate governance brought in by globalisation bring enormous benefits to them in the form of:
  - *(a)* enhancing wealth creation;
  - *(b)* ensuring the efficacious maagement of wealth and

---

1 From speech delivered by Shri GN Bajpai Chairman SEBI at the Global Governance Forum's meeting held on November 4, 2003 at Paris (SEBI Bulletin November 4, 2003)

(c) equitable sharing of wealth amongst all stakeholders.

- Recent corporate scandals, such as Enron and World.com have rocked the global financial markets and shaken the confidence of investors. The authorities and the regulators all lover the world are burning midnight's oil to prevent recurrence of such sandals. Though efforts are being made to instill good governance practices and rebuild confidence, it is easier said than done.
- Some of the key institutions and actors are corporate law, securities laws, securities regulations, listing requirements, judicial system, professional associations, business associations, fiancial accounting standards, stock tendering requirements, prescription of self-dealing.
- Public disclosure, auditing standards etc; these institutions and actors impose three kinds of discipline on the corporates: self-discipline, market discipline, regulatory discipline.
- Raising the-quality of corporate governance is a challenge that involves all the market participants-issuer's director's regulators, policy makers, auditors, advisors, educators and investors. We all have to work together to make this work.

CORPORATE GOVERNANCE: A STRATEGIC TOOL TO BUILD COMPETITIVENESS, MANISH BANSAL[2]

Management and boards in today's organisations face more dramatic demands, challenges, and opportunities than ever before. Building competitiveness is, unequivocally, at the top of the agenda of many corporations. Adopting corporate governance as a strategic tool to build competitiveness is something corporations must look into....

- Perspective is being widened to look at the stakeholders rather than just the shareholders. Stakeholders essentially mean all, who have stake in the business including shareholders, debt holders, suppliers, distributors, customers, employees, bankers, consultants etc. In a broader perspective, the whole nation is a stakeholder as the corporates create national wealth at the end of the day. This wider perspective helps corporations focus on the value creation for the big universe rather than a small segment.
- Good corporate governance helps build confidence among stakeholders. Once the corporates widen their perspective and take every stakeholder's interest into consideration, while weaving the strategies, they would end up creating very different image for themselves. Further, openness, trasnsparency, disclosures and value sharing build up an environment of incredible confidence across the value chain. People stick to the corporations even during their bad times. Think of Infosys again, where number of people across the organisation are millionaire. I think, good corporate governance practices make the stakeholders business partners; in that case stakeholders enroll themselves in the vision and the business philosophy of the corporates. Once it happens, it becomes easier for the

2 *Source*: SEBI Bulletin December 2003.

corporates to build a competitive differentiation and accomplish their strategic goals with long-term perspective.

- Another point to be understood clearly is that corporate governance is not the only tool but just a tool for building competitiveness. For success in any field, one needs the competitiveness at the different fronts. Let us look at the success of Walmart in US and other markets. It is not the competitiveness of Walmart at some specific front/fronts but the overall competitiveness of its business model, which includes ideal locations, range of merchandise, pricing strategy, customer reach, logistics management, customer relationship, high morale of employees etc. Now corporate governance is becoming one of the essential ingredients of business models in the corporate circles.

REAL CARROT IS NOT GOVERNANCE BUT RETURNS[3]

"The true test for investors is the carrot of growth prospects and returns.

How do they react when governance becomes a question mark?

They tend to sell their holdings rather than challenge management". Does that portrayal of investors as jumping bunnies puncture their power bubble image or simply present a matter-of-fact-we knew all along? Experts opine that corporate governance has to be voluntary, though it would help if you had vocal shareholders and alert media. On the latter, McKinsey mentions, as examples, China's Caijing and Malaysia's The Edge, for exposing corporate malfeasance and questionable practices. CLP (Hong Kong), POSCO (South Korea), Public Bank (Malaysia), Siam Cement (Thailand) and Singapore Telecommunications (Singapore) get good certificates for governance. So does Infosys: It "discloses the extent of its compliance with 10 corporate governance codes, reconciles its financial statements with eight accounting standards (including the US and the UK generally accepted accounting principles), and has a board with a majority of independent directors as well as wholly independent audit, nominations and compensation committees".

While mentioning reforms in accounting, the article states: "Accounting standards in many Asian jurisdictions remain weak. Not enough professionals have an in-depth understanding of local or international accounting standards. The accounting self-regulatory organisations are lax. As a result of all this, reported earnings, cash flows, and balance sheets can be quite unreliable. Since the general perception of Asian accounts rubs on us too, the Institute of Chartered Accountants of India may have to do more selling to get noticed globally.

---

3 *Source*: The Hindu Business Line, April 18, 2004.

Ministry of Company Affairs (MCA) Highlights of Significant Achievements during the Year 2004-05

The UPA Government has upgraded the erstwhile Department of Company Affairs to the level of Ministry under the charge of Minister of State (Independent charge).

VISION OF THE NEW MINISTRY

- Self- regulation within broad contours of law and public policy
- Effectively protecting interests of investors as promised in NCMP
- Promoting good corporate governance amongst the companies
- Institutional reforms in terms of decentralization, simplification, transparency, accountability and e-governance.

ACTIONS TAKEN IN THE FIRST YEAR

- **COMPREHENSIVE REVISION OF THE COMPANIES ACT, 1956 TO SIMPLIFY, RATIONALIZE & REDUCING THE SIZE BY TWO THIRD**
  - Consultative and participative approach adopted.
  - Concept paper launched on 4th August, 2004.
  - Large number of suggestions received.
  - Initiative welcomed by all concerned including CII, FICCI, ASSOCHAM, PHD Chambers, ICSI, ICAI and ICWAI.
  - Constituted Expert Group having Dr. J.J. Irani as head.
  - Report expected by 31st May.
  - Further time bound action-plan drawn.
- **PROTECTION OF INTERESTS OF INVESTORS–A PROMISE IN NCMP**
  - Responsive and action oriented approach
  - Investors complaints now being acknowledged within 48 hours and timely action taken
  - Investor protection cells opened and made functional at three levels
  - On-line Investors Grievances Redressal System developed, introduced and made functional
  - Investor Education and Protection Fund activated
  - Website www.watchoutinvestors.com which is a national registry of economic defaulters launched
  - Detailed Action Plan for 2005-06 drawn
- **CRUSADE AGAINST VANISHING COMPANIES**
  - Number reduced from 229 to 115
  - Inspections ordered in 109 cases

- Prosecutions launched in 177 and 157 cases in two different categories
- FIRs tiled in 100 cases
- Persons arrested at least 21
- Support of reputed NGOs enlisted
- Certain defaulting companies started refunding the money
- Further action in full swing

• **MCA21 E-GOVERNANCE PROJECT**

- Launched w.e.f. 1.3.2005 – the largest ever e-Governance initiative of a Mission Mode Project of the Government of India in public-private partnership
- Aim-paperless, transparent, hassle-free services to corporates and others
- Results will start showing within a year

• **SIMPLIFIED EXIT SCHEME, 2005 (SES 2005)**

- About 2 lakh defunct companies exist on the registers of ROCs Launched "Simplified Exit Scheme, 2005" (SES 2005) w.e.f. 1.2.2005 to be in operation for 6 months
- This will give much awaited relief to small, non-functional, defunct companies who do not wish to continue as such

• **REDUCING LITIGAT16N**

- About 50,000 prosecutions pending under Companies Act for many years
- Many of these relating to technical and procedural violations are pending in different courts for long
- Expert Group under the chairmanship of Shri O.P. Vaish, Sr. Advocate constituted to suggest measures within 2 months
- Successful implementation of the initiative likely to reduce the largely unproductive litigation in the Ministry substantially

• **NATIONAL FOUNDATION FOR CORPORATE GOVERNANCE (NFCG)**

- Activated NFCG for promoting good corporate governance practices on the lines of best international practices
- Shri N. R. Narayana Murthy, Chairman and Chief Mentor, Infosys Technologies Limited taken as vice-chairman
- Launched a web site of the Foundation namely-www.nfcgindia.org.

• **LAWS GOVERNING PROFESSIONAL INSTITUTES–ICAI, ICSI & ICWAI BEING RATIONALISED**

- Bills pertaining to revision of the Chartered Accountants Act, 1949, Cost and Works Accountants Act, 1959 and Company Secretaries Act, 1980 being pursued

– Recommendations of the Parliamentary Standing Committee on Finance duly considered

– Expected to be presented before the Monsoon Session, 2005.

- **ENFORCEMENT MACHINERY STRENGTHENED–SERIOUS FRAUD INVESTIGATION OFFICE (SFIO) ACTIVATED**

– 23 investigations and 210 inspections ordered during the year 2004-05 as against only 9 investigations and 46 inspections ordered during 2003-04

– SFIO fully activated-26 cases referred-4 completed

- **NEW INSTITUTIONAL FRAME WORK BEING BROUGHT INTO EXISTENCE**

– The Competition Commission of India to replace MRTPC

– NCLT & NCLAT to replace CLB.

References

1. Blake, Allan, Dynamic Directors: Aligning Board Structure for Business Success (Macmillan Press Ltd., London 1999).
2. Chinn, Richard and Jones, Martyn E (Eds.) The Corporate Governance Handbook (Geo Publishing Ltd., London, 1999).
3. Ginman P. The Guide to Directors' Duties and Responsibilities–Your Questions Answered (Kogan Page, London 1992).
4. Institute of Directors, Assessing Board Effectiveness (The Director Publications, London 1998).
5. Institute of Directors, Business in Ethics (The Director Publications London, 1999).
6. Corporate Governance Reporting: Best Practices, The Institute of Company Secretaries of India, New Delhi.
7. Boards and Governance: the new agenda ICFAI University.
8. Corporate Governance: Eds. PP Arya, BB Tandon and AK Vashisht Deep and Deep Publications New Delhi.
9. Corporate Governance, Concept and Dimensions Sanjiv Agarwal. Snowwhite, Bombay.
10. Directors and corporate governance, R Rajagopalan Company Law Institute, Chennai.